W9-ASX-633

ULTIMATE
Comfort Food

Taste
of Home
BOOKS

RDA ENTHUSIAST BRANDS, LLC
MILWAUKEE, WI

Taste of Home

Reader's digest

A TASTE OF HOME/READER'S DIGEST BOOK

©2014 RDA Enthusiast Brands, LLC, 1610 N. 2nd St., Suite 102, Milwaukee WI 53212-3906. All rights reserved.
Taste of Home and Reader's Digest are registered trademarks of The Reader's Digest Association, Inc.

EDITORIAL

Editor-in-Chief: Catherine Cassidy
Creative Director: Howard Greenberg
Editorial Operations Director: Kerri Balliet

Managing Editor, Print & Digital Books: Mark Hagen
Associate Creative Director: Edwin Robles Jr.

Editors: Heather Ray, Jan Briggs
Associate Editor: Molly Jasinski
Art Director: Jessie Sharon
Contributing Art Director: Lonnie Turner
Contributing Layout Designer: Siya Motamedi
Editorial Production Manager: Dena Ahlers
Copy Chief: Deb Warlaumont Mulvey
Copy Editor: Mary-Liz Shaw
Contributing Copy Editor: Valerie Phillips
Content Operations Manager: Colleen King
Content Operations Assistant: Shannon Stroud
Executive Assistant: Marie Brannon

Chief Food Editor: Karen Berner
Food Editors: James Schend; Peggy Woodward, RD
Associate Food Editor: Krista Lanphier
Recipe Editors: Mary King; Annie Rundle; Jenni Sharp, RD; Irene Yeh

Test Kitchen & Food Styling Manager: Sarah Thompson
Test Cooks: Nicholas Iverson (lead), Matthew Hass, Lauren Knoelke
Food Stylists: Kathryn Conrad (senior), Leah Rekau, Shannon Roum
Prep Cooks: Megumi Garcia, Melissa Hansen, Bethany Van Jacobson, Sara Wirtz

Photography Director: Stephanie Marchese
Photographers: Dan Roberts, Jim Wieland
Photographer/Set Stylist: Grace Natoli Sheldon
Set Stylists: Stacey Genaw, Melissa Haberman, Dee Dee Jacq
Creative Contributors: Mark Derse (photography), Pam Stasney (set stylist)

Editorial Business Manager: Kristy Martin
Billing Specialist: Mary Ann Koebernik

BUSINESS

Vice President, Chief Sales Officer: Mark S. Josephson
Vice President, Business Development & Marketing: Alain Begun
General Manager, Taste of Home Cooking School: Erin Puariea
Vice President, Digital Experience & E-Commerce: Jennifer Smith
Vice President, Direct to Consumer Marketing: Dave Fiegel

THE READER'S DIGEST ASSOCIATION, INC.

President and Chief Executive Officer: Bonnie Kintzer
Vice President, Chief Operating Officer, North America: Howard Halligan
Vice President, Enthusiast Brands, Books & Retail: Harold Clarke
Vice President, North American Operations: Philippe Cloutier
Vice President, Chief Marketing Officer: Leslie Doty
Vice President, North American Human Resources: Phyllis E. Gebhardt, SPHR
Vice President, Consumer Marketing Planning: Jim Woods

For other **Taste of Home** books and products, visit us at **tasteofhome.com.**

For more **Reader's Digest** products and information,
visit **rd.com** (in the United States) or **rd.ca** (in Canada).

Library of Congress Number: 2014904007

International Standard Book Number: 978-1-61765-321-6

Cover Photographer: Dan Roberts
Set Stylist: Stacey Genaw
Food Stylist: Kathryn Conrad

Pictured on front cover: Double-Cheese Mac with Bacon, page 140
Pictured on spine: Mini Maple Cinnamon Rolls, page 48
Pictured on back cover: Lemon-Berry Shortcake, page 256,
Best-Ever Meat Loaf, page 115, Guacamole, page 16

1 3 5 7 9 10 8 6 4 2
Printed in China

PAGE 265

CONTENTS

PAGE 162

PAGE 43

PAGE 180

PAGE 202

PAGE 15

LIKE US
facebook.com/tasteofhome

SHOP WITH US
shoptasteofhome.com

TWEET US
@tasteofhome

SHARE A RECIPE
tasteofhome.com/submit

FOLLOW US
pinterest.com/taste_of_home

Let's Dig In!

TURKEY POTPIES, PAGE 146

From dinners to desserts, this one-of-a-kind collection offers hundreds of recipes guaranteed to warm the soul—even on the chilliest of days. Whether dipping your fork into a golden potpie or sinking your teeth into a freshly baked brownie, you'll find more than **475 simple joys** within the pages of *Taste of Home Ultimate Comfort Food*. Best of all, each satisfying specialty is sure to make you stop and savor every delicious moment.

FUDGE NUT BROWNIES, PAGE 285

look for these icons

ULTIMATE *Comfort*
Favored classics you know and love.

kid FRIENDLY
Suggested for picky eaters.

❝There's no brownie recipe or mix I've ever tried that's better than this! You can mix it in one bowl in just a few minutes. My husband's grandmother passed the recipe on; now our son makes these brownies for after-school snacks.❞

—BECKY ALBRIGHT NORWALK, OH

Appetizers, Snacks & Beverages

SMALL PLATES AND SOOTHING DRINKS—SO SATISFYING YOU COULD MAKE A MEAL OUT OF THEM.

SAUSAGE SLIDERS WITH CRAN-APPLE SLAW
PAGE 10

SWEET 'N' TANGY CHICKEN WINGS
PAGE 18

HOT COCOA
PAGE 28

Bacon-Wrapped Appetizers

Water chestnuts lend a wonderful and unexpected crunch to the classic snack, while the pineapple's sweetness is perfect with sweet-and-sour sauce. The appetizer is always a hit at birthdays and Christmas.

—**NANCY HARROLD** BROKEN BOW, NE

PREP: 25 MIN. • **BAKE:** 25 MIN.
MAKES: ABOUT 2½ DOZEN

- 1 **pound sliced bacon**
- 1 **can (8 ounces) whole water chestnuts, drained**
- 1 **can (8 ounces) unsweetened pineapple chunks, drained**
- 1 **jar (10 ounces) sweet-and-sour sauce**

1. Cut each slice of bacon in half widthwise. Wrap a strip around each chestnut or pineapple chunk; secure with toothpicks. Place in an ungreased 15-in. x 10-in. x 1-in. baking pan. Bake at 400° for 25-35 minutes or until bacon is crisp.

2. Pour sweet-and-sour sauce into a microwave-safe bowl. Cover and microwave on high for 1-2 minutes or until heated through. Serve with appetizers.

Shrimp Spread

Reminiscent of the 60s, shrimp cocktail is the kind of appetizer you never get tired of tasting. In this fun variation, it becomes a creamy spread to serve on crackers or sliced bread.

—**NORENE WRIGHT** MANILLA, IN

START TO FINISH: 15 MIN.
MAKES: 20 SERVINGS

- 1 **package (8 ounces) reduced-fat cream cheese**
- ½ **cup reduced-fat sour cream**
- ¼ **cup reduced-fat mayonnaise**
- 1 **cup seafood cocktail sauce**
- 2 **cups (8 ounces) shredded part-skim mozzarella cheese**
- 1 **can (6 ounces) small shrimp, rinsed and drained**
- 3 **green onions, sliced**
- 1 **medium tomato, finely chopped Sliced Italian bread or assorted crackers**

1. In a small bowl, beat the cream cheese, sour cream and mayonnaise until smooth. Spread onto a 12-in. round serving plate; top with seafood sauce. Sprinkle with cheese, shrimp, onions and tomato.

2. Chill until serving. Serve with bread or crackers.

Mini Chicken Empanadas

Refrigerated pie pastry makes quick work of assembling these bite-size appetizers that are loaded with chicken and cheese. I've made them several times since receiving the recipe from a friend.

—BETTY FULKS ONIA, AR

PREP: 30 MIN. • **BAKE:** 15 MIN./BATCH
MAKES: ABOUT 2½ DOZEN

- 1 cup finely chopped cooked chicken
- ⅔ cup shredded Colby-Monterey Jack cheese
- 3 tablespoons cream cheese, softened
- 4 teaspoons chopped sweet red pepper
- 2 teaspoons chopped seeded jalapeno pepper
- 1 teaspoon ground cumin
- ½ teaspoon salt
- ⅛ teaspoon pepper
- 1 package (14.1 ounces) refrigerated pie pastry

1. In a small bowl, combine the first eight ingredients. On a lightly floured surface, roll each pastry sheet into a 15-in. circle. Cut with a floured 3-in. round biscuit cutter.

2. Place about 1 teaspoon filling on one half of each circle. Moisten pastry edges with water. Fold pastry over filling. Press edges with a fork to seal.

3. Transfer to greased baking sheets. Bake at 400° for 12-15 minutes or until golden brown. Remove to wire racks. Serve warm.

NOTE *Wear disposable gloves when cutting hot peppers; the oils can burn skin. Avoid touching your face.*

Warm Cider

This recipe came from a friend in Fort Wayne, IN, where we lived for many years. The cider is warm, wonderful and nonalcoholic, so we've even served it at church. It's also perfect for a holiday open house.

—MARYELLEN HAYS WOLCOTTVILLE, IN

START TO FINISH: 30 MIN.
MAKES: 10-12 SERVINGS (2½ QUARTS)

- 2 quarts apple cider
- 1½ cups orange juice
- ¾ cup pineapple juice
- 1 tablespoon brown sugar
- ½ teaspoon lemon juice
- 2 cinnamon sticks (3 inches)
    Dash ground cinnamon
    Dash ground cloves

In a large saucepan, combine all of the ingredients. Bring to a boil. Reduce heat; cover and simmer for 20-30 minutes. Discard cinnamon sticks. Serve hot in mugs.

top tip

Spice Surplus

Cinnamon sticks can last for 2-3 years if stored in an airtight container in a cool and dry place. But what can you do with extras? Use them as stirrers for hot chocolate and cider; tie them to food gifts; or cook them with rice.

kid FRIENDLY

Mozzarella Sticks

Crunchy on the outside with gooey, melted cheese on the inside… this favorite appetizer is unbelievably easy to make. Even the kids can help wrap the string cheese.

—**SHIRLEY WARREN** THIENSVILLE, WI

START TO FINISH: 20 MIN.
MAKES: 1 DOZEN

- 12 **pieces string cheese**
- 12 **egg roll wrappers**
  Oil for deep-fat frying
  Marinara or spaghetti sauce

1. Place a piece of string cheese near the bottom corner of one egg roll wrapper (keep remaining wrappers covered with a damp paper towel until ready to use). Fold bottom corner over cheese. Roll up halfway; fold sides toward center over cheese. Moisten remaining corner with water; roll up tightly to seal. Repeat with remaining wrappers and cheese.
2. In an electric skillet, heat ½ in. of oil to 375°. Fry sticks, a few at a time, for 30-60 seconds on each side or until golden brown. Drain on paper towels. Serve with marinara sauce.

Easy Antipasto Kabobs

PREP: 30 MIN. + MARINATING
MAKES: 12 KABOBS

- 1 **cup refrigerated cheese tortellini**
- ½ **cup balsamic vinegar**
- ¼ **cup grated Parmesan cheese**
- ¼ **cup minced fresh basil**
- 2 **tablespoons Dijon mustard**
- 1 **tablespoon olive oil**
- 2 **teaspoons honey**
- ¼ **teaspoon pepper**
- 1 **can (14 ounces) water-packed artichoke hearts, rinsed and drained**
- 1 **large green pepper, cut into 1-inch pieces**
- 1 **cup grape tomatoes**
- 1 **cup pitted ripe olives**
- ¼ **pound thinly sliced deli ham, cut into 1-inch strips**
- 12 **wooden skewers (6 inches)**

1. Cook tortellini according to package directions.
2. Meanwhile, in a large resealable plastic bag, combine the vinegar, cheese, basil, mustard, oil, honey and pepper. Add the artichokes, green pepper, tomatoes, olives and ham. Drain and rinse tortellini in cold water; add to bag. Seal bag and turn to coat. Refrigerate for 4 hours or overnight.
3. Drain and discard marinade. For each kabob, thread tortellini, artichokes, green pepper, tomatoes, olives and folded ham onto a skewer.

? **Did you know?**
According to a Cornell University study, women tend to consider sugary foods comforting, whereas men prefer savory options, such as steak and soup.

I found a marinade recipe that wasn't very heavy on oil and I modified it to suit my taste. But what I love about these kabobs is that they are easy to put together and there is no need to turn on the oven. —**KENDRA DOSS** COLORADO SPR INGS, CO

ULTIMATE *Comfort*
Sausage Sliders with Cran-Apple Slaw

The best things come in small packages, as these tasty sliders prove. The filling is so good, you'll want to have a fork on hand for any yummy tidbits that get away.

—**PRISCILLA YEE** CONCORD, CA

START TO FINISH: 25 MIN.
MAKES: 4 SERVINGS

- ⅔ cup coleslaw mix or shredded cabbage
- ⅓ cup chopped apple
- 3 tablespoons dried cranberries
- 3 tablespoons chopped pecans, toasted
- 4 teaspoons mayonnaise
- 4 teaspoons barbecue sauce

SLIDERS

- 1 pound bulk pork sausage
- 4 slices sharp cheddar cheese, halved
- 8 dinner rolls, halved and toasted
- 3 tablespoons spicy brown mustard
- 8 lettuce leaves

1. In a large bowl, combine the first six ingredients. Chill until serving.
2. Shape sausage into eight patties. In a large skillet, cook patties over medium heat for 3-4 minutes on each side or until a meat thermometer reads 160° and juices run clear, adding cheese slices during the last 1-2 minutes of cooking time.
3. Spread rolls with mustard; top each with a sausage patty, lettuce and 2 tablespoons coleslaw mixture. Replace roll tops.

Iced Coffee Latte

This is a great alternative to regular hot coffee and is much more economical than store-bought coffee drinks. Sweetened condensed milk and a hint of chocolate give it a special touch.

—**HEATHER NANDELL** JOHNSTON, IA

START TO FINISH: 10 MIN.
MAKES: 8 SERVINGS

- ½ cup instant coffee granules
- ½ cup boiling water
- 4 cups chocolate milk
- 2 cups cold water
- 1 can (14 ounces) sweetened condensed milk
  Ice cubes

In a large bowl, dissolve coffee in boiling water. Stir in the chocolate milk, cold water and condensed milk. Serve over ice.

Mini Muffuletta

Mediterranean meets comfort food when French rolls are slathered with olive spread and stuffed with layers of salami and cheese. You can make these muffulettas the night before and cut them into appetizer-size slices just before serving.

—**GARETH CRANER** MINDEN, NV

PREP: 25 MIN. + CHILLING
MAKES: 3 DOZEN

- 1 jar (10 ounces) pimiento-stuffed olives, drained and chopped
- 2 cans (4¼ ounces each) chopped ripe olives
- 2 tablespoons balsamic vinegar
- 1 tablespoon red wine vinegar
- 1 tablespoon olive oil
- 3 garlic cloves, minced
- 1 teaspoon dried basil
- 1 teaspoon dried oregano
- 6 French rolls, split
- ½ pound thinly sliced hard salami
- ¼ pound sliced provolone cheese
- ½ pound thinly sliced cotto salami
- ¼ pound sliced part-skim mozzarella cheese

1. In a large bowl, combine the first eight ingredients; set aside. Hollow out tops and bottoms of rolls, leaving ¾-in. shells (discard removed bread or save for another use).

2. Spread olive mixture over tops and bottoms of rolls. On roll bottoms, layer with hard salami, provolone cheese, cotto salami and mozzarella cheese. Replace tops.

3. Wrap tightly in plastic wrap. Refrigerate overnight. Cut each into six wedges; secure with toothpicks.

Easy Three-Cheese Pesto Pizza

Using a ready-made crust, pizza can be on a serving tray in half an hour. This triple-cheese version is meatless and makes a hearty appetizer for casual gatherings.

—**PAT STEVENS** GRANBURY, TX

START TO FINISH: 30 MIN.
MAKES: 16 SLICES

- ½ cup finely chopped red onion
- ½ cup finely chopped sweet red pepper
- 1 tablespoon olive oil
- 1 prebaked 12-inch pizza crust
- ½ cup prepared pesto
- 1 cup (4 ounces) crumbled feta cheese
- 1 cup (4 ounces) shredded part-skim mozzarella cheese
- 1 cup (4 ounces) shredded Parmesan cheese
- 1 can (4¼ ounces) chopped ripe olives
- 1 medium tomato, thinly sliced

1. In a small skillet, saute onion and red pepper in oil until tender. Remove from the heat; set aside.

2. Place crust on an ungreased 14-in. pizza pan. Spread pesto to within ½ in. of edges. Layer with cheeses, onion mixture, olives and tomato.

3. Bake at 400° for 15-18 minutes or until cheese is melted.

Aussie Sausage Rolls

I was born and raised in Australia, but moved to the U.S. when I married my husband. When I long for a taste of my homeland, I bake up a batch of these sausage rolls and share them with neighbors or co-workers.

—**MELISSA LANDON** PORT CHARLOTTE, FL

PREP: 15 MIN. • **BAKE:** 20 MIN.
MAKES: 3 DOZEN

- 1¼ **pounds bulk pork sausage**
- 1 **medium onion, finely chopped**
- 2 **teaspoons minced chives**
- 2 **teaspoons minced fresh basil or ½ teaspoon dried basil**
- 2 **garlic cloves, minced**
- 1 **teaspoon paprika, divided**
- ½ **teaspoon salt**
- ¼ **teaspoon pepper**
- 1 **package (17.3 ounces) frozen puff pastry, thawed**

1. In a large bowl, combine the sausage, onion, chives, basil, garlic, ¾ teaspoon paprika, salt and pepper. Unfold pastry onto a lightly floured surface. Roll each pastry sheet into an 11-in. x 10½-in. rectangle. Cut widthwise into 3½-in. strips.

2. Spread ½ cup of sausage mixture down the center of each strip. Fold pastry over and press edges together to seal. Cut each roll into six pieces.

3. Place seam side down on a rack in a shallow baking pan. Sprinkle with remaining paprika. Bake at 350° for 20-25 minutes or until golden brown.

Sausage-Stuffed Jalapenos

If you like foods that have a little kick, you'll love these zippy, cheese-and-sausage-filled jalapenos. The recipe is one of my favorites for parties.

—**RACHEL OSWALD** GREENVILLE, MI

PREP: 20 MIN. • **BAKE:** 15 MIN.
MAKES: 44 APPETIZERS

- 1 **pound bulk pork sausage**
- 1 **package (8 ounces) cream cheese, softened**
- 1 **cup (4 ounces) shredded Parmesan cheese**
- 22 **large jalapeno peppers, halved lengthwise and seeded**
  Ranch salad dressing, optional

1. In a large skillet, cook the sausage over medium heat until no longer pink; drain. In a small bowl, combine the cream cheese and Parmesan cheese; fold in sausage.

2. Spoon about 1 tablespoonful into each jalapeno half. Place in two ungreased 13-in. x 9-in. baking dishes. Bake, uncovered, at 425° for 15-20 minutes or until filling is lightly browned and bubbly. Serve with ranch dressing if desired.

NOTE *Wear disposable gloves when cutting hot peppers; the oils can burn skin. Avoid touching your face.*

Party Time Mini Cheeseburgers

Party-goers will love the fun of mini burgers. Juiced up with pickle relish and topped with cheese, these sliders will disappear in no time. You can even serve them with different shapes of cheese cutouts for holidays and themed events.

—TASTE OF HOME TEST KITCHEN

START TO FINISH: 30 MIN.
MAKES: 10 SERVINGS

- 1　egg, lightly beaten
- 2　tablespoons dill pickle relish
- 2　tablespoons ketchup
- 2　teaspoons Worcestershire sauce
- 2　teaspoons prepared mustard
- ¼　cup quick-cooking oats
- ¼　teaspoon pepper
- ⅛　teaspoon garlic powder
- 1　pound ground beef
- 3　to 4 slices process American cheese
- 10　dinner rolls, split

1. In a large bowl, combine the first eight ingredients. Crumble beef over mixture and mix well. Shape into 10 patties. Broil 3-4 in. from the heat for 4-6 minutes on each side or until a meat thermometer reads 160° and juices run clear.

2. Meanwhile, using a 1-in. pumpkin-shaped cookie cutter, cut out 10 pumpkin shapes from cheese slices or cut slices into thirds. Immediately place on burgers; serve on rolls.

Orange Julius

Orange Julius makes a refreshing drink year-round, but it also is a fun beverage to serve around the holidays. It's a tasty alternative to soft drinks, too.

—RITA SWANSON THREE HILLS, AB

START TO FINISH: 10 MIN.
MAKES: 4-5 SERVINGS

- 1　can (6 ounces) frozen orange juice concentrate, thawed
- 1　cup milk
- 1　cup water
- ¼　cup sugar
- 1　teaspoon vanilla extract
- 10　to 12 ice cubes

In a blender, combine the orange juice, milk, water, sugar and vanilla. Cover and blend until smooth. With blender running, add ice cubes, one at a time, through the opening in lid. Blend until smooth. Serve immediately.

top tip

Julius Review

This tasted just like the ones I used to get at the mall! I doubled the amount of ice, used the orange juice concentrate in its frozen state and used fat-free milk and Stevia instead of sugar.

—KGBURGESS TASTEOFHOME.COM

Stromboli Sandwich

Stromboli is a meal in itself, but it also makes a satisfying appetizer when sliced into strips.

—LEIGH LAUER HUMMELSTOWN, PA

PREP: 20 MIN. + RISING • **BAKE:** 30 MIN.
MAKES: 8-10 SERVINGS

- 2 **loaves (1 pound each) frozen bread dough, thawed**
- ¼ **pound sliced ham**
- ¼ **pound sliced pepperoni**
- ¼ **cup chopped onion**
- ¼ **cup chopped green pepper**
- 1 **jar (14 ounces) pizza sauce, divided**
- ¼ **pound sliced mozzarella cheese**
- ¼ **pound sliced bologna**
- ¼ **pound sliced hard salami**
- ¼ **pound sliced Swiss cheese**
- 1 **teaspoon dried basil**
- 1 **teaspoon dried oregano**
- ¼ **teaspoon garlic powder**
- ¼ **teaspoon pepper**
- 2 **tablespoons butter, melted**

1. Let dough rise in a warm place until doubled. Punch down. Roll loaves together into one 15x12-in. rectangle.
2. Layer ham and pepperoni on half of the dough (lengthwise). Sprinkle with onion and green pepper. Top with ¼ cup of pizza sauce. Layer mozzarella, bologna, salami and Swiss cheese over sauce. Sprinkle with basil, oregano, garlic powder and pepper. Spread another ¼ cup of pizza sauce on top. Fold plain half of dough over filling and seal edges well. Place on a greased 15x10x1-in. baking pan.
3. Bake at 375° for 30-35 minutes or until golden brown. Brush with melted butter. Heat the remaining pizza sauce and serve with sliced stromboli.

ULTIMATE Comfort Hot Bacon Cheese Spread

This creamy spread, made with Monterey Jack and Parmesan cheeses, is sure to warm up your next party. Guests never wander too far from the table when I put this out.

—BONNIE HAWKINS ELKHORN, WI

PREP: 10 MIN. • **BAKE:** 1 HOUR
MAKES: 2 CUPS

- 1 **unsliced round loaf (1 pound) Italian bread**
- 2 **cups (8 ounces) shredded Monterey Jack cheese**
- 1 **cup (4 ounces) shredded Parmesan cheese**
- 1 **cup mayonnaise**
- ¼ **cup chopped onion**
- 5 **bacon strips, cooked and crumbled**
- 1 **garlic clove, minced**

1. Cut top fourth off loaf of bread; carefully hollow out bottom, leaving a 1-in. shell. Cube removed bread and set aside. Combine the remaining ingredients; spoon into bread bowl. Replace top. Place on an ungreased baking sheet.
2. Bake at 350° for 1 hour or until heated through. Serve with reserved bread cubes.

Guacamole

Lemon or lime juice will keep the dip looking fresh and prevent discoloration until serving. Or, before chilling, you can place plastic wrap directly on the dip and lightly press so there isn't any air between the dip and the wrap.

—**ANNE TIPPS** DUNCANVILLE, TX

START TO FINISH: 10 MIN.
MAKES: ABOUT 1½ CUPS

- 1 **medium ripe avocado, halved, seeded and peeled**
- 4½ **teaspoons lemon juice**
- 1 **small tomato, seeded and finely chopped**
- ¼ **cup finely chopped onion**
- 1 **tablespoon finely chopped green chilies**
- 1 **garlic clove, minced**
- ¼ **teaspoon salt, optional**
  Tortilla chips

In a large bowl, mash avocado with lemon juice. Stir in the tomato, onion, chilies, garlic and salt if desired. Cover; chill. Serve with tortilla chips.

kid FRIENDLY Mini Corn Dogs

Summertime means county fairs and corn dogs! I make my own by wrapping cornmeal dough around mini hot dogs. Kids and the young at heart love them.

—**GERALYN HARRINGTON** FLORAL PARK, NY

START TO FINISH: 30 MIN.
MAKES: 2 DOZEN

- 1⅔ **cups all-purpose flour**
- ⅓ **cup cornmeal**
- 3 **teaspoons baking powder**
- 1 **teaspoon salt**
- 3 **tablespoons cold butter**
- 1 **tablespoon shortening**
- 1 **egg**
- ¾ **cup 2% milk**
- 24 **miniature hot dogs**
  HONEY MUSTARD SAUCE
- ⅓ **cup honey**
- ⅓ **cup prepared mustard**
- 1 **tablespoon molasses**

1. In a large bowl, combine the first four ingredients. Cut in butter and shortening until mixture resembles coarse crumbs. Beat egg and milk; stir into dry ingredients until a soft dough forms.

2. Turn onto a lightly floured surface; knead 6-8 times or until smooth. Roll out to ¼-in. thickness. Cut with a 2¼-in. biscuit cutter. Fold each dough circle over a hot dog and press edges to seal (dough will be sticky). Place on greased baking sheets.

3. Bake at 450° for 10-12 minutes or until golden brown. In a small bowl, combine the sauce ingredients. Serve with corn dogs.

Crab Spread

My family has fond memories of traveling to my parents' house for Christmas dinner. After a 12-hour drive, we would be welcomed in the door with Mom's special seafood spread.

—**BARBARA BIDDLE** HARRISBURG, PA

START TO FINISH: 20 MIN.
MAKES: 2 CUPS

- 1 **package (8 ounces) cream cheese, softened**
- 1 **can (6 ounces) crabmeat, drained, flaked and cartilage removed**
- 2 **tablespoons mayonnaise**
- 1 **teaspoon Dijon mustard**
- ½ **teaspoon lemon-pepper seasoning**
- ¼ **teaspoon minced garlic**
  Paprika
  Assorted crackers or vegetables

1. In a small bowl, combine the first six ingredients. To serve chilled, cover and refrigerate until serving. Sprinkle with paprika.

2. To serve warm, spoon into a greased 3-cup baking dish. Bake, uncovered, at 375° for 15 minutes or until heated through. Serve with crackers or vegetables.

Banana Split Shakes

These velvety smooth shakes make a special treat. They taste like an ice cream sundae, but you can sip them with a straw.

—**MARY DETWEILER** MIDDLEFIELD, OH

START TO FINISH: 10 MIN.
MAKES: 5 SERVINGS

- ½ **cup milk**
- 1 **small ripe banana, cut into chunks**
- 10 **maraschino cherries**
- 1 **tablespoon baking cocoa**
- ½ **teaspoon coconut extract**
- 3 **cups vanilla ice cream, softened**

Place the first five ingredients in a blender; cover and process until smooth. Add ice cream; cover and process until blended. Pour into chilled glasses. Serve immediately.

Sweet 'n' Tangy Chicken Wings

Here's a festive recipe that's perfect for parties. Put the wings in before you prepare for the party, and in a few hours, you'll have wonderful appetizers.

—IDA TUEY SOUTH LYON, MI

PREP: 20 MIN. • **COOK:** 3¼ HOURS
MAKES: ABOUT 2½ DOZEN

- 3 **pounds chicken wingettes (about 30)**
- ½ **teaspoon salt, divided**
  Dash pepper
- 1½ **cups ketchup**
- ¼ **cup packed brown sugar**
- ¼ **cup red wine vinegar**
- 2 **tablespoons Worcestershire sauce**
- 1 **tablespoon Dijon mustard**
- 1 **teaspoon minced garlic**
- 1 **teaspoon liquid smoke, optional**
  Sesame seeds, optional

1. Sprinkle chicken wings with a dash of salt and pepper. Broil 4-6 in. from the heat for 5-10 minutes on each side or until golden brown. Transfer to a greased 5-qt. slow cooker.

2. Combine the ketchup, brown sugar, vinegar, Worcestershire sauce, mustard, garlic, optional liquid smoke and remaining salt; pour over wings. Toss to coat.

3. Cover and cook on low for 3¼ to 3¾ hours or until chicken juices run clear. Sprinkle with sesame seeds if desired.

Did you know?

According to the National Chicken Council, wings became popular in the 1980s when consumers started eating boneless breast meat. Wings were the inexpensive byproduct.

Caramel Pretzel Sticks

Homemade caramel, smooth candy coating and chopped nuts make these pretzel rods sinfully delicious. When you carry these pretzels into a party, you will barely have time to place them on the table before they are snatched up.

—MARY BOWN EVANSTON, WY

PREP: 2 HOURS • **COOK:** 35 MIN.
MAKES: ABOUT 2½ DOZEN

- 2 **cups sugar**
- 1 **cup light corn syrup**
- 1 **cup butter, cubed**
- 1 **can (14 ounces) sweetened condensed milk**
- 1 **package (10 ounces) pretzel rods**
- 6 **to 12 ounces white candy coating**
- 6 **to 12 ounces milk chocolate candy coating**
- ¾ **cup finely chopped walnuts, optional**

1. In a large heavy saucepan, combine the sugar, corn syrup and butter. Bring just to a boil over medium heat, stirring constantly. Continue boiling, without stirring, at a moderate-steady rate for 4 minutes. Remove from the heat; stir in milk. Return to the heat. Reduce to medium-low; cook and stir until a candy thermometer reads 245° (firm-ball stage). Keep warm.

2. Pour 2 cups caramel mixture into a 2-cup glass measuring cup. Quickly dip each pretzel halfway into caramel. Allow excess to drip off. Place on well-buttered baking sheets; let stand until hardened.

3. In a microwave, melt white candy coating; stir until smooth. Dip half of the caramel-coated pretzels into coating. Melt milk chocolate coating; dip remaining pretzels. Drizzle white-coated pretzels with milk chocolate coating; drizzle milk chocolate-coated pretzels with white coating. Sprinkle with walnuts if desired. Store in an airtight container.

EDITOR'S NOTE *We recommend that you test your candy thermometer before each use by bringing water to a boil; the thermometer should read 212°. Adjust your recipe temperature up or down based on your test. Any remaining caramel mixture may be poured into a well-buttered 8x4x2-in. loaf pan. Cool to room temperature before cutting into squares and wrapping in waxed paper.*

Bacon Quiche Tarts

Flavored with vegetables, cheese and bacon, these memorable morsels are bound to be winners at any brunch. The tarts are impressive but also quite easy to make.

—KENDRA SCHERTZ NAPPANEE, IN

PREP: 15 MIN. • **BAKE:** 20 MIN.
MAKES: 8 SERVINGS

- 2 **packages (3 ounces each) cream cheese, softened**
- 5 **teaspoons 2% milk**
- 2 **Eggland's Best® Eggs**
- ½ **cup shredded Colby cheese**
- 2 **tablespoons chopped green pepper**
- 1 **tablespoon finely chopped onion**
- 1 **tube (8 ounces) refrigerated crescent rolls**
- 5 **bacon strips, cooked and crumbled**

1. In a small bowl, beat cream cheese and milk until smooth. Add the eggs, cheese, green pepper and onion.

2. Separate dough into eight triangles; press onto the bottom and up the sides of greased muffin cups. Sprinkle half of the bacon into cups. Pour egg mixture over bacon; top with remaining bacon.

3. Bake, uncovered, at 375° for 18-22 minutes or until a knife inserted near the center comes out clean. Serve warm.

Pepperoni Pinwheels

These golden brown pinwheels have lots of pepperoni flavor and are easy to make. This is the kind of recipe that makes entertaining simple and delicious.

—**VIKKI REBHOLZ** WEST CHESTER, OH

PREP: 20 MIN. • **BAKE:** 15 MIN.
MAKES: 2 DOZEN

- ½ **cup diced pepperoni**
- ½ **cup shredded part-skim mozzarella cheese**
- ¼ **teaspoon dried oregano**
- 1 **egg, separated**
- 1 **tube (8 ounces) refrigerated crescent rolls**

1. In a small bowl, combine the pepperoni, cheese, oregano and egg yolk. In another small bowl, whisk egg white until foamy; set aside. Separate crescent dough into four rectangles; seal perforations.

2. Spread pepperoni mixture over each rectangle to within ¼ in. of edges. Roll up jelly-roll style, starting with a short side; pinch seams to seal. Cut each into six slices.

3. Place cut side down on greased baking sheets; brush tops with egg white. Bake at 375° for 12-15 minutes or until golden brown. Serve warm. Refrigerate leftovers.

Beefy Taco Dip

PREP: 25 MIN. + CHILLING
COOK: 5 MIN. + COOLING
MAKES: 16-20 SERVINGS

- 1 **package (8 ounces) cream cheese, softened**
- 1 **cup (8 ounces) sour cream**
- ¾ **cup mayonnaise**
- 1 **pound ground beef**
- 1 **envelope taco seasoning**
- 1 **can (8 ounces) tomato sauce**
- 2 **cups (8 ounces) shredded cheddar or Mexican cheese blend**
- 4 **cups shredded lettuce**
- 2 **medium tomatoes, diced**
- 1 **small onion, diced**
- 1 **medium green pepper, diced**
  Tortilla chips

1. In a small bowl, beat the cream cheese, sour cream and mayonnaise until smooth. Spread on a 12 – to 14-in. pizza pan or serving dish. Refrigerate for 1 hour.

2. In a saucepan over medium heat, brown beef; drain. Add taco seasoning and tomato sauce; cook and stir for 5 minutes. Cool completely. Spread over cream cheese layer. Refrigerate.

3. Just before serving, sprinkle with cheese, lettuce, tomatoes, onion and green pepper. Serve with chips.

top tip

Meatless Dip

For those who don't like ground meat, I use refried beans with a packet of taco seasoning to add to the bottom layer. Can't go wrong.

—**KRISTANPOWELL,**
TASTEOFHOME.COM

Here's a taco dip that is a combination of several of my friends' recipes. I experimented until I came up with my favorite. It's always a hit, no matter where I take it! —**FAYE PARKER** BEDFORD, NS

Party Cheese Bread

You can't go wrong with this recipe. It looks fantastic and people just flock to it! It's great with pasta, too. It's cheesy, buttery and finger-lickin' good; no one can resist pulling off a piece of this bread.
—**KAREN GRANT** TULARE, CA

PREP: 25 MIN. • **BAKE:** 25 MIN.
MAKES: 8 SERVINGS

- ½ cup butter, melted
- 2 tablespoons lemon juice
- 2 tablespoons Dijon mustard
- 1½ teaspoons garlic powder
- ½ teaspoon onion powder
- ½ teaspoon celery salt
- 1 round loaf sourdough bread (1 pound)
- 1 pound Monterey Jack cheese, thinly sliced

1. In a small bowl, combine the first six ingredients; set aside. Cut bread diagonally into 1-in. slices to within ½ in. of bottom of loaf. Repeat cuts in opposite direction. Arrange cheese slices in cuts. Drizzle butter mixture over bread.

2. Wrap loaf in foil; place on a baking sheet. Bake at 350° for 15 minutes. Uncover; bake 10 minutes longer or until cheese is melted.

Chocolate-Covered Bacon

Feeling adventurous? It's easy to make this state fair hit at home. The salty-sweet concoction takes bacon to a new level by coating it with chocolate.
—**TASTE OF HOME TEST KITCHEN**

PREP: 20 MIN. • **BAKE:** 20 MIN.
MAKES: 1 DOZEN

- 12 thick-sliced bacon strips (about 1 pound)
- 12 wooden skewers (12 inches)
- 6 ounces white candy coating, chopped
- 1 cup semisweet chocolate chips
- 1 tablespoon shortening

Optional toppings: chopped dried apple chips, apricots and crystallized ginger, finely chopped pecans and pistachios, toasted coconut, kosher salt, brown sugar, cayenne pepper and coarsely ground black pepper

1. Thread each bacon strip onto a wooden skewer. Place on a rack in a large baking pan. Bake at 400° for 20-25 minutes or until crisp. Cool completely.

2. In a microwave, melt candy coating; stir until smooth. Combine chocolate chips and shortening; melt in a microwave and stir until smooth.

3. With pastry brushes, coat bacon on both sides with melted coatings. Top each strip as desired. Place on waxed paper-lined baking sheets. Refrigerate until firm. Store in the refrigerator.

Frappe Mocha

This fun recipe starts by making ice cubes with coffee. Make a tray the night before so you can whip up a batch of Frappe Mochas in the morning.

—BEVERLY COYDE GASPORT, NY

PREP: 5 MIN. + FREEZING
MAKES: 2 SERVINGS

- 1 **teaspoon instant coffee granules**
- ¼ **cup boiling water**
- 1 **cup fat-free milk**
- 4½ **teaspoons chocolate syrup**
- ½ **cup crushed ice**
  Whipped topping and additional chocolate syrup, optional

1. In a small bowl, dissolve coffee granules in water. Pour into an ice cube tray; freeze.
2. In a blender, combine the milk, chocolate syrup and coffee ice cubes. Cover and process until smooth. Add crushed ice; blend. Pour into chilled glasses; serve immediately. Garnish with whipped topping and additional chocolate syrup if desired.

ULTIMATE *Comfort* # Cheese-Trio Artichoke & Spinach Dip

No appetizer spread is complete without at least one amazing dip, and this is it! Creamy, cheesy, garlicky and packed full of veggies, it will quickly become your new go-to snack.

—DIANE SPEARE KISSIMMEE, FL

PREP: 20 MIN. • **COOK:** 2 HOURS
MAKES: 4 CUPS

- 1 **cup chopped fresh mushrooms**
- 1 **tablespoon butter**
- 2 **garlic cloves, minced**
- 1½ **cups mayonnaise**
- 1 **package (8 ounces) cream cheese, softened**
- 1 **cup plus 2 tablespoons grated Parmesan cheese, divided**
- 1 **cup (4 ounces) shredded part-skim mozzarella cheese, divided**
- 1 **can (14 ounces) water-packed artichoke hearts, rinsed, drained and chopped**
- 1 **package (10 ounces) frozen chopped spinach, thawed and squeezed dry**
- ¼ **cup chopped sweet red pepper**
  Toasted French bread baguette slices

1. In a large skillet, saute mushrooms in butter until tender. Add garlic; cook 1 minute longer.
2. In a large bowl, combine the mayonnaise, cream cheese, 1 cup Parmesan cheese and ¾ cup mozzarella cheese. Add the mushroom mixture, artichokes, spinach and red pepper.
3. Transfer to a 3-qt. slow cooker. Sprinkle with remaining cheeses. Cover and cook on low for 2-3 hours or until heated through. Serve with baguette slices.

Chai Tea Mix

One year, my sister-in-law mixed up this drink for a family gathering. I asked for the recipe and have been enjoying its warm, spicy flavor ever since. It goes great with a warm blanket and a good book!

—DEE FALK STROMSBURG, NE

START TO FINISH: 15 MIN.
MAKES: ABOUT 5 CUPS MIX (26 SERVINGS)

- 3 cups nonfat dry milk powder
- 1½ cups sugar
- 1 cup unsweetened instant tea
- ¾ cup vanilla powdered nondairy creamer
- 1½ teaspoons ground ginger
- 1½ teaspoons ground cinnamon
- ½ teaspoon ground cardamom
- ½ teaspoon ground cloves

OPTIONAL GARNISH

- Whipped cream

In a food processor, combine all dry ingredients; cover and process until powdery. Store in an airtight container in a cool dry place for up to 6 months.
TO PREPARE 1 SERVING *Dissolve 3 tablespoons of mix in ¾ cup boiling water; stir well. Dollop with whipped cream if desired.*

Easy Buffalo Chicken Dip

With three simple ingredients, you can turn leftover chicken into the ultimate game-day snack. I often serve this fun dip with crackers or celery.

—JANICE FOLTZ HERSHEY, PA

START TO FINISH: 30 MIN.
MAKES: 4 CUPS

- 1 package (8 ounces) reduced-fat cream cheese
- 1 cup (8 ounces) reduced-fat sour cream
- ½ cup Louisiana-style hot sauce
- 3 cups shredded cooked chicken breast
  Assorted crackers

1. In a large bowl, beat the cream cheese, sour cream and hot sauce until smooth; stir in chicken.
2. Transfer to an 8-in. square baking dish coated with cooking spray. Cover and bake at 350° for 18-22 minutes or until heated through. Serve warm with crackers.

Sweet 'n' Salty Popcorn

This popcorn recipe is a family favorite on weekend movie nights, thanks to the classic salty and sweet flavor. The secret is using instant vanilla pudding mix.

—HILARY KERR HAWKS, MI

PREP: 10 MIN. • **BAKE:** 25 MIN. + COOLING
MAKES: 10 CUPS

- 10 **cups air-popped popcorn**
- 1 **tablespoon butter**
- 5 **tablespoons instant vanilla pudding mix**
- ⅓ **cup light corn syrup**
- 1 **teaspoon vanilla extract**
  Dash salt

1. Place popcorn in a large bowl. In a small microwave-safe bowl, melt butter; whisk in the pudding mix, corn syrup, vanilla and salt until smooth.
2. Microwave, uncovered, for 45 seconds or until bubbly. Pour over popcorn; toss to coat. Spread in two 15-in. x 10-in. x 1-in. baking pans coated with cooking spray.
3. Bake at 250° for 25-30 minutes or until crisp, stirring once. Remove popcorn from pans to waxed paper to cool. Break into clusters. Store in airtight containers.
NOTE *This recipe was tested in a 1,100-watt microwave.*

Pop on...

To keep unpopped kernels out of my popcorn treats, I pour the popped corn into a big bowl, shake it a bit, and the kernels drop to the bottom. Then I transfer the popped corn to another bowl and proceed.
—CORRINE LANCE GOLD BAR, WA

Cranberry Chili Meatballs

Using packaged meatballs saves time in the kitchen and these are just as tasty as homemade. My friends look forward to enjoying these meatballs at our holiday gatherings, and there are never any leftovers!

—AMY SCAMERHORN INDIANAPOLIS, IN

START TO FINISH: 30 MIN.
MAKES: ABOUT 6 DOZEN

- 1 **can (14 ounces) jellied cranberry sauce**
- 1 **bottle (12 ounces) chili sauce**
- ¾ **cup packed brown sugar**
- ½ **teaspoon chili powder**
- ½ **teaspoon ground cumin**
- ¼ **teaspoon cayenne pepper**
- 1 **package (32 ounces) frozen fully cooked homestyle meatballs, thawed**

In a large saucepan over medium heat, combine the first six ingredients; stir until sugar is dissolved. Add meatballs; cook for 20-25 minutes or until heated through, stirring occasionally.

For entertaining, this shrimp can be prepared well in advance. I get a lot of requests for it when I make it for a party.
—**MARGARET DELONG** LAKE BUTLER, FL

Simple Marinated Shrimp

PREP: 10 MIN. + MARINATING
MAKES: 14 SERVINGS

- 2 **pounds cooked medium shrimp, peeled and deveined**
- 1 **medium red onion, sliced and separated into rings**
- 2 **medium lemons, cut into slices**
- 1 **cup pitted ripe olives, drained**
- ½ **cup olive oil**
- ⅓ **cup minced fresh parsley**
- 3 **tablespoons lemon juice**
- 3 **tablespoons red wine vinegar**
- 1 **garlic clove, minced**
- 1 **bay leaf**
- 1 **tablespoon minced fresh basil or 1 teaspoon dried basil**
- 1 **teaspoon salt**
- 1 **teaspoon ground mustard**
- ¼ **teaspoon pepper**

1. In a 3-qt. glass serving bowl, combine the shrimp, onion, lemons and olives. In a jar with a tight-fitting lid, combine the remaining ingredients; shake well. Pour over shrimp mixture and stir gently to coat.
2. Cover and refrigerate for 24 hours, stirring occasionally. Discard bay leaf before serving.

Ranch Snack Mix

This is a wonderful fast-fix munchie when you crave a salty snack. The recipe makes a generous 24 cups for sharing and doesn't involve any cooking—it's a cinch.
—**LINDA MURPHY** PULASKI, WI

START TO FINISH: 15 MIN.
MAKES: 6 QUARTS

- 1 **package (12 ounces) miniature pretzels**
- 2 **packages (6 ounces each) Bugles**
- 1 **can (10 ounces) salted cashews**
- 1 **package (6 ounces) bite-size cheddar cheese fish crackers**
- 1 **envelope ranch salad dressing mix**
- ¾ **cup canola oil**

In two large bowls, combine the pretzels, Bugles, cashews and crackers. Sprinkle with dressing mix; toss gently to combine. Drizzle with oil; toss until well coated. Store in airtight containers.

Appetizer Tortilla Pinwheels

A friend gave me the recipe for this fun and tasty appetizer. You can prepare the pinwheels in advance and slice just before serving to save time.
—**PAT WAYMIRE** YELLOW SPRINGS, OH

PREP: 20 MIN. + CHILLING
MAKES: ABOUT 4 DOZEN

- 1 **cup (8 ounces) sour cream**
- 1 **package (8 ounces) cream cheese, softened**
- 1 **can (4¼ ounces) chopped ripe olives**
- 1 **can (4 ounces) chopped green chilies, well drained**
- 1 **cup (4 ounces) shredded cheddar cheese**
- ½ **cup chopped green onions**
  Garlic powder to taste
  Seasoned salt to taste
- 5 **flour tortillas (10 inches), room temperature**
  Fresh parsley for garnish
  Salsa

1. In a large bowl, beat the first eight ingredients until blended. Spread over the tortillas; roll up tightly. Wrap each with plastic wrap, twisting ends; refrigerate for several hours.
2. Unwrap; cut into ½-in. to ¾-in. slices. (An electric knife works best.) Discard ends. Garnish with parsley. Serve with salsa if desired.

kid FRIENDLY

Hot Cocoa

Treat family and friends to a rich homemade cocoa. It will warm even the coldest winter's chill!

—VICKI HOLLOWAY JOELTON, TN

START TO FINISH: 15 MIN.
MAKES: 10 SERVINGS (2½ QUARTS)

- 1 **cup sugar**
- ⅔ **cup baking cocoa**
- ¼ **teaspoon salt**
- 8 **cups 2% milk**
- ⅔ **cup water**
- 2 **teaspoons vanilla extract**
- ½ **teaspoon almond extract**
     Miniature marshmallows, optional

In a large saucepan, combine the sugar, cocoa and salt. Stir in milk and water. Cook and stir over medium heat until heated through. Remove from the heat; stir in extracts. Serve in mugs with marshmallows if desired.

Cola Hot Wings

These are easy to make and they offer year-round versatility, from summer cookouts to autumn tailgates. My husband likes them so much, he'll stand out in the snow to grill them!

—LISA LINVILLE RANDOLPH, NE

PREP: 15 MIN. • **GRILL:** 40 MIN.
MAKES: ABOUT 2½ DOZEN

- 3 **pounds chicken wings**
- 1 **cup Louisiana-style hot sauce**
- 1 **can (12 ounces) cola**
- 1 **tablespoon soy sauce**
- ¼ **teaspoon cayenne pepper**
- ¼ **teaspoon pepper**
     Blue cheese salad dressing

1. Cut chicken wings into three sections; discard wing tip sections. In a small bowl, combine the hot sauce, cola, soy sauce, cayenne and pepper.
2. Prepare grill for indirect heat, using a drip pan. Moisten a paper towel with cooking oil; using long-handled tongs, lightly coat the grill rack. Grill chicken wings, covered, over indirect medium heat for 10 minutes. Grill 30-40 minutes longer, turning occasionally and basting frequently with sauce until wings are nicely glazed. Serve with salad dressing.
NOTE *Uncooked chicken wing sections (wingettes) may be substituted for whole chicken wings.*

Did you know?

Nationwide, ranch dressing is the most popular dip for wings. But according to the National Chicken Council, wing eaters in the Northeast are more likely to prefer blue cheese dressing than those in the Midwest or South.

Sausage-Stuffed Mushrooms

A few years back, I was looking for a snack that would suit my family's tastes. I combined three different recipes and came up with this one. They love the rich Parmesan flavor.

—**KATHY DEEZIK** HARTSTOWN, PA

START TO FINISH: 30 MIN.
MAKES: ABOUT 2 DOZEN

- 20 to 24 **large fresh mushrooms**
- 2 **tablespoons finely chopped onion**
- 1 **tablespoon butter**
- 2 to 3 **garlic cloves, minced**
- ¼ **pound bulk pork sausage, cooked, crumbled and drained**
- 3 **tablespoons seasoned bread crumbs**
- 3 **tablespoons grated Parmesan cheese**
- 1 **tablespoon dried parsley flakes**
- 1 **egg white**

1. Remove mushroom stems from caps. Set caps aside (discard stems or save for another use). In a small skillet, saute onion in butter until tender. Add garlic; cook 1 minute longer.

2. In a large bowl, combine the sausage, bread crumbs, cheese, parsley and egg white. Stir in onion mixture. Fill the mushroom caps; place in a lightly greased 15-in. x 10-in. x 1-in. baking pan.

3. Bake at 350° for 10-15 minutes or until mushrooms are tender and tops are browned.

2. Immediately spread onto waxed paper-lined baking sheet; let stand until set, about 20 minutes.

3. Break into pieces. Store in an airtight container.

Fruit Smoothies

I make smoothies often because my family likes them. Smoothies are just right for breakfast, dessert or afternoon snacks. It's fun to experiment with different fruits and berries.

—**SUSAN MCCARTNEY** ONALASKA, WI

START TO FINISH: 10 MIN.
MAKES: 4 SERVINGS

- 1 cup fat-free milk
- ½ cup plain yogurt
- ¼ teaspoon vanilla extract
- 1½ cups fresh or frozen strawberries, thawed
- ½ cup canned unsweetened pineapple chunks
- ¼ cup nonfat dry milk powder
- 4 ice cubes
- 2 tablespoons sugar

In a blender, combine all ingredients; cover and process for 30-45 seconds or until blended. Stir if necessary. Pour into chilled glasses; serve immediately.

kid FRIENDLY
Caramel Fruit Dip

What a tasty way to eat your fruit with this sweet, creamy dip. It's a wonderful treat in autumn when apples are in season.

—**TRISH GEHLHAR** YPSILANTI, ND

START TO FINISH: 10 MIN.
MAKES: 3 CUPS

- 2 packages (8 ounces each) cream cheese, softened
- 1 cup packed brown sugar
- ½ cup caramel ice cream topping
  Assorted fresh fruit

In a small bowl, beat cream cheese and brown sugar until smooth. Beat in caramel topping until blended. Serve with fruit. Refrigerate leftovers.

Blizzard Party Mix

This sweet-salty snack mix is sure to be popular. It's perfect for a party, munching at home or giving away as a gift.

—**KELLEY SCOTT** PARMA, OH

START TO FINISH: 30 MIN.
MAKES: 6 CUPS

- 2 cups Corn Chex
- 2 cups miniature pretzels
- 1 cup dry roasted peanuts
- 20 caramels, coarsely chopped
- 1 package (10 to 12 ounces) white baking chips

1. In a large bowl, combine the first four ingredients. In a microwave, melt chips; stir until smooth. Pour over cereal mixture and toss to coat.

Breakfast & Brunch

RISE AND SHINE WITH 36 THINGS TO BE HAPPY
ABOUT FIRST THING IN THE MORNING.

**BLUEBERRY
SOUR CREAM PANCAKES**
PAGE 41

**MAPLE-GLAZED
SAUSAGES**
PAGE 43

**OMELET
CROISSANTS**
PAGE 47

Cinnamon Peach Kuchen

With its flaky, buttery crust and sweet peach topping, this is one of my favorite treats. It can be served warm or cold. It's a tried and true recipe from my mother.

—**RACHEL GARCIA** FORT KNOX, KY

PREP: 25 MIN. • **BAKE:** 45 MIN. + COOLING
MAKES: 10 SERVINGS

- 2 **cups all-purpose flour**
- 2 **tablespoons sugar**
- ½ **teaspoon salt**
- ¼ **teaspoon baking powder**
- ½ **cup cold butter, cubed**
- 2 **cans (15¼ ounces each) peach halves, drained and patted dry**
- 1 **cup packed brown sugar**
- 1 **teaspoon ground cinnamon**
- 2 **egg yolks, lightly beaten**
- 1 **cup heavy whipping cream**

1. In a small bowl, combine the flour, sugar, salt and baking powder; cut in butter until crumbly. Press onto the bottom and 1½ in. up the sides of a greased 9-in. springform pan.

2. Place pan on a baking sheet. Arrange peach halves, cut side up, in the crust. Combine brown sugar and cinnamon; sprinkle over peaches.

3. Bake at 350° for 20 minutes. Combine egg yolks and cream; pour over peaches. Bake 25-30 minutes longer or until top is set. Cool on a wire rack. Refrigerate leftovers.

Strawberry Cream Crepes

PREP: 25 MIN. + CHILLING • **COOK:** 1 HOUR
MAKES: 22 CREPES

- 1½ **cups milk**
- 3 **eggs**
- 2 **tablespoons butter, melted**
- ½ **teaspoon lemon extract**
- 1¼ **cups all-purpose flour**
- 2 **tablespoons sugar**
  Dash salt
- **TOPPING**
- ½ **cup sugar**
- 2 **tablespoons cornstarch**
- ¾ **cup water**
- 1 **tablespoon lemon juice**
- 1 **teaspoon strawberry extract**
- ¼ **teaspoon red food coloring, optional**
- 4 **cups sliced fresh strawberries**
- **FILLING**
- 1 **cup heavy whipping cream**
- 1 **package (8 ounces) cream cheese, softened**
- 2 **cups confectioners' sugar**
- 1 **teaspoon vanilla extract**

1. In a large bowl, combine the milk, eggs, butter and extract. Combine the flour, sugar and salt; add to milk mixture and mix well. Cover and refrigerate for 1 hour. Heat a lightly greased 8-in. nonstick skillet over medium heat; pour 2 tablespoons batter into the center of skillet. Lift and tilt pan to coat bottom evenly. Cook until top appears dry; turn and cook 15-20 seconds longer. Remove to a wire rack. Repeat with remaining batter, greasing skillet as needed. When cool, stack crepes separated by paper towels or pieces of wax paper.

2. In a small saucepan, combine sugar and cornstarch; stir in water and lemon juice until smooth. Bring to a boil over medium heat; cook and stir for 1 minute or until thickened. Stir in extract and food coloring if desired. Cool. Add strawberries.

3. In a small bowl, beat the cream until stiff peaks form; set aside. In a large bowl, beat the cream cheese, confectioners' sugar and vanilla until smooth; fold in whipped cream. Spoon 2 rounded tablespoons of filling down the center of each crepe; roll up. Top with strawberry topping.

I always feel like a French chef when I serve these pretty crepes. Although they take a little time to prepare, they're well worth the effort.

—DEBRA LATTA PORT MATILDA, PA

Crunchy Apple Salad

With fiber-rich fruit, light dressing and crunchy walnuts, this is a great munchie you can feel good about.

—**KATHY ARMSTRONG** POST FALLS, ID

START TO FINISH: 15 MIN.
MAKES: 5 SERVINGS

- 6 **tablespoons fat-free sugar-free vanilla yogurt**
- 6 **tablespoons reduced-fat whipped topping**
- ¼ **teaspoon plus ⅛ teaspoon ground cinnamon, divided**
- 2 **medium red apples, chopped**
- 1 **large Granny Smith apple, chopped**
- ¼ **cup dried cranberries**
- 2 **tablespoons chopped walnuts**

In a large bowl, combine the yogurt, whipped topping and ¼ teaspoon cinnamon. Add apples and cranberries; toss to coat. Refrigerate until serving. Sprinkle with walnuts and remaining cinnamon before serving.

Spiced Bacon Twists

Whenever I share this recipe, I have to issue a caveat that bacon might become even more addictive after your first bite. Don't say I didn't warn you!

—**GLENDA EVANS WITTNER** JOPLIN, MO

PREP: 10 MIN. • **BAKE:** 25 MIN.
MAKES: 5 SERVINGS

- ¼ **cup packed brown sugar**
- 1½ **teaspoons ground mustard**
- ⅛ **teaspoon ground cinnamon**
- ⅛ **teaspoon ground nutmeg**
   Dash cayenne pepper
- 10 **center-cut bacon strips**

1. Preheat oven to 350°. Combine first five ingredients; rub over bacon on both sides. Twist bacon; place on a rack in a 15x10x1-in. baking pan.
2. Bake 25-30 minutes or until firm; bake longer if desired.

Did you know?

Bacon has been comforting diners since 1500 B.C. Preserving and salting pork bellies began in China around that time, and the Greeks and Romans kept up the tasty tradition.

Blueberry Sour Cream Coffee Cake

Holiday breakfasts would not be the same at our house without this delicious coffee cake. Whenever I take it anywhere, everyone wants the recipe, and I'm happy to share it.

—**SUSAN WALSCHLAGER** ANDERSON, IN

PREP: 25 MIN. • **BAKE:** 55 MIN. + COOLING
MAKES: 10-12 SERVINGS

- ¾ cup butter, softened
- 1½ cups sugar
- 4 eggs
- 1 teaspoon vanilla extract
- 3 cups all-purpose flour
- 1½ teaspoons baking powder
- ¾ teaspoon baking soda
- ¼ teaspoon salt
- 1 cup (8 ounces) sour cream

FILLING

- ¼ cup packed brown sugar
- 1 tablespoon all-purpose flour
- ½ teaspoon ground cinnamon
- 2 cups fresh or frozen blueberries

GLAZE

- 1 cup confectioners' sugar
- 2 to 3 tablespoons 2% milk

1. In a large bowl, cream butter and sugar until light and fluffy. Add eggs, one at a time, beating well after each addition. Beat in vanilla. Combine the flour, baking powder, baking soda and salt; add to creamed mixture alternately with sour cream, beating well after each addition.

2. Spoon a third of the batter into a greased and floured 10-in. tube pan. Combine brown sugar, flour and cinnamon; sprinkle half over batter. Top with half of the berries. Repeat layers. Top with remaining batter.

3. Bake at 350° for 55-65 minutes or until a toothpick inserted near the center comes out clean. Cool for 10 minutes before removing from pan to a wire rack to cool completely. Combine glaze ingredients; drizzle over warm coffee cake.

NOTE *If using frozen blueberries, use without thawing to avoid discoloring the batter.*

Cherry Chip Scones

These buttery scones, dotted with dried cherries and vanilla chips, are so sweet and flaky that I even serve them for dessert.

—**PAM BROOKS SOUTH** BERWICK, ME

PREP: 15 MIN. • **BAKE:** 20 MIN.
MAKES: 8 SERVINGS

- 3 cups all-purpose flour
- ½ cup sugar
- 2½ teaspoons baking powder
- ½ teaspoon baking soda
- 6 tablespoons cold butter
- 1 cup (8 ounces) vanilla yogurt
- ¼ cup plus 2 tablespoons milk, divided
- 1⅓ cups dried cherries
- ⅔ cup white baking chips
  Coarse sugar, optional

1. In a large bowl, combine the flour, sugar, baking powder and baking soda. Cut in butter until the mixture resembles coarse crumbs. Combine yogurt and ¼ cup milk; stir into crumb mixture just until moistened. Knead in the cherries and chips.

2. On a greased baking sheet, pat the dough into a 9-in. circle. Cut into eight wedges; separate wedges. Brush with remaining milk. If desired, sprinkle with sugar. Bake at 400° for 20-25 minutes or until golden brown. Serve warm.

NOTE *If using frozen blueberries, use without thawing to avoid discoloring the batter.*

Amish Breakfast Casserole

We enjoyed a hearty breakfast bake during a visit to an Amish inn. When I asked for the recipe, one of the ladies told me the ingredients right off the top of her head. I modified it to create this version my family loves.

—**BETH NOTARO** KOKOMO, IN

PREP: 15 MIN. • **BAKE:** 35 MIN. + STANDING
MAKES: 12 SERVINGS

- 1 pound sliced bacon, diced
- 1 medium sweet onion, chopped
- 6 eggs, lightly beaten
- 4 cups frozen shredded hash brown potatoes, thawed
- 2 cups (8 ounces) shredded cheddar cheese
- 1½ cups (12 ounces) 4% cottage cheese
- 1¼ cups shredded Swiss cheese

1. In a large skillet, cook bacon and onion until bacon is crisp; drain. In a large bowl, combine the remaining ingredients; stir in bacon mixture. Transfer to a greased 13-in. x 9-in. baking dish.

2. Bake, uncovered, at 350° for 35-40 minutes or until a knife inserted near the center comes out clean. Let stand for 10 minutes before cutting.

---

kid FRIENDLY

Fruity Baked Oatmeal

This is my husband's favorite breakfast treat and such a comfort food. It's warm, filling and always a hit when I serve it to guests. Kids love the fruity mix-ins.

—**KAREN SCHROEDER** KANKAKEE, IL

PREP: 15 MIN. • **BAKE:** 35 MIN.
MAKES: 9 SERVINGS

- 3 cups quick-cooking oats
- 1 cup packed brown sugar
- 2 teaspoons baking powder
- 1 teaspoon salt
- ½ teaspoon ground cinnamon
- 2 eggs, lightly beaten
- 1 cup fat-free milk
- ½ cup butter, melted
- ¾ cup chopped peeled tart apple
- ⅓ cup chopped fresh or frozen peaches
- ⅓ cup fresh or frozen blueberries
  Additional fat-free milk, optional

1. In a large bowl, combine the oats, brown sugar, baking powder, salt and cinnamon. Combine the eggs, milk and butter; add to the dry ingredients. Stir in the apple, peaches and blueberries.

2. Pour into an 8-in. square baking dish coated with cooking spray. Bake, uncovered, at 350° for 35-40 minutes or until a knife inserted near the center comes out clean. Cut into squares. Serve with milk if desired.

NOTE *If using frozen blueberries, use without thawing to avoid discoloring the batter.*

ULTIMATE *Comfort* Biscuits and Sausage Gravy

This is an old Southern recipe that I've adapted. It's the kind of hearty breakfast that will warm you right up.

—**SUE BAKER** JONESBORO, AR

START TO FINISH: 15 MIN.
MAKES: 2 SERVINGS

- ¼ **pound bulk pork sausage**
- 2 **tablespoons butter**
- 2 **to 3 tablespoons all-purpose flour**
- ¼ **teaspoon salt**
- ⅛ **teaspoon pepper**
- 1¼ **to 1⅓ cups milk**
  Warm biscuits

In a small skillet, cook sausage over medium heat until no longer pink; drain. Add butter and heat until melted. Add the flour, salt and pepper; cook and stir until blended. Gradually add the milk, stirring constantly. Bring to a boil; cook and stir for 2 minutes or until thickened. Serve with biscuits.

Orange Zucchini Muffins

Orange juice and peel infuse these soft muffins with a pleasant citrus flavor. We enjoy them fresh from the oven.

—**CHRIS SNYDER** BOULDER, CO

PREP: 15 MIN. • **BAKE:** 20 MIN.
MAKES: 10 MUFFINS.

- 1 **cup shredded zucchini**
- 1¼ **cups all-purpose flour**
- ¾ **teaspoon ground nutmeg, divided**
- ½ **teaspoon baking powder**
- ½ **teaspoon baking soda**
- ½ **teaspoon ground cinnamon**
- ¼ **teaspoon salt**
- 2 **eggs**
- ¾ **cup packed brown sugar**
- ⅓ **cup canola oil**
- 2 **tablespoons orange juice**
- 1 **teaspoon grated orange peel**
- 1 **teaspoon vanilla extract**
- ½ **cup raisins**
- 1 **tablespoon sugar**

1. Squeeze zucchini until dry; set aside. In a large bowl, combine the flour, ½ teaspoon nutmeg, baking powder, baking soda, cinnamon and salt. In another bowl, whisk the eggs, brown sugar, oil, orange juice, orange peel and vanilla. Stir into dry ingredients just until moistened. Fold in raisins and reserved zucchini.

2. Fill paper-lined muffin cups two-thirds full. Combine sugar and remaining nutmeg; sprinkle over batter. Bake at 350° for 18-22 minutes or until a toothpick inserted near the center comes out clean. Cool for 5 minutes before removing from pan to a wire rack. Serve warm.

TO FREEZE MUFFINS *Wrap individually in foil, transfer to a resealable plastic freezer bag and freeze for up to 3 months. To use frozen muffins, remove foil and thaw at room temperature. Warm in oven or microwave if desired.*

These tasty morsels are perfect with almost any egg dish or as finger foods that party guests can just pop into their mouths. Try them with your favorite egg bake.

—**PAT WAYMIRE** YELLOW SPRINGS, OH

Sausage Bacon Bites

PREP: 20 MIN. + CHILLING • **BAKE:** 35 MIN.
MAKES: ABOUT 3½ DOZEN

- ¾ **pound sliced bacon**
- 2 **packages (8 ounces each) frozen fully cooked breakfast sausage links, thawed**
- ½ **cup plus 2 tablespoons packed brown sugar, divided**

1. Cut bacon strips widthwise in half; cut sausage links in half. Wrap a piece of bacon around each piece of sausage. Place ½ cup brown sugar in a shallow bowl; roll sausages in sugar. Secure each with a toothpick. Place in a foil-lined 15-in. x 10-in. x 1-in. baking pan. Cover and refrigerate for 4 hours or overnight.

2. Sprinkle with 1 tablespoon brown sugar. Bake at 350° for 35-40 minutes or until bacon is crisp, turning once. Sprinkle with remaining brown sugar.

kid FRIENDLY Caramel-Pecan Monkey Bread

You can either cut this bread into generous slices, or have your guests pick off the gooey pieces themselves, just like monkeys! No one can resist this tender, caramel-coated bread.

—TASTE OF HOME TEST KITCHEN

PREP: 20 MIN. + CHILLING
BAKE: 30 MIN. + COOLING
MAKES: 1 LOAF (20 SERVINGS)

- 1 **package (¼ ounce) active dry yeast**
- ¼ **cup water (110° to 115°)**
- 1¼ **cups warm 2% milk (110° to 115°)**
- ⅓ **cup butter, melted**
- ¼ **cup sugar**
- 2 **eggs**
- 1 **teaspoon salt**
- 5 **cups all-purpose flour**

CARAMEL
- ⅔ **cup packed brown sugar**
- ¼ **cup butter, cubed**
- ¼ **cup heavy whipping cream**

ASSEMBLY
- ¾ **cup chopped pecans**
- 1 **cup sugar**
- 1 **teaspoon ground cinnamon**
- ½ **cup butter, melted**

1. In a large bowl, dissolve yeast in warm water. Add the milk, butter, sugar, eggs, salt and 3 cups flour. Beat on medium speed for 3 minutes. Stir in enough remaining flour to form a firm dough.

2. Turn onto a floured surface; knead until smooth and elastic, about 6-8 minutes. Place in a greased bowl, turning once to grease the top. Cover and refrigerate overnight.

3. For caramel, in a small saucepan, bring the brown sugar, butter and cream to a boil. Cook and stir for 3 minutes. Pour half into a greased 10-in. fluted tube pan; sprinkle with half of the pecans.

4. Punch dough down; shape into 40 balls (about 1¼-in. diameter). In a shallow bowl, combine sugar and cinnamon. Place melted butter in another bowl. Dip balls in butter, then roll in sugar mixture.

5. Place 20 balls in the tube pan; top with remaining caramel and pecans. Top with remaining balls. Cover and let rise until doubled, about 45 minutes.

6. Bake at 350° for 30-35 minutes or until golden brown. (Cover loosely with foil if top browns too quickly.) Cool for 10 minutes before inverting onto a serving plate. Serve warm.

Dad's Quick Bagel Omelet Sandwich

To give my kids a hearty start to the day, I wrap these tasty sandwiches in foil and hand them out as the kids run for the school bus!

—ANDREW NODOLSKI WILLIAMSTOWN, NJ

START TO FINISH: 20 MIN.
MAKES: 4 SERVINGS

- ¼ cup finely chopped onion
- 1 tablespoon butter
- 4 eggs
- ¼ cup chopped tomato
- ⅛ teaspoon salt
- ⅛ teaspoon hot pepper sauce
- 4 slices Canadian bacon
- 4 plain bagels, split
- 4 slices process American cheese

1. In a large skillet, saute onion in butter until tender. Whisk the eggs, tomato, salt and pepper sauce. Add egg mixture to skillet (mixture should set immediately at edges).
2. As eggs set, push cooked edges toward the center, letting uncooked portion flow underneath. Cook until eggs are set. Meanwhile, heat bacon in the microwave and toast bagels if desired.
3. Layer bagel bottoms with cheese. Cut omelet into fourths and serve on bagels with bacon.

Fiesta Scrambled Eggs

I love to fix this spicy scrambled egg dish for friends and family. It's a meal in itself, but I serve it with muffins or biscuits, fresh fruit juice and coffee.

—KAY KROPFF CANYON, TX

START TO FINISH: 30 MIN.
MAKES: 6 SERVINGS

- ½ cup chopped onion
- ¼ cup chopped sweet red pepper
- 1 jalapeno pepper, seeded and chopped
- 8 bacon strips, cooked and crumbled
- 8 eggs, lightly beaten
- 1 cup (4 ounces) shredded cheddar cheese, divided
- ½ teaspoon salt
- ⅛ teaspoon pepper
  Salsa

In a large nonstick skillet coated with cooking spray, saute the onion and peppers until tender. Sprinkle with bacon. Pour eggs over the top; sprinkle with ½ cup cheese, salt and pepper. Cook over medium heat, stirring occasionally, until eggs are completely set. Sprinkle with remaining cheese. Serve with salsa.

NOTE *Wear disposable gloves when cutting hot peppers; the oils can burn skin. Avoid touching your face.*

top tip — Make It Quick

To make this omelet sandwich quicker, we toss two eggs into a small round container about the size of the bagel and zap on high for 2 minutes. The Canadian Bacon cooks in the microwave with the egg for the last 30 seconds.

—CSBOWER TASTEOFHOME.COM

2. Fill greased or paper-lined muffin cups three-fourths full. Bake at 350° for 18-22 minutes or until a toothpick inserted in muffin comes out clean. Cool for 5 minutes before removing from pans to wire racks.

ULTIMATE *Comfort* Blueberry Sour Cream Pancakes

When our family of 10 goes blueberry picking, we have a bounty of berries in no time. We especially enjoy them in these melt-in your mouth pancakes topped with a rich blueberry sauce.

—**PAULA HADLEY** SOMERVILLE, LA

PREP: 20 MIN. • **COOK:** 5MIN./BATCH
MAKES: ABOUT 20 PANCAKES
(3½ CUPS TOPPING)

- ½ **cup sugar**
- 2 **tablespoons cornstarch**
- 1 **cup cold water**
- 4 **cups fresh or frozen blueberries**

PANCAKES

- 2 **cups all-purpose flour**
- ¼ **cup sugar**
- 4 **teaspoons baking powder**
- ½ **teaspoon salt**

- 2 **eggs, lightly beaten**
- 1½ **cups 2% milk**
- 1 **cup (8 ounces) sour cream**
- ⅓ **cup butter, melted**
- 1 **cup fresh or frozen blueberries**

1. In a large saucepan, combine sugar and cornstarch. Stir in water until smooth. Add blueberries. Bring to a boil over medium heat; cook and stir for 2 minutes or until thickened. Remove from the heat; cover and keep warm.

2. For pancakes, in a large bowl, combine the flour, sugar, baking powder and salt. Combine the eggs, milk, sour cream and butter. Stir into dry ingredients just until moistened. Fold in blueberries.

3. Pour batter by ¼ cupful onto a greased hot griddle. Turn when bubbles form on top; cook until the second side is golden brown. Serve with blueberry topping.

NOTE *If using frozen blueberries, use without thawing to avoid discoloring the batter.*

Apple Bran Muffins

My mom taught me how to make these soft and spicy muffins. The recipe makes a big batch, so you can freeze the extras or share with co-workers, family or friends.

—**KELLY KIRBY** SHAWNIGAN LAKE, BC

PREP: 25 MIN. • **BAKE:** 20 MIN. + COOLING
MAKES: 2 DOZEN

- 3 **cups all-purpose flour**
- 2 **teaspoons baking powder**
- 2 **teaspoons ground cinnamon**
- 1 **teaspoon salt**
- ½ **teaspoon baking soda**
- ¼ **teaspoon ground nutmeg**
- 1½ **cups 2% milk**
- 4 **eggs**
- ⅔ **cup packed brown sugar**
- ½ **cup canola oil**
- 2 **teaspoons vanilla extract**
- 3 **cups All-Bran**
- 2 **cups shredded peeled tart apples**
- 1 **cup chopped walnuts**
- 1 **cup raisins**

1. In a large bowl, combine the first six ingredients. In another bowl, combine the milk, eggs, brown sugar, oil and vanilla. Stir into dry ingredients just until moistened. Fold in remaining ingredients.

Sunny Morning Doughnuts

I love, love, love doughnuts, but buying them can get expensive. This recipe is economical and delicious. It beats any store-bought doughnut.

—SHERRY FLAQUEL CUTLER BAY, FL

PREP: 30 MIN. + CHILLING
COOK: 5 MIN./BATCH
MAKES: 20 DOUGHNUTS

- 4½ to 5 cups all-purpose flour
- 1¼ cups sugar
- 4 teaspoons baking powder
- 1 teaspoon salt
- 3 eggs, lightly beaten
- 1 cup 2% milk
- ¼ cup canola oil
- 2 tablespoons orange juice
- 4 teaspoons grated orange peel
  Oil for deep-fat frying
  Confectioners' sugar

1. In a large bowl, combine 4½ cups flour, sugar, baking powder and salt.

2. Combine the eggs, milk, oil, orange juice and peel; stir into dry ingredients just until moistened. Stir in enough remaining flour to form a soft dough. Cover and refrigerate for at least 1 hour.

3. Turn onto a floured surface; roll to ½-in. thickness. Cut with a floured 2½-in. doughnut cutter.

4. In an electric skillet or deep-fat fryer, heat oil to 375°. Fry doughnuts, a few at a time, until golden brown on both sides. Drain on paper towels. Dust warm doughnuts with confectioners' sugar.

TO FREEZE DOUGHNUTS *Wrap doughnuts in foil; transfer to a resealable plastic freezer bag. May be frozen for up to 3 months. To use frozen doughnuts, remove foil and thaw at room temperature. Warm if desired.*

Raspberry Cheese Danish

Your guests will think you made these yummy rolls from scratch...or bought them from a specialty bakery. No one needs to know the recipe calls for refrigerated dough!

—**KAREN WEIR** LITCHFIELD, CT

START TO FINISH: 25 MIN.
MAKES: 8 SERVINGS

- 4 **ounces cream cheese, softened**
- ¼ **cup plus ½ cup confectioners' sugar, divided**
- 1 **can (8 ounces) refrigerated crescent rolls**
- ½ **cup seedless raspberry jam**
- 2 **teaspoons 2% milk**

1. In a small bowl, beat cream cheese and ¼ cup confectioners' sugar until smooth. Unroll crescent dough and separate into four rectangles; seal perforations. Cut each rectangle in half, making eight squares.
2. Transfer squares to a parchment paper-lined baking sheet. Spread 1 tablespoon cream cheese mixture diagonally across each square. Top with 1 tablespoon jam. Bring two opposite corners of dough over filling; pinch together firmly to seal.
3. Bake at 375° for 10-12 minutes or until golden brown. Combine milk and remaining confectioners' sugar; drizzle over pastries. Serve warm. Refrigerate leftovers.

? Did you know?

Canada supplies nearly 80 percent of the maple syrup in the world. Now consider this: It takes 40 gallons of sugar maple tree sap to produce 1 gallon of maple syrup—and it's worth every drop.

Maple-Glazed Sausages

It's so easy to simmer up a sugar-and-spice syrup to cover a skillet full of breakfast sausages. They go well with eggs, French toast and pancakes.

—**TRUDIE HAGEN** ROGGEN, CO

START TO FINISH: 20 MIN.
MAKES: 10 SERVINGS

- 2 **packages (6.4 ounces each) frozen fully cooked breakfast sausage links**
- 1 **cup maple syrup**
- ½ **cup packed brown sugar**
- 1 **teaspoon ground cinnamon**

In a large skillet, brown sausage links. In a small bowl, combine the syrup, brown sugar and cinnamon; pour over sausages. Bring to a boil. Reduce heat; simmer, uncovered, until sausages are glazed.

Caramel Apple Strata

PREP: 20 MIN. + CHILLING
BAKE: 50 MIN. + STANDING
MAKES: 12 SERVINGS

- 2 **cups packed brown sugar**
- ½ **cup butter, cubed**
- ¼ **cup corn syrup**
- 3 **large apples, peeled and chopped**
- 2 **tablespoons lemon juice**
- 1 **tablespoon sugar**
- 1 **teaspoon apple pie spice**
- 1 **loaf (1 pound) day-old cinnamon bread**
- ½ **cup chopped pecans**
- 10 **eggs**
- 1 **cup 2% milk**
- 1 **teaspoon salt**
- 1 **teaspoon vanilla extract**

1. In a small saucepan, combine brown sugar, butter and corn syrup. Bring to a boil over medium heat, stirring constantly. Cook and stir 2 minutes or until thickened. Set aside.
2. In a small bowl, combine apples, lemon juice, sugar and pie spice. Arrange half the bread slices in a greased 13x9-in. baking dish. Spoon apples over bread; drizzle with half the caramel sauce. Sprinkle with pecans; top with remaining bread.
3. In a large bowl, combine eggs, milk, salt and vanilla. Pour over top. Cover and refrigerate overnight. Cover and refrigerate remaining caramel sauce.
4. Remove strata from refrigerator 30 minutes before baking. Preheat oven to 350°. Bake, uncovered, 50-55 minutes or until a knife inserted near center comes out clean. Let stand 10 minutes before cutting.
5. In a small microwave-safe dish, microwave reserved sauce, uncovered, 1-2 minutes or until heated through. Drizzle over strata.

kid FRIENDLY
Easy Morning Waffles

Making your own fluffy waffles from scratch takes no time at all, and the touch of cinnamon in these beats any store-bought frozen version.
—TASTE OF HOME TEST KITCHEN

PREP: 20 MIN. • **COOK:** 5 MIN./BATCH
MAKES: 14 WAFFLES (1 CUP SYRUP)

- 2 **cups all-purpose flour**
- 1 **tablespoon brown sugar**
- 2 **teaspoons baking powder**
- ½ **teaspoon salt**
- ½ **teaspoon ground cinnamon**
- 3 **eggs, separated**
- 2 **cups 2% milk**
- ¼ **cup canola oil**
- ¾ **teaspoon vanilla extract**
SYRUP
- ½ **cup butter, cubed**
- ½ **cup honey**
- 1 **teaspoon ground cinnamon**

1. In a large bowl, combine the flour, brown sugar, baking powder, salt and cinnamon. In a small bowl, whisk the egg yolks, milk, oil and vanilla; stir into dry ingredients just until moistened. In a small bowl, beat egg whites until stiff peaks form; fold into batter.
2. Bake in a preheated waffle iron according to manufacturer's directions until golden brown.
3. In a microwave, melt the butter, honey and cinnamon; stir until smooth. Serve over waffles.

TO FREEZE WAFFLES AND SYRUP
Arrange waffles in a single layer on sheet pans. Freeze overnight or until frozen. Transfer to a resealable plastic freezer bag. Pour remaining syrup into a freezer container. Waffles and syrup may be frozen for up to 2 months. To use frozen waffles and syrup, reheat waffles in a toaster. Microwave syrup until heated through and serve with waffles.

The flavors associated with autumn put an unexpected twist on a classic strata. This is great for brunch.

—**KELLY BOE** WHITELAND, IN

Sausage-Mushroom Breakfast Bake

My mom shared this delicious recipe when I needed to bring a dish to a breakfast potluck. Everyone loved it.

—**DIANE BABBITT** LUDLOW, MA

PREP: 25 MIN. • **BAKE:** 50 MIN. + STANDING
MAKES: 12 SERVINGS

- 1 **pound bulk pork sausage**
- 2 **cups sliced fresh mushrooms**
- 6 **cups cubed bread**
- 2 **cups (8 ounces) shredded sharp cheddar cheese**
- 1 **cup chopped fresh tomatoes**
- 10 **eggs, lightly beaten**
- 3 **cups milk**
- 2 **teaspoons ground mustard**
- ½ **teaspoon salt**
- ¼ **teaspoon pepper**

1. In a large skillet, cook sausage and mushrooms over medium heat until meat is no longer pink; drain.

2. Place half of the bread cubes in a greased 13-in. x 9-in. baking dish; top with 2 cups sausage mixture and half of the cheese and tomatoes. Repeat layers. In a large bowl, whisk the eggs, milk, mustard, salt and pepper; pour over bread mixture.

3. Bake, uncovered, at 350° for 50-55 minutes or until a knife inserted near the center comes out clean. Let stand for 10 minutes before serving.

ULTIMATE *Comfort* Baked Apple French Toast

This is a simply wonderful brunch recipe that tastes special and will have your guests asking for seconds. I serve it with whipped topping, maple syrup and additional nuts.

—**BEVERLY JOHNSTON** RUBICON, WI

PREP: 20 MIN. + CHILLING • **BAKE:** 35 MIN.
MAKES: 10 SERVINGS

- 20 **slices French bread (1 inch thick)**
- 1 **can (21 ounces) apple pie filling**
- 8 **eggs, lightly beaten**
- 2 **cups 2% milk**
- 2 **teaspoons vanilla extract**
- ½ **teaspoon ground cinnamon**
- ½ **teaspoon ground nutmeg**

TOPPING
- 1 **cup packed brown sugar**
- ½ **cup cold butter, cubed**
- 1 **cup chopped pecans**
- 2 **tablespoons corn syrup**

1. Arrange 10 slices of bread in a greased 13-in. x 9-in. baking dish. Spread with pie filling; top with remaining bread. In a large bowl, whisk the eggs, milk, vanilla, cinnamon and nutmeg. Pour over bread. Cover and refrigerate overnight.

2. Remove from the refrigerator 30 minutes before baking. Meanwhile, place brown sugar in a small bowl. Cut in butter until mixture resembles coarse crumbs. Stir in pecans and corn syrup. Sprinkle over French toast.

3. Bake, uncovered, at 350° for 35-40 minutes or until a knife inserted near the center comes out clean.

Raspberry Cream Muffins

It took me a couple of batches to perfect these muffins, but my family thinks this version is the best! I have to agree, since the muffins always disappear in a flash.

—STEPHANIE MOON BOISE, ID

PREP: 15 MIN. • **BAKE:** 25 MIN.
MAKES: 1 DOZEN

- 1 cup fresh raspberries
- ¾ cup plus 2 tablespoons sugar, divided
- ¼ cup butter, softened
- 1 egg
- ½ teaspoon almond extract
- ½ teaspoon vanilla extract
- 2¼ cups all-purpose flour
- 3 teaspoons baking powder
- ½ teaspoon salt
- 1 cup half-and-half cream
- 1 cup finely chopped vanilla or white chips
- 2 tablespoons brown sugar

1. In a small bowl, toss raspberries with ¼ cup sugar; set aside. In a large bowl, cream butter and ½ cup sugar until light and fluffy. Beat in egg and extracts. Combine the flour, baking powder and salt; add to creamed mixture alternately with cream, just until moistened. Stir in chips and reserved raspberries.

2. Pour into greased or paper-lined muffin cups to ¾ full. Combine brown sugar and remaining sugar; sprinkle over batter. Bake at 375° for 25-30 minutes or until a toothpick inserted near the center comes out clean. Cool for 5 minutes before removing from pan to a wire rack. Serve warm.

Omelet Croissants

Bacon and eggs never tasted so good, stacked with cheese, greens, tomato and more in this grilled meal-in-one.

—EDNA COBURN TUCSON, AZ

START TO FINISH: 30 MIN.
MAKES: 2 SERVINGS

- 3 eggs
- 1 tablespoon water
- 1 teaspoon chicken bouillon granules
- 1 green onion, finely chopped
- 2 tablespoons finely chopped sweet red pepper
- ¼ teaspoon lemon-pepper seasoning
- ½ teaspoon butter
- 2 croissants, split
- 4½ teaspoons ranch salad dressing
- 4 slices Canadian bacon
- 4 slices Muenster cheese
- ½ cup fresh arugula
- 4 thin slices tomato

1. In a small bowl, whisk the eggs, water and bouillon; set aside.

2. In a small nonstick skillet over medium heat, cook the onion, red pepper and lemon-pepper in butter until tender.

3. Add egg mixture. As eggs set, push cooked edges toward the center, letting uncooked portion flow underneath. When eggs are completely set, fold omelet in half and cut into two wedges.

4. Spread croissants with salad dressing. On croissant bottoms, layer with bacon, omelet, cheese, arugula and tomato. Replace croissant tops.

5. Cook on a panini maker or indoor grill for 2-4 minutes or until cheese is melted.

kid FRIENDLY Mini Maple Cinnamon Rolls

Maple syrup sweetens these lovely cinnamon buns. I make the dough in my bread machine before popping the rolls in the oven. My husband prefers them warm.
—**JUANITA CARLSEN** NORTH BEND, OR

PREP: 20 MIN. + RISING • **BAKE:** 20 MIN.
MAKES: 2 DOZEN

- ⅔ **cup milk**
- ⅓ **cup maple syrup**
- ⅓ **cup butter, softened**
- 1 **egg**
- ¾ **teaspoon salt**
- 3 **cups bread flour**
- 1 **package (¼ ounce) active dry yeast**

TOPPING

- ½ **cup packed brown sugar**
- 2 **tablespoons bread flour**
- 4 **teaspoons ground cinnamon**
- 6 **tablespoons cold butter**

MAPLE ICING

- 1 **cup confectioners' sugar**
- 3 **tablespoons butter, melted**
- 3 **tablespoons maple syrup**
- 1 **to 2 teaspoons milk**

1. In bread machine pan, place the first seven ingredients in order suggested by manufacturer. Select dough setting (check dough after 5 minutes of mixing; add 1 to 2 tablespoons of water or bread flour if needed).

2. When the cycle is completed, turn dough onto a lightly floured surface. Roll into two 12-in. x 7-in. rectangles. In a small bowl, combine the brown sugar, flour and cinnamon; cut in butter until mixture resembles coarse crumbs. Sprinkle half over each rectangle. Roll up jelly-roll style, starting from a long side; pinch seam to seal.

3. Cut each roll into 12 slices. Place cut side down in one greased 13x9-in. baking pan. Cover and let rise in a warm place until doubled, about 20 minutes.

4. Bake at 375° for 20-25 minutes or until golden brown. Cool on a wire rack for 5 minutes. Meanwhile, in a small bowl, combine the confectioners' sugar, butter, syrup and enough milk to achieve desired consistency. Spread over warm rolls.

NOTE *We recommend you do not use a bread machine's time-delay feature for this recipe.*

Berry-Filled Doughnuts

Check out how short the ingredient list is for these sweet treats. Friends and family will never guess that refrigerated buttermilk biscuits are the base for golden jelly-filled doughnuts.
—**GINNY WATSON** BROKEN ARROW, OK

START TO FINISH: 25 MIN.
MAKES: 10 SERVINGS

- 4 **cups canola oil**
- 1 **tube (7½ ounces) refrigerated buttermilk biscuits, separated into 10 biscuits**
- ¾ **cup seedless strawberry jam**
- 1 **cup confectioners' sugar**

1. In an electric skillet or deep-fat fryer, heat oil to 375°. Fry biscuits, a few at a time, for 1-2 minutes on each side or until golden brown. Drain on paper towels.

2. Cut a small hole in the corner of a pastry or plastic bag; insert a very small tip. Fill bag with jam. Push the tip through the side of each doughnut to fill with jam. Dust with confectioners' sugar while warm. Serve immediately.

Oh-So-Good Oatmeal

My two boys demand seconds of this homey and comforting breakfast. It's loaded with all the traditional mix-ins and gets even better when lightly drizzled with pure maple syrup.

—DANIELLE PEPA ELGIN, IL

START TO FINISH: 20 MIN.
MAKES: 4 SERVINGS

- 3 cups water
- 2 medium tart apples, chopped
- 1½ cups old-fashioned oats
  Dash salt
- ¼ cup packed brown sugar
- ½ teaspoon ground cinnamon
- ½ teaspoon vanilla extract
- ¼ cup chopped almonds
  Maple syrup and/or fat-free milk, optional

1. In a large saucepan over medium heat, bring water to a boil. Add the apples, oats and salt; cook and stir for 5 minutes.

2. Remove from the heat; stir in the brown sugar, cinnamon and vanilla. Cover and let stand for 2 minutes. Sprinkle each serving with almonds. Serve with maple syrup and/or milk if desired.

Big-Batch Oatmeal

top tip

Having a hot breakfast daily doesn't mean you have to set your alarm any earlier. Did you know cooked oatmeal lasts remarkably well in the refrigerator for 3 to 4 days? It's easy to make in big batches and reheat in the morning as needed.

Italian Sausage Quiche

This—my most popular recipe—is made with mild Italian sausage crafted especially for us by our local butcher. For the best flavor, choose sausage that is not too heavily spiced.

—LEE ANN MILLER MILLERSBURG, OH

PREP: 30 MIN. • **BAKE:** 35 MIN. + STANDING
MAKES: 6 SERVINGS

  Pastry for single-crust pie (9 inches)
- 1 pound bulk Italian sausage
- ¼ cup chopped onion
- ¼ cup chopped green pepper
- 4 teaspoons chopped seeded jalapeno pepper
- 1 cup (4 ounces) shredded sharp cheddar cheese
- 3 eggs
- 1 cup heavy whipping cream
- 1 teaspoon minced fresh parsley
- 1 teaspoon minced fresh basil
- ¼ teaspoon pepper
- ⅛ teaspoon salt
  Dash garlic powder
  Dash cayenne pepper

1. Preheat oven to 450°. Roll out pastry to fit a 9-in. pie plate. Transfer pastry to pie plate. Trim pastry to ½ in. beyond edge of plate; flute edges. Line unpricked pastry with a double thickness of heavy-duty foil. Fill with dried beans, uncooked rice or pie weights.

2. Bake 8 minutes. Remove foil and weights; bake 5 minutes longer. Cool on a wire rack. Reduce oven temperature to 375°.

3. Meanwhile, in a large skillet, cook sausage, onion, green pepper and jalapeno over medium heat until meat is no longer pink; drain. Spoon into shell and sprinkle with cheese.

4. In a large bowl, whisk remaining ingredients; pour over cheese. Bake 35-40 minutes or until a knife inserted near center comes out clean. Let stand 10 minutes before cutting.

FREEZE OPTION *Cover and freeze unbaked quiche. To use, remove from freezer 30 minutes before baking (do not thaw). Preheat oven to 375°. Place quiche on a baking sheet; cover edge loosely with foil. Bake as directed, increasing time as necessary for a knife inserted near the center to come out clean.*

NOTE *Wear disposable gloves when cutting hot peppers; the oils can burn skin. Avoid touching your face.*

This tender, nutty coffee cake is one of my favorite brunch treats. It looks and tastes so special, people won't believe you made it yourself. It's good that the recipe makes two! —
BETTY CLAYCOMB ALVERTON, PA

Almond Pastry Puffs

PREP: 40 MIN. • **BAKE:** 20 MIN. + COOLING
MAKES: 2 PASTRIES (11 SERVINGS EACH)

- 2 **cups all-purpose flour, divided**
- ¼ **teaspoon salt**
- 1 **cup cold butter, divided**
- 2 **tablespoons plus 1 cup cold water, divided**
- ¼ **teaspoon almond extract**
- 3 **eggs**

FROSTING

- 1½ **cups confectioners' sugar**
- 2 **tablespoons butter, softened**
- 4 **teaspoons water**
- ¼ **teaspoon almond extract**
- ⅔ **cup chopped almonds, toasted**

1. In a large bowl, combine 1 cup flour and salt; cut in ½ cup butter until mixture resembles coarse crumbs. Add 2 tablespoons cold water; stir with a fork until blended. Shape dough into a ball; divide in half. Place dough 3 in. apart on an ungreased baking sheet; pat each into a 12-in. x 3-in. rectangle.

2. In a large saucepan, bring remaining butter and water to a boil. Remove from the heat; stir in extract and remaining flour until a smooth ball forms. Remove from the heat; let stand for 5 minutes. Add eggs, one at a time, beating well after each addition. Continue beating until mixture is smooth and shiny.

3. Spread over rectangles. Bake at 400° for 18-20 minutes or until topping is lightly browned. Cool for 5 minutes before removing from pan to wire racks.

4. For frosting, in a small bowl, combine the confectioners' sugar, butter, water and extract; beat until smooth. Spread over pastries; sprinkle with almonds.

Breakfast Burritos

You can make a batch of these burritos in advance and freeze them for busy mornings when you want a hot breakfast. This is my family's favorite filling combination, but you could try replacing the bacon with cooked breakfast sausage.
—**AUDRA NIEDERMAN** ABERDEEN, SD

PREP: 20 MIN. + FREEZING
MAKES: 10 BURRITOS

- 12 **bacon strips, diced**
- 12 **eggs, lightly beaten**
  Salt and pepper to taste
- 10 **flour tortillas (8 inches)**
- 1½ **cups (6 ounces) shredded cheddar cheese**
- ½ **cup thinly sliced green onions**

1. In a large skillet, cook bacon until crisp; remove to paper towels. Drain, reserving 1-2 tablespoons drippings. Add eggs, salt and pepper to drippings; cook and stir over medium heat until the eggs are completely set.

2. Spoon about ¼ cup of egg mixture down the center of each tortilla; sprinkle with cheese, onions and reserved bacon. Fold bottom and sides of each tortilla over filling. Wrap each in waxed paper and aluminum foil. Freeze for up to 1 month.

TO USE FROZEN BURRITOS *Remove foil. Place waxed paper-wrapped burritos on a microwave-safe plate. Microwave at 60% power for 1 to 1½ minutes or until heated through. Let stand for 20 seconds.*
NOTE *This recipe was tested in a 1,100-watt microwave.*

Caramel French Toast

This scrumptious breakfast has been a favorite of mine for years. I like that I can assemble it the night before. I try to keep my mornings as simple as possible since I am a night owl and not a morning person!

—SHERRI-JO CAPODIFERRO
BRIGHTWATERS, NY

PREP: 15 MIN. + CHILLING • **BAKE:** 20 MIN.
MAKES: 2 SERVINGS

- ½ cup packed brown sugar
- ¼ cup butter, cubed
- 1 tablespoon corn syrup
- 3 slices white bakery bread (1 inch thick), halved
- 3 eggs
- ¾ cup half-and-half cream
- ½ teaspoon vanilla extract
- ¼ teaspoon ground cinnamon
- ¼ teaspoon salt

1. In a small saucepan, bring the brown sugar, butter and corn syrup to a boil over medium heat, stirring constantly. Remove from the heat. Pour into an 8-in. square baking dish coated with cooking spray. Arrange bread over caramel.

2. In a small bowl, whisk the eggs, cream, vanilla, cinnamon and salt; pour over top. Cover and refrigerate overnight.

3. Remove from the refrigerator 30 minutes before baking. Bake, uncovered, at 350° for 20-25 minutes or until a knife inserted near the center comes out clean.

? Did you know?

The origins of French toast are not traced back to France, but in fact to 4th-century Rome. The dish was developed as a way to use stale bread and prevent food waste.

Sausage Hash Brown Bake

Pork sausage is sandwiched between layers of hash browns and flavored with cream of chicken soup and French onion dip. Cheddar cheese tops the all-in-one breakfast casserole.

—ESTHER WRINKLES VANZANT, MO

PREP: 15 MIN. • **BAKE:** 55 MIN.
MAKES: 10-12 SERVINGS

- 2 pounds bulk pork sausage
- 2 cups (8 ounces) shredded cheddar cheese, divided
- 1 can (10¾ ounces) condensed cream of chicken soup, undiluted
- 1 cup (8 ounces) sour cream
- 1 carton (8 ounces) French onion dip
- 1 cup chopped onion
- ¼ cup chopped green pepper
- ¼ cup chopped sweet red pepper
- ⅛ teaspoon pepper
- 1 package (30 ounces) frozen shredded hash brown potatoes, thawed

1. In a large skillet, cook sausage over medium heat until no longer pink; drain on paper towels. In a large bowl, combine 1¾ cups cheese and the next seven ingredients; fold in potatoes.

2. Spread half into a greased shallow 3-qt. baking dish. Top with sausage and remaining potato mixture. Sprinkle with remaining cheese. cover and bake at 350° for 45 minutes. Uncover; bake 10 minutes longer or until heated through.

Jumbo Blueberry Muffins

In Michigan there are lots of blueberries, so I enjoy trying new recipes with them. Being jumbo, these muffins always stand out!

—**JACKIE HANNAHS** BRETHREN, MI

PREP: 15 MIN. • **BAKE:** 20 MIN.
MAKES: 8 JUMBO MUFFINS.

- ½ **cup butter, softened**
- 1 **cup sugar**
- 2 **eggs**
- ½ **cup buttermilk**
- 1 **teaspoon vanilla extract**
- 2 **cups all-purpose flour**
- 2 **teaspoons baking powder**
- ¼ **teaspoon salt**
- 2 **cups fresh or frozen blueberries**

TOPPING

- 3 **tablespoons sugar**
- ⅛ **teaspoon ground cinnamon**
- ⅛ **teaspoon ground nutmeg**

1. Preheat oven to 400°. In a large bowl, cream butter and sugar until light and fluffy. Add eggs, one at a time, beating well after each addition. Beat in buttermilk and vanilla. In another bowl, whisk flour, baking powder and salt. Add to creamed mixture; stir just until moistened. Fold in blueberries.

2. Pour into greased or paper-lined jumbo muffin cups to ⅔ full. Mix topping ingredients; sprinkle over tops. Bake 20-25 minutes or until a toothpick inserted in center comes out clean. Cool 5 minutes before removing from pan to a wire rack. Serve warm.

FOR STANDARD-SIZE MUFFINS
Make batter as directed; pour into greased or paper-lined standard muffin cups to ⅔ full. Bake in a preheated 400° oven for 15-20 minutes or until a toothpick comes out clean. Yield: 16 standard muffins.

Sour Cream Coffee Cake

I like that I can use delicious Wisconsin sour cream in this recipe. The coffee cake tastes wonderful and feeds a bunch, and it's just what the crowd will be craving with their coffee.

—SANDRA MUNYON WATERTOWN, WI

PREP: 15 MIN. • **BAKE:** 40 MIN.
MAKES: 12-15 SERVINGS

- ½ **cup butter, softened**
- 1 **cup sugar**
- 2 **eggs**
- 1 **cup (8 ounces) sour cream**
- 1 **teaspoon vanilla extract**
- 2 **cups all-purpose flour**
- 1 **teaspoon baking powder**
- 1 **teaspoon baking soda**
- ¼ **teaspoon salt**

TOPPING

- ¼ **cup sugar**
- ⅓ **cup packed brown sugar**
- 2 **teaspoons ground cinnamon**
- ½ **cup chopped pecans**

1. In a large bowl, cream butter and sugar until light and fluffy. Beat in the eggs, sour cream and vanilla. Combine the flour, baking powder, baking soda and salt; add to creamed mixture and beat until combined. Pour half the batter into a greased 13-in. x 9-in. baking pan.

2. In a small bowl, combine topping ingredients; sprinkle half of topping over batter. Add remaining batter and topping. Bake at 325° for 40 minutes or until a knife inserted near the center comes out clean. Cool on a wire rack.

Favorite Banana Chip Muffins

One of the first things my husband, Maj. John Duda Jr., gets hungry for when he's home from army deployment is a banana chip muffin. I make sure to have the overripe bananas ready to make the batter. These muffins are a family tradition.

—KIMBERLY DUDA SANFORD, NC

PREP: 20 MIN. • **BAKE:** 20 MIN.
MAKES: 1 DOZEN

- 1½ **cups all-purpose flour**
- ⅔ **cup sugar**
- 1 **teaspoon baking soda**
- ¼ **teaspoon ground cinnamon**
- ⅛ **teaspoon salt**
- 1 **egg**
- 1⅓ **cups mashed ripe bananas (about 3 medium)**
- ⅓ **cup butter, melted**
- 1 **teaspoon vanilla extract**
- ½ **cup semisweet chocolate chips**

1. Preheat oven to 375°. In a large bowl, whisk flour, sugar, baking soda, cinnamon and salt. In another bowl, whisk egg, bananas, melted butter and vanilla until blended. Add to flour mixture; stir just until moistened. Fold in chocolate chips.

2. Fill greased or paper-lined muffin cups three-fourths full. Bake 17-20 minutes or until a toothpick inserted in center comes out clean. Cool 5 minutes before removing from pan to a wire rack. Serve warm.

Stovetop Suppers

WHEN YOUR OVEN NEEDS THE NIGHT OFF, YOU'VE GOT CHOICES...
MORE THAN 75 OF THEM.

**BACON-CHICKEN
SANDWICHES**
PAGE 62

**CHUCK WAGON
TORTILLA STACK**
PAGE 64

**HEARTY
HUNTER'S STEW**
PAGE 78

Savory Spaghetti Sauce

I find this fresh-tasting spaghetti sauce is a real crowd-pleaser. With a husband and 12 kids to feed every day, I rely on this recipe often. It tastes especially good in the summer with fresh garden herbs.
—**ANNE HEINONEN** HOWELL, MI

PREP: 5 MIN. • **COOK:** 70 MIN.
MAKES: 4-6 SERVINGS (ABOUT 1 QUART)

- 1 **pound ground beef**
- 1 **large onion, chopped**
- 2 **cans (15 ounces each) tomato sauce**
- 1 **garlic clove, minced**
- 1 **bay leaf**
- 1 **tablespoon minced fresh basil or 1 teaspoon dried basil**
- 2 **teaspoons minced fresh oregano or ¾ teaspoon dried oregano**
- 2 **teaspoons sugar**
- ½ **to 1 teaspoon salt**
- ½ **teaspoon pepper**
  Hot cooked spaghetti
  Fresh oregano, optional

1. In a Dutch oven, cook ground beef and onion until meat is no longer pink and onion is tender; drain. Add the next eight ingredients; bring to a boil.
2. Reduce heat; cover and simmer for 1 hour, stirring occasionally. Remove the bay leaf. Serve with spaghetti. Garnish with oregano if desired.

ULTIMATE *Comfort*
Cheesy Ham Chowder

This soothing soup is a favorite of my five children. It's full of potatoes, carrots and ham. The best part is that I can get it on the table in a half-hour.
—**JENNIFER TRENHAILE** EMERSON, NE

PREP: 30 MIN. • **COOK:** 20 MIN.
MAKES: 10 SERVINGS

- 10 **bacon strips, diced**
- 1 **large onion, chopped**
- 1 **cup diced carrots**
- 3 **tablespoons all-purpose flour**
- 3 **cups milk**
- 1½ **cups water**
- 2½ **cups cubed potatoes**
- 1 **can (15¼ ounces) whole kernel corn, drained**
- 2 **teaspoons chicken bouillon granules**
  Pepper to taste
- 3 **cups (12 ounces) shredded cheddar cheese**
- 2 **cups cubed fully cooked ham**

1. In a Dutch oven, cook the bacon over medium heat until crisp. Using a slotted spoon, remove to paper towels to drain. In the drippings, saute onion and carrots until tender. Stir in flour until blended. Gradually add milk and water. Bring to a boil; cook and stir for 2 minutes or until thickened.
2. Add the potatoes, corn, bouillon and pepper. Reduce heat; simmer, uncovered, for 20 minutes or until potatoes are tender. Add cheese and ham; heat until cheese is melted. Stir in bacon.

Favorite Cola Chicken

Everyone who tries this chicken asks for the recipe. People are surprised to hear that soda is the secret ingredient.

—JEAN JARVIS WAUTOMA, WI

PREP: 5 MIN. • **COOK:** 70 MIN.
MAKES: 4 SERVINGS

- 1 can (12 ounces) diet cola
- ½ cup ketchup
- 2 to 4 tablespoons finely chopped onion
- ¼ teaspoon dried oregano
- ¼ teaspoon garlic powder
- 8 bone-in chicken thighs, skin removed

1. In a large skillet, combine first five ingredients. Bring to a boil; boil for 1 minute. Add chicken; stir to coat. Reduce heat to medium; cover and simmer for 20 minutes.
2. Uncover; simmer for 45 minutes or until a meat thermometer reads 180°.

Shredded Beef 'n' Slaw Sandwiches

I have served these tangy, hearty sandwiches for family gatherings and to many work crews. They have always gone over quite well.

—MARY JOHNSON WHITEHOUSE, OH

PREP: 20 MIN. • **COOK:** 2¾ HOURS
MAKES: 30 SANDWICHES

- 4 pounds beef stew meat, cut into 1-inch cubes
- 2 cups water
- 2 cups ketchup
- ½ to ¾ cup Worcestershire sauce
- 2 tablespoons lemon juice
- 2 tablespoons prepared horseradish
- 1 tablespoon prepared mustard
- 2 teaspoons salt
- 8 cups shredded cabbage
- 30 sandwich buns, split

1. In a Dutch oven, bring beef and water to a boil. Reduce heat; cover and simmer for 2 hours or until tender.
2. Remove beef with a slotted spoon; shred with two forks and set aside. Skim fat from cooking liquid. Stir in the ketchup, Worcestershire sauce, lemon juice, horseradish, mustard and salt. Add shredded beef and cabbage. Bring to a boil. Reduce heat; cover and simmer for 45 minutes or until cabbage is tender.
3. Spoon ⅓ cup onto each sandwich bun.

Did you know?

In addition to being the secret ingredient in Jean Jarvis' Favorite Cola Chicken, regular cola is an excellent ingredient in marinades for beef, poultry, pork or lamb because the acids help tenderize the meat.

No one will love fajita night more than you after you get a taste of this. And to think you're just 25 minutes away from this sizzling dinner.

—**JULIE STERCHI** CAMPBELLSVILLE, KY

Chicken Fajitas

PREP: 20 MIN. + MARINATING • **COOK:** 5 MIN.
MAKES: 6 SERVINGS

- 4 tablespoons canola oil, divided
- 2 tablespoons lemon juice
- 1½ teaspoons seasoned salt
- 1½ teaspoons dried oregano
- 1½ teaspoons ground cumin
- 1 teaspoon garlic powder
- ½ teaspoon chili powder
- ½ teaspoon paprika
- ½ teaspoon crushed red pepper flakes, optional
- 1½ pounds boneless skinless chicken breast, cut into thin strips
- ½ medium sweet red pepper, julienned
- ½ medium green pepper, julienned
- 4 green onions, thinly sliced
- ½ cup chopped onion
- 6 flour tortillas (8 inches), warmed
   Shredded cheddar cheese, taco sauce, salsa, guacamole and sour cream

1. In a large resealable plastic bag, combine 2 tablespoons oil, lemon juice and seasonings; add the chicken. Seal and turn to coat; refrigerate for 1-4 hours.

2. In a large skillet, saute peppers and onions in remaining oil until crisp-tender. Remove and keep warm.

3. Discard marinade. In the same skillet, cook chicken over medium-high heat for 5-6 minutes or until no longer pink. Return pepper mixture to pan; heat through.

4. Spoon filling down the center of tortillas; fold in half. Serve with cheese, taco sauce, salsa, guacamole and sour cream.

Beef Ragu with Ravioli

Here's a no-stress pasta sauce that tastes like it was simmering all day. Serve it over your favorite refrigerated or frozen ravioli for an easy meal.

—TASTE OF HOME TEST KITCHEN

PREP: 15 MIN. • **COOK:** 40 MIN.
MAKES: 4 SERVINGS

- 1 pound ground beef
- ½ cup chopped onion
- 1 pound plum tomatoes, diced
- 1 cup beef broth
- ½ cup red wine or additional beef broth
- 1 can (6 ounces) tomato paste
- 2 teaspoons minced fresh rosemary
- 1 teaspoon sugar
- 1 teaspoon minced garlic
- ½ teaspoon salt
- 1 package (20 ounces) refrigerated cheese ravioli
   Grated Parmesan cheese, optional

1. In a large skillet, cook beef and onion over medium heat until meat is no longer pink; drain. Add the tomatoes, broth, wine, tomato paste, rosemary, sugar, garlic and salt. Bring to a boil. Reduce heat; simmer, uncovered, for 30 minutes.

2. Cook ravioli according to package directions; drain. Serve with meat sauce. Sprinkle with cheese if desired.

Lemon Teriyaki Chicken

My easy stovetop chicken features mild and delicate family-pleasing flavors. It's fantastic with rice and a green vegetable like broccoli.

—CLARA COULSON MINNEY

WASHINGTON COURT HOUSE, OH

START TO FINISH: 25 MIN.
MAKES: 4 SERVINGS

- 4 boneless skinless chicken breast halves (4 ounces each)
- 2 tablespoons all-purpose flour
- 3 tablespoons butter
- ¼ cup reduced-sodium teriyaki sauce
- 2 tablespoons lemon juice
- ¾ teaspoon minced garlic
- ½ teaspoon sugar

1. Flatten chicken to ½-in. thickness; coat with flour. In a large skillet, cook chicken in butter over medium heat for 4-5 minutes on each side or until a thermometer reads 170°. Remove and set aside.

2. Add the teriyaki sauce, lemon juice, garlic and sugar to the skillet; stir to loosen browned bits. Return chicken to the pan and heat through.

Dagwood Burgers

You definitely need a knife and fork to dig into these stacked open-faced burgers. They make a fun weekend lunch or weeknight dinner.

—RUBY BERRY BRADENTON, FL

START TO FINISH: 25 MIN.
MAKES: 4 SERVINGS

- 1 pound ground beef
- ¼ cup prepared coleslaw salad dressing
- 4 thick slices bread, toasted
- 4 bacon strips, cooked and drained
- 4 slices Swiss cheese
- 4 slices tomato
- 4 slices onion
- 8 slices unpeeled cucumber
- 4 slices dill pickle
- 4 pitted jumbo ripe olives
- ¼ cup salad dressing of your choice, optional

1. Shape beef into four patties. Broil 4-in. from the heat or cook in a large skillet over medium heat for 6-8 minutes on each side or until a thermometer reads 160° and juices run clear; drain.

2. Spread coleslaw dressing over bread. Top each slice with a beef patty, bacon, cheese, tomato, onion, two cucumber slices, pickle and olive. Secure with a toothpick. Serve with additional salad dressing if desired.

EDITOR'S NOTE *Vary the flavor of Dagwood Burgers by combining different salad dressings and cheese. For instance, pair Thousand Island with Swiss, ranch with American or creamy Italian with mozzarella.*

Monte Cristos

Monte Cristos never fail to please even the biggest sandwich fans. They come together quickly with deli meats, packaged sliced cheese and bottled salad dressing.

—**DEBBIE BRUNSSEN** RANDOLPH, NE

START TO FINISH: 25 MIN.
MAKES: 4 SERVINGS

- ¼ **cup mayonnaise**
- 2 **teaspoons Thousand Island salad dressing**
- 1 **teaspoon Dijon mustard**
- 8 **slices white bread**
- ¼ **pound thinly sliced deli turkey**
- ¼ **pound thinly sliced deli ham**
- 4 **slices Swiss cheese**
- 2 **eggs, beaten**
- 1 **cup half-and-half cream**
- ¼ **teaspoon ground mustard**
- 2 **tablespoons butter**
- ¼ **cup strawberry preserves**

1. In a small bowl, combine the mayonnaise, salad dressing and Dijon mustard; spread over one side of each slice of bread. On four slices, layer the turkey, ham and Swiss cheese; top with remaining bread. In a shallow bowl, combine the eggs, cream and ground mustard. Dip sandwiches in egg mixture.

2. On a griddle or large skillet, melt butter. Toast sandwiches over medium heat for 2-3 minutes on each side or until bread is golden brown. Serve with preserves.

Did you know?

Monte Cristo sandwiches are a modern variation of an early 20th-century French appetizer called Croque Monsieur. Today they are commonly served with a side of jam.

Southwest Black Bean Soup

A friend brought her soup to a gathering, and it's been a hit with my family ever since! I use brown rice for more fiber and whole-grain goodness.

—**JILL HEATWOLE** PITTSVILLE, MD

PREP: 15 MIN. • **COOK:** 35 MIN.
MAKES: 6 SERVINGS

- 1 **medium sweet red pepper, chopped**
- 2 **celery ribs, chopped**
- 1 **small onion, chopped**
- 1 **tablespoon canola oil**
- 2 **cans (15 ounces each) black beans, rinsed and drained**
- 1 **can (14½ ounces) reduced-sodium chicken broth**
- 1 **can (14½ ounces) diced tomatoes, undrained**
- 1 **can (4 ounces) chopped green chilies**
- ¾ **teaspoon ground cumin**
- 1½ **cups cooked instant brown rice**
- 6 **tablespoons reduced-fat sour cream**

1. In a large nonstick saucepan, saute the pepper, celery and onion in oil until tender. Add the beans, broth, tomatoes, chilies and cumin. Bring to a boil. Reduce heat; simmer, uncovered, for 30 minutes or until thickened.

2. Divide rice among six soup bowls; top with soup and sour cream.

Bacon-Chicken Sandwiches

Everyone likes these tasty sandwiches. Flattening the chicken breasts helps them cook faster, and the mango chutney and other toppings make them better than anything you could ever order in a restaurant.

—**AGNES WARD** STRATFORD, ON

START TO FINISH: 25 MIN.
MAKES: 4 SERVINGS

- 4 boneless skinless chicken breast halves (5 ounces each)
- ½ teaspoon salt
- ½ teaspoon pepper
- 2 teaspoons canola oil
- 4 tomato slices
- 4 slices process Swiss cheese
- ¼ cup mango chutney
- 3 tablespoons mayonnaise
- 4 kaiser rolls, split and toasted
- 1 cup fresh baby spinach
- 8 slices ready-to-serve fully cooked bacon, warmed

1. Flatten chicken to ½-in. thickness; sprinkle with salt and pepper. In a large skillet over medium heat, cook chicken in oil for 4-5 minutes on each side or until chicken juices run clear. Top each chicken breast half with a tomato and cheese slice; cover and cook for 2-3 minutes or until cheese is melted.
2. Combine the chutney and mayonnaise; spread over roll bottoms. Layer with spinach, chicken and bacon; replace tops.

Chili con Carne

If you don't have a ton of people to feed and you're craving a thick, meaty chili, this recipe makes two generous bowls. Because it only takes 20 minutes, it's handy for whipping up a hot lunch.

—**MARLINE EMMAL** VANCOUVER, BC

START TO FINISH: 20 MIN.
MAKES: 2 SERVINGS

- ½ pound lean ground beef (90% lean)
- 1½ cups reduced-sodium tomato juice
- ¾ cup kidney beans, rinsed and drained
- 2 tablespoons chopped onion
- 1 teaspoon chili powder
- ¼ teaspoon ground cumin
- ¼ teaspoon minced garlic
- 2 to 3 drops hot pepper sauce

GARNISH
- Thinly sliced green onion, optional

In a large saucepan, cook beef over medium heat until no longer pink; drain. Stir in the remaining ingredients. Bring to a boil. Reduce heat; simmer, uncovered, for 10 minutes or until slightly thickened, stirring occasionally. Garnish with green onion if desired.

top tip | On a Roll

We loved the Bacon-Chicken Sandwiches! Lots of flavor—but you need to serve them on heavier rolls. We used sandwich buns, which were not sturdy enough to hold everything together, but they still tasted great.

—**CRAIGC3** TASTEOFHOME.COM

Taco Salad

When I brought this salad to a party, people were scrambling to figure out who made it. I took home an empty bowl, and each guest went home with a full stomach!

—**LISA HOMER** AVON, NY

PREP: 25 MIN. • **COOK:** 10 MIN.
MAKES: 26 SERVINGS (1⅓ CUPS EACH)

- 1½ pounds ground beef
- 2 envelopes taco seasoning, divided
- 1 medium head iceberg lettuce
- 1 package (12½ ounces) nacho tortilla chips, coarsely crushed
- 2 pints grape tomatoes, halved
- 2 cans (16 ounces each) kidney beans, rinsed and drained
- 3 cans (2¼ ounces each) sliced ripe olives, drained
- 1½ cups (6 ounces) shredded cheddar cheese
- 1 large sweet onion, chopped
- 2 cans (4 ounces each) chopped green chilies
- 1½ cups Thousand Island salad dressing
- 1⅓ cups salsa
- ⅓ cup sugar

1. In a Dutch oven over medium heat, cook beef with 1 envelope plus 2 tablespoons taco seasoning until no longer pink; drain.

2. In a very large serving bowl, combine the lettuce, chips, tomatoes, beans, olives, cheese, onion, chilies and beef mixture.

3. In a small bowl, combine the salad dressing, salsa, sugar and remaining taco seasoning; pour over salad and toss to coat.

Chuck Wagon Tortilla Stack

Piling on loads of hearty flavor at mealtime is easy when I roll out this skillet specialty. I layer the meat mixture with tortillas in a deep skillet and let it simmer. It's easy to cut and spoon out of the pan.

—**BERNICE JANOWSKI** STEVENS POINT, WI

PREP: 15 MIN. • **COOK:** 40 MIN.
MAKES: 4-6 SERVINGS

- 1 **pound ground beef**
- 2 **to 3 garlic cloves, minced**
- 1 **can (16 ounces) baked beans**
- 1 **can (14½ ounces) stewed tomatoes, undrained**
- 1 **can (11 ounces) whole kernel corn, drained**
- 1 **can (4 ounces) chopped green chilies**
- ¼ **cup barbecue sauce**
- 4½ **teaspoons chili powder**
- 1½ **teaspoons ground cumin**
- 4 **flour tortillas (10 inches)**
- 1⅓ **cups (about 5 ounces) shredded pepper jack cheese**
  Shredded lettuce, chopped red onion, sour cream and/or chopped tomatoes, optional

1. In a large skillet, cook beef until meat is no longer pink; drain. Add the garlic, beans, tomatoes, corn, chilies, barbecue sauce, chili powder and cumin. Bring to a boil. Reduce heat; simmer, uncovered, for 10-12 minutes or until liquid is reduced.

2. Coat a large deep skillet with cooking spray. Place one tortilla in skillet; spread with 1½ cups meat mixture. Sprinkle with ⅓ cup cheese. Repeat layers three times. Cover and cook on low for 15 minutes or until cheese is melted and tortillas are heated through. Cut into wedges. Serve with toppings of your choice.

Grilled Bacon-Tomato Sandwiches

My family loves these sandwiches and they are very easy to prepare. Fresh basil, tangy Italian dressing and melted cheese meld perfectly in this simple sandwich.

—**BETTY SNODDY** FRANKLIN, MO

START TO FINISH: 20 MIN.
MAKES: 2 SERVINGS

- 4 **slices Italian bread (½ inch thick)**
- 4 **slices provolone cheese (1 ounce each)**
- 4 **slices tomato**
- 4 **bacon strips, cooked and halved**
- 2 **teaspoons minced fresh basil or ½ teaspoon dried basil**
- 2 **tablespoons Italian salad dressing**

1. Top two slices of bread with a slice of cheese; layer with tomato, bacon, basil and remaining cheese. Top with remaining bread. Brush dressing over outsides of sandwiches.

2. In a large skillet over medium heat, toast sandwiches for 2-3 minutes on each side or until cheese is melted.

Balsamic Pork Scallopine

I developed this delightful dish by tweaking my veal scallopine recipe. Thinly sliced pork is an economical alternative to veal, and it was a tasty success!

—**MARY COKENOUR** MONTICELLO, UT

PREP: 25 MIN. • **COOK:** 30 MIN.
MAKES: 12 SERVINGS

- 3 **pounds pork sirloin cutlets**
- 1½ **cups all-purpose flour**
- ½ **cup olive oil**
- 2 **tablespoons butter**
- 1 **medium onion, chopped**
- ½ **cup chopped roasted sweet red peppers**
- 6 **garlic cloves, minced**
- 1 **can (14½ ounces) reduced-sodium chicken broth**
- ½ **cup minced fresh basil or 2 tablespoons dried basil**
- ½ **cup balsamic vinegar**
- ½ **teaspoon pepper**

NOODLES

- 1 **package (16 ounces) egg noodles**
- ½ **cup half-and-half cream**
- ¼ **cup grated Romano cheese**
- ¼ **cup butter, cubed**
- ½ **teaspoon pepper**
- ¼ **teaspoon garlic powder**

1. Dredge pork cutlets in flour. Heat oil and butter in a large skillet over medium-high heat; add pork and brown in batches. Set aside.

2. Add onion and red peppers to the pan; saute until onion is tender. Add garlic; cook 1 minute longer. Add the broth, basil, vinegar and pepper. Return pork to the pan, layering if necessary.

3. Cover and cook over low heat for 15-20 minutes or until meat is tender.

4. Meanwhile, in a Dutch oven, cook noodles according to package directions. Drain; stir in the cream, cheese, butter, pepper and garlic powder. Serve with pork.

ULTIMATE *Comfort* Country Fried Chicken

This is one of our favorite recipes to take along on a picnic. We like to eat the chicken cold, along with a salad and watermelon.

—**REBEKAH MILLER** ROCKY MOUNT, VA

PREP: 20 MIN. • **COOK:** 40 MIN.
MAKES: 4 SERVINGS

- 1 **cup all-purpose flour**
- 2 **teaspoons garlic salt**
- 2 **teaspoons pepper**
- 1 **teaspoon paprika**
- ½ **teaspoon poultry seasoning**
- 1 **egg**
- ½ **cup milk**
- 1 **broiler/fryer chicken (3 to 3½ pounds), cut up**
    Oil for frying

1. In a large resealable plastic bag, combine the flour and seasonings. In a shallow bowl, beat egg and milk. Dip chicken pieces into egg mixture, then add to bag, a few pieces at a time, and shake to coat.

2. In a large skillet, heat ¼ in. of oil; fry chicken in oil until browned on all sides. Cover and simmer for 35-40 minutes or until juices run clear and chicken is tender, turning occasionally. Uncover and cook 5 minutes longer. Drain on paper towels.

Peppercorn Steaks

These tender peppered steaks get plenty of zip from a quick-to-fix sauce flavored with mustard and Worcestershire.

—TASTE OF HOME TEST KITCHEN

START TO FINISH: 30 MIN.
MAKES: 2 SERVINGS

- 1 tablespoon whole black peppercorns, crushed
- 2 boneless beef top loin steaks (8 ounces each)
- 2 to 3 tablespoons butter, melted
- 1 to 2 garlic cloves, minced
- 1 tablespoon Worcestershire sauce
- ½ cup red wine or beef broth
- 1 teaspoon ground mustard
- ½ teaspoon sugar
- 2 teaspoons cornstarch
- 1 tablespoon water

1. Rub pepper over both sides of steaks. Refrigerate for 15 minutes. In an ungreased skillet, brown steaks on both sides over medium-high heat. Reduce heat to medium; add butter and garlic; cook for 4-6 minutes, turning steaks once. Add Worcestershire sauce; cook 4-6 minutes longer, turning once, or until meat reaches desired doneness (for medium-rare, a meat thermometer should read 145°; medium, 160°; well-done, 170°). Remove steaks and keep warm.

2. Combine wine or broth, mustard and sugar; add to the pan. Stir to loosen browned bits. Combine cornstarch and water until smooth; add to pan. Bring to a boil; cook and stir for 2 minutes or until thickened. Serve with the steaks.

NOTE *Top loin steak may be labeled as strip steak, KS City steak, NY strip steak, ambassador steak or boneless club steak in your region.*

Shrimp Gumbo

A crisp green salad and crusty French bread complete this shrimp gumbo meal for me. I have found that the instant microwave rice packages make it easier.

—JO ANN GRAHAM OVILLA, TX

PREP: 30 MIN. • **COOK:** 1 HOUR
MAKES: 11 SERVINGS

- ¼ cup all-purpose flour
- ¼ cup canola oil
- 3 celery ribs, chopped
- 1 medium green pepper, chopped
- 1 medium onion, chopped
- 1 carton (32 ounces) chicken broth
- 3 garlic cloves, minced
- 1 teaspoon salt
- 1 teaspoon pepper
- ½ teaspoon cayenne pepper
- 2 pounds uncooked large shrimp, peeled and deveined
- 1 package (16 ounces) frozen sliced okra
- 4 green onions, sliced
- 1 medium tomato, chopped
- 1½ teaspoons gumbo file powder
  Hot cooked rice

1. In a Dutch oven over medium heat, cook and stir flour and oil until caramel-colored, about 12 minutes (do not burn). Add the celery, green pepper and onion; cook and stir for 5-6 minutes or until tender. Stir in the broth, garlic, salt, pepper and cayenne; bring to a boil. Reduce heat; cover and simmer for 30 minutes.

2. Stir in the shrimp, okra, green onions and tomato. Return to a boil. Reduce heat; cover and simmer for 10 minutes or until shrimp turn pink. Stir in file powder. Serve with rice.

EDITOR'S NOTE *Gumbo file powder, used to thicken and flavor Creole recipes, is available in spice shops. If you don't want to use gumbo file powder, combine 2 tablespoons each cornstarch and cold water until smooth. Gradually stir into gumbo. Bring to a boil; cook and stir for 2 minutes or until thickened.*

kid FRIENDLY

Cheeseburger Soup

A local restaurant serves a similar soup but the chef wouldn't share the recipe. So I developed my own, modifying a recipe for potato soup. I was really pleased at how well this all-American soup turned out.

—JOANIE SHAWHAN MADISON, WI

PREP: 45 MIN. • **COOK:** 10 MIN.
MAKES: 8 SERVINGS (2¼ QUARTS)

- ½ pound ground beef
- ¾ cup chopped onion
- ¾ cup shredded carrots
- ¾ cup diced celery
- 1 teaspoon dried basil
- 1 teaspoon dried parsley flakes
- 4 tablespoons butter, divided
- 3 cups chicken broth
- 4 cups diced peeled potatoes (1¾ pounds)
- ¼ cup all-purpose flour
- 2 cups (8 ounces) process cheese (Velveeta), cubed
- 1½ cups milk
- ¾ teaspoon salt
- ¼ to ½ teaspoon pepper
- ¼ cup sour cream

1. In a 3-qt. saucepan, brown beef; drain and set aside. In the same saucepan, saute the onion, carrots, celery, basil and parsley in 1 tablespoon butter until vegetables are tender, about 10 minutes. Add broth, potatoes and beef; bring to a boil. Reduce heat; cover and simmer for 10-12 minutes or until potatoes are tender.

2. Meanwhile, in a small skillet, melt remaining butter. Add flour; cook and stir for 3-5 minutes or until bubbly. Add to soup; bring to a boil. Cook and stir for 2 minutes. Reduce heat to low. Stir in the cheese, milk, salt and pepper; cook and stir until cheese melts. Remove from the heat; blend in sour cream.

Honey Lemon Schnitzel

These pork cutlets are coated in a sweet sauce with honey, lemon juice and butter. I made this dish for a New Year's Eve dinner and it was a big hit. It's an easy recipe to double for guests.

—CAROLE FRASER NORTH YORK, ON

START TO FINISH: 25 MIN.
MAKES: 4 SERVINGS

- 2 tablespoons all-purpose flour
- ½ teaspoon salt
- ½ teaspoon pepper
- 4 pork sirloin cutlets (4 ounces each)
- 2 tablespoons butter
- ¼ cup lemon juice
- ¼ cup honey

1. In a large resealable plastic bag, combine the flour, salt and pepper. Add pork, two pieces at a time, and shake to coat. In a large skillet, cook pork in butter over medium heat for 3-4 minutes on each side or until juices run clear. Remove and keep warm.
2. Add lemon juice and honey to the skillet; cook and stir for 3 minutes or until thickened. Return pork to pan; cook 2-3 minutes longer or until heated through.

Get Your Honey's Worth

For measuring sticky liquids such as molasses, corn syrup or honey, spray the measuring cup with nonstick cooking spray before adding the liquid. This will make it easier to pour out the liquid and clean the cup.

Skillet Chicken Burritos

Here's one of my go-to dishes when I'm in a rush to make dinner. Preparing them in the skillet not only saves time, it gives the burritos a crispy outside and a warm gooey filling.

—SCARLETT ELROD NEWNAN, GA

START TO FINISH: 30 MIN.
MAKES: 8 SERVINGS

- 1 cup (8 ounces) reduced-fat sour cream
- ¼ cup chopped fresh cilantro
- 2 tablespoons chopped pickled jalapeno slices
- 2 teaspoons chopped onion
- 2 teaspoons Dijon mustard
- 1 teaspoon grated lime peel

BURRITOS

- 2 cups cubed cooked chicken breast
- 1 can (15 ounces) black beans, rinsed and drained
- 1 can (11 ounces) Mexicorn, drained
- 1 cup (4 ounces) shredded reduced-fat cheddar cheese
- ¼ teaspoon salt
- 8 whole wheat tortillas (8 inches), warmed
  Cooking spray
  Salsa, optional

1. In a small bowl, combine the first six ingredients. In a large bowl, combine the chicken, beans, corn, cheese, salt and ½ cup sour cream mixture. Spoon ½ cup chicken mixture on each tortilla. Fold sides and ends over filling and roll up. Spritz both sides with cooking spray.
2. In a large nonstick skillet or griddle coated with cooking spray, cook burritos in batches over medium heat for 3-4 minutes on each side or until golden brown. Serve with remaining sour cream mixture and salsa if desired.

A gyro is typically made of meat, often lamb, roasted on a spit and served sandwich-style in folded pita bread. It's topped with tomato, onion and Greek yogurt. Tradition takes a slight twist with the use of ground beef, spinach and ripe olives in this simple version. Opa!
—MARY JOHNSON COLOMA, WI

Beef & Spinach Gyros

START TO FINISH: 25 MIN.
MAKES: 6 SERVINGS

- 1 **pound lean ground beef (90% lean)**
- 1 **package (10 ounces) frozen chopped spinach, thawed and squeezed dry**
- 6 **green onions, chopped**
- 1 **can (2¼ ounces) sliced ripe olives, drained**
- 2 **teaspoons lemon-pepper seasoning, divided**
- 1 **large tomato, chopped**
- 1 **cup (8 ounces) fat-free plain yogurt**
- ½ **cup reduced-fat mayonnaise**
- 6 **pita breads (6 inches), halved**
- 12 **lettuce leaves**
- 1 **cup (4 ounces) crumbled feta cheese**

1. In a large skillet, cook beef over medium heat until no longer pink. Add the spinach, onions, olives and 1 teaspoon lemon-pepper; heat through. Stir in tomato; set aside.

2. In a small bowl, combine the yogurt, mayonnaise and remaining lemon-pepper. Line pita halves with lettuce; fill with beef mixture and feta cheese. Serve with yogurt sauce.

Italian Sausage Minestrone

My family asks for this soup every year after the cold weather sets in. I like to serve it with crusty French bread to dip into the broth.
—ELIZABETH RENTERIA VANCOUVER, WA

PREP: 20 MIN. + FREEZING
COOK: 1¼ HOURS
MAKES: 13 SERVINGS (3¼ QUARTS)

- 1 **pound bulk Italian sausage**
- 2 **large carrots, chopped**
- 2 **celery ribs, chopped**
- 1 **medium onion, chopped**
- 6 **garlic cloves, minced**
- 3 **tablespoons olive oil**
- 7 **cups reduced-sodium chicken broth**
- 2 **cans (15 ounces each) cannellini or white kidney beans, rinsed and drained**
- 2 **cans (14½ ounces each) fire-roasted diced tomatoes, undrained**
- 2 **bay leaves**
- 1 **tablespoon Italian seasoning**
- 1 **tablespoon tomato paste**

ADDITIONAL INGREDIENTS

- 1 **cup ditalini or other small pasta**
  Shredded or shaved Parmesan cheese

1. In a Dutch oven, cook sausage over medium heat until no longer pink; drain.

2. In the same pan, saute the carrots, celery, onion and garlic in oil until tender. Stir in the broth, beans, tomatoes, bay leaves, Italian seasoning, tomato paste and sausage. Bring to a boil. Reduce heat; cover and simmer for 30 minutes.

3. Cool soup; transfer to freezer containers. Freeze for up to 3 months.
TO USE FROZEN SOUP *Thaw in the refrigerator overnight. Transfer to a Dutch oven. Bring to a boil. Stir in ditalini; return to a boil. Reduce heat and cook, uncovered, for 6-8 minutes or until pasta is tender. Serve with cheese.*

ULTIMATE *Comfort*
Ranch Mac 'n' Cheese

I came up with the recipe for this creamy and satisfying macaroni and cheese—it has a tasty twist. My husband requests it often.

—**MICHELLE ROTUNNO** INDEPENDENCE, MO

START TO FINISH: 30 MIN.
MAKES: 8 SERVINGS

- 1 package (16 ounces) elbow macaroni
- 1 cup 2% milk
- ¼ cup butter, cubed
- 1 envelope ranch salad dressing mix
- 1 teaspoon garlic salt
- 1 teaspoon garlic pepper blend
- 1 teaspoon lemon-pepper seasoning
- 1 cup (4 ounces) shredded Monterey Jack cheese
- 1 cup (4 ounces) shredded Colby cheese
- 1 cup (8 ounces) sour cream
- ½ cup crushed saltines
- ⅓ cup grated Parmesan cheese

1. Cook macaroni according to package directions. Meanwhile, in a Dutch oven, combine the milk, butter, dressing mix and seasonings; heat through. Stir in Monterey Jack and Colby cheeses until melted. Stir in sour cream.

2. Drain macaroni; stir into cheese sauce with the saltines. Sprinkle with Parmesan cheese.

Sweet 'n' Tangy Shrimp

With its delightfully sweet-tangy flavor, this easy entree is destined to become a hit with your family. My husband and I adapted the recipe from one in a magazine, and we just love it.

—**KATHLEEN DAVIS** NORTH BEND, WA

START TO FINISH: 30 MIN.
MAKES: 4 SERVINGS

- ½ cup ketchup
- 2 tablespoons sugar
- 2 tablespoons cider vinegar
- 2 tablespoons reduced-sodium soy sauce
- 1 teaspoon sesame oil
- ¼ teaspoon crushed red pepper flakes
- 1½ pounds uncooked medium shrimp, peeled and deveined
- 1 tablespoon minced fresh gingerroot
- 1 tablespoon canola oil
- 3 garlic cloves, minced
- 2 green onions, sliced
- 1 teaspoon sesame seeds, toasted
      Hot cooked rice, optional

1. In a small bowl, combine the first six ingredients; set aside. In a large nonstick skillet or wok, stir-fry shrimp and ginger in oil until shrimp turn pink. Add garlic; cook 1 minute longer.

2. Add the ketchup mixture; cook and stir for 2-3 minutes or until heated through. Sprinkle with onions and sesame seeds. Serve with rice if desired.

Heartwarming Chili

A touch of baking cocoa gives this chili a rich flavor without adding sweetness. When I was growing up in the North, we served chili over rice. But after I married a Texan, I began serving it with chopped onions, shredded cheese and, of course, corn bread!

—AUDREY BYRNE LILLIAN, TX

PREP: 10 MIN. • **COOK:** 20 MIN. + SIMMERING
MAKES: 4 SERVINGS

- 1 pound ground beef
- 1 large onion, chopped
- 2 cans (16 ounces each) kidney beans, rinsed and drained
- 2 cans (14½ ounces each) diced tomatoes
- 1 can (8 ounces) tomato sauce
- 1 medium green pepper
- 3 tablespoons chili powder
- 1 tablespoon ground cumin
- 2 garlic cloves, minced
- 1 teaspoon baking cocoa
- 1 teaspoon dried oregano
- 1 teaspoon Worcestershire sauce, optional
  Salt and pepper to taste

In a large saucepan, cook beef and onion over medium heat until the meat is no longer pink; drain. Add the remaining ingredients; bring to a boil. Reduce heat; cover and simmer for 3 hours, stirring occasionally.

Italian Sausage with Bow Ties

Italian sausage paired with creamy tomato sauce is requested monthly in our home. Not only is this dish simple to make, it tastes like you slaved over a hot stove for hours and hours!

—JANELLE MOORE FEDERAL WAY, WA

START TO FINISH: 25 MIN.
MAKES: 5 SERVINGS

- 1 package (16 ounces) bow tie pasta
- 1 pound bulk Italian sausage
- ½ cup chopped onion
- 1½ teaspoons minced garlic
- ½ teaspoon crushed red pepper flakes
- 2 cans (14½ ounces each) Italian stewed tomatoes, drained and chopped
- 1½ cups heavy whipping cream
- ½ teaspoon salt
- ¼ teaspoon dried basil
  Shredded Parmesan cheese

1. Cook pasta according to package directions. Meanwhile, in a Dutch oven, cook the sausage, onion and pepper flakes over medium heat for 4-5 minutes or until meat is no longer pink. Add garlic; cook 1 minute longer. Drain.

2. Stir in the tomatoes, cream, salt and basil. Bring to a boil over medium heat. Reduce heat; simmer, uncovered, for 6-8 minutes or until thickened, stirring occasionally. Drain pasta; toss with sausage mixture. Garnish with cheese.

Chicken Melts

The secret to these toasty sandwiches is to use cinnamon-raisin bread for a touch of sweetness and jalapeno jelly for a little zip. You could also sub in brick cheese.

—**DIANE HALFERTY** CORPUS CHRISTI, TX

START TO FINISH: 10 MIN.
MAKES: 2 SERVINGS

- 4 **slices cinnamon-raisin bread**
- 2 **tablespoons jalapeno pepper jelly**
- 1 **package (6 ounces) thinly sliced deli smoked chicken breast**
- 3 **ounces Havarti cheese, sliced**
- 1 **tablespoon butter, softened**

1. Spread two bread slices with jelly. Layer with chicken and cheese; top with remaining bread. Butter outsides of sandwiches.
2. In a large skillet over medium heat, toast sandwiches for 2-3 minutes on each side or until cheese is melted.

kid FRIENDLY Soda Pop Chops with Smashed Potatoes

Root beer gives this family-friendly recipe a tangy taste kids will love. Served alongside the smashed potatoes, this makes a scrumptious stick-to-the-ribs meal any night of the week.

—**TASTE OF HOME TEST KITCHEN**

PREP: 25 MIN. • **COOK:** 15 MIN.
MAKES: 4 SERVINGS

- 1½ **pounds small red potatoes, halved**
- 1 **cup root beer**
- 1 **cup ketchup**
- 1 **tablespoon brown sugar**
- 2 **teaspoons chili powder**
- 2 **teaspoons Worcestershire sauce**
- ¼ **teaspoon garlic powder**
- 2 **tablespoons all-purpose flour**
- ¾ **teaspoon pepper, divided**
- ½ **teaspoon salt, divided**
- 4 **bone-in pork loin chops (7 ounces each)**
- 2 **tablespoons olive oil**
- 2 **tablespoons butter**
- ¼ **teaspoon garlic powder**

1. Place potatoes in a large saucepan and cover with water. Bring to a boil. Reduce heat; cover and cook for 15-20 minutes or until tender.
2. Meanwhile, in a small bowl, combine the root beer, ketchup, brown sugar, chili powder, Worcestershire sauce and garlic powder; set aside. In a large resealable plastic bag, combine the flour, ½ teaspoon pepper and ¼ teaspoon salt. Add pork chops, one at a time, and shake to coat.
3. In a large skillet, cook chops in oil over medium heat for 2-3 minutes on each side or until chops are lightly browned; drain. Add root beer mixture. Bring to a boil. Reduce heat; cover and simmer for 6-8 minutes or until a thermometer reads 145°. Remove pork and keep warm. Let stand for 5 minutes before serving.
4. Bring sauce to a boil; cook until liquid is reduced by half. Meanwhile, drain potatoes; mash with butter, garlic powder and remaining salt and pepper. Serve with pork chops and sauce.

Hungarian Goulash

With tender beef and a rich flavorful sauce, this entree is an old favorite with my family. We like it served over hot noodles.
—JOAN ROSE LANGLEY, BC

PREP: 20 MIN. • **COOK:** 1½ HOURS
MAKES: 6-8 SERVINGS

- 1 **pound beef stew meat, cut into 1-inch cubes**
- 1 **pound lean boneless pork, cut into 1-inch cubes**
- 2 **large onions, thinly sliced**
- 2 **tablespoons canola oil**
- 2 **cups water**
- 2 **tablespoons paprika**
- ½ **teaspoon salt**
- ½ **teaspoon dried marjoram**
- 1 **tablespoon all-purpose flour**
- 1 **cup (8 ounces) sour cream**
  Hot cooked noodles

1. In a large skillet, brown beef, pork and onions in oil over medium heat; drain. Add the water, paprika, salt and marjoram; bring to a boil. Reduce heat; cover and simmer for 1½ hours or until meat is tender.
2. Just before serving, combine flour and sour cream until smooth; stir into meat mixture. Bring to a boil over medium heat; cook and stir for 1-2 minutes or until thickened and bubbly. Serve over noodles.

EDITOR'S NOTE *You can use additional beef stew meat for the pork in this recipe.*

Did you know?

Creole and Cajun are sometimes used interchangeably, but there's a difference—the biggest being tomatoes. Creole jambalaya, for example, uses tomatoes, whereas the Cajun version does not.

Favorite Jiffy Jambalaya

Your family will love this smoky dish that comes together in a snap. A basic red beans and rice mix gets a quick makeover for a deliciously filling meal.
—TASTE OF HOME TEST KITCHEN

START TO FINISH: 30 MIN.
MAKES: 4 SERVINGS

- 1 **package (8 ounces) red beans and rice mix**
- ½ **pound smoked sausage, sliced**
- ½ **cup chopped onion**
- 1 **tablespoon olive oil**
- ½ **pound cooked medium shrimp, peeled and deveined**
- 1 **can (14½ ounces) diced tomatoes, drained**
- 1 **teaspoon brown sugar**
- ¼ **teaspoon Louisiana-style hot sauce, optional**

1. Cook red beans and rice mix according to package directions.
2. Meanwhile, in a large skillet, saute sausage and onion in oil until onion is tender. Add the shrimp, tomatoes, brown sugar and hot sauce if desired. Cook for 3-4 minutes or until heated through. Stir in rice mixture.

Hearty Sausage Stew

My daughters shared this recipe with me, and I've since shared it with many others. I had almost given up on cooking until I discovered quick and easy dinners like this.

—NELLIE LAMB MUSKOGEE, OK

START TO FINISH: 30 MIN.
MAKES: 7 SERVINGS

- ½ **pound fresh kielbasa or Polish sausage links**
- ½ **pound Italian sausage links**
- 1 **medium onion, chopped**
- 1 **medium green pepper, chopped**
- 3½ **cups beef broth**
- 1 **can (14½ ounces) diced tomatoes, undrained**
- 1 **cup apple juice**
- 1 **tablespoon minced fresh parsley**
- 1 **garlic clove, minced**
- ¼ **teaspoon dried basil**
- ¼ **teaspoon dried oregano**
- 4 **ounces uncooked spiral pasta**

1. In a large saucepan, cook sausages over medium heat until a thermometer reads 160°. Remove with a slotted spoon; drain, reserving 2 tablespoons drippings. Cut sausages into ½-inch slices; set aside.

2. In the drippings, saute onion and pepper until crisp-tender. Stir in the broth, tomatoes, apple juice, parsley, garlic, basil, oregano and sausages. Bring to a boil; add pasta. Reduce heat; cover and simmer for 10-15 minutes or until pasta is tender.

3. Serve immediately or cool and freeze in freezer containers for up to 3 months.

TO USE FROZEN STEW *Thaw in the refrigerator overnight. Transfer to a saucepan; add water to thin if necessary. Cover and cook over medium heat until hot and bubbly, stirring occasionally.*

Fish Tacos

A cool sauce with just a bit of zing tops these crispy, spicy fish tacos. It's great, guilt-free and doesn't break the bank.

—LENA LIM SEATTLE, WA

PREP: 30 MIN. • **COOK:** 20 MIN.
MAKES: 8 SERVINGS

- ¾ **cup fat-free sour cream**
- 1 **can (4 ounces) chopped green chilies**
- 1 **tablespoon fresh cilantro leaves**
- 1 **tablespoon lime juice**
- 4 **tilapia fillets (4 ounces each)**
- ½ **cup all-purpose flour**
- 1 **egg white, beaten**
- ½ **cup panko (Japanese) bread crumbs**
- 1 **tablespoon canola oil**
- ½ **teaspoon salt**
- ½ **teaspoon each white pepper, cayenne pepper and paprika**
- 8 **corn tortillas (6 inches), warmed**
- 1 **large tomato, finely chopped**

1. Place the sour cream, chilies, cilantro and lime juice in a food processor; cover and process until blended. Set aside.

2. Cut each tilapia fillet lengthwise into two portions. Place the flour, egg white and bread crumbs in separate shallow bowls. Dip tilapia in flour, then egg white, then crumbs.

3. In a large skillet over medium heat, cook tilapia in oil in batches for 4-5 minutes on each side or until fish flakes easily with a fork. Combine the seasonings; sprinkle over fish.

4. Place a portion of fish on each tortilla; top with about 2 tablespoons of sour cream mixture. Sprinkle with tomato.

Chicken a la King

Home-style Chicken a la King has a thick and creamy sauce that's perfect over biscuits. I've been making this for 30 years. 's a wonderful way to create a quick lunch r dinner with leftover chicken.

—**RUTH LEE** TROY, ON

TART TO FINISH: 25 MIN.
MAKES: 4 SERVINGS

- 4 **individually frozen biscuits**
- 1¾ **cups sliced fresh mushrooms**
- ¼ **cup chopped onion**
- ¼ **cup chopped celery**
- ⅓ **cup butter, cubed**
- ¼ **cup all-purpose flour**
- ⅛ **to ¼ teaspoon salt**
- 1 **cup chicken broth**
- 1 **cup milk**
- 2 **cups cubed cooked chicken**
- 2 **tablespoons diced pimientos**

Bake biscuits according to package irections. Meanwhile, in a large killet, saute the mushrooms, onion nd celery in butter until crisp-tender. tir in flour and salt until blended. radually stir in broth and milk. Bring a boil; cook and stir for 2 minutes or ntil thickened.

Add chicken and pimientos; heat hrough. Serve with biscuits.

Sweet-and-Sour Pork

I stir up a homemade sweet-and-sour sauce for this colorful combination of tender pork, crunchy vegetables and tangy pineapple. Serve it with rice, chow mein noodles or both!

—**ELEANOR DUNBAR** PEORIA, IL

PREP : 25 MIN. + MARINATING
COOK: 10 MIN. • **MAKES:** 4 SERVINGS

- ⅔ **cup packed brown sugar**
- ⅔ **cup cider vinegar**
- ⅔ **cup ketchup**
- 2 **teaspoons reduced-sodium soy sauce**
- 1 **pound boneless pork loin, cut into 1-inch cubes**
- 1 **tablespoon canola oil**
- 1 **medium onion, cut into chunks**
- 2 **medium carrots, sliced**
- 1 **medium green pepper, cut into 1-inch pieces**
- ¼ **teaspoon ground ginger**
- ½ **teaspoon minced garlic**
- 1 **can (8 ounces) pineapple chunks, drained**
  Hot cooked rice, optional

1. In a small bowl, combine the brown sugar, vinegar, ketchup, and soy sauce. Pour half into a large resealable plastic bag; add pork. Seal bag and turn to coat; refrigerate for 30 minutes. Set remaining marinade aside.

2. Drain pork and discard its marinade. In a large skillet, cook pork in oil over medium heat for 2-3 minutes on all sides or until meat is lightly browned; drain. Add the onion, carrots, green pepper, and ginger. Add garlic; cook 1 minute longer.

3. Cover and simmer for 6-8 minutes or until pork is tender. Add reserved marinade. Bring to a boil; cook for 1 minute or until heated through. Stir in pineapple. Serve with rice if desired.

Hearty Hunter's Stew

PREP: 25 MIN. • **COOK:** 2 HOURS 50 MIN.
MAKES: 8 SERVINGS

- 2 **pounds boneless venison or beef chuck roast, cut in 1-inch cubes**
- 2 **tablespoons canola oil**
- 4¼ **cups water, divided**
- ½ **cup tomato juice**
- 2 **medium onions, cut in wedges**
- 2 **celery ribs, sliced**
- 1 **teaspoon Worcestershire sauce**
- 2 **bay leaves**
- 2 **to 3 teaspoons salt**
- ½ **teaspoon pepper**
- 6 **medium carrots, quartered**
- 1 **large rutabaga, peeled and cubed**
- 6 **medium potatoes, peeled and quartered**
- 1 **cup frozen peas**
- 1 **tablespoon cornstarch**

1. In a Dutch oven, brown meat in oil over medium heat. Add 4 cups water and scrape to loosen any browned drippings from pan. Add the tomato juice, onions, celery, Worcestershire sauce, bay leaves, salt and pepper. Bring to a boil. Reduce heat; cover and cook for 2 hours, stirring occasionally.
2. Discard bay leaves; add the carrots, rutabaga and potatoes. Cover and cook for 40-60 minutes.
3. Stir in the peas; cook for 10 minutes Combine cornstarch and remaining water until smooth; stir into stew. Bring to a boil. Cook and stir for 2 minutes or until thickened.

Did you know?

Polish Hunter's Stew, known as *bigos,* is traditionally made with meat and cabbage and is a common dish throughout Poland in winter.

Pork Chop Supper

You can let this simmer while you do other things. This was a regular on washday when I was growing up.
—**RUTH ANDREWSON** LEAVENWORTH, WA

PREP: 25 MIN. • **COOK:** 40 MIN.
MAKES: 6 SERVINGS

- ½ **cup all-purpose flour**
- 6 **bone-in pork loin chops (¾ inch thick and 8 ounces each)**
- 2 **tablespoons olive oil**
- 2 **teaspoons dried thyme**
- 2 **teaspoons salt**
- ¼ **teaspoon pepper**
- 4 **large potatoes (about 2¼ pounds)**
- 5 **medium carrots, sliced ¼ inch thick**
- 1 **medium onion, cut into wedges**
- 3 **cups beef broth**

1. Place flour in a large resealable plastic bag. Add chops, a few at a time, and shake to coat. In a large skillet; brown the chops in oil on both sides. Sprinkle with thyme, salt and pepper.
2. Peel potatoes and cut into ¾-in. cubes. Add the potatoes, carrots and onion to the skillet. Pour broth over all; bring to a boil. Reduce heat; cover and simmer for 40-50 minutes or until a meat thermometer reads 160°.

Tender meat and thick, rich gravy are the hallmarks of this rustic stew. This is winter comfort at its finest. —JOYCE WORSECH CATAWBA, WI

Skinny Turkey-Vegetable Soup

My daughters and I love this soothing soup. I often make it after the holidays using the leftover turkey.

—**CHARLOTTE WELCH** UTICA, NY

PREP: 30 MIN. • **COOK:** 35 MIN.
MAKES: 6 SERVINGS (2¼ QUARTS)

- 2 medium onions, chopped
- 2 medium carrots, halved and thinly sliced
- 2 celery ribs, chopped
- ½ cup chopped sweet red pepper
- 1 tablespoon olive oil
- 3 garlic cloves, minced
- 4 cups water
- 1 can (10 ounces) diced tomatoes and green chilies, undrained
- ½ cup frozen peas
- 1 bay leaf
- 4 teaspoons sodium-free chicken bouillon granules
- ½ teaspoon dried basil
- ½ teaspoon dried thyme
- ¼ teaspoon ground cumin
- ¼ teaspoon pepper
- ¼ to ½ teaspoon hot pepper sauce, optional
- ½ cup uncooked whole wheat orzo pasta
- 2 cups cubed cooked turkey breast
- 1 tablespoon minced fresh cilantro

1. In a large saucepan, saute the onions, carrots, celery and red pepper in oil until tender. Add garlic; cook 2 minutes longer. Stir in the water, tomatoes, peas, bay leaf, bouillon, basil, thyme, cumin, pepper and pepper sauce if desired. Bring to a boil. Reduce heat; simmer, uncovered, for 15 minutes.

2. Meanwhile, cook orzo according to package directions; drain. Stir orzo and turkey into soup; heat through. Discard bay leaf. Sprinkle with cilantro.

FREEZE OPTION *Freeze cooled soup in freezer containers. To use, partially thaw in refrigerator overnight. Heat through in a saucepan, stirring occasionally and adding a little broth, water or milk if necessary.*

Cincinnati Chili

Cinnamon and cocoa give a rich brown color to this hearty chili. This dish will warm you up on a cold day.

—**EDITH JOYCE** PARKMAN, OH

PREP: 20 MIN. • **COOK:** 1¾ HOURS
MAKES: 8 SERVINGS

- 1 pound ground beef
- 1 pound ground pork
- 4 medium onions, chopped
- 6 garlic cloves, minced
- 2 cans (16 ounces each) kidney beans, rinsed and drained
- 1 can (28 ounces) crushed tomatoes
- ¼ cup white vinegar
- ¼ cup baking cocoa
- 2 tablespoons chili powder
- 2 tablespoons Worcestershire sauce
- 4 teaspoons ground cinnamon
- 3 teaspoons dried oregano
- 2 teaspoons ground cumin
- 2 teaspoons ground allspice
- 2 teaspoons hot pepper sauce
- 3 bay leaves
- 1 teaspoon sugar
   Salt and pepper to taste
   Hot cooked spaghetti
   Shredded cheddar cheese, sour cream, chopped tomatoes and green onions

1. In a Dutch oven, cook the beef, pork and onions over medium heat until meat is no longer pink. Add garlic; cook 1 minute longer. Drain. Add the beans, tomatoes, vinegar, cocoa and seasonings; bring to a boil. Reduce heat; cover and simmer for 1½ hours or until heated through.

2. Discard bay leaves. Serve with spaghetti. Garnish with cheese, sour cream, tomatoes and onions.

Hungarian Chicken

Ever since I discovered this chicken in an old church cookbook, it's been a favorite for both family and company dinners. Everyone asks for seconds.

—CRYSTAL GARZA SHAMROCK, TX

PREP: 10 MIN. • **COOK:** 1 HOUR
MAKES: 4-6 SERVINGS

- 6 **tablespoons all-purpose flour**
  Salt and pepper to taste
- 1 **broiler/fryer chicken (about 3½ pounds), cut up**
- ¼ **cup butter, divided**
- 1 **large onion, chopped**
- ⅔ **cup tomato juice**
- 1 **to 2 tablespoons paprika**
- 1 **teaspoon sugar**
- 1 **teaspoon salt**
- 1 **bay leaf**
- ⅔ **cup chicken broth**
- ⅔ **cup sour cream**
  Hot cooked egg noodles

1. Combine flour, salt and pepper in a large resealable plastic bag. Add chicken, a few pieces at a time, and shake to coat.

2. Melt 1 tablespoon butter in a large skillet. Add onion and cook until tender. Remove from pan and set aside. In the same skillet, melt remaining butter and brown chicken on all sides.

3. Combine tomato juice, paprika, sugar and salt; add to chicken. Add bay leaf, broth and onion. Cover and simmer 45-60 minutes or until chicken is tender.

4. Remove chicken to a platter; keep warm. Reduce heat to low, remove bay leaf and stir in sour cream. Heat through (do not boil). Pour sauce over chicken. Serve with noodles.

Parmesan Pork Chops

Everyone is amazed at how tender this pork is, and the golden brown coating on these chops is full of Parmesan flavor.

—**TERRI MCKITRICK** DELAFIELD, WI

START TO FINISH: 30 MIN.
MAKES: 4 SERVINGS

- ¼ cup biscuit/baking mix
- 1 egg, lightly beaten
- 1 cup shredded Parmesan cheese
- ¼ cup dry bread crumbs
- 2 teaspoons minced fresh rosemary
- 4 boneless pork loin chops (½ inch thick and 6 ounces each)
- 2 tablespoons canola oil

1. Place biscuit mix and egg in separate shallow bowls. In another shallow bowl, combine the cheese, bread crumbs and rosemary. Coat pork chops with biscuit mix, dip in egg, then coat with cheese mixture.

2. In a large skillet, brown pork chops on both sides in oil. Cook, uncovered, over medium heat for 10-15 minutes or until juices run clear, turning once.

Southwest Frito Pie

I got a real culture shock when we moved to New Mexico several years ago, but we grew to love the food. Now that we're back in South Carolina, we find ourselves craving New Mexican dishes, and this is one of my favorites.

—**JANET SCOGGINS** NORTH AUGUSTA, SC

PREP: 20 MIN. • **COOK:** 25 MIN.
MAKES: 6 SERVINGS

- 2 pounds lean ground beef (90% lean)
- 3 tablespoons chili powder
- 2 tablespoons all-purpose flour
- 1 teaspoon salt
- 1 teaspoon garlic powder
- 2 cups water
- 1 can (15 ounces) pinto beans, rinsed and drained, optional
- 4½ cups corn chips
- 2 cups shredded lettuce
- 1½ cups (6 ounces) shredded cheddar cheese
- ¾ cup chopped tomatoes
- 6 tablespoons finely chopped onion Sour cream and minced fresh cilantro, optional

1. In a Dutch oven, cook beef over medium heat until no longer pink; drain. Stir in the chili powder, flour, salt and garlic powder until blended; gradually stir in water.

2. Add the beans, if desired. Bring to a boil. Reduce heat; simmer, uncovered, for 12-15 minutes or until thickened, stirring occasionally.

3. To serve, divide chips among six serving bowls. Top with beef mixture, lettuce, cheese, tomatoes and onion; garnish with sour cream and cilantro, if desired.

Chicken-Fried Steaks

These crispy steaks will have people gushing about how good they are when you serve them for dinner. My husband asks me to prepare this recipe regularly. I like it because it's so easy to make.

—DENICE LOUK GARNETT, KS

START TO FINISH: 25 MIN.
MAKES: 4 SERVINGS (2 CUPS GRAVY)

- 2¼ cups all-purpose flour, divided
- 2 teaspoons baking powder
- ¾ teaspoon each salt, onion powder, garlic powder, chili powder and pepper
- 2 eggs, lightly beaten
- 1⅔ cups buttermilk, divided
- 4 beef cubed steaks (4 ounces each)
  Oil for frying
- 1½ cups 2% milk

1. In a shallow bowl, combine 2 cups flour, baking powder and seasonings. In another shallow bowl, combine eggs and 1 cup buttermilk. Dip each cubed steak in buttermilk mixture, then roll in flour mixture. Let stand for 5 minutes.

2. In a large skillet, heat ½ in. of oil on medium-high. Fry steaks for 5-7 minutes. Turn carefully; cook 5 minutes longer or until coating is crisp and meat is no longer pink. Remove steaks and keep warm.

3. Drain, reserving ⅓ cup drippings; stir remaining flour into drippings until smooth. Cook and stir over medium heat for 2 minutes. Gradually whisk in milk and remaining buttermilk. Bring to a boil; cook and stir for 2 minutes or until thickened. Serve with steaks.

kid FRIENDLY Pizza Pasta Toss

I needed a quick one-skillet dish to put on the table. I thought if I added pizza sauce, pepperoni and mozzarella cheese to pasta, it might appeal to my daughter's selective palate. I was right!

—LORI DANIELS BEVERLY, WV

START TO FINISH: 30 MIN.
MAKES: 4 SERVINGS

- 2 cups uncooked spiral pasta
- 1 pound ground beef
- 1 cup sliced fresh mushrooms
- ½ cup chopped green pepper
- 1 can (15 ounces) tomato puree
- ½ cup diced pepperoni
- 4½ teaspoons sugar
- 1 teaspoon Italian seasoning
- ½ teaspoon salt
- ½ teaspoon garlic powder
- ½ teaspoon dried oregano
- ¼ teaspoon onion powder
- 2 cups (8 ounces) shredded part-skim mozzarella cheese

1. Cook pasta according to package directions. Meanwhile, in a large skillet, cook the beef, mushrooms and green pepper over medium heat until meat is no longer pink; drain. Add the tomato puree, pepperoni, sugar and seasonings; cook and stir for 5 minutes.

2. Drain pasta; stir into meat mixture. Heat through. Sprinkle with cheese. Remove from the heat; cover and let stand until cheese is melted.

Swiss Tuna Melts

These hot, melty sandwiches pair perfectly with your favorite homemade soup. You'll love the crunch the celery gives to the creamy tuna filling. If you'd like to boost the flavor a bit, add a pinch of garlic powder and dill relish.

—KAREN OWEN RISING SUN, IN

START TO FINISH: 20 MIN.
MAKES: 4 SERVINGS

- 1 **can (6 ounces) light water-packed tuna, drained and flaked**
- ¾ **cup shredded Swiss cheese**
- ¼ **cup chopped onion**
- ¼ **cup chopped celery**
- ½ **cup sour cream**
- ½ **cup mayonnaise**
  Pepper to taste
- 8 **slices bread**
- 2 **to 3 tablespoons butter, softened**

1. In a large bowl, combine the tuna, cheese, onion and celery. In a small bowl, combine sour cream and mayonnaise. Pour over tuna mixture and toss to coat. Spread about ½ cup over four slices of bread; top with remaining bread. Butter the outsides of sandwiches.

2. On a griddle or in a large skillet over medium heat, toast sandwiches for 4-5 minutes on each side or until lightly browned.

Potato Kielbasa Skillet

Smoky kielbasa steals the show in this hearty home-style meal. This is perfect on those cold late fall and early winter nights.

—TASTE OF HOME TEST KITCHEN

START TO FINISH: 30 MIN.
MAKES: 4 SERVINGS

- 1 **pound red potatoes, cubed**
- 3 **tablespoons water**
- ¾ **pound smoked kielbasa or Polish sausage, cut into ¼-inch slices**
- ½ **cup chopped onion**
- 1 **tablespoon olive oil**
- 2 **tablespoons brown sugar**
- 2 **tablespoons cider vinegar**
- 1 **tablespoon Dijon mustard**
- ½ **teaspoon dried thyme**
- ¼ **teaspoon pepper**
- 4 **cups fresh baby spinach**
- 5 **bacon strips, cooked and crumbled**

1. Place potatoes and water in a microwave-safe dish. Cover and microwave on high for 4 minutes or until tender; drain.

2. In a large skillet, saute kielbasa and onion in oil until onion is tender. Add potatoes; saute 3-5 minutes longer or until kielbasa and potatoes are lightly browned.

3. Combine the brown sugar, vinegar, mustard, thyme and pepper; stir into skillet. Bring to a boil. Reduce heat; simmer, uncovered, for 2-3 minutes or until heated through. Add spinach and bacon; cook and stir until spinach is wilted.

Fried Chicken Tenders

Sesame crackers give these chicken tenders a crunchy coating with lots of nutty flavor. I use a simple gravy mix to make a dipping sauce. It's better than any take-out chicken tenders you've ever had.
—**SHIRLEY LITTLE** ALVORD, TX

START TO FINISH: 25 MIN.
MAKES: 4 SERVINGS

- **2 eggs**
- **1 tablespoon water**
- **1 pound boneless skinless chicken breasts, cut into 1-inch strips**
- **1 package (8 ounces) sesame crackers, crushed (about 4 cups)**
- **¼ to ½ cup canola oil**
- **1 envelope instant chicken gravy mix, optional**

1. In a shallow bowl, combine eggs and water. Dip chicken in egg mixture, then coat with cracker crumbs. In an electric skillet, heat oil to 375°. Fry chicken strips, a few at a time, for 5-6 minutes or until golden brown. Drain on paper towels.

2. Meanwhile, prepare gravy mix according to package directions if desired. Serve with chicken strips.

Cashew Chicken

There are lots of recipes for cashew chicken, but my family thinks this one stands alone. We love the flavor from the fresh ginger and the crunch of the cashews. Another plus is that it's easy to prepare.
—**OMA ROLLISON** EL CAJON, CA

PREP: 20 MIN. • **COOK:** 15 MIN.
MAKES: 4-6 SERVINGS

- **2 tablespoons cornstarch**
- **1 tablespoon brown sugar**
- **1¼ cups chicken broth**
- **2 tablespoons soy sauce**
- **1½ pounds boneless skinless chicken breasts, cubed**
- **3 tablespoons canola oil, divided**
- **½ pound sliced fresh mushrooms**
- **1 small green pepper, julienned**
- **4 green onions, sliced**
- **1½ teaspoons grated fresh gingerroot**
- **1 can (8 ounces) sliced water chestnuts, drained**
- **¾ cup salted cashews**
  Hot cooked rice

1. In a small bowl, combine the cornstarch, brown sugar, broth and soy sauce until smooth; set aside. In a large skillet or wok, stir-fry chicken in 2 tablespoons oil until no longer pink. Remove and keep warm.

2. In the same skillet, stir-fry the mushrooms, green pepper, onions and ginger in remaining oil until green pepper is crisp-tender, about 5 minutes. Stir in the chicken, water chestnuts and cashews; heat through.

3. Stir broth mixture and add to the pan. Bring to a boil; cook and stir for 1-2 minutes or until thickened. Serve with rice.

kid FRIENDLY
Nacho Mac 'n' Cheese

Beefy, cheesy, creamy and crunchy—what family wouldn't love this comforting dinner? And since most of the ingredients are mixed in one pot, clean-up is a breeze.
—TASTE OF HOME TEST KITCHEN

START TO FINISH: 25 MIN.
MAKES: 6 SERVINGS

- 3 cups uncooked gemelli or spiral pasta
- 1 pound ground beef
- 2 cups chopped sweet red peppers
- ¼ cup butter, cubed
- ¼ cup all-purpose flour
- 1 envelope taco seasoning
- ¼ teaspoon pepper
- 2¼ cups 2% milk
- 2 cups (8 ounces) shredded cheddar cheese
- 1 cup frozen corn, thawed
- 1 cup coarsely crushed tortilla chips

1. Cook gemelli according to package directions. Meanwhile, in a Dutch oven, cook beef and red peppers over medium heat until meat is no longer pink; drain.

2. Stir in the butter, flour, taco seasoning and pepper until blended. Gradually stir in milk. Bring to a boil; cook and stir for 2 minutes or until thickened. Remove from the heat. Stir in cheese and corn until cheese is melted.

3. Drain gemelli; add to beef mixture and stir to coat. Sprinkle with tortilla chips.

Glazed Pork Medallions

When my husband was told to lower his cholesterol, he worried that trimming the fat would mean losing the flavor. This lean and flavorful entree proves that fish isn't the only option when it comes to keeping fat in check.
—MICHELE FLAGEL SHELLSBURG, IA

START TO FINISH: 30 MIN.
MAKES: 4 SERVINGS

- 1 pork tenderloin (1¼ pounds)
- ¼ teaspoon salt
- ⅓ cup reduced-sugar orange marmalade
- 2 teaspoons cider vinegar
- 2 teaspoons Worcestershire sauce
- ½ teaspoon minced fresh gingerroot
- ⅛ teaspoon crushed red pepper flakes

Cut pork into 1-in. slices and flatten to ¼-in. thickness; sprinkle with salt. Cook pork in batches over medium-high heat in a large nonstick skillet coated with cooking spray until tender. Reduce heat to low; return all meat to the pan. Combine the remaining ingredients; pour over pork and turn to coat. Heat through.

top tip
Frozen Ginger to the Rescue

You can freeze fresh ginger. Just wrap it well and place it in a plastic bag. Peel and grate what you need from the frozen piece and return remaining ginger to the freezer. I always keep some in the freezer. You will not believe the difference it makes in recipes, especially pumpkin pie.
—NANCY65757 TASTEOFHOME.COM

Kid FRIENDLY Taco Macaroni

came up with this dish when I went to make stuffed peppers and realized the peppers had gone bad. So instead I added macaroni pasta to the filling and it was a big it! For a saucier version, use two cans of omato sauce.

—MARISSA UNDERCOFLER HOWARD, PA

TART TO FINISH: 30 MIN.
MAKES: 6 SERVINGS

- 1 package (16 ounces) elbow macaroni
- 1 pound ground beef
- ¾ cup chopped onion
- 1 can (14½ ounces) diced tomatoes, undrained
- 1 can (10¾ ounces) condensed tomato soup, undiluted
- 1 can (8 ounces) tomato sauce
- 1 envelope taco seasoning
  Shredded cheddar cheese

. Cook macaroni according to package directions. Meanwhile, in a Dutch oven, cook beef and onion over medium heat until meat is no longer pink; drain.

. Stir in the tomatoes, soup, tomato sauce and taco seasoning. Bring to a boil. Reduce heat; simmer, uncovered, or 8-10 minutes or until thickened.

. Drain macaroni; stir into meat mixture and heat through. Sprinkle with cheese.

Shredded Barbecue Chicken over Grits

There's nothing like juicy meat and grits. And the pumpkin in these grits makes them taste like a spicy, comforting bowl of fall flavors. Your family will come running to the table for this one.

—ERIN RENOUF MYLROIE SANTA CLARA, UT

PREP: 20 MIN. • **COOK:** 25 MIN.
MAKES: 6 SERVINGS

- 1 pound boneless skinless chicken breasts
- ¼ teaspoon pepper
- 1 can (14½ ounces) reduced-sodium chicken broth, divided
- 1 cup hickory smoke-flavored barbecue sauce
- ¼ cup molasses
- 1 tablespoon ground ancho chili pepper
- ½ teaspoon ground cinnamon
- 2¼ cups water
- 1 cup quick-cooking grits
- 1 cup canned pumpkin
- ¾ cup shredded pepper Jack cheese
- 1 medium tomato, seeded and chopped
- 6 tablespoons reduced-fat sour cream
- 2 green onions, chopped
- 2 tablespoons minced fresh cilantro

1. Sprinkle chicken with pepper; place in a large nonstick skillet coated with cooking spray.

2. In a large bowl, combine 1 cup broth, barbecue sauce, molasses, chili pepper and cinnamon; pour over chicken. Bring to a boil. Reduce heat; cover and simmer for 20-25 minutes or until a meat thermometer reads 170°. Shred meat with two forks and return to the skillet.

3. Meanwhile, in a large saucepan, bring water and remaining broth to a boil. Slowly stir in grits and pumpkin. Reduce heat; cook and stir for 5-7 minutes or until thickened. Stir in cheese until melted.

4. Divide grits among six serving bowls; top each with ½ cup chicken mixture. Serve with tomato, sour cream, green onions and cilantro.

For a slightly heartier chicken soup, try adding white beans and greens. This soothing version promises to keep the whole family warm.
—**ROSEMARY GOETZ** HUDSON, NY

Tuscan Chicken Soup

PREP: 15 MIN. • **COOK:** 20 MIN.
MAKES: 4 SERVINGS

- 1 small onion, chopped
- 1 small carrot, sliced
- 1 tablespoon olive oil
- 2 cans (14½ ounces each) chicken broth
- 1 cup water
- ¾ teaspoon salt
- ¼ teaspoon pepper
- 1 can (15 ounces) white kidney or cannellini beans, rinsed and drained
- ⅔ cup uncooked small spiral pasta
- 3 cups thinly sliced fresh escarole or spinach
- 2 cups shredded cooked chicken

1. In a large saucepan, saute onion and carrot in oil until onion is tender. Add the broth, water, salt and pepper; bring to a boil. Stir in beans and pasta; return to a boil.

2. Reduce heat; cover and simmer for 15 minutes or until pasta and vegetables are tender, stirring occasionally. Add escarole and chicken; heat through.

Salisbury Steak Deluxe

I've always liked Salisbury steak, but I had to search a long time to find a recipe this tasty. It's handy, too, because it can be prepared ahead, kept in the refrigerator and warmed up later.

—DENISE BARTEET SHREVEPORT, LA

START TO FINISH: 30 MIN.
MAKES: 6 SERVINGS

- 1 can (10¾ ounces) condensed cream of mushroom soup, undiluted
- 1 tablespoon prepared mustard
- 2 teaspoons Worcestershire sauce
- 1 teaspoon prepared horseradish
- 1 egg
- ¼ cup dry bread crumbs
- ¼ cup finely chopped onion
- ½ teaspoon salt
  Dash pepper
- 1½ pound ground beef
- 1 to 2 tablespoons canola oil
- ½ cup water
- 2 tablespoons chopped fresh parsley

1. In a small bowl, combine the soup, mustard, Worcestershire sauce and horseradish. Set aside. In another bowl, lightly beat the egg. Add the bread crumbs, onion, salt, pepper and ¼ cup of the soup mixture. Crumble beef over mixture and mix well. Shape into six patties.

2. In a large skillet, brown the patties in oil; drain. Combine remaining soup mixture with water; pour over patties. Cover and cook over low heat for 10-15 minutes or until meat is no longer pink and a thermometer reads 160°. Remove patties to a serving platter; serve sauce with meat. Sprinkle with parsley.

Parmesan-Crusted Tilapia

I usually serve this crispy fish with tartar sauce and seasoned steamed veggies. It's like a Friday night fish fry without all the calories!

—**CHRISTI MCELROY** NEENAH, WI

START TO FINISH: 25 MIN.
MAKES: 4 SERVINGS

- ½ cup all-purpose flour
- 1 egg, beaten
- ½ cup crushed butter-flavored crackers (about 10 crackers)
- ¼ cup grated Parmesan cheese
- ½ teaspoon salt
- 4 tilapia fillets (5 ounces each)
- 2 tablespoons olive oil
  Lemon wedges

1. Place flour and egg in separate shallow bowls. In another shallow bowl, combine the crackers, cheese and salt. Dip fillets in the flour, egg, then cracker mixture.
2. In a large skillet, cook fillets in oil over medium heat for 3-5 minutes on each side or until golden brown and fish flakes easily with a fork. Serve with lemon wedges.

ULTIMATE *Comfort* Beef & Bacon Stroganoff

Warm and saucy, this stovetop Stroganoff is real comfort food. You'll love the unexpected kick it gets from prepared horseradish.

—**MELISSA MILLWOOD** LYMAN, SC

PREP: 20 MIN. • **COOK:** 20 MIN.
MAKES: 6 SERVINGS

- 1 pound lean ground beef (90% lean)
- 5 thick-sliced bacon strips, chopped
- 1 cup sliced fresh mushrooms
- 1 medium onion, chopped
- 2 garlic cloves, minced
- 2 tablespoons all-purpose flour
- 1 can (14½ ounces) beef broth
- 1 can (10¾ ounces) condensed cream of mushroom with roasted garlic soup, undiluted
- 2 tablespoons Worcestershire sauce
- 1 teaspoon pepper
- ¼ teaspoon salt
- ¼ teaspoon paprika
- 6 cups uncooked egg noodles
- 1 cup (8 ounces) sour cream
- 2 teaspoons prepared horseradish
- ½ cup shredded white cheddar cheese
  Minced fresh parsley, optional

1. In a large skillet over medium heat, cook the beef, bacon, mushrooms and onion until beef is no longer pink. Add garlic; cook 1 minute longer. Drain. Stir in flour until blended. Add the broth, soup, Worcestershire sauce, pepper, salt and paprika. Bring to a boil. Reduce heat; simmer, uncovered, for 10-15 minutes, stirring occasionally.
2. Meanwhile, cook noodles according to package directions; drain.
3. Stir sour cream and horseradish into beef mixture; heat through (do not boil). Serve with noodles. Sprinkle with cheese. Garnish with parsley if desired.

Sweet-and-Sour Popcorn Chicken

Precooked, frozen popcorn chicken simmered in a thick, homemade sweet-and-sour sauce is the secret to this fast and fabulous entree. And what a great way to dress up frozen chicken nuggets! This is one menu item you'll find yourself returning to again and again.

—**AMY CORLEW-SHERLOCK** LAPEER, MI

START TO FINISH: 25 MIN.
MAKES: 4 SERVINGS

- 1 medium green pepper, cut into 1-inch pieces
- 1 small onion, thinly sliced
- 1 tablespoon canola oil
- 1 can (20 ounces) unsweetened pineapple chunks
- 3 tablespoons white vinegar
- 2 tablespoons soy sauce
- 2 tablespoons ketchup
- ⅓ cup packed brown sugar
- 2 tablespoons cornstarch
- 1 package (12 ounces) frozen popcorn chicken

1. In a large skillet or wok, stir-fry green pepper and onion in oil for 3-4 minutes or until crisp-tender. Drain pineapple, reserving the juice in a 2-cup measuring cup; set pineapple aside. Add enough water to the juice to measure 1⅓ cups; stir in the vinegar, soy sauce and ketchup.

2. In a large bowl, combine brown sugar and cornstarch. Stir in pineapple juice mixture until smooth. Gradually add to the skillet. Bring to a boil; cook and stir for 2 minutes or until thickened. Stir in pineapple and heat through.

3. Meanwhile, microwave chicken according to package directions. Stir into pineapple mixture. Serve immediately.

New England Clam Chowder

In the Pacific Northwest, we dig our own razor clams and I grind them for the chowder. Since these aren't readily available, you can use canned clams to make this creamy soup.

—**SANDY LARSON** PORT ANGELES, WA

PREP: 20 MIN. • **COOK:** 35 MIN.
MAKES: 5 SERVINGS

- 4 center-cut bacon strips
- 2 celery ribs, chopped
- 1 large onion, chopped
- 1 garlic clove, minced
- 3 small potatoes, peeled and cubed
- 1 cup water
- 1 bottle (8 ounces) clam juice
- 3 teaspoons reduced-sodium chicken bouillon granules
- ¼ teaspoon white pepper
- ¼ teaspoon dried thyme
- ⅓ cup all-purpose flour
- 2 cups fat-free half-and-half, divided
- 2 cans (6½ ounces each) chopped clams, undrained

1. In a Dutch oven, cook bacon over medium heat until crisp. Remove to paper towels to drain; set aside. Saute celery and onion in the drippings until tender. Add garlic; cook 1 minute longer. Stir in the potatoes, water, clam juice, bouillon, pepper and thyme. Bring to a boil. Reduce heat; simmer, uncovered, for 15-20 minutes or until potatoes are tender.

2. In a small bowl, combine flour and 1 cup half-and-half until smooth. Gradually stir into soup. Bring to a boil; cook and stir for 1-2 minutes or until thickened.

3. Stir in clams and remaining half-and-half; heat through (do not boil). Crumble the reserved bacon; sprinkle over each serving.

Creamy Noodle Casserole

My husband, Ronald, works long hours and frequently won't arrive home until past 7 p.m. But this casserole is still tasty after it's been warmed in the microwave.

—BARB MARSHALL PICKERINGTON, OH

START TO FINISH: 25 MIN.
MAKES: 8 SERVINGS

- 1 **package (12 ounces) egg noodles**
- 1 **package (16 ounces) frozen broccoli cuts**
- 3 **cups cubed fully cooked ham**
- 1 **cup (4 ounces) shredded part-skim mozzarella cheese**
- 1 **cup (4 ounces) shredded Parmesan cheese**
- ⅓ **cup butter, cubed**
- ½ **cup half-and-half cream**
- ¼ **teaspoon each garlic powder, salt and pepper**

1. In a Dutch oven, cook noodles in boiling water for 5 minutes. Add broccoli and ham; cook 5-10 minutes longer or until noodles are tender.

2. Drain; return to pan. Stir in the remaining ingredients. Cook and stir over low heat until butter is melted and mixture is heated through.

FREEZE OPTION *Freeze cooled noodle mixture in freezer containers. To use, partially thaw in refrigerator overnight. Microwave, covered, on high in a microwave-safe dish until heated through, gently stirring and adding a little broth or milk if necessary.*

Did you know?

Broccoli is a type of cruciferous vegetable, so named because the flowers have four petals and resemble a Greek cross.

Beef Rouladen

Until I entered kindergarten, we spoke German in our home and kept many old-world customs. We always enjoyed the food of our family's homeland. Mom usually prepared this for my birthday dinner.

—HELGA SCHLAPE FLORHAM PARK, NJ

PREP: 30 MIN. • **COOK:** 1½ HOURS
MAKES: 6 SERVINGS

- 3 **pounds beef top round steak (½ inch thick)**
- ½ **teaspoon salt**
- ¼ **teaspoon pepper**
- 6 **bacon strips**
- 3 **whole dill pickles, halved lengthwise**
- 2 **tablespoons canola oil**
- 2 **cups water**
- 1 **medium onion, chopped**
- 2 **tablespoons minced fresh parsley**
- 2 **teaspoons beef bouillon granules, optional**
- ¼ **cup all-purpose flour**
- ½ **cup cold water**
- ½ **teaspoon browning sauce, optional**

- Cut steak into six serving-size pieces; pound to ¼-in. thickness. Sprinkle with salt and pepper. Place a bacon strip down the center of each piece; arrange a pickle half on one edge. Roll up and secure with a toothpick.

- In a large skillet, heat oil over medium-high heat. Brown beef on all sides. Add the water, onion, parsley and bouillon if desired. Bring to a boil. Reduce heat; cover and simmer for 1½ to 2 hours or until meat is tender. Remove to a serving platter and keep warm.

- For gravy, skim fat from drippings. Combine the flour, water and browning sauce if desired; stir into drippings. Bring to a boil; cook and stir for 2 minutes or until thickened. Serve with beef.

Vegetarian White Bean Soup

We simmered this fresh-tasting meatless soup with two kinds of beans for a satisfying entree. Round out the meal with warm dinner rolls.

—TASTE OF HOME TEST KITCHEN

START TO FINISH: 30 MIN.
MAKES: 7 SERVINGS

- 2 **small zucchini, quartered lengthwise and sliced**
- 1 **cup each chopped onion, celery and carrot**
- 2 **tablespoons canola oil**
- 3 **cans (14½ ounces each) vegetable broth**
- 1 **can (15½ ounces) great northern beans, rinsed and drained**
- 1 **can (15 ounces) white kidney or cannellini beans, rinsed and drained**
- 1 **can (14½ ounces) diced tomatoes, undrained**
- ½ **teaspoon dried thyme**
- ½ **teaspoon dried oregano**
- ¼ **teaspoon pepper**

In a large saucepan, saute the zucchini, onion, celery and carrot in oil for 5-7 minutes or until crisp-tender. Add the remaining ingredients. Bring to a boil. Reduce heat; cover and simmer for 15 minutes or until vegetables are tender.

Hearty Sausage 'n' Hash Browns

Turn frozen hash browns into a satisfying supper by adding smoked sausage and green peppers. It's a simple meal-in-one that works any time of day.

—**VIOLET BEARD** MARSHALL, IL

START TO FINISH: 30 MIN.
MAKES: 3 SERVINGS

    4 cups frozen cubed hash brown
       potatoes
    ¼ cup chopped green pepper
    ⅓ cup canola oil
    ¼ pound smoked sausage, halved
       lengthwise and cut into ¼-inch
       slices
    3 slices process American cheese

In a large skillet, cook potatoes and pepper in oil over medium heat until potatoes are golden brown. Stir in sausage; heat through. Remove from heat; top with cheese. Cover and let stand for 5 minutes or until cheese is melted.

ULTIMATE *Comfort* Patty Melts

My husband often orders patty melts at restaurants, so I started fixing them at home. I added horseradish to give them more zip, and now he loves them my way.

—**LEAH ZIMMERMAN** EPHRATA, PA

START TO FINISH: 30 MIN.
MAKES: 2 SERVINGS

   10 thin slices sweet onion
    2 tablespoons butter, softened,
       divided
    ½ pound lean ground beef (90% lean)
    ¼ teaspoon salt
    ¼ teaspoon pepper
    4 slices rye bread
    2 tablespoons Thousand Island salad
       dressing
    2 teaspoons prepared horseradish
    2 slices process American cheese or
       Swiss cheese

1. In a large nonstick skillet, saute onion in 1 tablespoon butter until tender. Remove and keep warm.

2. Shape beef into two oval patties; sprinkle with salt and pepper. In the same skillet, cook patties over medium heat for 3-4 minutes on each side or until a meat thermometer reads 160 and meat juices run clear; drain. Remove and keep warm.

3. Spread remaining butter over one side of each slice of bread. Place in skillet, buttered side down, and toast until lightly browned.

4. Combine salad dressing and horseradish. On two slices of toast, layer a slice of cheese, a beef patty, half of the onion and dressing mixture. Top with remaining toast.

Glazed Ham Slices

Besides being a great cook, my mom could put a meal together in no time at all. We have ham quite often, and this is our favorite thing to make with leftover slices.
—LEONA LUECKING WEST BURLINGTON, IA

START TO FINISH: 15 MIN.
MAKES: 2 SERVINGS

- ¼ cup packed brown sugar
- 1½ teaspoons all-purpose flour
- ½ teaspoon ground mustard
- 2 tablespoons ginger ale
- 1 tablespoon cider vinegar
- 2 boneless fully cooked ham slices (½ to ¾ pound and ½ inch thick)

In a skillet, combine the brown sugar, flour, mustard, ginger ale and vinegar. Bring to a boil over low heat; cook and stir for 2 minutes or until sugar is dissolved and sauce is thickened. Add ham slices and heat through.

Chicken & Dumplings

After a very long week, I needed some comfort food, so I made this meal on a whim. Rotisserie chicken drastically cuts the prep time, so we don't have to wait long for dinner to be ready.
—JESSICA REHS CUYAHOGA FALLS, OH

PREP: 25 MIN. • **COOK:** 35 MIN.
MAKES: 6 SERVINGS

- 6 cups reduced-sodium chicken broth
- 3 bay leaves
- 5 fresh thyme sprigs
- 4 garlic cloves, peeled
- 1 teaspoon crushed red pepper flakes
- 1 cup chopped carrots
- 1 cup chopped celery
- 3 tablespoons olive oil
- 2 tablespoons butter
- 3 garlic cloves, minced
- 2 tablespoons all-purpose flour
- 1 cup frozen peas
- 1 rotisserie chicken, shredded
- ¼ cup heavy whipping cream

DUMPLINGS
- 2 cups all-purpose flour
- 1 tablespoon baking powder
- 1 teaspoon salt
- 1 teaspoon cayenne pepper
- 1 cup buttermilk
- 2 eggs, lightly beaten
- ¼ cup minced chives

1. In a large saucepan, combine the first five ingredients. Bring to a boil. Reduce heat; simmer, uncovered, for 30 minutes. Strain and set aside.
2. In a Dutch oven, saute carrots and celery in oil and butter until tender. Add minced garlic; cook 1 minute longer. Stir in flour until blended; gradually add prepared broth. Bring to a boil; cook 2 minutes or until thickened, stirring frequently.
3. Add peas; return to a boil. Cook 3 to 5 minutes or until peas are tender. Stir in chicken and cream; heat through.
4. For dumplings, combine the flour, baking powder, salt and cayenne in a large bowl. In another bowl, combine buttermilk and eggs; stir into dry ingredients just until moistened.
5. Drop by tablespoonfuls onto simmering chicken mixture. Cover and simmer for 15-20 minutes or until a toothpick inserted in a dumpling comes out clean. Garnish with chives before serving.

ULTIMATE *Comfort*
Batter-Up Walleye

Nothing is more rewarding than celebrating our day's catch with friends by sharing this battered fish with everyone. It gets gobbled up as fast as I can fry them!
—**ALESHA OSTER** WILLISTON, ND

START TO FINISH: 30 MIN.
MAKES: 4 SERVINGS

- 1 cup biscuit/baking mix
- 1 tablespoon garlic powder
- 1 tablespoon onion powder
- 1 tablespoon Cajun seasoning
- 1½ teaspoons pepper
- 1 teaspoon salt
- ½ cup 2% milk
  Oil for frying
- 1 pound walleye fillets, skin removed
  Lemon wedges

1. In a shallow bowl, mix the first six ingredients. Place milk in a separate shallow bowl. In an electric skillet, heat ¼ in. of oil to 375°.

2. In batches, dip fish in milk, then coat with baking mix mixture; fry for 5 minutes on each side or until golden brown and fish flakes easily with a fork. Serve immediately with lemon wedges.

Chicken Piccata

This is a comforting yet low-fat, low-sodium dish. With the lemon juice added, you don't miss the salt. I usually serve this with rice or pasta, although either one takes longer to cook than the chicken!
—**CAROL COTTRILL** RUMFORD, ME

START TO FINISH: 25 MIN.
MAKES: 2 SERVINGS

- 2 boneless skinless chicken breast halves (4 ounces each)
- 2 tablespoons all-purpose flour
- ¼ teaspoon salt
- ⅛ teaspoon pepper
- 1 tablespoon canola oil
- 2 tablespoons white wine or reduced-sodium chicken broth
- 1 garlic clove, minced
- ⅓ cup reduced-sodium chicken broth
- 1 tablespoon lemon juice
- 1½ teaspoons capers
- 1½ teaspoons butter
- 2 thin lemon slices

1. Flatten chicken to ½-in. thickness. In a large plastic resealable bag, combine the flour, salt and pepper; add the chicken, one piece at a time. Seal bag and toss to coat.

2. In a small skillet, brown chicken in oil for 2-3 minutes on each side or until no longer pink. Remove and keep warm.

3. Add wine and garlic to the pan; cook and stir for 30 seconds. Add the broth, lemon juice and capers. Bring to a boil; cook for 1-2 minutes or until slightly thickened. Stir in butter and lemon slices. Return chicken to the pan; heat through.

Polish Sausage and Veggies

Looking for something different to prepare with Polish sausage, I created this entree one afternoon. My family liked it so much that I've made it again and again.

—RITA KODET CHULA VISTA, CA

START TO FINISH: 30 MIN.
MAKES: 6 SERVINGS

- 4 **cups cubed peeled potatoes (about 2½ pounds)**
- 1 **pound smoked Polish sausage or smoked kielbasa, cut into ¼-inch slices**
- ½ **cup chopped onion**
- ½ **cup julienned sweet yellow pepper**
- ½ **cup julienned sweet red pepper**
- 1½ **teaspoons Cajun seasoning**
- 1 **tablespoon canola oil**
- 1 **tablespoon butter**

In a large skillet over medium heat, cook the potatoes, sausage, onion, peppers and Cajun seasoning in oil and butter for 15-20 minutes or until potatoes are tender, stirring occasionally.

Catfish Po'boys

When my neighbor prepared these full-flavored sandwiches, I had to have the recipe. Strips of catfish are treated to a zesty Cajun cornmeal breading, then served on a bun with packaged broccoli coleslaw mix dressed in a homemade sauce.

—MILDRED SHERRER FORT WORTH, TX

START TO FINISH: 30 MIN.
MAKES: 4 SERVINGS

- 2 **tablespoons fat-free mayonnaise**
- 1 **tablespoon fat-free sour cream**
- 1 **tablespoon white wine vinegar**
- 1 **teaspoon sugar**
- 2 **cups broccoli coleslaw mix**
- ¼ **cup cornmeal**
- 2 **teaspoons Cajun seasoning**
- ½ **teaspoon salt**
- ⅛ **teaspoon cayenne pepper**
- 1 **pound catfish fillets, cut into 2½-inch strips**
- 2 **tablespoons fat-free milk**
- 2 **teaspoons olive oil**
- 4 **kaiser rolls, split**

1. In a small bowl, whisk the mayonnaise, sour cream, vinegar and sugar until smooth. Add coleslaw mix; toss to coat. Set aside.

2. In a large resealable plastic bag, combine the cornmeal, Cajun seasoning, salt and cayenne. Place the milk in a shallow bowl. Dip the catfish in milk and place in bag, a few pieces at a time; seal bag and shake to coat.

3. In a large nonstick skillet, cook catfish over medium heat in oil for 4-5 minutes on each side or until fish flakes easily with a fork and coating is golden brown. Spoon coleslaw onto rolls; top with catfish.

kid FRIENDLY Beef Taco Skillet

Busy day? Save time and money with a stovetop supper the whole family will love. It calls for handy convenience products, so it can be on the table in minutes.

—**KELLY RODER** FAIRFAX, VA

START TO FINISH: 20 MIN.
MAKES: 6 SERVINGS

- 1 pound ground beef
- 1 small red onion, chopped
- 1 can (15¼ ounces) whole kernel corn, drained
- 10 corn tortillas (6 inches), cut into 1-inch pieces
- 1 bottle (8 ounces) taco sauce
- 1¼ cups shredded cheddar cheese, divided
  Hot pepper sauce, optional

In a large skillet, cook beef and onion over medium heat until meat is no longer pink; drain. Add the corn, tortillas, taco sauce and 1 cup cheese; heat through. Sprinkle with remaining cheese. Serve with pepper sauce if desired.

Mushroom Pepper Steak

Bell peppers, mushrooms and ginger provide the bulk of the flavor in this stir-fry. It's not too saucy and goes great over hot rice.

—**BILLIE MOSS** WALNUT CREEK, CA

PREP: 15 MIN. + MARINATING
COOK: 15 MIN. • **MAKES:** 4 SERVINGS

- 6 tablespoons reduced-sodium soy sauce, divided
- ⅛ teaspoon pepper
- 1 pound beef top sirloin steak, cut into thin strips
- 1 tablespoon cornstarch
- ½ cup reduced-sodium beef broth
- 1 garlic clove, minced
- ½ teaspoon minced fresh gingerroot
- 3 teaspoons canola oil, divided
- 1 cup julienned sweet red pepper
- 1 cup julienned green pepper
- 2 cups sliced fresh mushrooms
- 2 medium tomatoes, cut into wedges
- 6 green onions, sliced
  Hot cooked rice, optional

1. In a large resealable plastic bag, combine 3 tablespoons soy sauce and pepper; add beef. Seal bag and turn to coat; refrigerate for 30-60 minutes. In a small bowl, combine the cornstarch, broth and remaining soy sauce until smooth; set aside.

2. Drain beef and discard marinade. In a large nonstick skillet or wok, stir-fry the garlic and ginger in 2 teaspoons oil for 1 minute. Add the beef; stir-fry for 4-6 minutes or until no longer pink. Remove beef and keep warm.

3. Stir-fry the peppers in remaining oil for 1 minute. Add mushrooms; stir-fry 2 minutes longer or until peppers are crisp-tender. Stir broth mixture and add to vegetable mixture. Bring to a boil; cook and stir for 2 minutes or until thickened. Return beef to pan; add tomatoes and onions. Cook for 2 minutes or until heated through. Serve over rice if desired.

Shrimp Scampi with Lemon Couscous

With just a few minutes of prep work, you can make an eye-catching entree. I sometimes add a handful of halved grape tomatoes to the pan during the last minute of cooking.

—DIANA SANTOSPAGO ISLE AU HAUT, ME

START TO FINISH: 20 MIN.
MAKES: 6 SERVINGS

- 1 cup chicken broth
- 3 tablespoons lemon juice, divided
- 1 cup uncooked couscous
- 5 tablespoons butter, divided
- 3 tablespoons minced fresh parsley, divided
- 1 teaspoon grated lemon peel
- 2 tablespoons olive oil
- 1½ teaspoons minced garlic
- 2 pounds cooked jumbo shrimp, peeled and deveined
- ⅓ cup white wine or additional chicken broth
- ¼ teaspoon salt
- ⅛ teaspoon pepper
- ¼ cup shredded Asiago cheese

1. In a small saucepan, bring broth and 1 tablespoon lemon juice to a boil. Stir in couscous, 1 tablespoon butter, 1 tablespoon parsley and lemon peel. Cover and remove from the heat; let stand for 5 minutes or until liquid is absorbed.

2. Meanwhile, in a large skillet, stir oil and remaining butter over medium-high heat until butter is melted. Add garlic; cook and stir until tender. Add shrimp; cook for 1 minute on each side or until shrimp turn pink.

3. Add the wine, salt, pepper and remaining lemon juice; cook 2-3 minutes longer or until heated through. Serve with couscous. Sprinkle with cheese and remaining parsley.

Italian Wedding Soup Supper

Classic wedding soup is a combination of green vegetables and meat in a chicken-based broth. This hearty version includes chicken and meatballs along with pasta and carrots for a colorful variation.

—PATRICIA HARMON BADEN, PA

PREP: 25 MIN. • **COOK:** 15 MIN.
MAKES: 6 SERVINGS

- 2 cups small pasta shells
- ½ pound boneless skinless chicken breasts, cut into ¾-inch cubes
- 2 tablespoons olive oil, divided
- 1 medium onion, chopped
- 1 medium carrot, finely chopped
- 1 celery rib, chopped
- 1 package (12 ounces) frozen fully cooked Italian meatballs, thawed
- 1 can (10¾ ounces) reduced-fat reduced-sodium condensed cream of chicken soup, undiluted
- 1 package (10 ounces) frozen chopped spinach, thawed and squeezed dry
- 1 cup reduced-sodium chicken broth
- 2 teaspoons minced fresh thyme or ½ teaspoon dried thyme
- ½ teaspoon salt
- ⅛ teaspoon pepper
- ¾ cup shredded Asiago cheese

1. Cook pasta according to package directions. Meanwhile, in a large skillet, saute chicken in 1 tablespoon oil until no longer pink; remove and keep warm.

2. In the same skillet, saute the onion, carrot and celery in remaining oil until tender. Add the meatballs, soup, spinach, broth, thyme, salt, pepper and reserved chicken; cover and cook for 4-6 minutes or until heated through.

3. Drain pasta; stir into skillet. Sprinkle with cheese.

kid FRIENDLY Brief Burritos

As a busy mom, my evenings are often hectic. I can put these quick burritos together after school and still have time to run back out after dinner for evening activities. Best of all, my kids love them.
—**GINGER BUROW** FREDERICKSBURG, TX

START TO FINISH: 15 MIN.
MAKES: 8 BURRITOS

- **1 pound ground beef**
- **1 can (16 ounces) refried beans**
- **1 can (10 ounces) diced tomatoes and green chilies, drained**
- **½ cup chili sauce**
- **8 flour tortillas (10 inches), warmed**
- **½ cup shredded cheddar cheese**
- **½ cup sour cream**

1. In a large skillet, cook beef over medium heat until no longer pink; drain. Stir in the refried beans, tomatoes and chili sauce; heat through.
2. Spoon about ½ cup down the center of each tortilla; top with cheese and sour cream. Fold ends and sides over filling. Serve immediately.

Chicken & Shrimp Fettuccine

START TO FINISH: 30 MIN.
MAKES: 5 SERVINGS

- **8 ounces uncooked fettuccine**
- **4 bacon strips, chopped**
- **¾ pound boneless skinless chicken breasts, cubed**
- **1 can (14½ ounces) diced tomatoes with garlic and onion, drained**
- **2 cups fresh baby spinach, coarsely chopped**
- **¾ cup heavy whipping cream**
- **½ teaspoon dried sage leaves**
- **½ cup grated Parmesan cheese, divided**
- **¾ pound peeled and deveined cooked medium shrimp**

1. Cook fettuccine according to package directions. Meanwhile, in a large skillet, cook bacon over medium heat until crisp. Remove to paper towels with a slotted spoon; drain, reserving 2 teaspoons drippings.
2. In the same skillet, saute chicken in reserved drippings until chicken juices run clear. Remove and keep warm.
3. Add the tomatoes, spinach, cream, sage and ¼ cup cheese to the skillet; cook and stir over medium heat until slightly thickened and spinach is wilted. Drain fettuccine and add to skillet. Stir in the chicken and shrimp; heat through. Remove from the heat. Sprinkle with bacon and remaining cheese.

Because sometimes you just want a big plate of pasta. If you want a lighter version, you can replace the cream with half-and-half, and use turkey bacon instead of regular bacon.
—TASTE OF HOME TEST KITCHEN

Vegetable Beef Bow Tie Skillet

Meaty and full of veggies, this one-pot wonder is loaded with flavor in every bite.

—TASTE OF HOME TEST KITCHEN

PREP: 15 MIN. • **COOK:** 25 MIN.
MAKES: 4 SERVINGS

- 1 **pound ground beef**
- 1 **cup chopped onion**
- 1 **can (14½ ounces) beef broth**
- 1½ **cups uncooked bow tie pasta**
- ½ **cup water**
- 1 **teaspoon Italian seasoning**
- 1 **teaspoon chili powder**
- ½ **teaspoon salt**
- ½ **teaspoon garlic powder**
- ¼ **teaspoon pepper**
- 1 **cup chopped sweet yellow pepper**
- 1 **cup chopped zucchini**
- 2 **cups chopped tomatoes**
- 1 **cup (4 ounces) shredded cheddar cheese**

1. In a large skillet, cook beef and onion over medium heat until meat is no longer pink; drain. Stir in the broth, pasta, water and seasonings. Bring to a boil. Reduce heat; cover and simmer for 15 minutes.

2. Add yellow pepper and zucchini; cover and cook 2-4 minutes longer or until pasta and vegetables are tender, stirring occasionally. Stir in tomatoes; sprinkle with cheese.

You "Can" Substitute

When we made this bow tie skillet, the whole family loved it. I ended up not having any fresh tomatoes, so I drained a can of diced tomatoes and tossed those in. It still came out great!

—WADDINGTON6 TASTEOFHOME.COM

---

kid FRIENDLY ## Sloppy Joe Sandwiches

Cooks will love this dish because it's quick, easy and inexpensive. Brown sugar adds a touch of sweetness. In addition to rolls, the beef mixture is tasty over rice, biscuits or baked potatoes.

—LAURIE HAUSER ROCHESTER, NY

PREP: 5 MIN. • **COOK:** 35 MIN.
MAKES: 4 SERVINGS

- 1 **pound ground beef**
- 1 **cup ketchup**
- ¼ **cup water**
- 2 **tablespoons brown sugar**
- 2 **teaspoons Worcestershire sauce**
- 2 **teaspoons prepared mustard**
- ½ **teaspoon garlic powder**
- ½ **teaspoon onion powder**
- ½ **teaspoon salt**
- 4 **hamburger buns, split**

In a large saucepan, cook beef over medium heat until no longer pink; drain. Stir in ketchup, water, brown sugar, Worcestershire sauce, mustard, garlic and onion powders and salt. Bring to a boil. Reduce heat; cover and simmer for 30-40 minutes. Serve on hamburger buns.

Casseroles & Oven Entrees

PREP AND BAKE. THAT'S ALL THERE IS
TO THESE HOT-DISH DINNERS.

**BAKED BARBECUE
PORK CHOPS**
PAGE 106

**SIMPLE CREAMY
CHICKEN ENCHILADAS**
PAGE 130

**KING RANCH
CASSEROLE**
PAGE 143

Creamy Tuna-Noodle Casserole

Tunafish is an excellent standby when you want a hot casserole on the table in a hurry, and this creamy version is loaded with peas and Parmesan. No tuna? Try chicken instead.

—EDIE DESPAIN LOGAN, UT

PREP: 25 MIN. • **BAKE:** 25 MIN.
MAKES: 6 SERVINGS

- 5 **cups uncooked egg noodles**
- 1 **can (10¾ ounces) reduced-fat reduced-sodium condensed cream of mushroom soup, undiluted**
- 1 **cup (8 ounces) fat-free sour cream**
- ⅔ **cup grated Parmesan cheese**
- ⅓ **cup 2% milk**
- ¼ **teaspoon salt**
- 2 **cans (5 ounces each) light water-packed tuna, drained and flaked**
- 1 **cup frozen peas, thawed**
- ¼ **cup finely chopped onion**
- ¼ **cup finely chopped green pepper**

TOPPING

- ½ **cup soft bread crumbs**
- 1 **tablespoon butter, melted**

1. Cook noodles according to package directions.

2. Meanwhile, in a large bowl, combine the soup, sour cream, cheese, milk and salt. Stir in the tuna, peas, onion and pepper. Drain noodles; add to soup mixture.

3. Transfer to an 11-in. x 7-in. baking dish coated with cooking spray. Combine topping ingredients; sprinkle over top. Bake, uncovered, at 350° for 25-30 minutes or until bubbly.

Grandma's Potpie

My husband and father-in-law are both picky eaters, but they do enjoy this savory meat pie with a flaky golden crust. The recipe is from my husband's grandmother.

—ANNETTE WHEATLEY SYRACUSE, NY

PREP: 30 MIN. • **BAKE:** 45 MIN.
MAKES: 6 SERVINGS

- 1½ **pounds ground beef**
- 1 **teaspoon onion powder**
  Salt to taste
- 1 **cup diced peeled potatoes**
- 1 **cup frozen mixed vegetables, thawed**
- ¼ **cup butter, cubed**
- ¼ **cup all-purpose flour**
- 1 **can (14½ ounces) beef broth**

CRUST

- 2 **cups all-purpose flour**
- 1 **tablespoon baking powder**
- 1 **teaspoon salt**
- ¼ **cup shortening**
- ¾ **cup milk**
- 1 **tablespoon butter, melted**

1. In a large skillet, cook beef over medium heat until no longer pink; drain. Stir in onion powder and salt. Transfer to a greased 9-in.-square baking dish. Top with potatoes and vegetables.

2. Meanwhile, in a small saucepan, melt the butter. Stir in flour until smooth; gradually add broth. Bring to a boil. Cook and stir for 2 minutes or until thickened. Pour over vegetables.

3. For crust, in a small bowl, combine the flour, baking powder and salt in a bowl. Cut in shortening until mixture resembles coarse crumbs. Stir in milk until a soft dough forms.

4. On a floured surface, roll dough into a 9-in. square. Place over filling; flute edges and cut slits in top. Brush with melted butter. Bake at 350° for 45 minutes or until golden brown.

Peppery Pizza Loaves

I often take these French bread pizzas to church picnics or potluck suppers and there are never any left. When I fix them for my family, I freeze the extra loaves in foil to enjoy later.

—**LOU STASNY** POPLARVILLE, MS

PREP: 20 MIN. • **BAKE:** 20 MIN.
MAKES: 8-12 SERVINGS

- 1½ **pounds ground beef**
- ½ **teaspoon garlic powder**
- ½ **teaspoon salt**
- 2 **loaves (8 ounces each) French bread, halved lengthwise**
- 1 **jar (8 ounces) process cheese sauce**
- 1 **can (4 ounces) mushroom stems and pieces, drained**
- 1 **cup chopped green onions**
- 1 **can (4 ounces) sliced jalapenos, drained**
- 1 **can (8 ounces) tomato sauce**
- ½ **cup grated Parmesan cheese**
- 4 **cups (16 ounces) shredded part-skim mozzarella cheese**

1. In a large skillet, cook beef over medium heat until no longer pink; drain. Stir in garlic powder and salt.
2. Place each bread half on a large piece of heavy-duty foil. Spread with cheese sauce. Top with beef mixture, mushrooms, onions and jalapenos. Drizzle with tomato sauce. Top with Parmesan and mozzarella cheeses. Wrap and freeze. May be frozen for up to 3 months.
TO BAKE *Unwrap loaves and thaw on baking sheets in the refrigerator. Bake at 350° for 18 minutes or until cheese is melted.*

ULTIMATE *Comfort*

Sunday Chicken

When Sunday rolled around my mother reached for her chicken recipe—hence the name. It can be prepared ahead of time and left to bake while you attend church. The leftovers also freeze well.

—**DON HARKSEN** DOTHAN, AL

PREP: 15 MIN. • **BAKE:** 2 HOURS
MAKES: 4-6 SERVINGS

- 1 can (10¾ ounces) condensed cream of mushroom soup, undiluted
- 1 can (10¾ ounces) condensed cream of celery soup, undiluted
- 1 can (10¾ ounces) condensed cream of chicken soup, undiluted
- ⅓ cup butter, melted, divided
- 1¼ cups quick-cooking rice
- 1 broiler/fryer chicken (3 to 4 pounds), cut up
  Salt and pepper to taste
  Paprika

1. In a large bowl, combine the soups, ¼ cup butter and rice. Pour into a greased 13-in. x 9-in. baking dish. Top with chicken pieces. Drizzle chicken with remaining butter. Sprinkle with salt, pepper and paprika.
2. Bake, uncovered, at 350° for 2 hours or until chicken juices run clear and rice is tender.

Baked Barbecue Pork Chops

My mom used to prepare these chops for dinner when I was growing up. Our whole family loved them. Now I enjoy preparing this same dish for my husband and our four children. They enjoy it as much as I did when I was a kid.

—**BONNIE SCHILTZ** OAKLEY, KS

PREP: 20 MIN. • **BAKE:** 15 MIN.
MAKES: 4 SERVINGS

- 4 boneless pork loin chops (¾ inch thick and 4 ounces each)
- ½ teaspoon salt, divided
- ¼ teaspoon pepper
- 2 teaspoons canola oil
- ⅓ cup water
- ¼ cup ketchup
- 2 tablespoons cider vinegar
- ¼ teaspoon celery seed
- ⅛ teaspoon ground nutmeg
- 1 bay leaf

1. Sprinkle pork chops with ¼ teaspoon salt and pepper. In a large nonstick skillet coated with cooking spray, cook chops in oil for 3-4 minutes on each side or until browned.
2. Transfer to an 8-in. square baking dish coated with cooking spray. In a small saucepan, combine the water, ketchup, vinegar, celery seed, nutmeg, bay leaf and remaining salt; bring to a boil. Pour over pork.
3. Cover and bake at 350° for 15-20 minutes or until a meat thermometer reads 160°. Discard bay leaf.

German Sauerbraten

Our family loves it when Mom prepares this wonderful old-world dish. The tender beef has a bold blend of mouthwatering seasonings. It smells great while it's cooking in the oven and tastes even better!

—CATHY ELAND HIGHSTOWN, NJ

PREP: 10 MIN. + MARINATING
COOK: 10 MIN. + SIMMERING
MAKES: 14 SERVINGS

- 2 teaspoons salt
- 1 teaspoon ground ginger
- 1 beef top round roast (4 pounds)
- 2½ cups water
- 2 cups cider vinegar
- ⅓ cup sugar
- 2 medium onions, sliced, divided
- 2 tablespoons mixed pickling spices, divided
- 1 teaspoon whole peppercorns, divided
- 8 whole cloves, divided
- 2 bay leaves, divided
- 2 tablespoons vegetable oil
- 14 to 16 gingersnaps, crushed

1. In a small bowl, combine salt and ginger; rub over roast. Place in a deep glass bowl. In a large bowl, combine the water, vinegar and sugar. Pour half of marinade into a large saucepan; add half of the onions, pickling spices, peppercorns, cloves and bay leaves. Bring to a boil. Pour over roast; turn to coat. Cover and refrigerate for 2 days, turning twice a day.

2. To the remaining marinade, add the remaining onions, pickling spices, peppercorns, cloves and bay leaves. Cover and refrigerate.

3. Drain roast and discard its marinade; pat roast dry. In a Dutch oven over medium-high heat, brown roast in oil on all sides. Pour 1 cup of reserved marinade with all of the onions and seasonings over roast (cover and refrigerate remaining marinade). Bring to a boil. Reduce heat; cover and simmer for 3 hours or until meat is tender.

4. Strain cooking juices, discarding onions and seasonings. Add enough reserved marinade to the cooking juices to measure 3 cups. Pour into a large saucepan; bring to a boil. Add gingersnaps; reduce heat and simmer until gravy is thickened. Slice roast and serve with gravy.

kid FRIENDLY

Cheeseburger Pockets

Ground beef is my favorite meat to cook with because it's inexpensive, and there's always a fun new recipe to try such as this one for cheesy burger biscuits.

—PAT CHAMBLESS CROWDER, OK

PREP: 30 MIN. • **BAKE:** 10 MIN.
MAKES: 5 SERVINGS

- ½ pound ground beef
- 1 tablespoon chopped onion
- ½ teaspoon salt
- ⅛ teaspoon pepper
- 1 tube (12 ounces) refrigerated buttermilk biscuits
- 5 slices process American cheese

1. In a large skillet, cook the beef, onion, salt and pepper over medium heat until meat is no longer pink; drain and cool.

2. Place two biscuits overlapping on a floured surface; roll out into a 5-in. oval. Place about ¼ cup of meat mixture on one side. Fold a cheese slice to fit over meat mixture. Fold dough over filling; press edges with a fork to seal. Repeat with remaining biscuits, meat mixture and cheese.

3. Place on a greased baking sheet. Prick tops with a fork. Bake at 400° for 10 minutes or until golden brown.

EDITOR'S NOTE *Pricking the tops of Cheeseburger Pockets helps steam escape during baking. If you don't do this, the pockets will puff up and may break open.*

This rich, cheesy pasta dish is a family tradition for holidays and special occasions. I was delighted the first time I tried this recipe–it has all the flavor of lasagna without the work of layering the ingredients.
—NANCY MUNDHENKE KINSLEY, KS

Mostaccioli

PREP: 15 MIN. • **BAKE:** 45 MIN.
MAKES: 10-12 SERVINGS

- 1 pound uncooked mostaccioli
- 1½ pounds bulk Italian sausage
- 1 jar (28 ounces) meatless spaghetti sauce
- 1 egg, lightly beaten
- 1 carton (15 ounces) ricotta cheese
- 2 cups (8 ounces each) shredded part-skim mozzarella cheese
- ½ cup grated Romano cheese

1. Cook pasta according to package directions; drain. Crumble sausage into a Dutch oven. Cook over medium heat until no longer pink; drain. Stir in spaghetti sauce and pasta. In a large bowl, combine the egg, ricotta cheese and mozzarella cheese.

2. Spoon half of the pasta mixture into a greased shallow 3-qt. baking dish; layer with cheese mixture and remaining pasta mixture.

3. Cover and bake at 375° for 40 minutes or until a meat thermometer reads 160°. Uncover; top with Romano cheese. Bake 5 minutes longer or until heated through.

Sausage Substitution

This Mostaccioli is an easy and flavorful casserole. I used 1 pound of ground beef and ½ pound of Italian sausage instead, because my children can't handle all the spices. But it was still quite tasty and not dry like some others I've tried.

—**ARSTEPHIA** TASTEOFHOME.COM

Sausage Pie

When I was growing up, Mom made this tasty casserole often for our family and guests. It's a great use of garden vegetables, and the sausage adds comforting flavor. I'm sure other families will enjoy it as much as we do.

—**SALLY HOLBROOK** PASADENA, CA

PREP: 20 MIN. • **BAKE:** 30 MIN.
MAKES: 6-8 SERVINGS

- 16 fresh pork sausage links (about 1 pound)
- ½ medium green pepper, chopped
- ½ medium sweet red pepper, chopped
- 1 tablespoon canola oil
- 3 cups cooked long grain rice
- 4 to 5 medium tomatoes, peeled and chopped
- 1 package (10 ounces) frozen corn, thawed
- 1 cup (4 ounces) shredded cheddar cheese
- 2 tablespoons minced fresh parsley
- 1 tablespoon Worcestershire sauce
- 1 teaspoon salt
- 1 teaspoon dried basil
- 1 cup soft bread crumbs
- 2 tablespoons butter, melted

1. Place sausages on a rack in a baking pan. Bake at 350° for 15 minutes or until lightly browned and no longer pink. Cut into 1-in. pieces; set aside.

2. In a large skillet, saute peppers in oil for 3 minutes or until crisp-tender. Transfer to a 3-qt. baking dish. Add the sausages and the next eight ingredients.

3. Combine bread crumbs and butter; sprinkle over top. Bake, uncovered, at 350° for 30-40 minutes or until heated through.

Hot Tuna Sandwiches

What makes this lunchtime classic stand out? Adding mixed veggies and ranch salad dressing to the tuna gives this sandwich a homey touch.

—TASTE OF HOME TEST KITCHEN

START TO FINISH: 25 MIN.
MAKES: 4 SERVINGS

- 1   **can (12 ounces) white water-packed tuna, drained and flaked**
- ½   **cup frozen mixed vegetables, thawed and chopped**
- ⅓   **cup mayonnaise**
- 2   **tablespoons finely chopped onion**
- 1   **tablespoon ranch salad dressing mix**
- 4   **hamburger buns, split**

1. In a large bowl, combine the first five ingredients. Spoon tuna mixture onto bun bottoms; replace tops.
2. Place each sandwich on a piece of heavy-duty foil (about 12 in. square). Fold foil around each sandwich and seal tightly; place packets on a baking sheet.
3. Bake at 400° for 10-15 minutes or until heated through.

ULTIMATE *Comfort* Chicken Potpie with Cheddar Biscuit Topping

With chunks of chicken, veggies and a golden biscuit topping, this potpie makes a hearty meal that will rival the one Mom used to make.

—SALA HOUTZER GOLDSBORO, NC

PREP: 20 MIN. • **BAKE:** 45 MIN.
MAKES: 9 SERVINGS

- 4   **cups cubed cooked chicken**
- 1   **package (12 ounces) frozen broccoli and cheese sauce**
- 1   **can (10¾ ounces) condensed cream of chicken and mushroom soup, undiluted**
- 1   **can (10¾ ounces) condensed cream of chicken soup, undiluted**
- 2   **medium potatoes, cubed**
- ¾   **cup chicken broth**
- ⅔   **cup sour cream**
- ½   **cup frozen peas**
- ¼   **teaspoon pepper**

TOPPING
- 1½ **cups biscuit/baking mix**
- ¾   **cup shredded sharp cheddar cheese**
- ¾   **cup 2% milk**
- 3   **tablespoons butter, melted**

1. In a Dutch oven, combine the first nine ingredients; bring to a boil. Transfer to a greased 13-in. x 9-in. baking dish.
2. In a small bowl, combine the topping ingredients; spoon over top. Bake, uncovered, at 350° for 40-45 minutes or until bubbly and topping is golden brown. Let stand for 10 minutes before serving.

Sweet & Spicy Chicken Drummies

A group of us were on a camping trip, and a young bachelor brought these chicken legs for dinner. They were fabulous! I was so impressed, I asked him for the recipe.

—**LYNETTE HANUS** FAYETTEVILLE, GA

PREP: 15 MIN. + MARINATING
BAKE: 50 MIN. • **MAKES:** 20 DRUMSTICKS

- 2 **cups sugar**
- ¼ **cup paprika**
- 2 **tablespoons salt**
- 2 **teaspoons pepper**
- 1 **teaspoon garlic powder**
- 1 **teaspoon chili powder**
- ½ **teaspoon cayenne pepper**
- 20 **chicken drumsticks**
  (5 ounces each)

1. In a large resealable plastic bag, combine the sugar, paprika, salt, pepper, garlic powder, chili powder and cayenne. Add drumsticks, a few at a time; seal and shake to coat.

2. Place chicken in two greased 15x10x1-in. baking pans. Cover and refrigerate for 8 hours or overnight. (A small amount of meat juices will form in the pan.)

3. Bake, uncovered, at 325° for 50-60 minutes or until chicken juices run clear and a meat thermometer reads 180°.

Lasagna Roll-Ups

This crowd-pleasing take on lasagna offers up a new way to enjoy a classic dish in individual portions. And it only requires 5 ingredients.

—**SUSAN SABIA** WINDSOR, CA

PREP: 20 MIN. • **BAKE:** 30 MIN.
MAKES: 10 SERVINGS

- 10 **uncooked lasagna noodles**
- 1 **package (19½ ounces) Italian turkey sausage links, casings removed**
- 1 **package (8 ounces) cream cheese, softened**
- 1 **jar (26 ounces) spaghetti sauce, divided**
- 1¾ **cups shredded cheddar cheese, divided**

1. Cook noodles according to package directions. Meanwhile, in a large skillet, cook sausage over medium heat until no longer pink; drain. Stir in cream cheese and ⅓ cup spaghetti sauce.

2. Drain the noodles; spread ¼ cup meat mixture on each noodle. Sprinkle each with 2 tablespoon cheese; carefully roll up.

3. Spread ⅔ cup spaghetti sauce into an ungreased 13-in. x 9-in. baking dish. Place roll-ups seam side down over sauce. Top with remaining sauce and cheese.

4. Cover and bake at 350° for 20 minutes. Uncover; bake 10-15 minutes longer or until bubbly.

Taco Corn Bread Casserole

A whole can of chiles adds fire to this corn bread casserole. For less heat, you can use just enough of the chilies for your taste.

—**LISA PAUL** TERRE HAUTE, IN

PREP: 15 MIN. • **BAKE:** 1 HOUR
MAKES: 8 SERVINGS

- 2 **pounds ground beef**
- 2 **envelopes taco seasoning**
- 2 **cans (14½ ounces each) diced tomatoes, drained**
- 1 **cup water**
- 1 **cup cooked rice**
- 1 **can (4 ounces) chopped green chilies**
- 2 **packages (8½ ounces each) corn bread/muffin mix**
- 1 **can (8¾ ounces) whole kernel corn, drained**
- 1 **cup (8 ounces) sour cream**
- 2 **cups corn chips**
- 2 **cups (8 ounces) shredded Mexican or cheddar cheese, divided**
- 1 **can (2¼ ounces) sliced ripe olives, drained**
  Shredded lettuce and chopped tomatoes, optional

1. Preheat oven to 400°. In a Dutch oven, cook beef over medium heat 8-10 minutes or until no longer pink, breaking into crumbles; drain. Stir in taco seasoning. Add tomatoes, water, rice and green chilies; heat through, stirring occasionally.

2. Meanwhile, prepare corn bread mix according to package directions; stir in corn. Pour half of the batter into a greased 13x9-in. baking dish. Layer with half of the meat mixture, all the sour cream, half of the corn chips and 1 cup cheese. Top with remaining batter, remaining meat mixture, olives and remaining corn chips.

3. Bake, uncovered, 55-60 minutes or until cornbread is cooked through. Sprinkle with remaining cheese; bake 3-5 minutes longer or until cheese is melted. If desired, serve with lettuce and chopped tomatoes.

Garlic-Roasted Chicken and Potatoes

This recipe has been in my favorites file for more than 20 years. My husband and I enjoyed it before we had kids, and now they love it, too. It's a real time-saver!

—**BETH ERBERT** LIVERMORE, CA

PREP: 20 MIN. • **BAKE:** 1 HOUR
MAKES: 6 SERVINGS

- 6 **bone-in chicken thighs (about 2¼ pounds)**
- 6 **chicken drumsticks**
- 6 **medium red potatoes (about 2 pounds), cut into 1-inch cubes**
- 24 **garlic cloves, peeled**
- ¼ **cup butter, melted**
- 1 **teaspoon salt, divided**
- ¼ **cup maple syrup**

1. Place the chicken, potatoes and garlic in a large roasting pan. Drizzle with butter; sprinkle with ¾ teaspoon salt. Toss to coat. Bake, uncovered, at 400° for 40 minutes.

2. Combine the syrup and remaining salt; drizzle over chicken. Spoon pan juices over potatoes and garlic. Bake 20 minutes longer or until a meat thermometer reads 180° and potatoes are tender.

Four-Cheese Baked Penne

Rich and cheesy with a slight heat from pepper flakes, this protein-packed pasta is a tasty vegetarian option to share with friends and family.

—SCARLETT ELROD NEWNAN, GA

PREP: 30 MIN. + COOLING • **BAKE:** 20 MIN.
MAKES: 6 SERVINGS

- 4 **cups uncooked whole wheat penne pasta**
- 1 **medium onion, chopped**
- 2 **teaspoons olive oil**
- 4 **garlic cloves, minced**
- 1 **can (15 ounces) crushed tomatoes**
- 1 **can (8 ounces) tomato sauce**
- 3 **tablespoons minced fresh parsley or 1 tablespoon dried parsley flakes**
- 1 **teaspoon dried oregano**
- 1 **teaspoon dried rosemary, crushed**
- ½ **teaspoon crushed red pepper flakes**
- ¼ **teaspoon pepper**
- 1½ **cups (12 ounces) 2% cottage cheese**
- 1¼ **cups (5 ounces) shredded part-skim mozzarella cheese, divided**
- 1 **cup part-skim ricotta cheese**
- ¼ **cup grated Parmesan cheese**

1. Cook penne according to package directions.

2. Meanwhile, in a large skillet, saute onion in oil until tender. Add garlic; cook 1 minute longer. Stir in the tomatoes, tomato sauce, parsley, oregano, rosemary, pepper flakes and pepper. Bring to a boil. Remove from the heat; cool for 15 minutes.

3. Drain penne; add to sauce. Stir in the cottage cheese, ½ cup mozzarella and all of the ricotta. Transfer to a 13-in. x 9-in. baking dish coated with cooking spray. Top with Parmesan cheese and remaining mozzarella.

4. Bake, uncovered, at 400° for 20-25 minutes or until bubbly.

Puffy Chile Rellenos Casserole

Here's a wonderfully zesty casserole that's much lower in fat and easier to assemble than traditional chile rellenos. I don't remember where I got the recipe, but I've enjoyed this layered entree for years.
—**MARILYN MOREY** MALLARD, IA

PREP: 20 MIN. • **BAKE:** 40 MIN. + STANDING
MAKES: 12 SERVINGS

- 6 cans (4 ounces each) whole green chilies, drained
- 8 flour tortillas (6 inches), cut into 1-inch strips
- 2 cups (8 ounces) shredded part-skim mozzarella cheese
- 2 cups (8 ounces) shredded reduced-fat cheddar cheese
- 3 cups egg substitute
- ¾ cup fat-free milk
- ½ teaspoon garlic powder
- ½ teaspoon ground cumin
- ½ teaspoon pepper
- ¼ teaspoon salt
- 1 teaspoon paprika
- 1 cup salsa

1. Cut along one side of each chili and open to lie flat. Coat a 13-in. x 9-in. baking dish with cooking spray. Layer half of the chilies, tortilla strips, mozzarella and cheddar cheeses in prepared dish. Repeat layers.
2. In a small bowl, beat the egg substitute, milk, garlic powder, cumin, pepper and salt. Pour over cheese. Sprinkle with paprika.
3. Bake, uncovered, at 350° for 40-45 minutes or until puffy and a knife inserted 2 in. from the edge of the pan comes out clean. Let stand for 10 minutes before cutting. Serve with salsa.
NOTE *Wear disposable gloves when cutting hot peppers; the oils can burn skin. Avoid touching your face.*

kid FRIENDLY

Cheese Enchiladas

You won't bring home leftovers when you bring these easy enchiladas to a potluck. With a homemade tomato sauce and cheesy filling, they always go fast. You can substitute any type of cheese you like.
—**ASHLEY SCHACKOW** DEFIANCE, OH

PREP: 25 MIN. • **BAKE:** 25 MIN.
MAKES: 16 ENCHILADAS

- 2 cans (15 ounces each) tomato sauce
- 1⅓ cups water
- 2 tablespoons chili powder
- 2 garlic cloves, minced
- 1 teaspoon dried oregano
- ½ teaspoon ground cumin
- 16 flour tortillas (8 inches), warmed
- 4 cups (16 ounces) shredded Monterey Jack cheese
- 2½ cups (10 ounces) shredded cheddar cheese, divided
- 2 medium onions, finely chopped
- 1 cup (8 ounces) sour cream
- ¼ cup minced fresh parsley
- ½ teaspoon salt
- ½ teaspoon pepper
  Shredded lettuce, sliced ripe olives and additional sour cream, optional

1. In a large saucepan, combine the first six ingredients. Bring to a boil. Reduce heat; simmer, uncovered, for 4-5 minutes or until thickened, stirring occasionally. Spoon 2 tablespoons sauce over each tortilla.
2. In a large bowl, combine the Monterey Jack, 2 cups cheddar cheese, onions, sour cream, parsley, salt and pepper. Place about ⅓ cup down the center of each tortilla. Roll up and place seam side down in two greased 13-in. x 9-in. baking dishes. Pour remaining sauce over top.
3. Bake, uncovered, at 350° for 20 minutes. Sprinkle with remaining cheddar cheese. Bake 4-5 minutes longer or until cheese is melted. Garnish with lettuce, olives and sour cream if desired.

Alfredo Chicken 'n' Biscuits

Full of veggies and topped off with golden-brown biscuits and Alfredo sauce, this is one complete meal that your family will finish in record time!

—**CHERYL MILLER** FORT COLLINS, CO

PREP: 20 MIN. • **BAKE:** 20 MIN.
MAKES: 4 SERVINGS

- 2 **cups chopped fresh broccoli**
- 1½ **cups sliced fresh carrots**
- 1 **cup chopped onion**
- 2 **tablespoons olive oil**
- 2 **cups cubed cooked chicken**
- 1 **carton (10 ounces) refrigerated Alfredo sauce**
- 1 **cup biscuit/baking mix**
- ⅓ **cup 2% milk**
- ¼ **teaspoon dill weed**

1. Preheat oven to 400°. In a large skillet, saute broccoli, carrots and onion in oil until crisp-tender. Stir in chicken and Alfredo sauce; heat through. Transfer to a lightly greased 8-in. square baking dish.
2. In a small bowl, combine baking mix, milk and dill just until moistened. Drop by rounded tablespoonfuls onto chicken mixture.
3. Bake, uncovered, 18-22 minutes or until bubbly and biscuits are golden brown.

ULTIMATE *Comfort*

Best-Ever Meat Loaf

There's a reason we call this the best-ever meat loaf. Adding a handful of shredded mozzarella cheese elevates the richness of each slice. Plus, the recipe is easy to double or cut in half to suit the number you're cooking for, and it also freezes well.

—**ANNA BAKER** BLAINE, WA

PREP: 15 MIN.
BAKE: 1¼ HOURS + STANDING
MAKES: 6 SERVINGS

- 2 **eggs**
- ⅔ **cup milk**
- 3 **slices bread, torn**
- ½ **cup chopped onion**
- ½ **cup grated carrot**
- 1 **cup (4 ounces) shredded cheddar or part-skim mozzarella cheese**
- 1 **tablespoon minced fresh parsley or 1 teaspoon dried parsley**
- 1 **teaspoon dried basil, thyme or sage, optional**
- 1 **teaspoon salt**
- ¼ **teaspoon pepper**
- 1½ **pounds lean ground beef**

TOPPING
- ½ **cup tomato sauce**
- ½ **cup packed brown sugar**
- 1 **teaspoon prepared mustard**

1. In a large bowl, beat eggs. Add milk and bread; let stand until liquid is absorbed. Stir in the onion, carrot, cheese and seasonings. Crumble beef over mixture and mix well.
2. Shape into a 7½-in. x 3½-in. x 2½-in. loaf in a shallow baking pan. Bake, uncovered, at 350° for 45 minutes.
3. Combine the topping ingredients; spoon half of the mixture over meat loaf. Bake 30 minutes longer or until meat is no longer pink and a meat thermometer reads 160°, occasionally spooning remaining topping over loaf. Let stand 10 minutes before serving.

kid FRIENDLY Hot Ham & Cheese Slices

Everything about these ham puffs is comforting and delicious. A cheesy center inside a buttery, flaky pastry—what's not to love?

—PAT STEVENS GRANBURY, TX

PREP: 15 MIN. • **BAKE:** 20 MIN.
MAKES: 8 SERVINGS

- 1 cup sliced fresh mushrooms
- 1 small sweet red pepper, chopped
- 2 green onions, chopped
- 2 tablespoons butter
- 1 package (17.3 ounces) frozen puff pastry, thawed
- ½ pound thinly sliced deli ham
- ½ pound sliced Swiss cheese

1. In a large skillet, saute the mushrooms, pepper and onions in butter until tender. Set aside.

2. Unfold pastry. Layer the ham, cheese and mushroom mixture off-center on each sheet of pastry. Fold pastry over filling; pinch seams to seal. Place in a greased 15x10x1-in. baking pan. Bake at 400° for 18-22 minutes or until golden brown. Let stand for 5 minutes. Cut each with a serrated knife into 4 slices.

top tip

Veggie Layer

I love the Hot Ham & Cheese Slices! But I highly recommend putting the layer of sauteed veggies between the ham and cheese layers; otherwise the pastry gets a little soggy on the bottom.

—FAITHQ_06 TASTEOFHOME.COM

Sausage and Pepperoni Pizza Pasta

PREP: 25 MIN. • **BAKE:** 25 MIN.
MAKES: 8 SERVINGS

- 4 cups uncooked penne pasta
- 3 Italian sausage links, cut into ½-inch slices
- 1 cup sliced fresh mushrooms
- 1 medium green pepper, chopped
- 1 medium onion, chopped
- 1 package (3½ ounces) sliced pepperoni
- 3½ cups water
- 2 cans (6 ounces each) tomato paste
- 2 envelopes thick and zesty spaghetti sauce mix
- 1 can (2¼ ounces) sliced ripe olives, drained
- ¼ cup olive oil
- ½ teaspoon garlic salt
- 1 cup (4 ounces) shredded part-skim mozzarella cheese

1. Cook penne according to package directions. Meanwhile, in a Dutch oven, cook the sausage, mushrooms, pepper and onion over medium heat until meat is no longer pink and the vegetables are tender; drain and remove from pan.

2. Cook pepperoni in the same pan until heated through. Return sausage mixture to the pan.

3. Stir in the water, tomato paste, spaghetti sauce mix, olives, oil and garlic salt. Bring to a boil. Reduce heat; simmer, uncovered, for 4-5 minutes to allow flavors to blend.

4. Drain pasta; stir into sausage mixture. Transfer to a greased 13-in. x 9-in. baking dish. Sprinkle with cheese.

5. Bake, uncovered, at 350° for 25-30 minutes or until bubbly.

Quick-prep veggies and simple seasonings get this saucy meat-lover's pizza casserole on the table pronto. It's great for potlucks, too, as it can easily be doubled or tripled to feed a large group. —JULIE GLISSON ZDERO RACINE, WI

ULTIMATE *Comfort* Hearty Shepherd's Pie

You can use real or instant mashed potatoes to make this family-pleasing classic. I like to make this on a cold day and serve it with a side of corn bread.

—**MELISSA HASS** GILBERT, SC

PREP: 35 MIN. • **BAKE:** 20 MIN.
MAKES: 6 SERVINGS

- 1 **pound lean ground beef (90% lean)**
- 1 **medium onion, chopped**
- 1 **can (10¾ ounces) condensed cream of celery soup, undiluted**
- 1 **can (8½ ounces) peas and carrots, drained**
- 1 **jar (4½ ounces) sliced mushrooms, drained**
- ¼ **cup water**
- 1 **tablespoon minced fresh rosemary or 1 teaspoon dried rosemary, crushed**
- 1 **teaspoon garlic powder, divided**
- ½ **teaspoon salt**
- ¼ **teaspoon pepper**
- 2 **cups prepared instant mashed potatoes**
- 1 **package (3 ounces) cream cheese, softened and cubed**
- ¼ **cup sour cream**
- ¼ **cup grated Parmesan cheese**

1. In a large skillet, cook beef and onion over medium heat until meat is no longer pink; drain. Stir in the soup, peas and carrots, mushrooms, water, rosemary, ½ teaspoon garlic powder, salt and pepper; heat through. Transfer to a greased 9-in. deep-dish pie plate.
2. In a large bowl, beat the mashed potatoes, cream cheese, sour cream and remaining garlic powder until blended. Spread over top. Sprinkle with Parmesan cheese.
3. Bake, uncovered, at 350° for 20-25 minutes or until heated through and potatoes are lightly browned.

Artichoke Shrimp Bake

I usually serve this dish with rice or baking powder biscuits. You can substitute frozen asparagus cuts for the artichokes and cream of asparagus soup for cream of shrimp.

—**JEANNE HOLT** MENDOTA HEIGHTS, MN

PREP: 20 MIN. • **BAKE:** 20 MIN.
MAKES: 4 SERVINGS

- 1 **pound cooked medium shrimp, peeled and deveined**
- 1 **can (14 ounces) water-packed quartered artichoke hearts, rinsed, drained**
- ⅔ **cup frozen pearl onions, thawed**
- 2 **cups sliced fresh mushrooms**
- 1 **small sweet red pepper, chopped**
- 2 **tablespoons butter**
- 1 **can (10¾ ounces) condensed cream of shrimp soup, undiluted**
- ½ **cup sour cream**
- ¼ **cup sherry or chicken broth**
- 2 **teaspoons Worcestershire sauce**
- 1 **teaspoon grated lemon peel**
- ⅛ **teaspoon white pepper**

TOPPING
- ½ **cup soft bread crumbs**
- ⅓ **cup grated Parmesan cheese**
- 1 **tablespoon minced fresh parsley**
- 1 **tablespoon butter, melted**
  Hot cooked rice, optional

1. Preheat oven to 375°. Place shrimp, artichokes and onions in a greased 11x7-in. baking dish; set aside.
2. In a large skillet, saute mushrooms and red pepper in butter until tender. Stir in soup, sour cream, sherry, Worcestershire sauce, lemon peel and white pepper; heat through. Pour over shrimp mixture.
3. In a small bowl, combine bread crumbs, cheese, parsley and butter; sprinkle over top.
4. Bake, uncovered, 20-25 minutes or until bubbly and topping is golden brown. Serve with rice if desired.

Salmon Loaf

During the Depression, Mom's tasty salmon loaf was a welcome change from the usual meat loaf everyone made to stretch a meal. I still enjoy a lot of the make-do meals of those days, but this loaf is one of my favorites.

—DOROTHY BATEMAN CARVER, MA

PREP: 20 MIN. • **BAKE:** 40 MIN. + STANDING
MAKES: 4 SERVINGS

- 1 can (14¾ ounces) salmon, drained, bones and skin removed
- 1 small onion, finely chopped
- ½ cup soft bread crumbs
- ¼ cup butter, melted
- 3 eggs, separated
- 2 teaspoons lemon juice
- 1 teaspoon minced fresh parsley
- ½ teaspoon salt
- ⅛ teaspoon pepper

OLIVE CREAM SAUCE

- 2 tablespoons butter
- 2 tablespoons all-purpose flour
- 1½ cups milk
- ¼ cup chopped pimiento-stuffed olives

1. In a large bowl, combine the salmon, onion, bread crumbs and butter. Stir in the egg yolks, lemon juice, parsley, salt and pepper.

2. In a small bowl, beat the egg whites on high speed until stiff peaks form. Fold into salmon mixture.

3. Transfer to a greased 8-in. x 4-in. loaf pan. Place in a larger baking pan. Add 1 in. of hot water to larger pan. Bake at 350° for 40-45 minutes or until a knife inserted near the center comes out clean. Let stand for 10 minutes before slicing.

4. Meanwhile, in a small saucepan, melt the butter. Stir in flour until smooth; gradually add milk. Bring to a boil; cook and stir for 1-2 minutes or until thickened. Stir in olives. Serve with salmon loaf.

Pork Tenderloin with Glazed Onions

My husband and I love pork, especially with sweet apricots and glazed onions—they go beautifully with the juicy meat.

—JANICE CHRISTOFFERSON EAGLE RIVER, WI

PREP: 20 MIN. • **BAKE:** 20 MIN.
MAKES: 8 SERVINGS

- 4 large sweet onions, sliced (about 8 cups)
- ¼ cup butter, cubed
- 1 cup chopped dried apricots or golden raisins
- ¼ cup packed brown sugar
- ¼ cup balsamic vinegar
- ½ teaspoon salt
- ½ teaspoon pepper
- 2 pork tenderloins (1 pound each)

1. In large skillet, saute onions in butter for 2 minutes. Stir in the apricots, brown sugar, vinegar, salt and pepper; cook until onions are tender.

2. Place pork tenderloins on a rack coated with cooking spray in a shallow roasting pan; top with onion mixture.

3. Bake, uncovered, at 425° for 20-27 minutes or until a thermometer reads 145°. Let stand for 5 minutes before slicing. Serve with onion mixture.

? Did you know?

Meat loaf became a common comfort food during the Great Depression, thanks to its economical ingredients, which served as a way to stretch an inexpensive cut of meat into a nourishing meal.

kid FRIENDLY

Easy Chicken Strips

I came up with these crispy strips one night when I was looking for a fast new way to serve chicken. They also make great appetizers, especially when served with barbecue or sweet-and-sour sauce for dunking.

—**CRYSTAL SHECKLES-GIBSON**
BEESPRING, KY

START TO FINISH: 30 MIN.
MAKES: 6 SERVINGS

- ¼ cup all-purpose flour
- ¾ teaspoon seasoned salt
- 1¼ cups crushed cornflakes
- ⅓ cup butter, melted
- 1½ pounds boneless skinless chicken breasts, cut into 1-inch strips

1. In a shallow bowl, combine flour and seasoned salt. Place cornflakes and butter in separate shallow bowls. Coat chicken with flour mixture, then dip in butter and coat with cornflakes.
2. Transfer to an ungreased baking sheet. Bake at 400° for 15-20 minutes or until no longer pink.

Roast Pork and Potatoes

We used to raise our own hogs. A fellow farmer who also had hogs and served pork frequently shared this delicious, home-style recipe with us.

—**DENISE COLLINS** CHILLICOTHE, OH

PREP: 20 MIN.
BAKE: 2½ HOURS + STANDING
MAKES: 8-10 SERVINGS

- 1 envelope onion soup mix
- 2 garlic cloves, minced
- 1 tablespoon dried rosemary, crushed
- ½ teaspoon salt
- ½ teaspoon pepper
- ¼ teaspoon ground cloves
- 3 cups water, divided
- 1 bone-in pork loin roast (4 to 5 pounds)
- 2 to 3 pounds small red potatoes, cut in half
- 1½ cups sliced onions

1. In a large bowl, combine the first six ingredients. Stir in ½ cup water; let stand for 3 minutes.
2. Place roast, fat side up, on a greased rack in a roasting pan. Pour remaining water into the pan. Combine potatoes and onions; spoon around the roast. Brush vegetables and roast with seasoning mixture.
3. Bake, uncovered, at 325° for 2½ to 3 hours or until a thermometer reads 160° and potatoes are tender. Baste and stir potatoes occasionally. Tent with foil if browning too fast. Thicken juices for gravy if desired. Let stand 10 minutes before slicing.

Barbecued Chicken

I still have the card for this recipe that a friend gave me 25 years ago—the stains on it attest to its frequent use! The chicken turns out juicy and tender, and the sauce makes a tasty gravy to serve with it.

—**NORMA HARDER** WEYAKWIN, SK

PREP: 20 MIN. • **BAKE:** 55 MIN.
MAKES: 4-6 SERVINGS

- 1 **broiler/fryer chicken (4 to 5 pounds), cut up**
- 1 **tablespoon canola oil**
- ½ **cup chicken broth**
- ½ **cup ketchup**
- ¼ **cup cider vinegar**
- 1 **tablespoon brown sugar**
- ½ **teaspoon curry powder**
- ½ **teaspoon paprika**
- ¼ **teaspoon salt**
- ¼ **teaspoon ground mustard**
- ⅛ **teaspoon chili powder**
  Pinch pepper
- 2 **tablespoons onion soup mix**

1. Preheat oven to 350°. In a large skillet, brown chicken on all sides in oil in batches; drain. Place the chicken in a greased 13x9-in. baking dish and an 8-in. square baking dish.

2. Combine broth, ketchup, vinegar, brown sugar, curry powder, paprika, salt, mustard, chili powder and pepper; pour over chicken. Sprinkle with soup mix. Cover and bake 55-65 minutes or until a thermometer inserted in thigh reads 180°.

Chili Cheese Dog Casserole

If you like corn bread with your chili, this is a must-try. It can easily be spiced up by adding a layer of sliced jalapenos.

—**TASTE OF HOME TEST KITCHEN**

PREP: 20 MIN. • **BAKE:** 30 MIN.
MAKES: 6 SERVINGS

- 1 **package (8½ ounces) corn bread/ muffin mix**
- 1 **cup chopped green pepper**
- ½ **cup chopped onion**
- ½ **cup chopped celery**
- 1 **tablespoon olive oil**
- 1 **package (1 pound) hot dogs, halved lengthwise and cut into bite-size pieces**
- 1 **can (15 ounces) chili with beans**
- 2 **tablespoons brown sugar**
- ½ **teaspoon garlic powder**
- ½ **teaspoon chili powder**
- 1 **cup (4 ounces) shredded cheddar cheese, divided**

1. Prepare corn bread batter according to package directions. Spread half the batter into a greased 8-in. square baking dish; set aside.

2. In a large skillet, saute the green pepper, onion and celery in oil until crisp-tender. Stir in hot dogs; saute 3-4 minutes longer or until lightly browned. Stir in the chili, brown sugar, garlic powder and chili powder; heat through. Stir in ¾ cup cheese.

3. Spoon over corn bread batter; top with remaining corn bread batter. Sprinkle remaining cheese over the top.

4. Bake, uncovered, at 350° for 28-32 minutes or until a toothpick inserted near the center comes out clean. Let stand for 5 minutes before serving.

Savory Stuffed Pork Chops

Who'd ever guess stuffed chops could be so simple? Baby spinach and stuffing mix are the secrets to this elegant entree, and they bake in the oven so they only take 10 minutes to prepare.

—**REBECCA NOSSAMAN** HURRICANE, WV

PREP: 10 MIN. • **BAKE:** 40 MIN.
MAKES: 8 SERVINGS

- 8 **boneless pork loin chops (1 inch thick and 8 ounces each</I>)**
- 1 **small onion, chopped**
- ½ **cup butter, cubed**
- 5 **cups fresh baby spinach**
- 1 **package (6 ounces) sage stuffing mix**
- 1½ **cups (12 ounces) sour cream**
- ½ **teaspoon rubbed sage**
- ½ **teaspoon lemon-pepper seasoning**

1. Using a sharp knife, cut a pocket in each pork chop. In a large skillet, saute onion in butter until tender. Add spinach, cook until wilted. Stir in the stuffing mix, sour cream and sage.
2. Fill each chop with about ⅓ cup stuffing mixture; secure with toothpicks if necessary. Place on a greased 15-in. x 10-in. x 1-in. baking pan. Sprinkle with lemon-pepper.
3. Bake, uncovered, at 350° for 35-40 minutes or until a meat thermometer reads 160°. Discard toothpicks.

Ham 'n' Noodle Hot Dish

Frozen green peas add lovely color to this comforting meal-in-one. The easy, cheesy dish is a terrific way to use up extra baked ham from a holiday feast or dinner party. No one feels like they're eating leftovers when I serve this.

—**RENEE SCHWEBACH** DUMONT, MN

PREP: 15 MIN. • **BAKE:** 30 MIN.
MAKES: 4 SERVINGS

- 3 **tablespoons butter, divided**
- 2 **tablespoons all-purpose flour**
- 1 **cup milk**
- 1 **cup (4 ounces) shredded process cheese (Velveeta)**
- ½ **teaspoon salt**
- 2 **cups diced fully cooked ham**
- 1½ **cups elbow macaroni or medium noodles, cooked and drained**
- 1 **cup frozen peas, thawed**
- ¼ **cup dry bread crumbs**
- ½ **teaspoon dried parsley flakes**

1. In a saucepan, melt 2 tablespoons butter; stir in flour until smooth. Gradually add milk. Bring to a boil over medium heat; cook and stir for 2 minutes. Remove from the heat; stir in cheese and salt until cheese is melted.
2. Add the ham, noodles and peas. Pour into a greased 1-qt. baking dish. Melt remaining butter; add bread crumbs and parsley. Sprinkle over casserole.
3. Bake, uncovered, at 350° for 30 minutes or until heated through.

Zesty Calzone

Calzones are great when you need a quick weekend lunch, but they also make cozy comfort food for watching the big game on TV.

—MARY ANN SAAM CRIDERSVILLE, OH

PREP: 10 MIN. • **BAKE:** 20 MIN. + STANDING
MAKES: 4 SERVINGS

- 1 tube (13.8 ounces) refrigerated pizza crust
- 2 tablespoons grated Parmesan cheese
- 8 thin slices deli ham
- 8 thin slices hard salami
- ¼ cup chopped onion
- ¼ cup chopped green pepper
- ¼ cup chopped tomato
- 1 cup (4 ounces) shredded part-skim mozzarella cheese

1. Preheat oven to 425°. In a greased 15x10x1-in. baking pan, pat dough into a 13x8-in. rectangle. Sprinkle Parmesan cheese to within ½ in. of edges.

2. On half of the dough, layer the ham, salami, onion, green pepper and tomato to within 1 in. of edges. Sprinkle with mozzarella cheese. Fold dough over filling; pinch edges to seal. Cut slits in top.

3. Bake 20-22 minutes or golden brown. Let stand 10 minutes. Cut into four pieces.

Seasoned Pork Loin Roast

This is a year-round dinner I like to make. In summer, I barbecue it when the weather is mild, and in winter I roast it in the oven.

—ELAINE SEIP MEDICINE HAT, AB

PREP: 20 MIN.
BAKE: 1½ HOURS + STANDING
MAKES: 18 SERVINGS

- 2 teaspoons garlic salt
- 2 teaspoons garlic-pepper blend
- 2 teaspoons lemon-pepper seasoning
- 1 boneless rolled pork loin roast (about 5 pounds)

BASTING SAUCE

- 3 cups water
- 2 tablespoons lemon juice
- 1½ teaspoons dried minced onion
- ½ teaspoon garlic salt
- ½ teaspoon garlic-pepper blend
- ½ teaspoon lemon-pepper seasoning
- ½ teaspoon crushed red pepper flakes
- ½ teaspoon grated lemon peel

1. Combine the garlic salt, garlic-pepper and lemon-pepper; rub over roast. Place on a rack in a shallow roasting pan. Bake, uncovered, at 325° for 1½ to 2 hours or until a thermometer reads 145°.

2. Meanwhile, in a large saucepan, combine the basting sauce ingredients. Bring to a boil; reduce heat. Simmer, uncovered, for 10 minutes. Brush over roast occasionally while baking. Let roast stand 10 minutes before slicing.

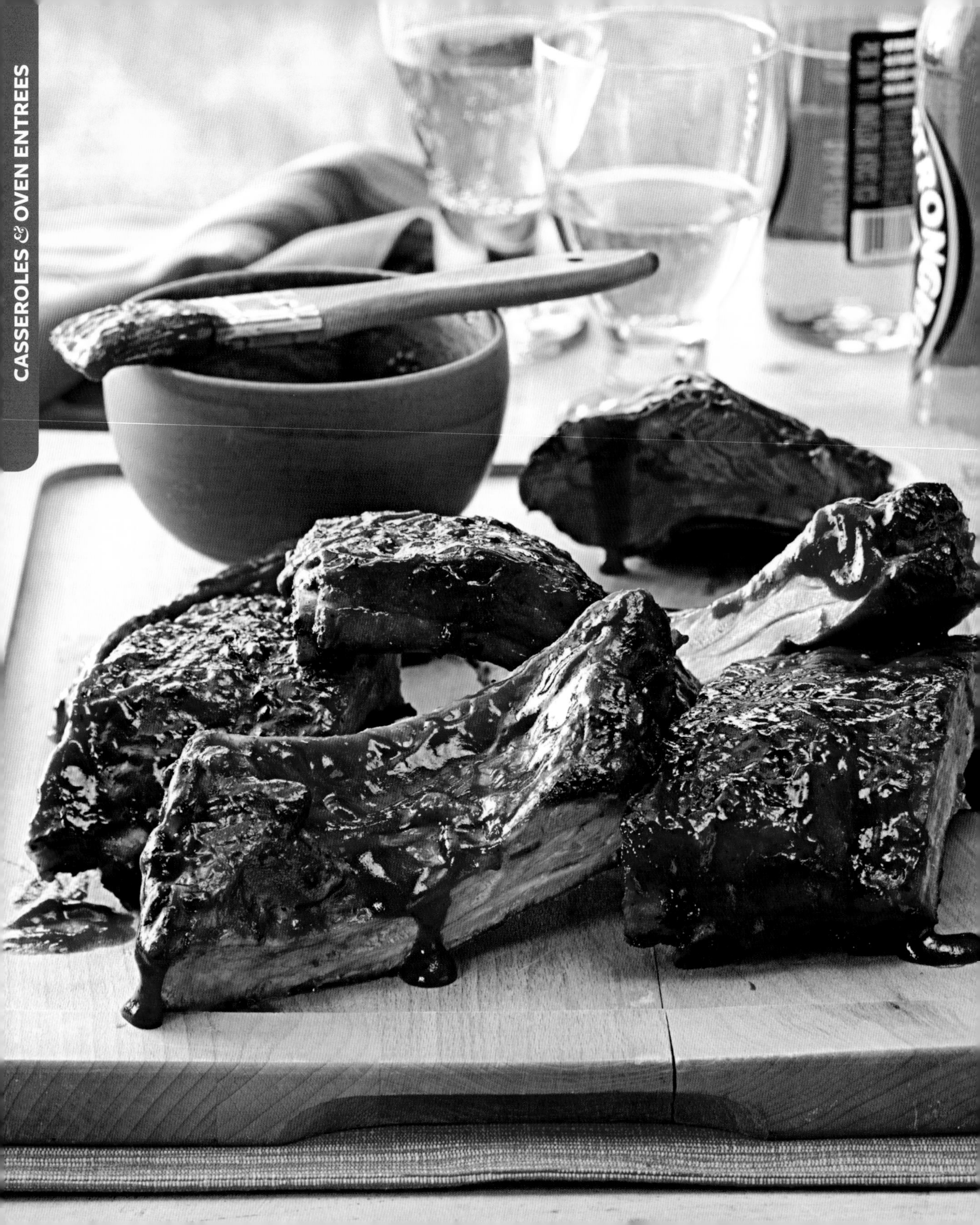

Honey-Beer Braised Ribs

My family just loves ribs, and this recipe is our all-time favorite! The darker the beer, the richer the taste, but you can also substitute beef broth for the beer.

—**TERRY SERENA** MCMURRAY, PA

PREP: 3½ HOURS • **GRILL:** 10 MIN.
MAKES: 6 SERVINGS

- ½ cup packed brown sugar
- 1 teaspoon pepper
- ¾ teaspoon salt
- 6 pounds pork baby back ribs
- ¼ cup honey
- 1 bottle (12 ounces) dark beer or beef broth
- ¼ cup cider vinegar
- 1 bottle (18 ounces) barbecue sauce

1. Combine the brown sugar, pepper and salt; rub over ribs. Place ribs bone side down on a rack in a large shallow roasting pan. Drizzle with honey.
2. Combine beer and vinegar; pour around ribs. Spoon some of the beer mixture over ribs. Cover tightly with foil and bake at 325° for 1 hour. Reduce heat to 250°; bake 2 hours longer or until tender.
3. Moisten a paper towel with cooking oil; using long-handled tongs, lightly coat the grill rack. Drain ribs. Grill, covered, over medium heat for 10-15 minutes or until browned, turning and basting occasionally with barbecue sauce. Serve with remaining barbecue sauce.

Did you know?

While many people use French salad dressing and Catalina salad dressing interchangeably, there is a subtle difference between the two. Catalina is described as darker, sweeter and moderately tangy.

Catalina Chicken

Using salad dressing to make this family favorite helps keep the prep time to only 10 minutes. I like to spoon extra sauce over the baked chicken just before serving.

—**FRANCES ROBERTS** SILVER SPRING, MD

PREP: 10 MIN. • **BAKE:** 25 MIN.
MAKES: 2 SERVINGS

- 2 boneless skinless chicken breast halves (5 ounces each)
- 2 teaspoons canola oil
- ¼ cup Catalina salad dressing
- 4½ teaspoons onion soup mix
- 1 tablespoon grape jelly

1. In a large nonstick skillet, brown chicken in oil. Transfer to a shallow baking dish coated with cooking spray. Combine the salad dressing, soup mix and jelly; pour over chicken.
2. Bake, uncovered, at 350° for 25-30 minutes or until a meat thermometer reads 170°.

Parmesan Chicken

Salty, savory Parmesan comes through in every bite of this chicken. Whenever I make it for dinner, we never have leftovers.

—SCHELBY THOMPSON

CAMDEN WYOMING, DE

PREP: 10 MIN. • **BAKE:** 25 MIN.
MAKES: 6-8 SERVINGS

- ½ cup butter, melted
- 2 teaspoons Dijon mustard
- 1 teaspoon Worcestershire sauce
- ½ teaspoon salt
- 1 cup dry bread crumbs
- ½ cup grated Parmesan cheese
- 6 boneless skinless chicken breast halves (7 ounces each)

1. Preheat oven to 350°. In a shallow bowl, combine butter, mustard, Worcestershire sauce and salt. Place bread crumbs and cheese in another shallow bowl. Dip chicken in butter mixture, then in bread crumb mixture, patting to help coating adhere.
2. Place in an ungreased 15x10x1-in. baking pan. Drizzle with any remaining butter mixture. Bake, uncovered, 25-30 minutes or until a thermometer reads 170°.

Teriyaki Beef Tenderloin

A beautiful glaze coats this fantastic tenderloin, and it's as easy to make as it is delicious. All you have to do is throw some ingredients together and let the marinade do all the work.

—LILY JULOW LAWRENCEVILLE, GA

PREP: 10 MIN. + MARINATING
BAKE: 45 MIN. + STANDING
MAKES: 8 SERVINGS

- 1 cup sherry or reduced-sodium beef broth
- ½ cup reduced-sodium soy sauce
- 1 envelope onion soup mix
- ¼ cup packed brown sugar
- 1 beef tenderloin roast (2 pounds)
- 2 tablespoons water

1. In a large bowl, combine the sherry, soy sauce, soup mix and brown sugar. Pour 1 cup into a large resealable plastic bag; add tenderloin. Seal bag and turn to coat; refrigerate for 5 hours or overnight. Cover and refrigerate remaining marinade.
2. Drain and discard marinade. Place tenderloin on a rack in a shallow roasting pan. Bake, uncovered, at 425° for 45-50 minutes or until meat reaches desired doneness (for medium-rare, a thermometer should read 145°; medium, 160°; well done, 170°), basting often with ⅓ cup reserved marinade. Let stand for 10-15 minutes.
3. Meanwhile, in a small saucepan, bring water and remaining marinade to a rolling boil for 1 minute or until sauce is slightly reduced. Slice beef; serve with sauce.

Salisbury Steak with Gravy

Here's a light twist on classic comfort food. The recipe was shared at a weight management meeting I attended, and my whole family really enjoys it. I like that it's so tasty and quick to prepare.

—DANELLE WEIHER VERNDALE, MN

PREP: 15 MIN. • **BAKE:** 50 MIN.
MAKES: 4 SERVINGS

- ½ cup fat-free milk
- 14 fat-free saltines, crushed
- 2 tablespoons dried minced onion
- 2 teaspoons dried parsley flakes
- 1 pound lean ground beef (90% lean)
- 1 jar (12 ounces) fat-free beef gravy
- 2 tablespoons ketchup
- 2 teaspoons Worcestershire sauce
- ¼ teaspoon pepper

1. In a large bowl, combine the milk, saltines, onion and parsley. Crumble beef over mixture and mix well. Shape into four patties. Place in an 8-in. square baking dish coated with cooking spray.

2. In a small bowl, combine the gravy, ketchup, Worcestershire and pepper; pour over patties. Bake, uncovered, at 350° for 50-55 minutes or until a thermometer reads 160°.

No Saltines? No Problem

The Salisbury Steak with Gravy gets 5 out of 5 stars from me—it's excellent. But I use Italian bread crumbs in place of the saltines.

—MEINJAS TASTEOFHOME.COM

Turkey Tetrazzini

Your family will flip over this turkey and mushroom casserole. In fact, the creamy Parmesan-topped tetrazzini is so satisfying that no one will suspect it's low in fat.

—IRENE BANEGAS LAS CRUCES, NM

PREP: 25 MIN. • **BAKE:** 25 MIN.
MAKES: 6 SERVINGS

- ½ pound uncooked spaghetti
- ¼ cup finely chopped onion
- 1 tablespoon butter
- 1 garlic clove, minced
- 3 tablespoons cornstarch
- 1 can (14½ ounces) reduced-sodium chicken broth
- 1 can (12 ounces) fat-free evaporated milk
- 2½ cups cubed cooked turkey breast
- 1 can (4 ounces) mushroom stems and pieces, drained
- ½ teaspoon seasoned salt
  Dash pepper
- 2 tablespoons grated Parmesan cheese
- ¼ teaspoon paprika

1. Cook spaghetti according to package directions; drain.

2. In a large saucepan, saute onion in butter until tender. Add garlic; cook 1 minute longer. Combine cornstarch and broth until smooth; stir into the onion mixture. Bring to a boil; cook and stir for 2 minutes or until thickened.

3. Reduce heat to low. Add milk; cook and stir for 2-3 minutes. Stir in the spaghetti, turkey, mushrooms, seasoned salt and pepper.

4. Transfer to an 8-in. square baking dish coated with cooking spray. Cover and bake at 350° for 20 minutes. Uncover; sprinkle with cheese and paprika. Bake 5-10 minutes longer or until heated through.

Creamy Pork Potpie

This hearty entree is made for cold weather, so huddle up with the family and enjoy! You might even have enough left over for lunch the next day.

—TASTE OF HOME TEST KITCHEN

PREP: 20 MIN. • **COOK:** 20 MIN.
MAKES: 6 SERVINGS

- ¼ cup butter, cubed
- ½ cup all-purpose flour
- 1 can (14½ ounces) chicken broth
- ¾ cup milk
- 2½ cups cubed cooked pork
- 2½ cups frozen broccoli-cauliflower blend
- 1½ cups (6 ounces) shredded cheddar cheese
- ½ teaspoon seasoned salt
  Dash pepper
- 1 sheet frozen puff pastry, thawed
- 1 egg, lightly beaten

1. In a large saucepan, melt butter. Stir in flour until smooth; gradually add broth and milk. Bring to a boil; cook and stir for 2 minutes or until thickened. Add the pork, vegetables, cheese, seasoned salt and pepper; heat through.
2. Transfer to a greased 11-in. x 7-in. baking dish. On a lightly floured surface, roll pastry into an 11-in. x 7-in. rectangle. Place over pork mixture. Brush with egg.
3. Bake, uncovered, at 425° for 18-22 minutes or until golden brown. Let stand for 5 minutes before cutting.

Oven Beef Stew

I love stew because everything comes together in one pot. Add a good loaf of bread and you're all set.

—BETTINA TURNER KERNERSVILLE, NC

PREP: 20 MIN. • **BAKE:** 2¼ HOURS
MAKES: 6 SERVINGS

- 6 tablespoons all-purpose flour, divided
- ¼ teaspoon salt, optional
- ½ teaspoon pepper, divided
- 1½ pounds boneless beef chuck roast, cut into 1-inch cubes
- 1 medium onion, chopped
- 1 tablespoon canola oil
- 3 garlic cloves, minced
- 3 cups beef broth
- 1 can (14½ ounces) stewed tomatoes, cut up
- ¾ teaspoon dried thyme
- 3 large potatoes, peeled and cut into 1-inch cubes
- 3 medium carrots, cut into ¼-inch slices
- ½ cup frozen peas, thawed

1. In a large resealable plastic bag, combine 4 tablespoons flour, salt if desired and ¼ teaspoon pepper. Add beef, a few pieces at a time, and shake to coat.
2. In a Dutch oven over medium-high heat, brown beef in oil in batches. Remove and set aside. Add onion to the pan and cook until tender. Add garlic; cook 1 minute longer. Stir in remaining flour and pepper until blended. Gradually stir in broth. Add the beef, tomatoes and thyme. Cover and bake at 350° for 1¼ hours.
3. Add the potatoes and carrots. Cover and bake 1 hour longer or until meat and vegetables are tender. Stir in peas; cover and let stand for 5 minutes before serving.

kid FRIENDLY Baked Ziti

I enjoy making this dish for family and friends. It's easy to prepare, and I like to get creative with the sauce. For example, sometimes I might add my home-canned tomatoes, mushrooms or vegetables.

—ELAINE ANDERSON NEW GALILEE, PA

PREP: 20 MIN. • **BAKE:** 45 MIN. + STANDING
MAKES: 6-8 SERVINGS

12	ounces uncooked ziti or small tube pasta
2	pounds ground beef
1	jar (24 ounces) spaghetti sauce
2	eggs, beaten
1	carton (15 ounces) ricotta cheese
2½	cups (10 ounces) shredded mozzarella cheese, divided
½	cup grated Parmesan cheese

1. Cook pasta according to package directions. Meanwhile, in a large skillet, cook beef over medium heat until no longer pink; drain. Stir in spaghetti sauce.

2. In a large bowl, combine the eggs, ricotta cheese, 1½ cups mozzarella cheese and the Parmesan cheese. Drain pasta; add to cheese mixture and stir until blended.

3. Spoon a third of the meat sauce into a greased 13-in. x 9-in. baking dish; top with half of the pasta mixture. Repeat layers. Top with remaining meat sauce.

4. Cover and bake at 350° for 40 minutes or until a thermometer reads 160°. Uncover; sprinkle with remaining mozzarella cheese. Bake 5-10 minutes longer or until cheese is melted. Let stand for 15 minutes before serving.

Simple Creamy Chicken Enchiladas

Shortly after we were married, I made these enchiladas for my husband. He was so impressed! We fix these creamy enchiladas for friends regularly.

—**MELISSA ROGERS** TUSCALOOSA, AL

PREP: 30 MIN. • **BAKE:** 30 MIN.
MAKES: 2 CASSEROLES (5 SERVINGS EACH)

- 1 rotisserie chicken
- 2 cans (14½ ounces each) diced tomatoes with mild green chilies, undrained
- 2 cans (10¾ ounces each) condensed cream of chicken soup, undiluted
- 1 can (10¾ ounces) condensed cheddar cheese soup, undiluted
- ¼ cup 2% milk
- 1 tablespoon ground cumin
- 1 tablespoon chili powder
- 2 teaspoons garlic powder
- 2 teaspoons dried oregano
- 1 package (8 ounces) cream cheese, cubed
- 20 flour tortillas (8 inches), warmed
- 4 cups shredded Mexican cheese blend

1. Remove meat from bones; discard bones. Shred chicken with two forks and set aside. In a large bowl, combine the tomatoes, soups, milk and seasonings. Transfer 3½ cups to another bowl; add chicken and cream cheese.

2. Spread ¼ cup soup mixture into each of two greased 13-in. x 9-in. baking dishes. Place ⅓ cup chicken mixture down the center of each tortilla. Roll up and place seam side down in baking dishes. Pour remaining soup mixture over tops; sprinkle with cheese.

3. Bake one casserole, uncovered, at 350° for 30-35 minutes or until heated through and cheese is melted. Cover and freeze remaining casserole for up to 3 months.

TO USE FROZEN CASSEROLE *Thaw in the refrigerator overnight. Cover and bake at 350° for 45 minutes. Uncover; bake 5-10 minutes longer or until heated through and cheese is melted.*

Beef Noodle Bake

My grandmother brought this recipe with her from Scotland. I like to make it for church suppers and picnics.

—**EVELYNE OLECHNOWICZ** VALENCIA, PA

PREP: 15 MIN. • **BAKE:** 35 MIN.
MAKES: 6 SERVINGS

- 1½ pounds ground beef
- 1 small onion, chopped
- 2 cans (8 ounces each) tomato sauce
- 1 cup (8 ounces) sour cream
- 1 package (3 ounces) cream cheese, cubed and softened
- 1 teaspoon sugar
- ½ to 1 teaspoon garlic salt
- 7 cups uncooked wide egg noodles, cooked and drained
- 1 cup (4 ounces) shredded cheddar cheese

1. In a large skillet, cook beef and onion until meat is no longer pink; drain. Remove from the heat; stir in the tomato sauce, sour cream, cream cheese, sugar and garlic salt.

2. Place half of the noodles in a greased 13-in. x 9-in. baking dish; top with half of the beef mixture. Repeat layers. Cover and bake at 350° for 30-35 minutes or until heated through. Sprinkle with cheese; bake 3-5 minutes longer or until cheese is melted.

Crab Melt Loaf

Our family loves seafood, and this recipe is a nice switch from traditional sandwiches. I've served big slices of it for lunch, Sunday brunch and as a light dinner with salad.

—LOUISE FAUTH FOREMOST, AB

START TO FINISH: 30 MIN.
MAKES: 8 SERVINGS

- 1 pound imitation crabmeat, chopped
- ½ cup mayonnaise
- ¼ cup thinly sliced green onions
- ¼ cup diced celery
- 2 cups (8 ounces) shredded part-skim mozzarella cheese
- ⅛ teaspoon salt
- ⅛ teaspoon pepper
- 1 loaf (1 pound) unsliced French bread, split

1. In a large bowl, combine the crab, mayonnaise, onions and celery. Stir in the cheese, salt and pepper. Spread over bread bottom; replace top.

2. Wrap in a large piece of heavy-duty foil. Place on an ungreased baking sheet. Bake at 400° for 20 minutes or until heated through. Cut into slices.

Saucy Garlic Chicken

Roasted garlic lends a rich flavor to this appetizing entree, and it complements the spinach nicely. Ideal for entertaining, the recipe can be assembled in advance and popped in the oven when guests arrive.

—JOANNA JOHNSON FLOWER MOUND, TX

PREP: 40 MIN. + COOLING • **BAKE:** 35 MIN.
MAKES: 6 SERVINGS

- 4 whole garlic bulbs
- 2 tablespoons olive oil, divided
- 1 package (9 ounces) fresh baby spinach
- ¾ teaspoon salt, divided
- ½ teaspoon coarsely ground pepper, divided
- 6 boneless skinless chicken breast halves (6 ounces each)
- 6 tablespoons butter, cubed
- 6 tablespoons all-purpose flour
- 3 cups 2% milk
- 2½ cups grated Parmesan cheese, divided
- ⅛ teaspoon nutmeg
  Hot cooked pasta
  Chopped tomato and minced fresh parsley, optional

1. Remove papery outer skin from garlic (do not peel or separate cloves). Cut tops off of garlic bulbs; brush bulbs with 1 tablespoon oil. Wrap each bulb in heavy-duty foil. Bake at 425° for 30-35 minutes or until softened. Cool for 10-15 minutes.

2. Meanwhile, place spinach in a greased 13-in. x 9-in. baking dish; sprinkle with ¼ teaspoon each of salt and pepper. In a large skillet, brown chicken in remaining oil on both sides; place over spinach.

3. In a large saucepan, melt butter. Stir in flour until smooth; gradually add milk. Bring to a boil; cook and stir for 1-2 minutes or until thickened. Stir in 2 cups cheese, nutmeg and remaining salt and pepper.

4. Transfer to a blender; squeeze softened garlic into blender. Cover and process until smooth. Pour mixture over chicken.

5. Cover and bake at 425° for 30-35 minutes or until a meat thermometer reads 170° and sauce is bubbly. Uncover; sprinkle with remaining cheese. Bake 5 minutes longer. Serve with pasta. Sprinkle with tomato and parsley if desired.

Cheese-Stuffed Shells

When I was living in California, I tasted this rich cheesy pasta dish at a neighborhood Italian restaurant. I got the recipe, made a few changes to it and now I think it's even better than the original!

—**LORI MECCA** GRANTS PASS, OR

PREP: 35 MIN. • **BAKE:** 50 MIN.
MAKES: 12 SERVINGS

- 1 pound bulk Italian sausage
- 1 large onion, chopped
- 1 package (10 ounces) frozen chopped spinach, thawed and squeezed dry
- 1 package (8 ounces) cream cheese, cubed
- 1 egg, lightly beaten
- 2 cups (8 ounces) shredded part-skim mozzarella cheese, divided
- 2 cups (8 ounces) shredded cheddar cheese
- 1 cup 4% cottage cheese
- 1 cup grated Parmesan cheese
- ¼ teaspoon salt
- ¼ teaspoon pepper
- ⅛ teaspoon ground cinnamon, optional
- 24 jumbo pasta shells, cooked and drained

SAUCE

- 1 can (29 ounces) tomato sauce
- 1 tablespoon dried minced onion
- 1½ teaspoons dried basil
- 1½ teaspoons dried parsley flakes
- 2 garlic cloves, minced
- 1 teaspoon sugar
- 1 teaspoon dried oregano
- ½ teaspoon salt
- ¼ teaspoon pepper

1. In a large skillet, cook sausage and onion over medium heat until meat is no longer pink; drain. Transfer to a large bowl. Stir in the spinach, cream cheese and egg. Add 1 cup mozzarella cheese, cheddar cheese, cottage cheese, Parmesan cheese, salt, pepper and cinnamon if desired.

2. Stuff pasta shells with sausage mixture. Arrange in two 11-in. x 7-in. baking dishes coated with cooking spray. Combine the sauce ingredients; spoon over shells.

3. Cover and bake at 350° for 45 minutes. Uncover; sprinkle with remaining mozzarella. Bake 5-10 minutes longer or until bubbly and cheese is melted. Let stand for 5 minutes before serving.

Perfect Prime Rib Roast

If you've never made prime rib before, you can't go wrong with this recipe. It comes from a chef at my favorite local restaurant.

—**PAULINE WAASDORP** FERGUS FALLS, MN

PREP: 5 MIN. + MARINATING
BAKE: 2½ HOURS + STANDING
MAKES: 8-10 SERVINGS

- ½ cup Worcestershire sauce
- 3 teaspoons garlic salt
- 3 teaspoons seasoned salt
- 3 teaspoons coarsely ground pepper
- 1 bone-in beef rib roast (5 to 6 pounds)

1. In a small bowl, combine the first four ingredients; rub half over the roast. Place roast in a large resealable plastic bag; seal and refrigerate overnight, turning often. Cover and refrigerate remaining marinade.

2. Drain roast and discard its marinade. Place roast fat side up in a large pan; pour reserved marinade over roast. Tent with foil. Bake at 350° for 1 hour. Uncover and bake 1½ hours longer or until meat reaches desired doneness (for medium-rare, a thermometer should read 145°; medium, 160°; well-done 170°). Let stand for 15 minutes before carving.

Horseradish Sauce

Here's an easy recipe to try: In a small bowl, beat ½ cup heavy whipping cream until stiff peaks form. Fold in ¼ cup fresh grated horseradish root, ½ teaspoon Dijon mustard and ¼ teaspoon salt. Cover the sauce and refrigerate for 15 minutes before serving.

Brown Sugar Glazed Salmon

I was not a fan of salmon until I tried it like this. The recipe is a simple way to serve a salmon fillet to a small group of friends.

—**RACHEL GARCIA** FORT KNOX, KY

PREP: 15 MIN. • **BAKE:** 20 MIN.
MAKES: 8 SERVINGS

- 1 tablespoon brown sugar
- 2 teaspoons butter
- 1 teaspoon honey
- 1 tablespoon olive oil
- 1 tablespoon Dijon mustard
- 1 tablespoon reduced-sodium soy sauce
- ½ to ¾ teaspoon salt
- ¼ teaspoon pepper
- 1 salmon fillet (2½ pounds)

1. In a small saucepan over medium heat, cook and stir the brown sugar, butter and honey until melted. Remove from the heat; whisk in the oil, mustard, soy sauce, salt and pepper. Cool for 5 minutes.

2. Place salmon in a large foil-lined baking pan; spoon brown sugar mixture over salmon. Bake, uncovered, at 350° for 20-25 minutes or until fish flakes easily with a fork.

Favorite Mexican Lasagna

Tortillas replace lasagna noodles in this enchilada-inspired casserole. With beef, refried beans, salsa, chilies and cheese, it's a fiesta of flavors.

—**TINA NEWHAUSER** PETERBOROUGH, NH

PREP: 25 MIN. • **BAKE:** 40 MIN. + STANDING
MAKES: 12 SERVINGS

- 1¼ pounds ground beef
- 1 medium onion, chopped
- 4 garlic cloves, minced
- 2 cups salsa
- 1 can (16 ounces) refried beans
- 1 can (15 ounces) black beans, rinsed and drained
- 1 can (10 ounces) enchilada sauce
- 1 can (4 ounces) chopped green chilies
- 1 envelope taco seasoning
- ¼ teaspoon pepper
- 6 flour tortillas (10 inches)
- 3 cups (12 ounces) shredded Mexican cheese blend, divided
- 2 cups crushed tortilla chips
  Sliced ripe olives, guacamole, chopped tomatoes and sour cream, optional

1. In a large skillet, cook beef and onion over medium heat until meat is no longer pink. Add garlic; cook 1 minute longer. Drain. Stir in the salsa, beans, enchilada sauce, chilies, taco seasoning and pepper; heat through.

2. Spread 1 cup meat mixture in a greased 13-in. x 9-in. baking dish. Layer with two tortillas, a third of the remaining meat mixture and 1 cup cheese. Repeat layers. Top with remaining tortillas and meat mixture.

3. Cover and bake at 375° for 30 minutes. Uncover; sprinkle with remaining cheese and top with tortilla chips.

4. Bake 10-15 minutes longer or until cheese is melted. Let stand for 10 minutes before serving. Garnish with olives, guacamole, tomatoes and sour cream if desired.

Pesto-Chicken Penne Casseroles

Pesto and Alfredo sauce give bold flavors to this rich pasta. This recipe makes two casseroles, so you can have one for dinner tonight and freeze one for later.
—**LAURA KAYSER** ANKENY, IA

PREP: 20 MIN. • **BAKE:** 40 MIN.
MAKES: 2 CASSEROLES (6 SERVINGS EACH)

- 1 package (16 ounces) penne pasta
- 6 cups cubed cooked chicken
- 4 cups (16 ounces) shredded Italian cheese blend
- 3 cups fresh baby spinach
- 1 can (15 ounces) crushed tomatoes
- 1 jar (15 ounces) Alfredo sauce
- 1½ cups 2% milk
- 1 jar (8.1 ounces) prepared pesto
- ½ cup seasoned bread crumbs
- ½ cup grated Parmesan cheese
- 1 tablespoon olive oil

1. Cook pasta according to package directions. Meanwhile, in a large bowl, combine the chicken, cheese blend, spinach, tomatoes, Alfredo sauce, milk and pesto. Drain pasta and add to chicken mixture; toss to coat.
2. Transfer to two greased 8-in. square baking dishes. In a small bowl, combine the bread crumbs, Parmesan cheese and oil; sprinkle over casseroles.
3. Cover and freeze one casserole for up to 3 months. Cover and bake the remaining casserole at 350° for 40-45 minutes or until bubbly.
TO USE FROZEN CASSEROLE *Thaw in the refrigerator overnight. Remove from the refrigerator 30 minutes before baking. Cover and bake at 350° for 50-60 minutes or until bubbly.*

Baked Mushroom Chicken

PREP: 20 MIN. • **BAKE:** 20 MIN.
MAKES: 4 SERVINGS

- 4 boneless skinless chicken breast halves (1 pound)
- ¼ cup all-purpose flour
- 3 tablespoons butter, divided
- 1 cup sliced fresh mushrooms
- ½ cup chicken broth
- ¼ teaspoon salt
- ⅛ teaspoon pepper
- ⅓ cup shredded part-skim mozzarella cheese
- ⅓ cup grated Parmesan cheese
- ¼ cup sliced green onions

1. Flatten each chicken breast half to ¼-in. thickness. Place flour in a resealable plastic bag; add chicken, a few pieces at a time. Seal and shake to coat.
2. In a large skillet, brown chicken in 2 tablespoons butter on both sides. Transfer to a greased 11-in. x 7-in. baking dish. In the same skillet, saute mushrooms in the remaining butter until tender. Add the broth, salt and pepper. Bring to a boil; cook for 5 minutes or until liquid is reduced to ½ cup. Spoon over chicken.
3. Bake, uncovered, at 375° for 15 minutes or until chicken is no longer pink. Sprinkle with cheeses and green onions. Bake 5 minutes longer or until cheese is melted.

 **Did you know?** The word casserole comes from the French word for "saucepan." But in Australia, New Zealand and the United Kingdom, these dishes are known as stews.

Dress up chicken breasts for a family dinner using fresh mushrooms, green onions and two kinds of cheese. I can count on this recipe for tender and flavorful chicken every time.

—**BARBARA MCCALLEY** ALLISON PARK, PA

Pizza Roll-Up

There's so much you can do with refrigerated pizza crust besides making an ordinary pizza. In this recipe, we stuff it with tasty fillings and roll it up into a loaf.

—JANICE CHRISTOFFERSON EAGLE RIVER, WI

PREP: 15 MIN. • **BAKE:** 25 MIN.
MAKES: 6 SERVINGS

- ½ pound lean ground beef (90% lean)
- 1 tube (13.8 ounces) refrigerated pizza crust
- 1 package (10 ounces) frozen chopped spinach, thawed and squeezed dry
- 1 jar (7 ounces) roasted sweet red peppers, drained and sliced
- 1 cup (4 ounces) shredded part-skim mozzarella cheese
- ½ teaspoon onion powder
- ½ teaspoon pepper
- ½ cup loosely packed basil leaves
  Cooking spray
- 1 tablespoon grated Parmesan cheese
- 1 can (8 ounces) pizza sauce, warmed

1. In a small nonstick skillet, cook beef over medium heat until no longer pink; drain.

2. Unroll dough into one long rectangle; top with spinach, beef, roasted peppers and mozzarella cheese. Sprinkle with onion powder and pepper. Top with basil.

3. Roll up jelly-roll style, starting with a short side; tuck ends under and pinch seam to seal. Place roll-up on a baking sheet coated with cooking spray; spritz top and sides with additional cooking spray. Sprinkle with Parmesan cheese.

4. Bake at 375° for 25-30 minutes or until golden brown. Let stand for 5 minutes. Cut into scant 1-in. slices. Serve with pizza sauce.

Swiss Steak with Dumplings

My mother was a great cook, and I learned so much from her. Ten years ago, I entered this steak and dumpling recipe in a contest and won. It's great all year, and one of our workers' favorites when I take it to the field during harvest.

—**PAT HABIGER** SPEARVILLE, KS

PREP: 25 MIN. • **BAKE:** 70 MIN.
MAKES: 6-8 SERVINGS

- 2 **pounds beef top round steak**
- ⅓ **cup all-purpose flour**
- 2 **tablespoons canola oil**
- 2 **cans (10¾ ounces each) condensed cream of chicken soup, undiluted**
- 1⅓ **cups water**
- ½ **teaspoon salt**
- ⅛ **teaspoon pepper**

DUMPLINGS
- ½ **cup dry bread crumbs**
- 5 **tablespoons butter, melted, divided**
- 1⅓ **cups all-purpose flour**
- 2 **teaspoons baking powder**
- ½ **teaspoon salt**
- ¼ **teaspoon poultry seasoning**
- ⅔ **cup milk**

1. Cut steaks into six or eight pieces. Place flour in a large resealable bag. Add beef, a few pieces at a time, and shake to coat. In a large skillet, brown meat in oil on both sides. Transfer to a greased 2½-qt. baking dish.

2. In the same skillet, combine the soup, water, salt and pepper; bring to a boil, stirring occasionally. Pour over steak. Cover and bake at 350° for 50-60 minutes or until meat is tender.

3. For dumplings, combine bread crumbs and 2 tablespoons butter in a small bowl; set aside. In another bowl, combine the flour, baking powder, salt and poultry seasoning. Stir in milk and remaining butter just until moistened.

4. Drop by rounded tablespoonfuls into the crumb mixture; roll until coated. Place dumplings over steak. Bake, uncovered, at 425° for 20-30 minutes or until dumplings are lightly browned and a toothpick inserted near the center comes out clean.

Creamy Beef Enchiladas

These American-style enchiladas are rich, creamy and loaded with cheese. They're not too spicy for kids but they have just a little kick from the green chilies.

—**BELINDA MORAN** WOODBURY, TN

PREP: 25 MIN. • **BAKE:** 20 MIN.
MAKES: 12 SERVINGS

- 2 **pounds lean ground beef (90% lean)**
- 1 **cup chopped onion**
- 1 **can (10¾ ounces) condensed cream of mushroom soup, undiluted**
- 1 **cup (8 ounces) sour cream**
- 1 **can (4 ounces) chopped green chilies**
- 3 **cups (12 ounces) shredded cheddar cheese, divided**
- 3 **cans (10 ounces each) enchilada sauce, divided**
- 12 **flour tortillas (8 inches), warmed**

1. In a Dutch oven, cook beef and onion over medium heat until meat is no longer pink; drain. Add the soup, sour cream, chilies, 1 cup cheese and ½ cup enchilada sauce; heat through.

2. Spread ¼ cup enchilada sauce into each of two ungreased 13-in. x 9-in. baking dishes. Place ½ cup beef mixture down the center of each tortilla. Roll up and place seam side down in prepared dishes.

3. Pour remaining enchilada sauce over top; sprinkle with remaining cheese. Bake, uncovered, at 350° for 20-25 minutes or until heated through.

Brisket in a Bag

This tender brisket is served with a savory cranberry gravy that's made right in the bag. You'll want to serve the slices with mashed potatoes just so you can drizzle the gravy over them.

—PEGGY STIGERS FORT WORTH, TX

PREP: 15 MIN. • **BAKE:** 2½ HOURS
MAKES: 12 SERVINGS

- 3 **tablespoons all-purpose flour, divided**
- 1 **large oven roasting bag**
- 1 **fresh beef brisket (5 pounds), trimmed**
- 1 **can (14 ounces) whole-berry cranberry sauce**
- 1 **can (10¾ ounces) condensed cream of mushroom soup, undiluted**
- 1 **can (8 ounces) tomato sauce**
- 1 **envelope onion soup mix**

1. Place 1 tablespoon flour in oven bag; shake to coat. Place bag in an ungreased 13x9-in. baking pan; place brisket in bag.

2. Combine the cranberry sauce, soup, tomato sauce, soup mix and remaining flour; pour over beef. Seal bag. Cut slits in top of bag according to package directions.

3. Bake at 325° for 2½ to 3 hours or until meat is tender. Carefully remove brisket from bag. Let stand 5 minutes before slicing. Thinly slice meat across the grain; serve with gravy.

NOTE *This is a fresh beef brisket, not corned beef.*

kid FRIENDLY

Cowboy Casserole

This quick and creamy Tater Tot bake is a great homey dinner, especially on a cold night. We don't think it's that pretty, but my family LOVES it!

—DONNA DONHAUSER REMSEN, NY

PREP: 15 MIN. • **BAKE:** 20 MIN.
MAKES: 2 SERVINGS

- ½ **pound lean ground beef (90% lean)**
- 1 **can (8¾ ounces) whole kernel corn, drained**
- ⅔ **cup condensed cream of chicken soup, undiluted**
- ½ **cup shredded cheddar cheese, divided**
- ⅓ **cup 2% milk**
- 2 **tablespoons sour cream**
- ¾ **teaspoon onion powder**
- ¼ **teaspoon pepper**
- 2 **cups frozen Tater Tots**

1. In a large skillet, cook beef over medium heat until no longer pink. Stir in the corn, soup, ¼ cup cheese, milk, sour cream, onion powder and pepper.

2. Place 1 cup Tater Tots in a greased 3-cup baking dish. Layer with beef mixture and remaining Tater Tots; sprinkle with remaining cheese. Bake, uncovered, at 375° for 20-25 minutes or until bubbly.

kid FRIENDLY Meatball Pizza

Keep meatballs and pizza crusts in the freezer to make this on the spur of the moment. Try it instead of pepperoni and see what a difference it makes.

—MARY HUMENIUK-SMITH PERRY HALL, MD

START TO FINISH: 25 MIN.
MAKES: 6-8 SLICES

- 1 prebaked 12-inch pizza crust
- 1 can (8 ounces) pizza sauce
- 1 teaspoon garlic powder
- 1 teaspoon Italian seasoning
- ¼ cup grated Parmesan cheese
- 1 small onion, halved and sliced
- 12 frozen fully cooked homestyle meatballs (½ ounce each), thawed and halved
- 1 cup (4 ounces) shredded part-skim mozzarella cheese
- 1 cup (4 ounces) shredded cheddar cheese

. Place the crust on an ungreased 2-in. pizza pan. Spread with pizza sauce; top with garlic powder, Italian seasoning, Parmesan cheese and onion. Arrange the meatball halves over top; sprinkle with cheeses.

2. Bake at 350° for 12-17 minutes or until heated through and cheese is melted.

Almond Chicken Casserole

A crispy golden topping of buttery cornflakes and sliced almonds gives this creamy chicken casserole a light crunch. I think it makes the perfect dish for a cozy potluck.

—MICHELLE KRZMARCZICK
REDONDO BEACH, CA

PREP: 15 MIN. • **BAKE:** 25 MIN.
MAKES: 6-8 SERVINGS

- 2 cups cubed cooked chicken
- 1 can (10¾ ounces) condensed cream of chicken soup, undiluted
- 1 cup (8 ounces) sour cream
- ¾ cup mayonnaise
- 2 celery ribs, chopped
- 3 hard-cooked eggs, chopped
- 1 can (4 ounces) mushroom stems and pieces, drained
- 1 can (8 ounces) water chestnuts, drained and chopped
- 1 tablespoon finely chopped onion
- 2 teaspoons lemon juice
- ½ teaspoon salt
- ¼ teaspoon pepper
- 1 cup (4 ounces) shredded cheddar cheese
- ½ cup crushed cornflakes
- 2 tablespoons butter, melted
- ¼ cup sliced almonds

1. In a large bowl, combine the first 12 ingredients. Transfer to a greased 13x9-in. baking dish; sprinkle with cheese.

2. Toss cornflakes with butter; sprinkle over cheese. Top with almonds. Bake, uncovered, at 350° for 25-30 minutes or until heated through.

ULTIMATE *Comfort* Double-Cheese Mac with Bacon

Inspired by traditional homemade mac 'n' cheese, we used cottage cheese and half-and-half for an extra creamy sauce and topped it with bread crumbs and bacon to make a fully loaded dish.

—**TASTE OF HOME TEST KITCHEN**

PREP: 25 MIN. • **BAKE:** 25 MIN.
MAKES: 12 SERVINGS (1 CUP EACH)

- 1 **package (16 ounces) elbow macaroni or small tube pasta**
- 3 **cups (24 ounces) 4% cottage cheese**
- ½ **cup plus 1 tablespoon butter, divided**
- ½ **cup all-purpose flour**
- 1 **teaspoon salt**
- ½ **teaspoon white pepper**
- ¼ **teaspoon garlic salt**
- 3 **cups half-and-half cream**
- 1 **cup milk**
- 4 **cups (16 ounces) shredded cheddar cheese**
- 1 **cup crumbled cooked bacon, divided**
- ⅓ **cup dry bread crumbs**

1. Preheat oven to 400°. Cook pasta according to package directions. Meanwhile, place cottage cheese in a food processor; cover and process until smooth. Set aside.
2. In a large saucepan, melt ½ cup butter. Stir in flour, salt, pepper and garlic salt until smooth. Gradually add cream and milk. Bring to a boil; cook and stir 2 minutes or until thickened.
3. Drain macaroni; transfer to a large bowl. Add cheddar cheese, cottage cheese, white sauce and ¾ cup bacon; toss to coat. Transfer to a greased 13x9-in. baking dish. (Dish will be full.) Melt remaining butter. Add bread crumbs; toss to coat. Sprinkle over casserole.
4. Bake, uncovered, 20 minutes. Sprinkle with remaining bacon. Bake 5 minutes or until bubbly.

COVER RECIPE

Sweet Potato Ham Casserole

If you like sweet potatoes, here's a great way to serve them. It's so easy to make this meal-in-one hot bake. I like to think of the marshmallows on top as dessert!

—**BARBARA SMITH** CANNON FALLS, MN

PREP: 20 MIN. • **BAKE:** 15 MIN.
MAKES: 2 SERVINGS

- 1 **large sweet potato, about (10 ounces)**
- ¼ **cup water**
- 1 **boneless fully cooked ham steaks (½ pound and ¾ inch thick)**
- 1 **tablespoon butter**
- ⅓ **cup unsweetened pineapple juice**
- 2 **tablespoons packed brown sugar**
- 1 **can (8 ounces) pineapple chunks, drained**
- ⅓ **cup miniature marshmallows**

1. Peel sweet potato and cut into chunks. Place in a microwave-safe dish; add water. Cover and microwave on high for 7-9 minutes or until tender; drain and set aside.
2. Cut ham into two pieces. In a skillet brown ham in butter on both sides. In a bowl, combine pineapple juice and brown sugar; stir until sugar is dissolved. Pour over ham. Bring to a boil. Reduce heat; simmer, uncovered, for 5-7 minutes or until slightly thickened.
3. Transfer ham to a greased shallow 1-qt. baking dish. Place sweet potato and pineapple around edge of dish. Pour brown sugar mixture over the top. Bake, uncovered, at 400° for 12-15 minutes or until heated through. Sprinkle marshmallows around edge. Bake 3-5 minutes longer or until the marshmallows are golden brown. **NOTE** *This recipe was tested in a 1,100-watt microwave.*

Ravioli Casserole

It takes less than 30 minutes to prep this hearty, crowd-pleasing meal. Nutmeg, white wine and basil give it an extra-special flavor you just can't help but love.

—**MARGIE WILLIAMS** MT. JULIET, TN

PREP: 25 MIN. • **BAKE:** 35 MIN. + STANDING
MAKES: 8 SERVINGS

- 1 package (25 ounces) frozen cheese ravioli
- ¼ cup butter, cubed
- ¼ cup all-purpose flour
- ¼ teaspoon salt
- ¼ teaspoon ground nutmeg
- 2 cups milk
- ¼ cup white wine or vegetable broth
- ½ cup minced fresh basil
- 3 cups (12 ounces) shredded part-skim mozzarella cheese, divided
- ¾ cup grated Parmesan cheese, divided
- 2½ cups marinara or spaghetti sauce

1. Cook ravioli according to package directions.
2. Meanwhile, in a large saucepan, melt butter. Stir in the flour, salt and nutmeg until smooth; gradually add milk and wine. Bring to a boil; cook and stir for 1 minute or until thickened. Remove from the heat. Stir in the basil, 1 cup mozzarella cheese and ¼ cup Parmesan cheese.
3. Drain ravioli; toss with sauce mixture. Transfer to a greased 13-in. x 9-in. baking dish. Top with 1 cup mozzarella cheese and marinara sauce; sprinkle with remaining cheeses.
4. Cover and bake at 375° for 30 minutes. Uncover; bake 5-10 minutes longer or until bubbly. Let stand for 15 minutes before serving.

Chicken Swiss Bundles

These yummy sandwich buns made with frozen dinner rolls are a favorite at our house. They're great hot from the oven but also freeze well. I serve them with tomato soup, and watch them disappear.

—**TRISHA KRUSE** EAGLE, ID

PREP: 30 MIN. • **BAKE:** 20 MIN.
MAKES: 12 SERVINGS

- 1 small onion, finely chopped
- ½ cup sliced fresh mushrooms
- 1½ teaspoons butter
- 1 garlic clove, minced
- 1 cup cubed cooked chicken breast
- ½ cup chopped roasted sweet red peppers
- 1 tablespoon honey mustard
- ¼ teaspoon salt
- ¼ teaspoon lemon-pepper seasoning
- ¼ teaspoon Italian seasoning
- 2 cups (8 ounces) shredded Swiss cheese
- 12 frozen bread dough dinner rolls, thawed
- 2 tablespoons butter, melted

1. In a large skillet, saute onion and mushrooms in butter until tender. Add garlic; cook 1 minute longer. Add the chicken, peppers, mustard and seasonings; heat through. Remove from the heat; stir in cheese.
2. Flatten each roll into a 5-in. circle. Place ¼ cup chicken mixture in the center of six circles. Brush edges with water; top with remaining circles. Press edges with a fork to seal.
3. Place on greased baking sheets; brush with butter. Bake at 350° for 18-22 minutes or until golden brown. Cut bundles in half to serve.

Crescent Turkey Casserole

Using mayonnaise to make the filling for this potpie casserole gives it a little extra tang and adds to the creaminess. Remember this recipe for the next time you have leftover turkey.

—**DANIELA ESSMAN** PERHAM, MN

START TO FINISH: 30 MIN.
MAKES: 4 SERVINGS

- ½ cup mayonnaise
- 2 tablespoons all-purpose flour
- 1 teaspoon chicken bouillon granules
- ⅛ teaspoon pepper
- ¾ cup 2% milk
- 1½ cups cubed cooked turkey breast
- 1 package (10 ounces) frozen mixed vegetables
- 1 tube (4 ounces) refrigerated crescent rolls

1. Preheat oven to 375°. In a large saucepan, combine mayonnaise, flour, bouillon and pepper. Gradually add milk; stir until smooth. Bring to a boil over medium heat; cook and stir 2 minutes or until thickened. Add turkey and vegetables; heat through. Spoon into a greased 8-in. square baking dish.
2. Unroll crescent dough and separate into two rectangles. Seal perforations. Place over turkey mixture. Bake 15-20 minutes or until golden brown.

Italian Sausage with Peppers

Local fairs in these parts are famous for sausage and pepper sandwiches. We like this version with mild sweet peppers.

—**BECKI CLEMETSON** SHARPSVILLE, PA

PREP: 40 MIN. • **BAKE:** 35 MIN.
MAKES: 8 SERVINGS

- 5 Hungarian wax peppers or Cubanelle peppers
- 1 large sweet yellow pepper
- 1 large sweet red pepper
- 2 medium sweet onions, chopped
- 2 tablespoons olive oil
- 1 can (14½ ounces) Italian diced tomatoes, undrained
- 1 can (6 ounces) tomato paste
- ½ cup water
- 4 garlic cloves, minced
- 2 bay leaves
- 1 tablespoon dried parsley flakes
- ½ teaspoon dried basil
- ½ teaspoon dried oregano
- ½ teaspoon salt
- ⅛ teaspoon white pepper
- 8 Italian sausage links (4 ounces each)
- 8 hoagie buns, split

1. Seed wax peppers if desired; cut wax and bell peppers into 2-in. pieces. In a large skillet, saute peppers and onions in oil until tender. Stir in the tomatoes, tomato paste, water, garlic, bay leaves and seasonings; heat through.
2. Meanwhile, in another large skillet, brown sausages. Transfer to an ungreased 13x9-in. baking dish. Top with pepper mixture.
3. Cover and bake at 350° for 35-40 minutes or until a thermometer reads 160°. Discard bay leaves. Serve on buns.
NOTE *Wear disposable gloves when cutting hot peppers; the oils can burn skin. Avoid touching your face.*

Pork Chops with Gravy

My daughter and I came up with this special recipe for pork chops, but our original version was much higher in fat. Since I started watching what I ate, I made a few changes to make it a little healthier for my family and me.

—**BETTY SLIVON** SUN CITY, AZ

PREP: 30 MIN. • **BAKE:** 10 MIN.
MAKES: 4 SERVINGS

- 1 egg
- 1¼ cups 2% milk, divided
- 1½ cups soft bread crumbs
- 3 teaspoons minced fresh parsley, divided
- 1 teaspoon minced fresh thyme
- 4 bone-in pork loin chops (7 ounces each)
- ¾ teaspoon salt, divided
- ½ teaspoon pepper, divided
- 3 tablespoons reduced-fat butter, divided
- 3 tablespoons plus 1 teaspoon all-purpose flour
- ⅓ cup half-and-half cream
- ⅓ cup reduced-sodium beef broth

1. In a shallow bowl, whisk egg and ½ cup milk. Combine the bread crumbs, 1 teaspoon parsley and thyme in another shallow bowl. Sprinkle pork chops with ½ teaspoon salt and ¼ teaspoon pepper. Dip chops in egg mixture, then crumb mixture.

2. In a large skillet over medium-high heat, cook pork chops in 2 tablespoons butter for 4 minutes on each side. Transfer to an ungreased 13-in. x 9-in. baking pan. Bake, uncovered, at 425° for 10-15 minutes or until a meat thermometer reads 160°.

3. Meanwhile, in the same skillet, melt remaining butter. Stir in flour and remaining salt and pepper until smooth; gradually stir in the cream, broth and remaining milk. Bring to a boil; cook and stir for 2 minutes or until thickened. Serve gravy with chops; sprinkle with remaining parsley.

NOTE *This recipe was tested with Land O'Lakes light stick butter.*

King Ranch Casserole

I'm so happy this Texas-style casserole was passed down to me. It's easy to make and freezes well, and if your family likes a little spice, this would be good topped with sliced jalapenos.

—**KENDRA DOSS** COLORADO SPRINGS, CO

PREP: 25 MIN. • **BAKE:** 30 MIN.
MAKES: 8 SERVINGS

- 1 large onion, finely chopped
- 2 celery ribs, finely chopped
- 1 medium green pepper, finely chopped
- 1 medium sweet red pepper, finely chopped
- 1 tablespoon canola oil
- 1 garlic clove, minced
- 3 cups cubed cooked chicken breast
- 1 can (10¾ ounces) reduced-fat reduced-sodium condensed cream of celery soup, undiluted
- 1 can (10¾ ounces) reduced-fat reduced-sodium condensed cream of chicken soup, undiluted
- 1 can (10 ounces) diced tomatoes and green chilies, undrained
- 1 tablespoon chili powder
- 12 corn tortillas (6 inches), cut into 1-inch strips
- 2 cups (8 ounces) shredded reduced-fat cheddar cheese, divided

1. In a large nonstick skillet coated with cooking spray, saute the onion, celery and peppers in oil until crisp-tender. Add garlic; cook 1 minute longer. Stir in the chicken, soups, tomatoes and chili powder.

2. Line the bottom of a 3-qt. baking dish with half of the tortilla strips; top with half of the chicken mixture and 1 cup cheese. Repeat layers. Bake, uncovered, at 350° for 30-35 minutes or until bubbly.

This hearty casserole takes advantage of garden-fresh vegetables and handy convenience items. My aunt originally made this for family gatherings. Now I fix it any night of the week.
—**KATE BECKMAN** HEMET, CA

Cheesy Kielbasa Bake

PREP: 55 MIN. • **BAKE:** 30 MIN.
MAKES: 2 CASSEROLES
(8-10 SERVINGS EACH)

- 12 ounces uncooked elbow macaroni
- 2 pounds kielbasa or Polish sausage, halved lengthwise and sliced
- 1 tablespoon olive oil
- 2 medium onions, chopped
- 2 medium zucchini, quartered and sliced
- 2 medium carrots, grated
- ½ teaspoon minced garlic
- 1 jar (26 ounces) spaghetti sauce
- 1 can (14½ ounces) stewed tomatoes
- 1 egg, lightly beaten
- 1 carton (15 ounces) ricotta cheese
- 2 cups (8 ounces) shredded cheddar cheese
- 2 cups (8 ounces) part-skim shredded mozzarella cheese
- 2 green onions, chopped

1. Cook macaroni according to package directions. Meanwhile, in a large skillet, brown sausage in oil over medium heat; drain. Add the onions, zucchini, carrots and garlic; cook and stir for 5-6 minutes or until crisp-tender.

2. Stir in spaghetti sauce and tomatoes. Bring to a boil. Reduce heat; simmer, uncovered, for 15 minutes. Drain macaroni.

3. In each of two greased 13-in. x 9-in. baking dishes, layer a fourth of the macaroni and meat sauce. Combine egg and ricotta cheese; spoon a fourth over sauce. Sprinkle with a fourth of the cheddar and mozzarella. Repeat layers. Top with green onions.

4. Cool one casserole; cover and freeze for up to 2 months. Cover and bake the remaining casserole at 350° for 15 minutes. Uncover; bake 15 minutes longer or until cheese is melted.

TO USE FROZEN CASSEROLE *Thaw in the refrigerator for 24 hours. Remove from the refrigerator 30 minutes before baking. Cover and bake at 350° for 35-40 minutes or until heated through.*

Meatball Pizza Subs

This is just one of the reasons I like having canned pizza sauce on hand. I made this one night with meatballs I had in the freezer and my whole family loved them.
—**ANN NOLTE** RIVERVIEW, FL

START TO FINISH: 25 MIN.
MAKES: 4 SERVINGS

- 1⅓ cups pizza sauce
- 4 submarine buns, split and toasted
- 1⅓ cups shredded part-skim mozzarella cheese
- 20 slices pepperoni
- 1 package (12 ounces) frozen fully cooked Italian meatballs, thawed
  Italian seasoning to taste

1. Spread ⅓ cup pizza sauce on the bottom of each bun. Top each with ⅓ cup cheese, five slices of pepperoni and three meatballs; sprinkle with Italian seasoning. Replace tops.

2. Wrap each sandwich in foil. Bake at 400° for 10-12 minutes or until heated through.

Mini Substitutions

When I make these, I cut the subs in half and put 2 meatballs in each. Anything you can put on a pizza would be good in these!
—**MAMAKNOWSBEST**
TASTEOFHOME.COM

Baked Salmon Cakes

Baked in muffin pans and served with sauce on the side, these cute cakes make a fantastic light meal. You can also bake a double batch and freeze some for a quick, healthful supper later in the month.

—**NIKKI HADDAD** GERMANTOWN, MD

START TO FINISH: 30 MIN.
MAKES: 4 SERVINGS

- 1 can (14¾ ounces) salmon, drained, bones and skin removed
- 1½ cups soft whole wheat bread crumbs
- ½ cup finely chopped sweet red pepper
- ½ cup egg substitute
- 3 green onions, thinly sliced
- ¼ cup finely chopped celery
- ¼ cup minced fresh cilantro
- 3 tablespoons fat-free mayonnaise
- 1 tablespoon lemon juice
- 1 garlic clove, minced
- ⅛ to ¼ teaspoon hot pepper sauce
SAUCE
- 2 tablespoons fat-free mayonnaise
- ¼ teaspoon capers, drained
- ¼ teaspoon dill weed
  Dash lemon juice

1. In a large bowl, combine the first 11 ingredients. Place ⅓ cup salmon mixture into eight muffin cups coated with cooking spray. Bake at 425° for 10-15 minutes or until a meat thermometer reads 160°.
2. Meanwhile, combine the sauce ingredients. Serve with salmon.

kid FRIENDLY Turkey Potpies

Some days, comfort-food cravings don't jive with busy schedules. The solution: Whip up a batch of these rich and creamy potpies when you have some time on the weekend. Then stash them in the freezer for when the mood strikes.

—**TASTE OF HOME TEST KITCHEN**

PREP: 30 MIN. • **BAKE:** 20 MIN.
MAKES: 4 SERVINGS

- 1 small onion, chopped
- 1 medium carrot, chopped
- ½ cup diced peeled potato
- ¼ cup chopped celery
- ¼ cup butter, cubed
- ⅓ cup all-purpose flour
- ½ teaspoon salt
- ½ teaspoon dried parsley flakes
- ¼ teaspoon dried rosemary, crushed
- ¼ teaspoon rubbed sage
- ¼ teaspoon pepper
- 1 cup 2% milk
- 1 cup chicken broth
- 2 cups cubed cooked turkey
- ½ cup frozen peas
- 1 sheet refrigerated pie pastry

1. In a large saucepan, saute the onion, carrot, potato and celery in butter until tender. Add the flour and seasonings until blended; gradually add milk and broth. Bring to a boil; cook and stir for 2 minutes or until thickened. Stir in turkey and peas; divide mixture among four ungreased 5-in. pie plates.
2. Divide pastry into quarters. On a lightly floured surface, roll each quarter into a 6-in. circle; place over filling. Trim, seal and flute edges; cut slits to vent.
3. Cover and freeze two potpies for up to 3 months. Bake the remaining potpies at 375° for 18-22 minutes or until golden brown. Let stand for 10 minutes before serving.
TO USE FROZEN POTPIES *Remove from the freezer 30 minutes before baking. Cover edges of crusts loosely with foil; place on a baking sheet. Bake at 375° for 30 minutes. Remove foil; bake 15-20 minutes longer or until golden brown and filling is bubbly.*

Cornmeal Oven-Fried Chicken

A coating of cornmeal and Parmesan cheese really perks up fried chicken. This recipe is crispier and less greasy because it's baked, not fried.

—DEBORAH WILLIAMS PEORIA, AZ

PREP: 20 MIN. • **BAKE:** 40 MIN.
MAKES: 6 SERVINGS

- ½ cup dry bread crumbs
- ½ cup cornmeal
- ⅓ cup grated Parmesan cheese
- ¼ cup minced fresh parsley or 4 teaspoons dried parsley flakes
- ¾ teaspoon garlic powder
- ½ teaspoon salt
- ½ teaspoon onion powder
- ½ teaspoon dried thyme
- ½ teaspoon pepper
- ½ cup buttermilk
- 1 broiler/fryer chicken (3 to 4 pounds), cut up and skin removed
- 1 tablespoon butter, melted

1. In a large resealable plastic bag, combine the first nine ingredients. Place the buttermilk in a shallow bowl. Dip chicken in buttermilk, then add to bag, a few pieces at a time, and shake to coat.

2. Place in a 13x9-in. baking pan coated with cooking spray. Bake at 375° for 10 minutes; drizzle with butter. Bake 30-40 minutes longer or until juices run clear.

? Did you know?

Portobello, cremini and white button mushrooms are all the same variety—the difference being age. The youngest is the white button, cremini (also called baby portobello) is in the middle, and portobellos are the most mature.

ULTIMATE *Comfort* Beef & Mushroom Braised Stew

Every spring, my family heads to our timber acreage to collect morel mushrooms for this stew. But it's also delicious with button mushrooms or baby portobellos.

—AMY WERTHEIM ATLANTA, IL

PREP: 35 MIN. • **BAKE:** 1½ HOURS
MAKES: 6 SERVINGS

- 1 boneless beef chuck roast (2 to 3 pounds), cut into 1-inch cubes
- ¼ teaspoon salt
- ¼ teaspoon pepper
- 3 tablespoons olive oil
- 1 pound sliced fresh mushrooms
- 2 medium onions, sliced
- 2 garlic cloves, minced
- 1 carton (32 ounces) beef broth
- 1 cup dry red wine or additional beef broth
- ½ cup brandy
- 1 tablespoon tomato paste
- ¼ teaspoon each dried parsley flakes, rosemary, sage leaves, tarragon and thyme
- 3 tablespoons all-purpose flour
- 3 tablespoons water
  Hot mashed potatoes

1. Preheat oven to 325°. Sprinkle beef with salt and pepper. In an ovenproof Dutch oven, heat oil over medium heat; brown beef in batches. Remove from pan.

2. In same pan, add mushrooms and onions; cook and stir until tender. Add garlic; cook 1 minute longer. Stir in broth, wine, brandy, tomato paste and herbs. Return beef to pan. Bring to a boil.

3. Bake, covered, 1 hour. In a small bowl, mix flour and water until smooth; gradually stir into stew. Bake, covered, 30 minutes longer or until sauce is thickened and beef is tender. Skim fat. Serve with mashed potatoes.

FREEZE OPTION *Freeze cooled stew in freezer containers. To use, partially thaw in refrigerator overnight. Heat through in a saucepan, stirring occasionally and adding a little broth or water if necessary.*

Scallop Mac & Cheese

A nice way to dress up this favorite feel-good food is to add scallops. They transform mac 'n' cheese into a delicious and sophisticated dish.

—LAURIE LUFKIN ESSEX, MA

PREP: 35 MIN. • **BAKE:** 15 MIN.
MAKES: 5 SERVINGS

- 2 cups uncooked medium pasta shells
- ½ cup butter, divided
- 1 cup French bread baguette crumbs
- 1 pound bay scallops
- 1 cup sliced fresh mushrooms
- 1 small onion, chopped
- 3 tablespoons all-purpose flour
- ¾ teaspoon dried thyme
- ¼ teaspoon salt
- ⅛ teaspoon pepper
- 2 cups whole milk
- ½ cup white wine or chicken broth
- 2 tablespoons sherry or chicken broth
- 1 cup (4 ounces) shredded Swiss cheese
- 1 cup (4 ounces) shredded sharp cheddar cheese

1. Cook pasta according to package directions. Meanwhile, in a small skillet, melt 4 tablespoons butter. Add bread crumbs; cook and stir until lightly toasted.

2. In a large skillet over medium heat, melt 2 tablespoons butter. Add scallops; cook and stir for 2 minutes or until firm and opaque. Remove and keep warm. Melt remaining butter in the pan; add mushrooms and onion. Cook and stir until tender. Stir in the flour, thyme, salt and pepper until blended.

3. Gradually add the milk, wine and sherry. Bring to a boil; cook and stir for 1-2 minutes or until thickened. Stir in cheeses until melted. Drain pasta; stir pasta and scallops into sauce.

4. Divide among five 10-oz. ramekins or custard cups. Sprinkle with bread crumbs. Place ramekins on a baking sheet. Bake, uncovered, at 350° for 15-20 minutes or until heated through. Spoon onto plates if desired.

Crumb-Topped Baked Fish

The coating on this cod is thicker than most, but the fish still comes out tender and flaky. It's the ideal contrast of textures

—JEAN BARCROFT CLARKSVILLE, MI

START TO FINISH: 25 MIN.
MAKES: 4 SERVINGS

- 4 haddock or cod fillets (6 ounces each)
  Salt and pepper to taste
- 1¼ cups seasoned bread crumbs
- ¼ cup shredded cheddar cheese
- ¼ cup butter, melted
- 1 tablespoon minced fresh parsley
- ½ teaspoon dried marjoram
- ¼ teaspoon garlic powder
- ¼ teaspoon dried rosemary, crushed

Preheat oven to 400°. Place fillets on a greased baking sheet; season with salt and pepper. In a small bowl, combine the remaining ingredients; pat onto fillets. Bake 15-20 minutes or until fish flakes easily with a fork.

White Cheddar & Ham Scalloped Potatoes

I've been tweaking my scalloped potatoes for more than eight years. After I added the thyme, ham and sour cream, my husband declared, "This is it!"

—**HOPE TOOLE** MUSCLE SHOALS, AL

PREP: 40 MIN. • **BAKE:** 70 MIN.
MAKES: 10 SERVINGS

- ¼ **cup butter**
- 1 **medium onion, finely chopped**
- ¼ **cup all-purpose flour**
- 1 **teaspoon salt**
- 1 **teaspoon dried parsley flakes**
- ½ **teaspoon dried thyme**
- ½ **teaspoon pepper**
- 3 **cups 2% milk**
- 1 **can (10¾ ounces) condensed cream of mushroom soup, undiluted**
- 1 **cup (8 ounces) sour cream**
- 8 **cups thinly sliced peeled potatoes**
- 3½ **cups cubed fully cooked ham**
- 2 **cups (8 ounces) shredded sharp white cheddar cheese**

1. Preheat oven to 375°. In a large saucepan, heat butter over medium-high heat. Add onion; cook and stir until tender. Stir in flour and seasonings until blended; gradually whisk in milk. Bring to a boil, stirring constantly; cook and stir 2 minutes or until thickened. Stir in soup. Remove from heat; stir in sour cream.
2. In a greased 13x9-in. baking dish, layer half of each of the following: potatoes, ham, cheese and sauce. Repeat layers.
3. Bake, covered, 30 minutes. Bake, uncovered, 40-50 minutes longer or until potatoes are tender.

Hamburger Casserole

This meat-and-potatoes recipe has traveled all around the country! My mother started making it in Pennsylvania, then I brought it to Texas when I married. Today, I still make it in California, and my daughter treats her friends to this oldie but goodie in Colorado.

—**HELEN CARMICHALL** SANTEE, CA

PREP: 10 MIN. • **COOK:** 45 MIN.
MAKES: 10 SERVINGS

- 2 **pounds lean ground beef (90% lean)**
- 4 **pounds potatoes, peeled and sliced ¼ inch thick**
- 1 **large onion, sliced**
- 1 **teaspoon salt, optional**
- ½ **teaspoon pepper**
- 1 **teaspoon beef bouillon granules**
- 1 **cup boiling water**
- 1 **can (28 ounces) diced tomatoes, undrained**
  Minced fresh parsley, optional

In a Dutch oven, layer half of the meat, potatoes and onion. Sprinkle with half of the salt if desired and pepper. Repeat layers. Dissolve bouillon in water; pour over all. Top with tomatoes. Cover and cook over medium heat for 45-50 minutes or until potatoes are tender. Garnish with parsley if desired.

Roasted Chicken with Rosemary

Herbs, garlic and butter give this hearty meal-in-one a classic flavor. It's a lot like pot roast, but it uses chicken instead of beef.

—**ISABEL ZIENKOSKY** SALT LAKE CITY, UT

PREP: 20 MIN. • **BAKE:** 2 HOURS + STANDING
MAKES: 9 SERVINGS

- ½ **cup butter, cubed**
- 4 **tablespoons minced fresh rosemary or 2 tablespoons dried rosemary, crushed**
- 2 **tablespoons minced fresh parsley**
- 3 **garlic cloves, minced**
- 1 **teaspoon salt**
- ½ **teaspoon pepper**
- 1 **whole roasting chicken (5 to 6 pounds)**
- 6 **small red potatoes, halved**
- 6 **medium carrots, halved lengthwise and cut into 2-inch pieces**
- 2 **medium onions, quartered**

1. In a small saucepan, melt butter; stir in the seasonings. Place chicken breast side up on a rack in a shallow roasting pan; tie drumsticks together with kitchen string. Spoon half of the butter mixture over chicken. Place the potatoes, carrots and onions around chicken. Drizzle remaining butter mixture over vegetables.

2. Cover and bake at 350° for 1½ hours, basting every 30 minutes. Uncover; bake 30-60 minutes longer or until a thermometer reads 180°, basting occasionally.

3. Cover with foil and let stand for 10-15 minutes before carving. Serve with vegetables.

From the Slow Cooker

IMAGINE WALKING THROUGH THE DOOR AFTER A BUSY DAY AND SMELLING THE AROMA OF A HOT SUPPER JUST WAITING TO BE SERVED.

CARAMELIZED ONION CHUCK ROAST
PAGE 152

ITALIAN PULLED PORK SANDWICHES
PAGE 173

SAUSAGE PASTA STEW
PAGE 179

Caramelized Onion Chuck Roast

Wonderfully fork-tender, this tasty roast with sweet onions makes the perfect comfort food at the end of a long day.

—JEANNIE KLUGH LANCASTER, PA

PREP: 25 MIN. • **COOK:** 8 HOURS
MAKES: 8 SERVINGS

- 1 cup water
- 1 cup beer or beef broth
- ½ cup beef broth
- ¼ cup packed brown sugar
- 3 tablespoons Dijon mustard
- 2 tablespoons cider vinegar
- 1 boneless beef chuck roast (4 pounds), trimmed
- 1 teaspoon onion salt
- 1 teaspoon coarsely ground pepper
- 1 tablespoon olive oil
- 3 large sweet onions, halved and sliced
- 2 tablespoons cornstarch
- 2 tablespoons cold water

1. In a large bowl, combine the first six ingredients; set aside. Sprinkle roast with onion salt and pepper. In a large skillet, brown meat in oil on all sides. Place onions and roast in a 5-qt. slow cooker; pour beer mixture over top. Cover and cook on low for 8-10 hours or until meat is tender.

2. Remove roast and onions and keep warm. Skim fat from cooking juices; transfer 2 cups to a small saucepan. Bring liquid to a boil. Combine cornstarch and water until smooth; gradually stir into the pan. Bring to a boil; cook and stir for 2 minutes or until thickened. Serve with roast.

Parmesan Pork Roast

Honey, soy sauce and Parmesan all slowly cooked together with a pork loin roast give this dinner a lip-smacking flavor. The juices are then used to make a tasty gravy you can drape over each slice of pork.

—KAREN WARNER LOUISVILLE, OH

PREP: 15 MIN. • **COOK:** 5½ HOURS
MAKES: 10 SERVINGS

- 1 boneless whole pork loin roast (4 pounds)
- ⅔ cup grated Parmesan cheese
- ½ cup honey
- 3 tablespoons soy sauce
- 2 tablespoons dried basil
- 2 tablespoons minced garlic
- 2 tablespoons olive oil
- ½ teaspoon salt
- 2 tablespoons cornstarch
- ¼ cup cold water

1. Cut roast in half. Transfer to a 3-qt. slow cooker. In a small bowl, combine the cheese, honey, soy sauce, basil, garlic, oil and salt; pour over pork. Cover and cook on low for 5½ to 6 hours or until a meat thermometer reads 160°.

2. Remove meat to a serving platter; keep warm. Skim fat from cooking juices; transfer to a small saucepan. Bring liquid to a boil. Combine cornstarch and water until smooth. Gradually stir into pan. Bring to a boil; cook and stir for 2 minutes or until thickened. Slice roast; serve with gravy.

Did you know?

Children who regularly eat dinner with their families are more likely to make healthier food decisions, consume higher amounts of vitamins and minerals, and eat more balanced meals.

kid FRIENDLY Sweet and Saucy Chicken

I can't remember where this recipe came from, but I've been making it for several years. Everyone who tries it enjoys it. When the chicken is done cooking, it's so tender it falls off the bone.

—PATRICIA WEIR CHILLIWACK, BC

PREP: 30 MIN. • **COOK:** 6 HOURS
MAKES: 6 SERVINGS

- 1 broiler/fryer chicken (4 pounds), cut up and skin removed
- ¾ cup packed brown sugar
- ¼ cup all-purpose flour
- ⅔ cup water
- ⅓ cup white vinegar
- ⅓ cup reduced-sodium soy sauce
- 2 tablespoons ketchup
- 1 tablespoon dried minced onion
- 1 teaspoon prepared mustard
- ¼ teaspoon garlic powder
- ¼ teaspoon salt
- ¼ teaspoon pepper
    Hot cooked rice or egg noodles, optional

1. Place chicken in a 3-qt. slow cooker. In a small saucepan, combine brown sugar and flour. Stir in the water, vinegar and soy sauce. Add the ketchup, onion, mustard, garlic powder, salt and pepper. Bring to a boil; cook and stir for 1-2 minutes or until thickened.

2. Pour over chicken. Cover and cook on low for 6-8 hours or until chicken juices run clear. Serve with rice or noodles if desired.

Melt-In-Your-Mouth Chuck Roast

My husband and I like well-seasoned foods, so this recipe is terrific. You'll also love how flavorful this roast turns out.

—**BETTE MCCUMBER** SCHENECTADY, NY

PREP: 20 MIN. • **COOK:** 5 HOURS
MAKES: 6 SERVINGS

- 1 large onion, sliced
- 1 medium green pepper, sliced
- 1 celery rib, chopped
- 1 boneless beef chuck roast (2 to 3 pounds)
- 1 can (14½ ounces) Italian stewed tomatoes
- ½ cup beef broth
- ½ cup ketchup
- 3 tablespoons brown sugar
- 2 tablespoons Worcestershire sauce
- 4½ teaspoons prepared mustard
- 3 garlic cloves, minced
- 1 tablespoon soy sauce
- 2 teaspoons pepper
- ¼ teaspoon crushed red pepper flakes
- 3 tablespoons cornstarch
- ¼ cup cold water

1. Place the onion, green pepper and celery in a 5-qt. slow cooker; add the roast. In a large bowl, combine the tomatoes, broth, ketchup, brown sugar, Worcestershire sauce, mustard, garlic, soy sauce, pepper and pepper flakes; pour over meat. Cover and cook on low for 5-6 hours or until meat is tender.
2. Remove meat and vegetables; keep warm. Skim fat from cooking juices if necessary; transfer to a small saucepan. Combine cornstarch and cold water until smooth; stir into cooking juices. Bring to a boil; cook and stir for 2 minutes or until thickened. Serve with roast.

Creole Chicken Thighs

Cajun seasoning gives this dish a wonderful spice. I like to serve it with crusty bread and a refreshing mint and ginger iced tea.

—**MATTHEW LAMAN** HUMMELSTOWN, PA

PREP: 30 MIN. • **COOK:** 7 HOURS
MAKES: 8 SERVINGS

- 8 bone-in chicken thighs (about 3 pounds), skin removed
- 3 tablespoons Cajun seasoning, divided
- 1 tablespoon canola oil
- 3½ cups chicken broth
- 1 can (16 ounces) red beans, rinsed and drained
- 1½ cups uncooked converted rice
- 2 medium tomatoes, finely chopped
- 1 medium green pepper, chopped
- 2 tablespoons minced fresh parsley

1. Sprinkle chicken with 1 tablespoon Cajun seasoning. In a large skillet, brown chicken in oil.
2. In a 5-qt. slow cooker, combine the broth, beans, rice, tomatoes, green pepper, parsley and remaining Cajun seasoning. Top with chicken. Cover and cook on low for 7-8 hours or until chicken is tender.

Honey-Glazed Ham

Here's an easy solution for feeding a large group. Slow-cooked ham is perfect for family dinners where time in the kitchen is as valuable as space in the oven.
—**JACQUIE STOLZ** LITTLE SIOUX, IA

PREP: 10 MIN. • **COOK:** 4½ HOURS
MAKES: 14 SERVINGS

- 1 **boneless fully cooked ham (4 pounds)**
- 1½ **cups ginger ale**
- ¼ **cup honey**
- ½ **teaspoon ground mustard**
- ½ **teaspoon ground cloves**
- ¼ **teaspoon ground cinnamon**

1. Cut ham in half; place in a 5-qt. slow cooker. Pour ginger ale over ham. Cover and cook on low for 4-5 hours or until heated through.

2. Combine the honey, mustard, cloves and cinnamon; stir until smooth. Spread over ham; cook 30 minutes longer.

ULTIMATE *Comfort*
French Dip au Jus

I created this sandwich because so many French Dip recipes seem bland or rely on a mix. Mine is simple to make and tastes better than a restaurant version.
—**LINDSAY EBERT** OREM, UT

PREP: 30 MIN. • **COOK:** 8 HOURS
MAKES: 8 SERVINGS

- 1½ **teaspoons beef base**
- 1 **teaspoon dried thyme**
- 1 **beef rump roast or bottom round roast (3 pounds), cut in half**
- 1 **medium onion, quartered**
- ½ **cup reduced-sodium soy sauce**
- 2 **garlic cloves, minced**
- 1 **bay leaf**
- ½ **teaspoon pepper**
- 8 **cups water**
- 2 **tablespoons Dijon mustard**
- 2 **loaves French bread (1 pound each), split and toasted**
- 12 **slices part-skim mozzarella cheese**
- 1 **jar (4½ ounces) sliced mushrooms, drained**

1. Combine beef base and thyme; rub over roast and place in a 5-qt. slow cooker. Combine the onion, soy sauce, garlic, bay leaf and pepper; pour over roast. Add water.

2. Cover and cook on low for 8-9 hours or until meat is tender. Remove roast to a cutting board; cool slightly. Strain cooking juices, reserving onion; skim fat from juices. Discard bay leaf. Thinly slice meat.

3. To assemble sandwiches, spread mustard over bread. Top each bottom with three slices cheese; layer with beef, remaining cheese, mushrooms and reserved onion. Replace tops. Cut each loaf into four slices; serve with reserved juices.

NOTE *Look for beef base near the broth and bouillon.*

Turkey Meatballs and Sauce

PREP: 40 MIN. • **COOK:** 6 HOURS
MAKES: 8 SERVINGS

- ¼ cup egg substitute
- ½ cup seasoned bread crumbs
- ⅓ cup chopped onion
- ½ teaspoon pepper
- ¼ teaspoon salt-free seasoning blend
- 1½ pounds lean ground turkey

SAUCE

- 1 can (15 ounces) tomato sauce
- 1 can (14½ ounces) diced tomatoes, undrained
- 1 small zucchini, chopped
- 1 medium green pepper, chopped
- 1 medium onion, chopped
- 1 can (6 ounces) tomato paste
- 2 bay leaves
- 2 garlic cloves, minced
- 1 teaspoon dried oregano
- 1 teaspoon dried basil
- 1 teaspoon dried parsley flakes
- ¼ teaspoon crushed red pepper flakes
- ¼ teaspoon pepper
- 1 package (16 ounces) whole wheat spaghetti

1. In a large bowl, combine the egg substitute, bread crumbs, onion, pepper and seasoning blend. Crumble turkey over mixture and mix well. Shape into 1-in. balls; place on a rack coated with cooking spray in a shallow baking pan. Bake at 400° for 15 minutes or until no longer pink.

2. Meanwhile, in a 4- or 5-qt. slow cooker, combine the tomato sauce, tomatoes, zucchini, green pepper, onion, tomato paste, bay leaves, garlic and seasonings. Stir in meatballs. Cover and cook on low for 6 hours. Cook spaghetti according to package directions; serve with meatballs and sauce.

Slow Cooker Jambalaya

Sausage, chicken and shrimp keep this dish hearty and satisfying. Made easy with canned items and other kitchen staples, it's perfect for casual get-togethers.

—SHERRY HUNTWORK GRETNA, NE

PREP: 20 MIN. • **COOK:** 6¼ HOURS
MAKES: 12 SERVINGS

- 1 pound smoked kielbasa or Polish sausage, sliced
- ½ pound boneless skinless chicken breasts, cut into 1-inch cubes
- 1 can (14½ ounces) beef broth
- 1 can (14½ ounces) diced tomatoes, undrained
- 2 celery ribs, chopped
- ⅓ cup tomato paste
- 4 garlic cloves, minced
- 1 tablespoon dried parsley flakes
- 1½ teaspoons dried basil
- 1 teaspoon cayenne pepper
- ½ teaspoon salt
- ½ teaspoon dried oregano
- 1 pound cooked medium shrimp, peeled and deveined
- 2 cups cooked rice

1. In a 4-qt. slow cooker, combine the first 12 ingredients. Cover and cook on low for 6-7 hours or until chicken is no longer pink.

2. Stir in shrimp and rice. Cover and cook 15 minutes longer or until heated through.

My sweetie and I have fought the battle of the bulge forever. This is my less-fattening take on meatballs. They're easy and full of flavor.

—**JANE MCMILLAN** DANIA BEACH, FL

Italian Sausage Dinner

My family loves this dish. It's easy to prepare before I go to work, and it makes the house smell so good at the end of the day.

—KATHY KASPROWICZ

ARLINGTON HEIGHTS, IL

PREP: 20 MIN. • **COOK:** 6 HOURS
MAKES: 5 SERVINGS

- 1 **pound small red potatoes**
- 2 **large zucchini, cut into 1-inch slices**
- 2 **large green peppers, cut into 1½-inch pieces**
- 1 **large onion, cut into wedges**
- ¼ **teaspoon salt**
- ¼ **teaspoon pepper**
- 1 **pound Italian sausage links, cut into 1½-inch pieces**
- 1 **tablespoon olive oil**
- ½ **cup white wine or chicken broth**
- 1 **tablespoon Italian seasoning**

Place the first six ingredients in a 6-qt. slow cooker. In a large skillet, brown sausages in oil. Reduce heat. Add wine and Italian seasoning, stirring to loosen browned bits from pan. Transfer to slow cooker. Cover and cook on low for 6-8 hours or until potatoes are tender.

White Chicken Chili

This slow-simmered chili features chicken, two kinds of beans and crunchy corn. It's quick, easy and tastes great. It's a family favorite that we enjoy with corn bread.

—LORI WEBER WENTZVILLE, MO

PREP: 25 MIN. • **COOK:** 5 HOURS
MAKES: 8 SERVINGS (2 QUARTS)

- ¾ **pound boneless skinless chicken breasts, cubed**
- 1 **medium onion, chopped**
- 1 **tablespoon canola oil**
- 1 **garlic clove, minced**
- 1½ **cups water**
- 1 **can (15 ounces) white kidney or cannellini beans, rinsed and drained**
- 1 **can (15 ounces) garbanzo beans or chickpeas, rinsed and drained**
- 1 **can (11 ounces) whole kernel white corn, drained or 1¼ cups frozen shoepeg corn**
- 1 **can (4 ounces) chopped green chilies**
- 1 **to 2 teaspoons chicken bouillon granules**
- 1 **teaspoon ground cumin**

1. In a large skillet, saute chicken and onion in oil until onion is tender. Add garlic; cook 1 minute longer. Transfer to a 3-qt. slow cooker. Stir in the remaining ingredients.

2. Cover and cook on low for 5-6 hours or until chicken is tender.

Chicken Stew with Gnocchi

My chicken stew fills the house with a comforting aroma as it gently bubbles in the slow cooker. One whiff and my family heads to the kitchen to see if it's ready.

—**MARGE DRAKE** JUNIATA, NE

PREP: 25 MIN. • **COOK:** 6½ HOURS
MAKES: 8 SERVINGS (3 QUARTS)

- **3** medium parsnips, peeled and cut into ½-inch pieces
- **2** large carrots, cut into ½-inch slices
- **2** celery ribs, chopped
- **1** large sweet potato, peeled and cut into 1-inch cubes
- **4** green onions, chopped
- **3** pounds bone-in chicken thighs, skin removed
- **½** teaspoon dried sage leaves
- **¼** teaspoon salt
- **¼** teaspoon pepper
- **4** cups chicken broth
- **1** cup water
- **3** tablespoons cornstarch
- **¼** cup cold water
- **1** package (16 ounces) potato gnocchi
  Hot pepper sauce, optional

1. Place the parsnips, carrots, celery, sweet potato and onions in a 5-qt. slow cooker. Top with chicken; sprinkle with the sage, salt and pepper. Add broth and water. Cover and cook on low for 6-8 hours or until chicken is tender.

2. Remove chicken; when cool enough to handle, remove meat from bones and discard bones. Cut meat into bite-size pieces and return to the slow cooker.

3. Mix cornstarch and cold water until smooth; stir into stew. Add gnocchi. Cover and cook on high for 30 minutes or until thickened. Season with hot pepper sauce if desired.

Spicy Goulash

Ground cumin, chili powder and a can of Mexican diced tomatoes jazz up my goulash recipe. Even the elbow macaroni is prepared in the slow cooker.

—**MELISSA POLK** WEST LAFAYETTE, IN

PREP: 25 MIN. • **COOK:** 5½ HOURS
MAKES: 12 SERVINGS

- **1** pound lean ground beef (90% lean)
- **4** cans (14½ ounces each) Mexican diced tomatoes, undrained
- **2** cans (16 ounces each) kidney beans, rinsed and drained
- **2** cups water
- **1** medium onion, chopped
- **1** medium green pepper, chopped
- **¼** cup red wine vinegar
- **2** tablespoons chili powder
- **1** tablespoon Worcestershire sauce
- **2** teaspoons beef bouillon granules
- **1** teaspoon dried basil
- **1** teaspoon dried parsley flakes
- **1** teaspoon ground cumin
- **¼** teaspoon pepper
- **2** cups uncooked elbow macaroni

1. In a large skillet, cook beef over medium heat until no longer pink; drain. Transfer to a 5-qt. slow cooker. Stir in the tomatoes, beans, water, onion, green pepper, vinegar, chili powder, Worcestershire sauce, bouillon and seasonings.

2. Cover and cook on low for 5-6 hours or until heated through.

3. Stir in macaroni; cover and cook 30 minutes longer or until macaroni is tender.

top tip

Spice Control

If you love hot food, this goulash is for you. When it says spicy, boy howdy, they weren't kidding. I'd use half the chili powder and some regular canned tomatoes or tomato sauce in place of the Mexican diced tomatoes.

—**LIBBY T.** TASTEOFHOME.COM

Herbed Beef with Noodles

Just a handful of ingredients and a sprinkling of spices go into this hearty dish. Even though it's very simple, it's full of subtle and creamy flavors. It would be just as good served over hot rice.

—ROSLYN HURST BELMONT, CA

PREP: 25 MIN. • **COOK:** 5 HOURS
MAKES: 8 SERVINGS

- 2 pounds beef top round steak
- ½ teaspoon salt
- ½ teaspoon pepper, divided
- 2 teaspoons canola oil
- 1 can (10¾ ounces) reduced-fat reduced-sodium condensed cream of celery soup, undiluted
- 1 medium onion, chopped
- 1 tablespoon fat-free milk
- 1 teaspoon dried oregano
- ½ teaspoon dried thyme
- 6 cups cooked wide egg noodles
  Chopped celery leaves, optional

1. Cut steak into serving-size pieces; sprinkle with salt and ¼ teaspoon pepper. In a large nonstick skillet coated with cooking spray, brown meat in oil on both sides. Transfer to a 3-qt. slow cooker.

2. In a small bowl, combine the soup, onion, milk, oregano, thyme and remaining pepper. Pour over meat. Cover and cook on low for 5-6 hours or until meat is tender.

3. Serve with noodles. Sprinkle with celery leaves if desired.

BBQ Beef Sandwiches

After years of searching, I found a recipe for shredded barbecue beef that's a hit with all my family and friends. It's easy to freeze for future meals, if there's any left!

—REBECCA ROHLAND MEDFORD, WI

PREP: 15 MIN. • **COOK:** 8 HOURS
MAKES: 14 SERVINGS

- 2 cups ketchup
- 1 medium onion, chopped
- ¼ cup cider vinegar
- ¼ cup molasses
- 2 tablespoons Worcestershire sauce
- 2 garlic cloves, minced
- ½ teaspoon salt
- ½ teaspoon ground mustard
- ½ teaspoon pepper
- ¼ teaspoon garlic powder
- ¼ teaspoon crushed red pepper flakes
- 1 boneless beef chuck roast (3 pounds)
- 14 sesame seed hamburger buns, split

1. In a large bowl, combine the first 11 ingredients. Cut roast in half; place in a 5-qt. slow cooker. Pour ketchup mixture over roast. Cover and cook on low for 8-10 hours or until meat is tender.

2. Remove meat and shred with two forks. Skim fat from cooking juices. Return meat to slow cooker; heat through. Using a slotted spoon, serve beef on buns.

Moist & Tender Turkey Breast

Turkey is notorious for being dry. Don't let that happen to yours. This slow-cooked version promises a fork-tender dinner your family will love.

—HEIDI VAWDREY RIVERTON, UT

PREP: 10 MIN. • **COOK:** 4 HOURS
MAKES: 12 SERVINGS

- 1   **bone-in turkey breast (6 to 7 pounds)**
- ½   **cup water**
- 4   **fresh rosemary sprigs**
- 4   **garlic cloves, peeled**
- 1   **tablespoon brown sugar**
- ½   **teaspoon coarsely ground pepper**
- ¼   **teaspoon salt**

Place turkey breast and water in a 6-qt. slow cooker. Place rosemary and garlic around turkey. Combine the brown sugar, pepper and salt; sprinkle over turkey. Cover and cook on low for 4-6 hours or until turkey is tender.

French Onion Portobello Brisket

I use this recipe when I go to winter potlucks and want something everyone will love. Though I have seen kids who scrape away the mushrooms and onion, they still rave about how the meat tastes and gobble it right up.

—AYSHA SCHURMAN AMMON, ID

PREP: 20 MIN. • **COOK:** 8 HOURS
MAKES: 9 SERVINGS

- 1   **fresh beef brisket (4 pounds)**
- 1¾ **cups sliced baby portobello mushrooms**
- 1   **small red onion, sliced**
- 2   **garlic cloves, minced**
- 2   **tablespoons butter**
- 1   **can (10½ ounces) condensed French onion soup**
- ¼   **cup dry white wine or beef broth**
- ½   **teaspoon coarsely ground pepper Fresh sage, optional**

1. Cut brisket in half; place in a 5-qt. slow cooker.

2. In a large saucepan, saute the mushrooms, onion and garlic in butter for 3-5 minutes or until onion is crisp-tender. Add the soup, wine and pepper; mix well.

3. Pour mushroom mixture over beef. Cover and cook on low for 8-10 hours or until meat is tender. Garnish with sage if desired.

NOTE *This is a fresh beef brisket, not corned beef.*

? Did you know?

The difference between beef brisket and corned beef is that corned beef is cured in a brine solution along with seasonings, whereas beef brisket simply refers to a cut of meat.

Slow-Cooked Lasagna

kid FRIENDLY

My scrumptious version of lasagna is made super-easy in a slow cooker. The finished dish cuts really well! I also like that it makes a smaller batch than most lasagnas.

—REBECCA O'BRYAN ALVATON, KY

PREP: 45 MIN.
COOK: 4¼ HOURS + STANDING
MAKES: 6 SERVINGS

- 1 pound ground beef
- 1 medium green pepper, chopped
- 1 medium onion, chopped
- 1 jar (24 ounces) herb and garlic pasta sauce
- 4 cups (16 ounces) shredded part-skim mozzarella cheese
- 1 carton (15 ounces) ricotta cheese
- 1 tablespoon Italian seasoning
- ½ teaspoon garlic powder
- ½ teaspoon salt
- ¼ teaspoon pepper
- 4 no-cook lasagna noodles
- 2 tablespoons shredded Parmesan cheese

1. In a large skillet, cook the beef, green pepper and onion over medium heat until meat is no longer pink; drain. Stir in pasta sauce; heat through. In a large bowl, combine the mozzarella and ricotta cheeses, Italian seasoning, garlic powder, salt and pepper.

2. Spread 1 cup meat sauce in an oval 3-qt. slow cooker. Break one lasagna noodle into three pieces. Layer 1⅓ noodles over sauce, breaking noodles to fit as necessary. Top with ⅔ cup meat sauce and 1⅓ cups cheese mixture. Repeat layers twice. Top with remaining sauce.

3. Cover and cook on low for 4-5 hours or until noodles are tender. Sprinkle with Parmesan cheese. Cover and cook 15 minutes longer. Let stand for 10 minutes before cutting.

Mexican Chicken Chili

Corn and black beans give this satisfying chili Mexican flair the whole family will love. Adjust the cayenne if you have small children or are looking for a little less zip.

—STEPHANIE RABBITT-SCHAPP

CINCINNATI, OH

PREP: 30 MIN. • **COOK:** 5 HOURS
MAKES: 6 SERVINGS

- 1 pound boneless skinless chicken breasts, cubed
- 1 tablespoon canola oil
- 2 cans (14½ ounces each) diced tomatoes, undrained
- 2 cups frozen corn
- 1 can (15 ounces) black beans, rinsed and drained
- 1 can (14½ ounces) reduced-sodium chicken broth
- 1 can (4 ounces) chopped green chilies
- 2 tablespoons chili powder
- 1 tablespoon ground cumin
- ½ teaspoon salt
- ¼ teaspoon cayenne pepper

In a small skillet, brown chicken in oil. Transfer to a 5-qt. slow cooker. Stir in the remaining ingredients. Cover and cook on low for 5-6 hours or until chicken is no longer pink.

Sweet and Savory Ribs

My husband, Randy, and I love barbecue ribs, but with our busy schedules, we rarely have time to fire up the grill. So we let the slow cooker do the work for us. By the time we get home from work, the ribs are tender, juicy and ready to devour.

—**KANDY BINGHAM** GREEN RIVER, WY

PREP: 10 MIN. • **COOK:** 8 HOURS
MAKES: 8 SERVINGS

- 1 large onion, chopped
- 4 pounds boneless country-style pork ribs
- 1 bottle (18 ounces) honey barbecue sauce
- ⅓ cup maple syrup
- ¼ cup spicy brown mustard
- ½ teaspoon salt
- ¼ teaspoon pepper

Place onion in a 5-qt. slow cooker. Top with ribs. In a small bowl, combine remaining ingredients; pour over ribs. Cook, covered, on low 8-9 hours or until meat is tender.

Reuben Brats

Sauerkraut gives these beer-simmered brats a big flavor boost, but it's the special chili sauce and melted cheese that puts them over the top. This sauce is also one to remember for burgers or chicken sandwiches.

—**ALANA SIMMONS** JOHNSTOWN, PA

PREP: 30 MIN. • **COOK:** 7¼ HOURS
MAKES: 10 SERVINGS

- 10 uncooked bratwurst links
- 3 cans (12 ounces each) light beer or nonalcoholic beer
- 1 large sweet onion, sliced
- 1 can (14 ounces) sauerkraut, rinsed and well drained
- ¾ cup mayonnaise
- ¼ cup chili sauce
- 2 tablespoons ketchup
- 1 tablespoon finely chopped onion
- 2 teaspoons sweet pickle relish
- 1 garlic clove, minced
- ⅛ teaspoon pepper
- 10 hoagie buns, split
- 10 slices Swiss cheese

1. In a large skillet, brown bratwurst in batches; drain. In a 5-qt. slow cooker, combine beer, sliced onion and sauerkraut; top with bratwurst. Cook, covered, on low 7-9 hours or until sausages are cooked through.

2. Preheat oven to 350°. In a small bowl, mix mayonnaise, chili sauce, ketchup, chopped onion, relish, garlic and pepper until blended. Spread over cut sides of buns; top with cheese, bratwurst and sauerkraut mixture. Place on an ungreased baking sheet. Bake 8-10 minutes or until cheese is melted.

My husband and I love this yummy dish! It's a breeze to prepare in the slow cooker, and it tastes just like a meal you'd have at your favorite Indian or Thai restaurant.
—**ANDI KAUFFMAN** BEAVERCREEK, OR

Coconut Curry Chicken

PREP: 20 MIN. • **COOK:** 5 HOURS
MAKES: 4 SERVINGS

- 2 medium potatoes, peeled and cubed
- 1 small onion, chopped
- 4 boneless skinless chicken breast halves (4 ounces each)
- 1 cup light coconut milk
- 4 teaspoons curry powder
- 1 garlic clove, minced
- 1 teaspoon reduced-sodium chicken bouillon granules
- ¼ teaspoon salt
- ¼ teaspoon pepper
- 2 cups hot cooked rice
- ¼ cup thinly sliced green onions
  Raisins, flaked coconut and chopped unsalted peanuts, optional

1. Place potatoes and onion in a 3- or 4-qt. slow cooker. In a large nonstick skillet coated with cooking spray, brown chicken on both sides.

2. Transfer to slow cooker. In a small bowl, combine the coconut milk, curry, garlic, bouillon, salt and pepper; pour over chicken. Cover and cook on low for 5-6 hours or until meat is tender.

3. Serve chicken and sauce with rice; sprinkle with green onions. Garnish with raisins, coconut and peanuts if desired.

Did you know?

Hominy is made by soaking corn kernels in a lye solution to remove the hull and germ. It's often used as an ingredient in soups and casseroles, but can be ground to make grits or mashed to make masa, the dough used to make tortillas.

Pork and Green Chile Stew

Tender pork, green chilies and hominy have roots in Southwestern cuisine, but they help bring the heat to the Midwest for those long winter nights. An easily adaptable recipe, this stew is ready in 4 hours if cooked on high in a slow cooker, or in about 8 hours if cooked on low.

—**PAUL SEDILLO** PLAINFIELD, IL

PREP: 40 MIN. • **COOK:** 7 HOURS
MAKES: 8 SERVINGS (2 QUARTS)

- 2 pounds boneless pork shoulder butt roast, cut into ¾-inch cubes
- 1 large onion, cut into ½-in. pieces
- 2 tablespoons canola oil
- 1 teaspoon salt
- 1 teaspoon coarsely ground pepper
- 4 large potatoes, peeled and cut into ¾-inch cubes
- 3 cups water
- 1 can (16 ounces) hominy, rinsed and drained
- 2 cans (4 ounces each) chopped green chilies
- 2 tablespoons quick-cooking tapioca
- 2 garlic cloves, minced
- ½ teaspoon dried oregano
- ½ teaspoon ground cumin
- 1 cup minced fresh cilantro
  Sour cream, optional

1. In a large skillet, brown pork and onion in oil in batches. Sprinkle with salt and pepper. Transfer to a 4-qt. slow cooker.

2. Stir in the potatoes, water, hominy, chilies, tapioca, garlic, oregano and cumin. Cover and cook on low for 7-9 hours or until meat is tender, stirring in cilantro during the last 30 minutes of cooking. Serve with sour cream if desired.

Taco Chili

Ranch dressing mix and taco seasoning give extra flavor to my chili.

—JULIE NEUHALFEN GLENWOOD, IA

PREP: 30 MIN. • **COOK:** 6 HOURS
MAKES: 11 SERVINGS (2¾ QUARTS)

- 2 pounds ground beef
- 1 can (16 ounces) kidney beans, rinsed and drained
- 1 can (15 ounces) pinto beans, rinsed and drained
- 1 can (15 ounces) black beans, rinsed and drained
- 1 can (14 ounces) hominy, rinsed and drained
- 1 can (10 ounces) diced tomatoes and green chilies, undrained
- 1 can (8 ounces) tomato sauce
- 1 small onion, chopped
- 1 envelope ranch salad dressing mix
- 1 envelope taco seasoning
- ½ teaspoon pepper
- 2 cans (14½ ounces each) diced tomatoes, undrained
- 1 can (4 ounces) chopped green chilies
  Corn chips, sour cream and shredded cheddar cheese, optional

1. In a large skillet, cook beef over medium heat until no longer pink; drain. Transfer to a 5-qt. slow cooker. Add the beans, hominy, tomatoes, tomato sauce, onion, salad dressing mix, taco seasoning and pepper.
2. In a blender, combine diced tomatoes and green chilies; cover and process until smooth. Add to the slow cooker. Cover and cook on low for 6-8 hours.
3. Serve with corn chips, sour cream and cheese if desired.

FREEZE OPTION *Freeze in a freezer container for up to 3 months. To use, thaw in the refrigerator. Transfer to a large saucepan; heat through, adding water to thin if desired.*

German-Style Beef Roast

My grandmother used to make this, and I adapted it for the slow cooker.

—LOIS STANLEY MYRTLE BEACH, SC

PREP: 10 MIN. • **COOK:** 8 HOURS
MAKES: 10 SERVINGS

- 1 boneless beef chuck roast (4 pounds), trimmed
- 1 teaspoon pepper
- 1 large onion, thinly sliced
- 1 bottle (12 ounces) beer or nonalcoholic beer
- 1 cup ketchup
- ¼ cup packed brown sugar
- ¼ cup all-purpose flour
- ¼ cup cold water

1. Cut roast in half; sprinkle with pepper. Place onion and roast in a 5-qt. slow cooker. In a small bowl, combine the beer, ketchup and brown sugar; pour over top. Cover and cook on low for 8-10 hours or until meat is tender.
2. Remove meat to a serving platter; keep warm. Skim fat from cooking juices; transfer to a small saucepan. Bring liquid to a boil.
3. Combine flour and water until smooth; gradually stir into the pan. Bring to a boil; cook and stir for 2 minutes or until thickened. Serve with roast.

top tip

What's on Tap?

I've been making the German-Style Beef Roast for years, and it's a huge hit with my family. Try it with pumpkin spice beer or an Oktoberfest to amp up the flavor. YUM!

—MSDISHTAC TASTEOFHOME.COM

Chicken and Red Potatoes

Try this juicy and tender chicken-and-potato dish with scrumptious gravy tonight. Just fix it early in the day, then forget about it until meal time.

—**MICHELE TRANTHAM** WAYNESVILLE, NC

PREP: 20 MIN. • **COOK:** 3½ HOURS
MAKES: 4 SERVINGS

- 3 tablespoons all-purpose flour
- 4 boneless skinless chicken breast halves (6 ounces each)
- 2 tablespoons olive oil
- 4 medium red potatoes, cut into wedges
- 2 cups fresh baby carrots, halved lengthwise
- 1 can (4 ounces) mushroom stems and pieces, drained
- 4 canned whole green chilies, cut into ½-inch slices
- 1 can (10¾ ounces) condensed cream of onion soup, undiluted
- ¼ cup 2% milk
- ½ teaspoon chicken seasoning
- ¼ teaspoon salt
- ¼ teaspoon dried rosemary, crushed
- ¼ teaspoon pepper

1. Place flour in a large resealable plastic bag. Add chicken, one piece at a time; shake to coat. In a large skillet, brown chicken in oil on both sides.
2. Meanwhile, place the potatoes, carrots, mushrooms and chilies in a greased 5-qt. slow cooker. In a small bowl, combine the remaining ingredients. Pour half of soup mixture over vegetables.
3. Transfer chicken to slow cooker; top with remaining soup mixture. Cover and cook on low for 3½ to 4 hours or until a thermometer reads 170°.
NOTE *This recipe was tested with McCormick's Montreal Chicken Seasoning. Look for it in the spice aisle.*

Swiss Steak Supper

Here's a satisfying dinner that's loaded with veggies. To save a step, I like to season the steak with peppered seasoned salt instead of using both seasoned salt and pepper.

—**KATHLEEN ROMANIUK** CHOMEDEY, PQ

PREP: 20 MIN. • **COOK:** 5 HOURS
MAKES: 6 SERVINGS

- 1½ pounds beef top round steak
- ½ teaspoon seasoned salt
- ¼ teaspoon coarsely ground pepper
- 1 tablespoon canola oil
- 3 medium potatoes
- 1½ cups fresh baby carrots
- 1 medium onion, sliced
- 1 can (14½ ounces) Italian diced tomatoes
- 1 jar (12 ounces) home-style beef gravy
- 1 tablespoon minced fresh parsley

1. Cut steak into six serving-size pieces; flatten to ¼-in. thickness. Rub with seasoned salt and pepper. In a large skillet, brown beef in oil on both sides; drain.
2. Cut each potato into eight wedges. In a 5-qt. slow cooker, layer the potatoes, carrots, beef and onion. Combine tomatoes and gravy; pour over the top.
3. Cover and cook on low for 5-6 hours or until meat and vegetables are tender. Sprinkle with parsley.

ULTIMATE *Comfort* **Barbecued Beef Short Ribs**

These tender slow-cooked ribs with a tangy sauce are a cinch to make. They're great for picnics and parties.

—ERIN GLASS WHITE HALL, MD

PREP: 25 MIN. • **COOK:** 4½ HOURS
MAKES: 8 SERVINGS

- 4 **pounds bone-in beef short ribs, trimmed**
- 2 **tablespoons canola oil**
- 1 **large sweet onion, halved and sliced**
- ½ **cup water**
- 1 **bottle (12 ounces) chili sauce**
- ¾ **cup plum preserves or preserves of your choice**
- 2 **tablespoons brown sugar**
- 2 **tablespoons red wine vinegar**
- 2 **tablespoons Worcestershire sauce**
- 2 **tablespoons Dijon mustard**
- ¼ **teaspoon ground cloves**

1. In a large skillet, brown ribs in oil in batches. Place onion and water in a 5-qt. slow cooker; add ribs. Cover and cook on low for 4 to 5 hours or until meat is tender.

2. In a small saucepan, combine the remaining ingredients; cook and stir until heated through.

3. Remove ribs from slow cooker. Discard cooking liquid. Return ribs to slow cooker; pour sauce over ribs. Cover and cook on high for 30 minutes or until sauce is thickened.

Veggie Meatball Soup

Loaded with veggies, meatballs and spices, this meal-in-one soup is hearty enough to warm up any cold winter day. It's a recipe you'll make again and again.

—PENNY FAGAN MOBILE, AL

PREP: 20 MIN. • **COOK:** 5½ HOURS
MAKES: 6 SERVINGS (2½ QUARTS)

- 1 **package (12 ounces) frozen fully cooked Italian meatballs**
- 1 **can (28 ounces) diced tomatoes, undrained**
- 3 **cups beef broth**
- 2 **cups shredded cabbage**
- 1 **can (16 ounces) kidney beans, rinsed and drained**
- 1 **medium zucchini, sliced**
- 1 **cup fresh green beans, cut into 1-inch pieces**
- 1 **cup water**
- 2 **medium carrots, sliced**
- 1 **teaspoon dried basil**
- ½ **teaspoon minced garlic**
- ¼ **teaspoon salt**
- ⅛ **teaspoon dried oregano**
- ⅛ **teaspoon pepper**
- 1 **cup uncooked elbow macaroni**
- ¼ **cup minced fresh parsley**
  Grated Parmesan cheese, optional

1. In a 5-qt. slow cooker, combine the first 14 ingredients. Cover and cook on low for 5-6 hours or until vegetables are almost tender.

2. Stir in macaroni and parsley; cook 30 minutes longer or until macaroni is tender. Serve with cheese if desired.

Chicken Thighs With Sausage

Whether you're serving your family or special guests, here's a delicious entree that hits the spot. Smoked turkey sausage adds an enormous amount of flavor to the chicken and veggies.

—**JOANNE IOVINO** KINGS PARK, NY

PREP: 25 MIN. • **COOK:** 6 HOURS
MAKES: 8 SERVINGS

- 2 **medium carrots, chopped**
- 2 **celery ribs, chopped**
- 1 **large onion, finely chopped**
- 8 **bone-in chicken thighs (about 3 pounds), skin removed**
- 1 **package (14 ounces) smoked turkey sausage, cut into ½-inch slices**
- ¼ **cup ketchup**
- 6 **garlic cloves, minced**
- 1 **tablespoon Louisiana-style hot sauce**
- 1 **teaspoon dried basil**
- 1 **teaspoon paprika**
- 1 **teaspoon dried thyme**
- ½ **teaspoon dried oregano**
- ½ **teaspoon pepper**
- ¼ **teaspoon ground allspice**
- 1 **teaspoon browning sauce, optional**

1. In a 4– or 5-qt. slow cooker, combine the carrots, celery and onion. Top with chicken and sausage.
2. In a small bowl, combine the ketchup, garlic, hot sauce, seasonings and, if desired, browning sauce. Spoon over meats. Cover and cook on low for 6-8 hours or until chicken is tender.

Lucky Corned Beef

It's not luck; it's just an amazing Irish recipe. With this in the slow cooker by sunrise, you can definitely fill the seats at the dinner table by sundown. Plus, this recipe makes two briskets, so you can have corned beef sandwiches the next day.

—**HEATHER PARRAZ** ROCHESTER, WA

PREP: 20 MIN. • **COOK:** 9 HOURS
MAKES: 5 SERVINGS PLUS LEFTOVERS

- 6 **medium red potatoes, quartered**
- 2 **medium carrots, cut into chunks**
- 1 **large onion, sliced**
- 2 **corned beef briskets with spice packets (3 pounds each)**
- ¼ **cup packed brown sugar**
- 2 **tablespoons sugar**
- 2 **tablespoons coriander seeds**
- 2 **tablespoons whole peppercorns**
- 4 **cups water**

1. In a 6-qt. slow cooker, combine the potatoes, carrots and onion. Add briskets (discard spice packets from corned beef or save for another use). Sprinkle the brown sugar, sugar, coriander and peppercorns over meat. Pour water over top.
2. Cover and cook on low for 9-11 hours or until meat is tender.
3. Remove meat and vegetables to a serving platter. Thinly slice one brisket across the grain and serve with vegetables. Save the remaining brisket for another use.

Spicy Chicken and Rice

As a working mom with two kids, I have little time to prepare something hearty during the week. This recipe is easily tossed together in the morning and fabulous to come home to at night. Both my picky eaters love it!

—**JESSICA COSTELLO** FITCHBURG, MA

PREP: 20 MIN. • **COOK:** 5½ HOURS
MAKES: 8 SERVINGS

- 4 **boneless skinless chicken breast halves (6 ounces each)**
- 2 **cans (14½ ounces each) diced tomatoes with mild green chilies, undrained**
- 2 **medium green peppers, chopped**
- 1 **medium onion, chopped**
- 1 **garlic clove, minced**
- 1 **teaspoon smoked paprika**
- ¾ **teaspoon salt**
- ½ **teaspoon ground cumin**
- ½ **teaspoon ground chipotle pepper**
- 6 **cups cooked brown rice**
- 1 **can (15 ounces) black beans, rinsed and drained**
- ½ **cup shredded cheddar cheese**
- ½ **cup reduced-fat sour cream**

1. Place chicken in a 4– or 5-qt. slow cooker. In a large bowl, combine the tomatoes, green peppers, onion, garlic, paprika, salt, cumin and chipotle pepper; pour over chicken. Cover and cook on low for 5-6 hours or until chicken is tender.

2. Remove chicken; cool slightly. Shred with two forks and return to the slow cooker. Stir in rice and beans; heat through. Garnish with cheese and sour cream.

ULTIMATE *Comfort* Mom's Italian Beef Sandwiches

PREP: 20 MIN. • **COOK:** 8 HOURS
MAKES: 16 SERVINGS

- 1 **boneless beef rump roast or bottom round roast (2 pounds), halved**
- 1 **boneless beef chuck roast (2 pounds), halved**
- 1 **beef sirloin tip roast (1 pound)**
- 2 **tablespoons canola oil**
- 2 **cups water**
- 1 **medium onion, chopped**
- 4 **garlic cloves, minced**
- 2 **envelopes Italian salad dressing mix**
- 1 **envelope zesty Italian salad dressing mix**
- 1 **envelope (0.87 ounce) brown gravy mix**
- 1 **to 2 tablespoons crushed red pepper flakes**
- 1 **tablespoon Italian seasoning**
- 2 **teaspoons Worcestershire sauce**
- 16 **hoagie buns, split**
  Sliced provolone cheese, optional
  Giardiniera, optional

1. In a large skillet, brown each roast in oil on all sides. Drain. Transfer meat to a 7-qt. slow cooker. Combine the water, onion, garlic, salad dressing and gravy mixes, pepper flakes, Italian seasoning and Worcestershire sauce; pour over beef. Cover and cook on low for 8-10 hours or until meat is tender.

2. Remove beef; cool slightly. Skim fat from cooking juices. Pour juices into a large bowl. Shred beef with two forks; add to bowl. Cool. Transfer to freezer containers. Freeze for up to 3 months.

TO USE FROZEN MEAT *Thaw in the refrigerator overnight. Place in a Dutch oven; heat through. Using a slotted spoon, place 1/2 cup on each bun. Top with cheese and giardiniera if desired.*

My mom made the best Italian beef. I've added to it over the years, but it's still her recipe. She made this for family reunions, and there were never leftovers. —**MARY MCVEY** COLFAX, NC

1. Place the first 12 ingredients in a large bowl; mix lightly to combine. Cut and discard tops from sweet peppers; remove seeds. Fill peppers with rice mixture.

2. In a small bowl, mix spaghetti sauce and water; pour half of the mixture into an oval 5-qt. slow cooker. Add filled peppers. Top with remaining sauce. Sprinkle with 2 tablespoons Parmesan cheese.

3. Cook, covered, on low 3½ to 4 hours or until heated through and peppers are tender. Sprinkle with remaining Parmesan cheese.

Chicken with Mushroom Gravy

A friend shared this recipe with me years ago, and I adapted it by adding a few new ingredients. I like to serve it over mashed potatoes or rice.

—**DAROLYN JONES** FISHERS, IN

PREP: 10 MIN. • **COOK:** 4¼ HOURS
MAKES: 4 SERVINGS

- 4 **boneless skinless chicken breast halves (6 ounces each)**
- 1 **can (12 ounces) mushroom gravy**
- 1 **cup 2% milk**
- 1 **can (8 ounces) mushroom stems and pieces, drained**
- 1 **can (4 ounces) chopped green chilies**
- 1 **envelope Italian salad dressing mix**
- 1 **package (8 ounces) cream cheese, cubed**

1. In a 3-qt. slow cooker, combine the chicken, gravy, milk, mushrooms, chilies and dressing mix. Cover and cook on low for 4-5 hours or until chicken is tender.

2. Stir in cream cheese; cover and cook 15 minutes longer or until cheese is melted.

Vegetarian Stuffed Peppers

These filling and flavorful peppers are an updated version of my mom's stuffed peppers, which were a favorite when I was growing up in upstate New York. Whenever I make them, I'm reminded of home.

—**MELISSA MCCABE** LONG BEACH, CA

PREP: 30 MIN. • **COOK:** 3½ HOURS
MAKES: 6 SERVINGS

- 2 **cups cooked brown rice**
- 3 **small tomatoes, chopped**
- 1 **cup frozen corn, thawed**
- 1 **small sweet onion, chopped**
- ¾ **cup cubed Monterey Jack cheese**
- 1 **can (4¼ ounces) chopped ripe olives**
- ⅓ **cup canned black beans, rinsed and drained**
- ⅓ **cup canned red beans, rinsed and drained**
- 4 **fresh basil leaves, thinly sliced**
- 3 **garlic cloves, minced**
- 1 **teaspoon salt**
- ½ **teaspoon pepper**
- 6 **large sweet peppers**
- ¾ **cup meatless spaghetti sauce**
- ½ **cup water**
- 4 **tablespoons grated Parmesan cheese, divided**

Italian Pulled Pork Sandwiches

Enjoy all the flavors of classic Italian sausage sandwiches with a healthier alternative that uses spicy and tender pulled pork instead.

—DELLARIO LIA MIDDLEPORT, NY

PREP: 20 MIN. • **COOK:** 8 HOURS
MAKES: 12 SERVINGS

- 1 tablespoon fennel seed, crushed
- 1 tablespoon steak seasoning
- 1 teaspoon cayenne pepper, optional
- 1 boneless pork shoulder butt roast (3 pounds)
- 1 tablespoon olive oil
- 2 medium green or sweet red peppers, thinly sliced
- 2 medium onions, thinly sliced
- 1 can (14½ ounces) diced tomatoes, undrained
- 12 whole wheat hamburger buns, split

1. In a small bowl, combine the fennel seed, steak seasoning and cayenne if desired. Cut roast in half. Rub seasoning mixture over pork. In a large skillet, brown roast in oil on all sides. Place in a 4– or 5-qt. slow cooker. Add the peppers, onions and tomatoes; cover and cook on low for 7-9 hours or until meat is tender.

2. Remove roast; cool slightly. Skim fat from cooking juices. Shred pork with two forks and return to slow cooker; heat through. Using a slotted spoon, place ½ cup meat mixture on each bun.

NOTE *This recipe was tested with McCormick's Montreal Steak Seasoning. Look for it in the spice aisle.*

Louisiana Red Beans and Rice

Smoked turkey sausage and red pepper flakes add zip to this saucy, slow-cooked version of the New Orleans classic. For extra heat, pass a jar of hot sauce around the table.

—**JULIA BUSHREE** GEORGETOWN, TX

PREP: 20 MIN. • **COOK:** 8 HOURS
MAKES: 8 SERVINGS

- 4 cans (16 ounces each) kidney beans, rinsed and drained
- 1 can (14½ ounces) diced tomatoes, undrained
- 1 package (14 ounces) smoked turkey sausage, sliced
- 3 celery ribs, chopped
- 1 large onion, chopped
- 1 cup chicken broth
- 1 medium green pepper, chopped
- 1 small sweet red pepper, chopped
- 6 garlic cloves, minced
- 1 bay leaf
- ½ teaspoon crushed red pepper flakes
- 2 green onions, chopped
  Hot cooked rice

1. In a 4- or 5-qt. slow cooker, combine the first 11 ingredients. Cook, covered, on low 8-10 hours or until vegetables are tender.

2. Stir before serving. Remove bay leaf. Serve with green onions and rice.

FREEZE OPTION *Discard bay leaf and freeze cooled bean mixture in freezer containers. To use, partially thaw in refrigerator overnight. Heat through in a saucepan, stirring occasionally and adding a little broth or water if necessary. Serve as directed.*

kid FRIENDLY

Home-Style Stew

My husband and I both work full time, so quick meals are important. Because this stew always tastes great, it's a regular menu item for us.

—**MARIE SHANKS** TERRE HAUTE, IN

PREP: 20 MIN. • **COOK:** 6 HOURS
MAKES: 5 SERVINGS

- 2 packages (16 ounces each) frozen vegetables for stew
- 1½ pounds beef stew meat, cut into 1-inch cubes
- 1 can (10¾ ounces) condensed cream of mushroom soup, undiluted
- 1 can (10¾ ounces) condensed tomato soup, undiluted
- 1 envelope reduced-sodium onion soup mix

1. Place vegetables in a 5-qt. slow cooker. In a large nonstick skillet coated with cooking spray, brown beef on all sides.

2. Transfer to slow cooker. Combine the remaining ingredients; pour over the top.

3. Cover and cook on low for 6-8 hours or until meat is tender.

Cola Beef Brisket

I use my slow cooker to make this fork-tender brisket; it keeps my kitchen cool during the warmer months. The leftovers are equally delicious, especially with reserved juice poured over the beef.

—**STEPHANIE STRONG** MT. JULIET, TN

PREP: 10 MIN. • **COOK:** 6 HOURS
MAKES: 7 SERVINGS (2 CUPS GRAVY)

- 1 **fresh beef brisket (3 pounds)**
- 1 **cup chili sauce**
- 1 **cup cola**
- 1 **envelope onion soup mix**
- 1 **tablespoon cornstarch**
- 1 **tablespoon cold water**

1. Cut brisket in half and place in a 5-qt. slow cooker. Combine chili sauce, cola and soup mix; pour over brisket. Cover and cook on low for 6-7 hours or until meat is tender.

2. Remove meat to a serving platter and keep warm. Skim fat from cooking juices; transfer to a small saucepan. Bring liquid to a boil.

3. Combine cornstarch and water until smooth. Gradually stir into the pan. Bring to a boil; cook and stir for 2 minutes or until thickened. Thinly slice meat across the grain; serve with gravy.

NOTE *This is a fresh beef brisket, not corned beef.*

Mac & Stew

top tip

Instead of using corn starch to thicken the Tuscan Pork Stew, I added 2 cups of low-carb dry macaroni pasta during the last 2 hours of cooking. It cooked perfectly and soaked up extra liquid.

—**BUGSYNANA** TASTEOFHOME.COM

Tuscan Pork Stew

Tender chunks of pork slowly cook in a nicely seasoned wine-infused sauce, which is the perfect consistency for serving over a bed of hot pasta.

—**PENNY HAWKINS** MEBANE, NC

PREP: 15 MIN. • **COOK:** 8½ HOURS
MAKES: 8 SERVINGS

- 1½ **pounds boneless pork loin roast, cut into 1-inch cubes**
- 2 **tablespoons olive oil**
- 2 **cans (14½ ounces each) Italian diced tomatoes, undrained**
- 2 **cups reduced-sodium chicken broth**
- 2 **cups frozen pepper stir-fry vegetable blend, thawed**
- ½ **cup dry red wine or additional reduced-sodium chicken broth**
- ¼ **cup orange marmalade**
- 2 **garlic cloves, minced**
- 1 **teaspoon dried oregano**
- ½ **teaspoon fennel seed**
- ½ **teaspoon pepper**
- ⅛ **teaspoon crushed red pepper flakes, optional**
- 2 **tablespoons cornstarch**
- 2 **tablespoons cold water**
  Hot cooked fettuccine, optional

1. In a large skillet, brown pork in oil; drain. Transfer to a 5-qt. slow cooker.

2. Stir in the tomatoes, broth, vegetable blend, wine, marmalade, garlic, oregano, fennel seed, pepper and pepper flakes if desired. Cover and cook on low for 8-10 hours or until meat is tender.

3. Combine cornstarch and water until smooth; gradually stir into stew. Cover and cook on high for 30 minutes or until thickened. Serve with fettuccine if desired.

Barbecue Meatballs

I whipped these up for my son's first birthday so I could serve something heartier alongside the cake and ice cream. They're delicious!

—**TARA REEDER** MASON, MI

PREP: 20 MIN. • **COOK:** 7 HOURS
MAKES: 6 SERVINGS

- 1 egg, beaten
- ½ cup shredded Colby-Monterey Jack cheese
- ¼ cup seasoned bread crumbs
- ¼ cup finely chopped onion
- 2 pounds ground beef

SAUCE

- 2 cups ketchup
- 2 tablespoons prepared mustard
- 1 tablespoon brown sugar
- 1 tablespoon cider vinegar
- 1 tablespoon lemon juice
- 1 tablespoon soy sauce

1. In a large bowl, combine the egg, cheese, bread crumbs and onion. Crumble beef over mixture and mix well. Shape into 1½-in. balls. Transfer to a 3-qt. slow cooker.

2. In a small bowl, combine the sauce ingredients; pour over meatballs. Cover and cook on low for 7-8 hours or until meat is no longer pink.

Slow-Cooked Lemon Chicken

A hint of lemon and fresh parsley brighten up everyday chicken. This is the perfect mid-winter recipe when you need a taste of spring.

—**WALTER POWELL** WILMINGTON, DE

PREP: 20 MIN. • **COOK:** 5¼ HOURS
MAKES: 6 SERVINGS

- 6 bone-in chicken breast halves (12 ounces each), skin removed
- 1 teaspoon dried oregano
- ½ teaspoon seasoned salt
- ¼ teaspoon pepper
- 2 tablespoons butter
- ¼ cup water
- 3 tablespoons lemon juice
- 2 garlic cloves, minced
- 1 teaspoon chicken bouillon granules
- 2 teaspoons minced fresh parsley
  Hot cooked rice

1. Pat chicken dry with paper towels. Combine the oregano, seasoned salt and pepper; rub over chicken. In a skillet over medium heat, brown the chicken in butter; transfer to a 5-qt. slow cooker. Add water, lemon juice, garlic and bouillon to the skillet; bring to a boil, stirring to loosen browned bits. Pour over chicken.

2. Cover and cook on low for 5-6 hours. Baste the chicken. Add parsley. Cover and cook 15-30 minutes longer or until meat juices run clear. If desired, remove chicken to a platter and keep warm; thicken cooking juices. Serve over chicken and rice.

Chicago-Style Beef Sandwiches

I'm originally from the Windy City, so I love Chicago-style beef. These delicious sandwiches have an authentic flavor, and they're too easy not to make.

—**LOIS SZYDLOWSKI** TAMPA, FL

PREP: 30 MIN. • **COOK:** 8 HOURS
MAKES: 12 SERVINGS

- 1 boneless beef chuck roast (4 pounds)
- 1 teaspoon salt
- ¾ teaspoon pepper
- 2 tablespoons olive oil
- ½ pound fresh mushrooms
- 2 medium carrots, cut into chunks
- 1 medium onion, cut into wedges
- 6 garlic cloves, halved
- 2 teaspoons dried oregano
- 1 carton (32 ounces) beef broth
- 1 tablespoon beef base
- 12 Italian rolls, split
- 1 jar (16 ounces) giardiniera, drained

1. Cut roast in half; sprinkle with salt and pepper. In a large skillet, brown meat in oil on all sides. Transfer to a 5-qt. slow cooker.

2. In a food processor, combine the mushrooms, carrots, onion, garlic and oregano. Cover and process until finely chopped. Transfer to slow cooker. Combine beef broth and base; pour over top. Cover and cook on low for 8-10 hours or until tender.

3. Remove meat and shred with two forks. Skim fat from cooking juices. Return meat to slow cooker; heat through. Using a slotted spoon, serve beef on buns; top with giardiniera.

NOTE Look for beef base near the broth and bouillon.

Red Clam Sauce

This luscious sauce tastes like you've worked on it all day. Instead, it cooks hands-free while you do other things. What a great way to change up pasta.

—**JOANN BROWN** LATROBE, PA

PREP: 25 MIN. • **COOK:** 3 HOURS
MAKES: 4 SERVINGS

- 1 medium onion, chopped
- 1 tablespoon canola oil
- 2 garlic cloves, minced
- 2 cans (6½ ounces each) chopped clams, undrained
- 1 can (14½ ounces) diced tomatoes, undrained
- 1 can (6 ounces) tomato paste
- ¼ cup minced fresh parsley
- 1 bay leaf
- 1 teaspoon sugar
- 1 teaspoon dried basil
- ½ teaspoon dried thyme
- 6 ounces linguine, cooked and drained

1. In a small skillet, saute onion in oil until tender. Add garlic; cook 1 minute longer.

2. Transfer to a 1½- or 2-qt. slow cooker. Stir in the clams, tomatoes, tomato paste, parsley, bay leaf, sugar, basil and thyme.

3. Cover and cook on low for 3-4 hours or until heated through. Discard bay leaf. Serve with linguine.

FREEZE OPTION *Cool before placing in a freezer container. Cover and freeze for up to 3 months. To use, thaw in the refrigerator overnight. Place in a large saucepan; heat through, stirring occasionally. Serve with linguine.*

I use my slow cooker to whip up a hearty pasta specialty. It's packed with turkey sausage, beans and veggies. My family inhales it without even realizing it's healthy. —SARA BOWEN UPLAND, CA

Sausage Pasta Stew

Kid FRIENDLY

PREP: 20 MIN. • **COOK:** 7¼ HOURS
MAKES: 8 SERVINGS

- 1 pound turkey Italian sausage links, casings removed
- 4 cups water
- 1 jar (24 ounces) meatless spaghetti sauce
- 1 can (16 ounces) kidney beans, rinsed and drained
- 1 medium yellow summer squash, halved lengthwise and cut into 1-inch pieces
- 2 medium carrots, sliced
- 1 medium sweet red or green pepper, diced
- ⅓ cup chopped onion
- 1½ cups uncooked spiral pasta
- 1 cup frozen peas
- 1 teaspoon sugar
- ½ teaspoon salt
- ¼ teaspoon pepper

1. In a nonstick skillet, cook sausage over medium heat until no longer pink; drain and place in a 5-qt. slow cooker. Stir in the water, spaghetti sauce, beans, summer squash, carrots, red pepper and onion.

2. Cover and cook on low for 7-9 hours or until vegetables are tender.

3. Stir in the pasta, peas, sugar, salt and pepper. Cover and cook on high for 15-20 minutes or until pasta is tender.

Did you know?

Rotini's spiral shape helps the pasta hold bits of meat, vegetables and cheese. That's what makes it an optimal choice for a hearty, chunky stew. Plus, kids love its twisted shape.

Pork Roast with Mashed Potatoes and Gravy

This home-style meal can be made ahead of time and reheated. Simply strain and skim the cooking juices and cover and store in the fridge. Then finish the gravy in a pan just before serving.

—LEE BREMSON KANSAS CITY, MO

PREP: 20 MIN. • **COOK:** 3 HOURS + STANDING
MAKES: 4 SERVINGS

- 1 boneless whole pork loin roast (3 to 4 pounds)
- 1 can (14½ ounces) chicken broth
- 1 cup julienned sweet red pepper
- ½ cup chopped onion
- ¼ cup cider vinegar
- 2 tablespoons Worcestershire sauce
- 1 tablespoon brown sugar
- 2 teaspoons Italian seasoning
- 1 teaspoon salt
- 1 teaspoon pepper
- 2 teaspoons cornstarch
- 2 teaspoons cold water
- 2 cups refrigerated mashed potatoes

1. Cut roast in half; transfer to a 5-qt. slow cooker. In a small bowl, combine the broth, red pepper, onion, vinegar, Worcestershire sauce, brown sugar and seasonings; pour over pork. Cover and cook on low for 3-4 hours or until meat is tender.

2. Remove pork; cut some into cubes measuring 2½ cups and save for another use. (Keep remaining pork warm.)

3. For gravy, strain cooking juices and skim fat; pour 1 cup into a small saucepan. Combine cornstarch and water until smooth; stir into cooking juices. Bring to a boil; cook and stir for 2 minutes or until thickened.

4. Meanwhile, in a small microwave-safe bowl, cook potatoes on high for 2-3 minutes or until heated through. Let meat stand for 10 minutes before slicing; serve with potatoes and gravy.
NOTE *This recipe was tested in a 1,100-watt microwave.*

2. Discard spice bag. Remove chicken cool slightly. Stir linguine into soup; cover and cook on high for 30 minutes or until tender. Cut chicken into piece and return to soup; heat through.

Fiesta Beef Bowls

This easy entree will knock your socks off. Zesty ingredients turn round steak into a phenomenal meal-in-one.

—**DEBORAH LINN** VALDEZ, AK

PREP: 25 MIN. • **COOK:** 8½ HOURS
MAKES: 6 SERVINGS

- 1½ **pounds boneless beef top round steak**
- 1 **can (10 ounces) diced tomatoes and green chilies**
- 1 **medium onion, chopped**
- 2 **garlic cloves, minced**
- 1 **teaspoon dried oregano**
- 1 **teaspoon chili powder**
- 1 **teaspoon ground cumin**
- ¼ **teaspoon salt**
- ¼ **teaspoon pepper**
- 2 **cans (15 ounces each) pinto beans rinsed and drained**
- 3 **cups hot cooked rice**
- ½ **cup shredded cheddar cheese**
- 6 **tablespoons sliced ripe olives**
- 6 **tablespoons thinly sliced green onions**
- 6 **tablespoons guacamole**

1. Place round steak in a 3-qt. slow cooker. In a small bowl, combine the tomatoes, onion, garlic and seasonings pour over steak. Cover and cook on low for 8-9 hours or until meat is tender.
2. Remove meat from slow cooker. Add beans to tomato mixture. Cover and cook on high for 30 minutes or until beans are heated through. When cool enough to handle, slice meat. In individual bowls, layer the rice, meat and bean mixture. Top with cheese, olives, onions and guacamole.

ULTIMATE *Comfort* **Slow-Cooked Chicken Noodle Soup**

This satisfying homemade soup with a hint of cayenne is brimming with vegetables, chicken and noodles. The recipe came from my father-in-law, but I made some adjustments to give it my own spin.

—**NORMA REYNOLDS** OVERLAND PARK, KS

PREP: 20 MIN. • **COOK:** 5½ HOURS
MAKES: 12 SERVINGS (3 QUARTS)

- 12 **fresh baby carrots, cut into ½-inch pieces**
- 4 **celery ribs, cut into ½-inch pieces**
- ¾ **cup finely chopped onion**
- 1 **tablespoon minced fresh parsley**
- ½ **teaspoon pepper**
- ¼ **teaspoon cayenne pepper**
- 1½ **teaspoons mustard seed**
- 2 **garlic cloves, peeled and halved**
- 1¼ **pounds boneless skinless chicken breast halves**
- 1¼ **pounds boneless skinless chicken thighs**
- 4 **cans (14½ ounces each) chicken broth**
- 1 **package (9 ounces) refrigerated linguine**

1. In a 5-qt. slow cooker, combine the first six ingredients. Place mustard seed and garlic on a double thickness of cheesecloth; bring up corners of cloth and tie with kitchen string to form a bag. Place in slow cooker. Add chicken and broth. Cover and cook on low for 5-6 hours or until meat is tender.

Side Dishes

WITH MORE THAN 50 BOLD WAYS TO ROUND OUT A MEAL,
IT WOULD BE A SHAME TO SETTLE FOR THE SAME OLD SIDE.

**MOM'S
FRIED RICE**
PAGE 188

**BAKED POTATO
CHEDDAR SOUP**
PAGE 195

**SPIRAL
PASTA SALAD**
PAGE 211

Bacon & Egg Potato Salad

Vinegar and lemon juice add a slightly tangy taste to this creamy potato salad. I think it is wonderful served with baked beans and barbecue.

—MELISSA DAVIES CLERMONT, FL

PREP: 15 MIN. • **COOK:** 25 MIN. + CHILLING
MAKES: 8 SERVINGS

- 6 **cups cubed red potatoes (about 2½ pounds)**
- 4 **hard-cooked eggs, sliced**
- 1 **small onion, chopped**
- 4 **bacon strips, cooked and crumbled**
- 1 **tablespoon minced fresh parsley**
- 1 **cup mayonnaise**
- 2 **tablespoons dill pickle relish**
- 3 **to 5 teaspoons prepared mustard**
- 1 **tablespoon white vinegar**
- 1 **tablespoon lemon juice**
- ½ **teaspoon salt**
- ½ **teaspoon celery seed**
- ½ **teaspoon dill weed**
- ½ **teaspoon pepper**

1. Place potatoes in a Dutch oven; cover with water. Bring to a boil. Reduce heat; cover and cook for 10-15 minutes or until tender. Drain and cool.

2. Place potatoes in a large bowl. Add the eggs, onion, bacon and parsley. In a small bowl, combine the mayonnaise, relish, mustard, vinegar, lemon juice and seasonings. Pour over potato mixture and toss gently to coat. Refrigerate until chilled.

Did you know?

Some of the earliest recipes for potato salad involve boiling the potatoes in wine or a mixture of vinegar and herbs.

Steakhouse Mushrooms

I got this recipe from a friend back when we were in nursing school. Whenever my husband is cooking meat on the grill, you can bet I'll be in the kitchen preparing these mushrooms.

—KENDA BURGETT RATTAN, OK

START TO FINISH: 20 MIN.
MAKES: 4 SERVINGS

- ¼ **cup butter, cubed**
- 1 **pound medium fresh mushrooms**
- 2 **teaspoons dried basil**
- ½ **teaspoon dried oregano**
- ½ **teaspoon seasoned salt**
- ¼ **teaspoon garlic powder**
- 1 **teaspoon browning sauce, optional**

In a large skillet, heat butter over medium-high heat. Add mushrooms; cook and stir until tender. Stir in seasonings and, if desired, browning sauce. Reduce heat to medium; cook, covered, for 3-5 minutes to allow flavors to blend.

Cheese Fries

kid FRIENDLY

I came up with this recipe after my daughter had cheese fries at a restaurant and couldn't stop talking about them. She loves that I can fix them so quickly at home.

—MELISSA TATUM GREENSBORO, NC

START TO FINISH: 20 MIN.
MAKES: 8-10 SERVINGS

- 1 **package (28 ounces) frozen steak fries**
- 1 **can (10¾ ounces) condensed cheddar cheese soup, undiluted**
- ¼ **cup 2% milk**
- ½ **teaspoon garlic powder**
- ¼ **teaspoon onion powder**
  Paprika

1. Arrange the steak fries in a single layer in two greased 15x10x1-in. baking pans. Bake at 450° for 15-18 minutes or until tender and golden brown.
2. Meanwhile, in a small saucepan, combine the soup, milk, garlic powder and onion powder; heat through. Drizzle over fries; sprinkle with paprika.

French Onion Soup

I like to serve up steaming bowlfuls of this all-time favorite. My version has a slightly sweet flavor that makes it unique.

—LISE THOMSON MAGRATH, AB

PREP: 30 MIN. • **COOK:** 30 MIN.
MAKES: 8 SERVINGS (2 QUARTS)

- 6 **cups thinly sliced onions**
- 1 **tablespoon sugar**
- ½ **teaspoon pepper**
- ⅓ **cup canola oil**
- 6 **cups beef broth**
- 8 **slices French bread (¾ inch thick), toasted**
- ½ **cup shredded Parmesan or Swiss cheese**

1. In a Dutch oven, saute the onions, sugar and pepper in oil until onions are softened. Reduce heat to medium-low; cook, stirring occasionally, for 30 minutes or until onions are a deep golden brown. Add broth; bring to a boil. Reduce heat; cover and simmer for 30 minutes.
2. Ladle soup into ovenproof bowls. Top each with a slice of French bread; sprinkle with cheese. Broil 4-6 in. from heat until cheese is melted. Serve immediately.

BLT Salad

This simple pasta salad is great for gatherings and a favorite of everyone who tries it. I like to keep the ingredients in separate containers in the fridge, and then toss them together for one or more servings whenever needed.

—MARY SIGFUSSON MANKATO, MN

PREP: 25 MIN. + CHILLING
MAKES: 6 SERVINGS

- 2 cups uncooked spiral pasta
- 1 package (1 pound) sliced bacon, chopped
- 1 large tomato, seeded and chopped
- ½ cup ranch salad dressing
- 3 cups torn romaine

1. Cook pasta according to package directions. Meanwhile, in a large skillet, cook bacon over medium heat until crisp. Remove to paper towels with a slotted spoon to drain.
2. Drain pasta and rinse in cold water; place in a large bowl. Add the bacon, tomato and dressing. Toss to coat. Refrigerate until serving.
3. Just before serving, add romaine and toss to coat.

ULTIMATE *Comfort* Summer Vegetable Cobbler

PREP: 40 MIN. • **BAKE:** 25 MIN.
MAKES: 4 SERVINGS

- 2 tablespoons butter
- 3 small zucchini, sliced
- 1 small sweet red pepper, finely chopped
- 1 small onion, finely chopped
- 2 garlic cloves, minced
- 2 tablespoons all-purpose flour
- 1 cup 2% milk
- ½ teaspoon salt
- ¼ teaspoon pepper

BISCUIT TOPPING

- 1 cup all-purpose flour
- 1 teaspoon baking powder
- ½ teaspoon salt
- 3 tablespoons cold butter
- ¼ cup shredded Parmesan cheese
- 3 tablespoons minced fresh basil
- ⅔ cup 2% milk

1. Preheat oven to 400°. In a large skillet, heat butter over medium-high heat. Add zucchini, red pepper and onion; cook and stir 10-12 minutes or until zucchini is crisp-tender. Add garlic; cook 1 minute longer.
2. In a small bowl, whisk flour, milk, salt and pepper; stir into vegetables. Bring to a boil, stirring constantly; cook and stir 2-3 minutes or until sauce is thickened. Spoon into a greased 8-in.-square baking dish.
3. For topping, in a small bowl, whisk flour, baking powder and salt. Cut in butter until mixture resembles coarse crumbs. Stir in cheese and basil. Add milk; stir just until moistened. Drop by rounded tablespoonfuls over filling. Bake 25-30 minutes or until filling is bubbly and biscuits are golden brown.

Here's a comforting vegetarian dish that uses a lot of garden produce. Try different squashes like pattypan and crookneck or zucchini.

—ELISABETH LARSEN PLEASANT GROVE, UT

Favorite Broccoli Salad

People always enjoy this salad whenever I take it to a church dinner. Although I use many other salad recipes, I'm especially fond of this one.

—ESTHER SHANK HARRISONBURG, VA

START TO FINISH: 20 MIN.
MAKES: 6-8 SERVINGS

- 1 bunch broccoli, separated into florets
- 1 head cauliflower, separated into florets
- 8 bacon strips, cooked and crumbled
- 1 cup chopped seeded tomatoes
- ⅓ cup chopped onion
- 2 hard-cooked eggs, sliced
- 1 cup mayonnaise
- ⅓ cup sugar
- 2 tablespoons cider vinegar

1. In a large salad bowl, combine the broccoli, cauliflower, bacon, tomatoes, onion and eggs; set aside.
2. In another bowl, combine the mayonnaise, sugar and vinegar. Just before serving, pour dressing over salad and toss to coat.

kid FRIENDLY Zucchini Fries for 2

I often make these fries for my husband and myself—especially when our garden is full of zucchini. Kids dig them when they're served with marinara or pizza sauce.

—SARAH GOTTSCHALK RICHMOND, IN

START TO FINISH: 30 MIN.
MAKES: 2 SERVINGS

- 2 small zucchini
- 1 egg white
- ¼ cup all-purpose flour
- 3 tablespoons cornmeal
- ½ teaspoon each salt, garlic powder, chili powder, paprika and pepper
  Cooking spray
  Marinara or spaghetti sauce, warmed

1. Cut zucchini into 3-in. x ½-in. x ½-in. pieces. In a shallow bowl, whisk egg white. In another shallow bowl, combine the flour, cornmeal and seasonings. Dip zucchini in egg white, then roll in flour mixture.
2. Place zucchini on a baking sheet coated with cooking spray; spray with additional cooking spray. Bake at 425° for 18-22 minutes or until golden brown, turning once. Serve with marinara sauce.

top tip — Customize Your Fries

These fries are delicious. I used ¼ teaspoon cayenne pepper instead of chili powder, a whole egg, and I dipped them in ranch dressing. I love that they're baked and not fried.

—JAGS58 TASTEOFHOME.COM

Seven-Layer Gelatin Salad

My mother makes this salad for Christmas dinner each year. You can use gelatin flavors to make color combinations for specific holidays or other gatherings.

—**JAN HEMNESS** STOCKTON, MO

PREP: 30 MIN. + CHILLING
MAKES: 15-20 SERVINGS

- 7 packages (3 ounces each) assorted flavored gelatin
- 4½ cups boiling water, divided
- 4½ cups cold water, divided
- 1 can (12 ounces) evaporated milk, divided
- 1 carton (8 ounces) frozen whipped topping, thawed
  Fresh mint, sliced strawberries and kiwifruit, optional

1. In a small bowl, dissolve one package of gelatin in ¾ cup boiling water. Add ¾ cup cold water; stir. Spoon into a 13-in. x 9-in. dish coated with cooking spray. Chill until set but not firm, about 40 minutes.
2. In another bowl, dissolve another package of gelatin in ½ cup boiling water. Add ½ cup cold water and ½ cup milk; stir. Spoon over the first layer. Chill until set but not firm, about 40 minutes.
3. Repeat five times, alternating plain gelatin layers with creamy gelatin layers. Chill each layer until set but not firm before spooning next layer on top. Refrigerate entire salad overnight. Just before serving, spread top with whipped topping. Cut into squares to serve. Garnish with mint and fruit if desired.
NOTE *This recipe takes time to prepare since each layer must be set before the next layer is added.*

Creamed Corn with Bacon

My family is absolutely addicted to this yummy, crunchy side. I like to make it in the summer with farm-fresh corn.

—**TINA REPAK MIRILOVICH** JOHNSTOWN, PA

START TO FINISH: 25 MIN.
MAKES: 6 SERVINGS

- 1 small onion, finely chopped
- 1 tablespoon butter
- 4 cups fresh or frozen corn, thawed
- 1 cup heavy whipping cream
- ¼ cup chicken broth
- 4 bacon strips, cooked and crumbled
- ¼ teaspoon pepper
- ¼ cup grated Parmesan cheese
- 2 tablespoons minced fresh parsley

1. In a large skillet, saute onion in butter for 3 minutes. Add corn; saute 1-2 minutes longer or until onion and corn are tender.
2. Stir in the cream, broth, bacon and pepper. Cook and stir for 5-7 minutes or until slightly thickened. Stir in cheese and parsley.

Mom's Fried Rice

I sometimes add pea pods for more color and crunch. Or if you want to turn this into a main dish, you can add chopped shrimp, chicken or steak. It always turns out great.

—CAREY HUNT PORTLAND, OR

START TO FINISH: 25 MIN.
MAKES: 4 SERVINGS

- 1 teaspoon canola oil
- 1 egg, beaten
- 8 bacon strips, chopped
- 1 cup chopped fresh mushrooms
- 8 green onions, thinly sliced
- 3 cups leftover cooked rice
- 1 cup bean sprouts
- 1 cup frozen peas, thawed
- ¼ cup reduced-sodium soy sauce

1. In a large skillet, heat oil over medium-high heat. Pour egg into the pan. As egg sets, lift edges, letting uncooked portion flow underneath. When egg is completely cooked, remove to a plate. Set aside.

2. In the same skillet, cook bacon over medium heat until crisp. Using a slotted spoon, remove to paper towels; drain, reserving 2 tablespoons drippings. Saute mushrooms and onions in the drippings. Stir in the rice, bean sprouts, peas, soy sauce and bacon. Chop egg into small pieces; stir into the pan and heat through.

Fourth of July Bean Casserole

The outstanding barbecue taste of these beans makes them a favorite for cookouts all summer and into the fall. It's a popular dish with everyone, even kids. Mixing in beef with the beans is so much better than plain pork and beans.

—DONNA FANCHER LAWRENCE, IN

PREP: 20 MIN. • **BAKE:** 1 HOUR
MAKES: 12 SERVINGS

- ½ pound bacon strips, diced
- ½ pound ground beef
- 1 cup chopped onion
- 1 can (28 ounces) pork and beans
- 1 can (16 ounces) kidney beans, rinsed and drained
- 1 can (15¼ ounces) lima beans
- ½ cup barbecue sauce
- ½ cup ketchup
- ½ cup sugar
- ½ cup packed brown sugar
- 2 tablespoons prepared mustard
- 2 tablespoons molasses
- 1 teaspoon salt
- ½ teaspoon chili powder

1. In a large skillet, cook bacon, beef and onion until meat is no longer pink; drain.

2. Transfer to a greased 2½-qt. baking dish; add all of the beans and mix well. In a small bowl, combine the remaining ingredients; stir into beef and bean mixture.

3. Cover and bake at 350° for 45 minutes. Uncover; bake 15 minutes longer.

Glazed Acorn Squash

With brown sugar, butter and honey, what's not to love about this sweet and yummy side dish? It's ready in no time from the microwave.

—KARA DE LA VEGA SANTA ROSA, CA

START TO FINISH: 20 MIN.
MAKES: 4 SERVINGS

- 2 **medium acorn squash**
- ¼ **cup packed brown sugar**
- 2 **tablespoons butter**
- 4 **teaspoons honey**
- ¼ **teaspoon salt**
- ¼ **teaspoon pepper**

1. Cut squash in half; discard seeds. Place squash cut side down in a microwave-safe dish. Cover and microwave on high for 10-12 minutes or until tender.

2. Turn squash cut side up. Fill centers of squash with brown sugar, butter and honey; sprinkle with salt and pepper. Cover and microwave on high for 2-3 minutes or until heated through.

NOTE *This recipe was tested in a 1,100-watt microwave.*

Sweet Potato Fries

Sweet potatoes lend a different flavor to these extra-crunchy fries. With the tasty chutney dip, this dish could double as a party appetizer.

—KELLY MCWHERTER HOUSTON, TX

PREP: 15 MIN. • **BAKE:** 25 MIN.
MAKES: 2 SERVINGS

- 2 **tablespoons beaten egg**
- 1 **tablespoon water**
- ⅓ **cup dry bread crumbs**
- 2 **tablespoons grated Parmesan cheese**
- ¼ **teaspoon cayenne pepper**
- ¼ **teaspoon pepper**
- 1 **large sweet potato (14 ounces), peeled**
- 2 **teaspoons olive oil**

MANGO CHUTNEY MAYONNAISE

- ¼ **cup mayonnaise**
- 2 **tablespoons mango chutney**
- ¼ **teaspoon curry powder**
  Dash salt
- 2 **teaspoons minced fresh parsley, optional**

1. In a shallow bowl, whisk egg and water. In a resealable plastic bag, combine the bread crumbs, cheese, cayenne and pepper. Cut sweet potato into ¼-in. strips. Add to egg mixture, a few at a time, and toss to coat. Add to the crumb mixture, a few at a time; seal bag and shake to coat.

2. Arrange potato strips in a single layer on a baking sheet coated with cooking spray; drizzle with oil. Bake at 450° for 25-30 minutes or until golden brown and crisp, turning occasionally.

3. In a small bowl, combine the mayonnaise, chutney, curry powder and salt. If desired, sprinkle parsley over fries. Serve with mango chutney mayonnaise.

kid FRIENDLY Creamy Parmesan Penne

Great for serving with chicken, this simple yet flavor-packed pasta recipe makes a single serving for a quick and easy side.

—**WENDY NUIS** STOKES BAY, ON

START TO FINISH: 25 MIN.
MAKES: 1 SERVING.

- ½ cup uncooked penne pasta
- 2 teaspoons all-purpose flour
- ¾ teaspoon chicken bouillon granules
- ¼ teaspoon garlic powder
- ¼ teaspoon dried parsley flakes
- Dash dried oregano
- Dash pepper
- 2 small fresh mushrooms, chopped
- 2 tablespoons chopped onion
- 1½ teaspoons diced sweet red pepper
- 1½ teaspoons olive oil
- ⅓ cup 2% milk
- 2 tablespoons shredded Parmesan cheese

1. Cook pasta according to package directions. Meanwhile, in a small bowl, combine the flour, bouillon, garlic powder, parsley, oregano and pepper.
2. In a small nonstick skillet, saute the mushrooms, onion and red pepper in oil until tender. Stir in flour mixture. Gradually add milk. Bring to a boil; cook and stir for 2 minutes or until thickened. Stir in Parmesan cheese. Drain pasta; add to mushroom mixture and stir to coat.

Ham and Bean Soup

I learned to make this soup when we lived in Pennsylvania near several Amish families. It's a great way to use up ham and mashed potatoes. It freezes well, too.

—**AMANDA REED** MILFORD, DE

PREP: 30 MIN. + SOAKING • **COOK:** 1½ HOURS
MAKES: 15 SERVINGS (3¾ QUARTS)

- 1 pound dried navy beans
- 2 medium onions, chopped
- 2 teaspoons canola oil
- 2 celery ribs, chopped
- 10 cups water
- 4 cups cubed fully cooked ham
- 1 cup mashed potatoes (without added milk and butter)
- ½ cup shredded carrot
- 2 tablespoons Worcestershire sauce
- 1 teaspoon salt
- ½ teaspoon dried thyme
- ½ teaspoon pepper
- 2 bay leaves
- 1 meaty ham bone or 2 smoked ham hocks
- ¼ cup minced fresh parsley

1. Place beans in a Dutch oven; add water to cover by 2 in. Bring to a boil; boil for 2 minutes. Remove from the heat; cover and let stand for 1 to 4 hours or until beans are softened. Drain and rinse beans, discarding liquid.
2. In the same pan, saute onions in oil for 2 minutes. Add celery; cook until tender. Stir in the beans, water, ham, potatoes, carrot, Worcestershire sauce, salt, thyme, pepper and bay leaves. Add ham bone. Bring to a boil. Reduce heat; cover and simmer for 1¼ to 1½ hours or until beans are tender.
3. Discard bay leaves. Remove ham bone; and set aside until cool enough to handle. Remove ham from bone and cut into cubes. Discard bone. Return ham to soup; heat through. Garnish soup with parsley.

Roasted Tomato Soup with Fresh Basil

Roasting the tomatoes first gives this soup a dimension of flavor that will have everyone saying mmm! I like to top it with fresh basil and croutons.

—MARIE FORTE RARITAN, NJ

PREP: 40 MIN. • **COOK:** 25 MIN.
MAKES: 6 SERVINGS

- 3½ pounds tomatoes (about 11 medium), halved
- 1 small onion, quartered
- 2 garlic cloves, peeled and halved
- 2 tablespoons olive oil
- 2 tablespoons fresh thyme leaves
- 1 teaspoon salt
- ¼ teaspoon pepper
- 12 fresh basil leaves
  Salad croutons, optional
  Julienned fresh basil, optional

1. Preheat oven to 400°. Place tomatoes, onion and garlic in a greased 15x10x1-in. baking pan; drizzle with oil. Sprinkle with thyme, salt and pepper; toss to coat. Roast 25-30 minutes or until tender, stirring once. Cool slightly.

2. Process tomato mixture and basil leaves in batches in a blender until smooth. Transfer to a large saucepan; heat through. If desired, top with croutons and julienned basil.

? Did you know?

Roasting tomatoes enhances the amount of cancer-fighting lycopene that can be absorbed by the body.

Toasted almonds add crunch to this timeless treatment for fresh beans. They get extra flavor from onion soup mix and Parmesan cheese.
—**EDNA HOFFMAN** HEBRON, IN

Buttery Almond Green Beans

START TO FINISH: 30 MIN.
MAKES: 8 SERVINGS

- 2 **pounds fresh green beans, trimmed**
- 2 **cups water**
- 1 **envelope onion soup mix**
- ⅔ **cup slivered almonds, toasted**
- 2 **tablespoons grated Parmesan cheese**
- 1 **teaspoon paprika**
- 6 **tablespoons butter, melted**

1. In a large saucepan, combine the beans, water and soup mix. Bring to a boil. Reduce heat; cover and simmer for 15-20 minutes or until beans are crisp-tender.

2. In a small bowl, combine the almonds, cheese and paprika. Drain beans; drizzle with butter and sprinkle with almond mixture. Toss to coat.

ULTIMATE *Comfort* Fried Green Tomatoes

These lightly battered plump tomato slices are gently fried before being baked to give them a crispy coating. I like to serve them with my homemade salsa.

—**INGRID PARKER** HATTIESBURG, MS

PREP: 30 MIN. • **COOK:** 25 MIN.
MAKES: 6 SERVINGS

- ½ **cup all-purpose flour**
- 1 **teaspoon sugar**
- 1 **teaspoon salt**
- ¾ **teaspoon cayenne pepper**
- 1 **egg**
- 1 **tablespoon fat-free milk**
- 1 **cup cornflake crumbs**
- 4 **medium green tomatoes, cut into ½-inch slices**
- ¼ **cup canola oil**

FRESH TOMATO SALSA

- 5 **medium red tomatoes, seeded and chopped**
- ½ **cup minced fresh cilantro**
- ¼ **cup chopped onion**
- 2 **jalapeno peppers, seeded and chopped**
- 4½ **teaspoons lime juice**
- 2 **teaspoons sugar**
- 1 **garlic clove, minced**
- ¼ **teaspoon salt**
- ¼ **teaspoon pepper**

1. In a shallow bowl, combine the flour, sugar, salt and cayenne. In another shallow bowl, beat egg and milk. Place cornflake crumbs in a third bowl. Pat green tomato slices dry. Coat with flour mixture, dip into egg

mixture, then coat with crumbs.

2. In a large nonstick skillet, heat 4 teaspoons oil over medium heat. Fry tomato slices, four at a time, for 3-4 minutes on each side or until golden brown, adding more oil as needed. Drain on paper towels.

3. Place fried tomatoes on an ungreased baking sheet. Bake at 375° for 4-5 minutes or until tender. Meanwhile, in a large bowl, combine salsa ingredients. Serve with the fried tomatoes.

NOTE *Wear disposable gloves when cutting hot peppers; the oils can burn skin. Avoid touching your face.*

ULTIMATE *Comfort* Twice-Baked Mashed Potatoes

Dress up an all-time favorite comfort food with savory fixings. This is an easy recipe that delivers big flavor. Better still, you can effortlessly double or triple it for a crowd.

—ANNA MAYER FORT BRANCH, IN

PREP: 30 MIN. • **BAKE:** 30 MIN.
MAKES: 6 SERVINGS

- 2½ **pounds medium potatoes, peeled**
- 1 **cup (8 ounces) sour cream**
- ¼ **cup milk**
- 2 **tablespoons butter, melted**
- 1½ **cups (6 ounces) shredded cheddar cheese, divided**
- ½ **cup chopped onion**
- 5 **bacon strips, cooked and crumbled**
- ½ **teaspoon salt**
- ⅛ **teaspoon pepper**

1. Place potatoes in a large saucepan and cover with water. Bring to a boil. Reduce heat; cover and cook for 15-20 minutes or until tender. Drain.
2. In a large bowl, mash potatoes. Add the sour cream, milk, butter and 1 cup cheese. Stir in the onion, bacon, salt and pepper. Spoon into a greased 2-qt. baking dish. Sprinkle with remaining cheese.
3. Bake, uncovered, at 350° for 30-35 minutes or until heated though.

Garlic Corn on the Cob

Every summer we look forward to fresh corn on the cob. The garlic-oil really makes the flavor of corn pop.

—HEATHER CARROLL

COLORADO SPRINGS, CO

START TO FINISH: 15 MIN.
MAKES: 4 SERVINGS

- 4 **garlic cloves, minced**
- 4 **teaspoons olive oil**
- 4 **medium ears sweet corn, husks removed**
- 1 **teaspoon sugar**

1. In a small bowl, combine garlic and oil; brush over corn. Sprinkle with sugar. Place each on a double thickness of heavy-duty foil (about 14 in. x 12. in.). Fold foil over corn and seal tightly.
2. Grill corn, covered, over medium heat for 10-15 minutes or until tender, turning occasionally. Open foil carefully to allow steam to escape.

Cauliflower Au Gratin

A lighter version of a classic white sauce coats this cauliflower. But in the end, it turns out thick and creamy with a golden brown top layer—and it tastes as comforting as it sounds.
—**TASTE OF HOME TEST KITCHEN**

PREP: 30 MIN. • **BAKE:** 30 MIN.
MAKES: 12 SERVINGS

- 3 packages (16 ounces each) frozen cauliflower, thawed
- 1 large onion, chopped
- ⅓ cup butter, cubed
- ⅓ cup all-purpose flour
- ½ teaspoon salt
- ¼ teaspoon ground mustard
- ¼ teaspoon pepper
- 2 cups fat-free milk
- ½ cup grated Parmesan cheese

TOPPING
- ½ cup soft whole wheat bread crumbs
- 2 tablespoons butter, melted
- ¼ teaspoon paprika

1. Place 1 in. of water in a Dutch oven; add cauliflower. Bring to a boil. Reduce heat; cover and cook for 4-6 minutes or until crisp-tender. Drain and pat dry.
2. Meanwhile, in a large saucepan, saute onion in butter until tender. Stir in the flour, salt, mustard and pepper until blended; gradually add milk. Bring to a boil; cook and stir for 1-2 minutes or until thickened. Remove from the heat. Add cheese; stir until melted.
3. Place cauliflower in a 13-in. x 9-in. baking dish coated with cooking spray. Pour sauce over top.
4. For topping, combine the bread crumbs, butter and paprika. Sprinkle over sauce. Bake, uncovered, at 350° for 30-35 minutes or until bubbly.

kid FRIENDLY Baked Potato Cheddar Soup

This creamy soup tastes like a loaded baked potato. We suggest using a high-quality cheddar cheese and topping it with fixings like bacon and green onions.
—**KRISTIN REYNOLDS** VAN BUREN, AR

START TO FINISH: 30 MIN.
MAKES: 4 SERVINGS

- ⅓ cup all-purpose flour
- 3 cups milk
- 2 large potatoes, baked, peeled and coarsely mashed (1½ pounds)
- ⅓ cup plus 2 tablespoons shredded cheddar cheese, divided
- ½ teaspoon salt
- ¼ teaspoon pepper
- ½ cup sour cream
- ½ cup thinly sliced green onions, divided
  Crumbled cooked bacon, optional

1. In a large saucepan, whisk flour and milk until smooth. Bring to a boil; cook and stir for 2 minutes or until thickened. Stir in the potatoes, ⅓ cup cheese, salt and pepper. Cook over medium heat for 2-3 minutes or until cheese is melted.
2. Remove from the heat. Stir in sour cream and ¼ cup onions until blended. Cover; cook over medium heat for 10-12 minutes or until heated through (do not boil). Garnish with remaining cheese, onions and, if desired, bacon.

Wisconsin Split Pea Soup

Field peas that have been dried (split peas) have been a staple soup ingredient for country cooks for years. Marjoram, garlic, potatoes and carrots blend nicely in this hearty and economical soup.

—LINDA ROCK STRATFORD, WI

PREP: 10 MIN. + COOLING
COOK: 3 HOURS + COOLING
MAKES: 12 SERVINGS (3 QUARTS)

- 1 pound dried green split peas
- 2½ quarts water
- 1 meaty ham bone or 2 smoked ham hocks
- 1½ cups chopped onion
- 1 cup each diced celery, carrots and potatoes
- 1 teaspoon dried parsley flakes
- ½ teaspoon pepper
- ¼ teaspoon garlic salt
- ¼ teaspoon dried marjoram
  Salt to taste

1. In a Dutch oven, add the peas, water and ham bone; bring to a boil. Reduce heat; cover and simmer for 2 hours, stirring occasionally.
2. Stir in the remaining ingredients. Bring to a boil. Reduce heat; cover and simmer for 30 minutes or until vegetables are tender.
3. Set aside ham bone until cool enough to handle. Remove meat from bone; discard bone. Cut ham into bite-size pieces. Return to the soup and heat through.

Chunky Garlic Mashed Potatoes

I like to dress up these mashed spuds with a whole bulb of roasted garlic. It may seem like overkill, but once cooked, any harshness mellows out and you're left with a sweet and delicate garlic flavor.

—JACKIE GREGSTON HALLSVILLE, TX

START TO FINISH: 30 MIN.
MAKES: 9 SERVINGS

- 3 pounds Yukon Gold potatoes, cut into quarters
- 1 whole garlic bulb, cloves separated and peeled
- ½ cup butter, cubed
- ½ cup half-and-half cream
- 2 tablespoons prepared horseradish
- ¾ teaspoon salt
- ¾ teaspoon pepper
  Fresh thyme leaves, optional

1. Place potatoes and garlic cloves in a large saucepan; cover with water. Bring to a boil. Reduce heat; cover and cook for 15-20 minutes or until potatoes are tender.
2. Meanwhile, in a small saucepan, heat butter and cream; keep warm. Drain potatoes and garlic; return to pan. Add the horseradish, salt, pepper and butter mixture; mash to reach desired consistency. Garnish with thyme if desired.

Broccoli Cheese Bake

Broccoli on the side doesn't have to be boring. This cheesy casserole for four is a simple and delicious way to round out a meal.

—DEBORAH PATRAUCHUK SICAMOUS, BC

PREP: 20 MIN. • **BAKE:** 25 MIN.
MAKES: 4 SERVINGS

- 1¾ cups fresh broccoli florets
- 1 tablespoon cornstarch
- ⅛ teaspoon salt
  Dash pepper
- ⅔ cup fat-free milk
- 1 medium onion, chopped
- ½ cup shredded cheddar cheese
- 2 tablespoons grated Parmesan cheese

1. Place 1 in. of water and broccoli in a small saucepan; bring to a boil. Reduce heat; cover and simmer for 3-5 minutes or until crisp-tender.
2. Meanwhile, in a small saucepan, combine the cornstarch, salt, pepper and milk until smooth. Bring to a boil; cook and stir for 1 minute or until thickened. Stir in onion and cheddar cheese until cheese is melted. Drain broccoli; stir into cheese sauce.
3. Transfer to a 1-qt. baking dish coated with cooking spray. Sprinkle with Parmesan cheese. Cover and bake at 350° for 25-30 minutes or until vegetables are tender.

Veggie Macaroni Salad

When I bring this super salad to church dinners, there is usually nothing to take home but the bowl. Add 2 or 3 cups of leftover turkey or chicken to create a filling main-dish salad. The dressing is so good that we use it on potato salads and even green salads.

—LYNN COLE SAGLE, ID

PREP: 35 MIN. + CHILLING
MAKES: 10 SERVINGS

- 2 cups uncooked elbow macaroni
- 1 large tomato, seeded and chopped
- 1 cup frozen peas, thawed
- ½ cup shredded reduced-fat cheddar cheese
- ½ cup chopped celery
- 1 hard-cooked egg, chopped
- 2 green onions, sliced

DRESSING

- ¾ cup reduced-fat mayonnaise
- 1 cup fat-free plain yogurt
- 2 tablespoons sugar
- 1 tablespoon prepared mustard
- ⅛ teaspoon celery seed

1. Cook macaroni according to package directions; drain and rinse in cold water. In a large bowl, combine the macaroni, tomato, peas, cheese, celery, egg and onions.
2. In a small bowl, combine the dressing ingredients. Pour over macaroni mixture and toss to coat. Refrigerate until serving.

ULTIMATE *Comfort*
Grandma's Chicken 'n' Dumpling Soup

I've enjoyed making this rich soup for over 40 years. Every time I serve it, I remember my grandma, who was very special to me and was a great cook.

—**PAULETTE BALDA** PROPHETSTOWN, IL

PREP: 20 MIN. + COOLING
COOK: 2¾ HOURS
MAKES: 12 SERVINGS (3 QUARTS)

- 1 broiler/fryer chicken (3½ to 4 pounds), cut up
- 2¼ quarts cold water
- 5 chicken bouillon cubes
- 6 whole peppercorns
- 3 whole cloves
- 1 can (10¾ ounces) condensed cream of chicken soup, undiluted
- 1 can (10¾ ounces) condensed cream of mushroom soup, undiluted
- 1½ cups chopped carrots
- 1 cup fresh or frozen peas
- 1 cup chopped celery
- 1 cup chopped peeled potatoes
- ¼ cup chopped onion
- 1½ teaspoons seasoned salt
- ¼ teaspoon pepper
- 1 bay leaf

DUMPLINGS
- 2 cups all-purpose flour
- 4 teaspoons baking powder
- 1 teaspoon salt
- ¼ teaspoon pepper
- 1 egg, beaten
- 2 tablespoons butter, melted
- ¾ to 1 cup milk
  Snipped fresh parsley, optional

1. Place the chicken, water, bouillon, peppercorns and cloves in a stockpot. Cover and bring to a boil; skim foam. Reduce heat; cover and simmer 45-60 minutes or until chicken is tender. Strain broth; return to stockpot.
2. Remove chicken and set aside until cool enough to handle. Remove meat from bones; discard bones and skin and cut chicken into chunks. Cool broth and skim off fat.

3. Return chicken to stockpot with soups, vegetables and seasonings; bring to a boil. Reduce heat; cover and simmer for 1 hour. Uncover; increase heat to a gentle boil. Discard bay leaf.
4. For dumplings, combine dry ingredients in a medium bowl. Stir in egg, butter and enough milk to make a moist stiff batter. Drop by teaspoonfuls into soup. Cover and cook without lifting the lid for 18-20 minutes. Sprinkle with parsley if desired.

Carrot Raisin Salad

This traditional salad is one of my mother-in-law's favorites. It's fun to eat because of its crunchy texture, and the raisins give it a slightly sweet flavor.

—**DENISE BAUMERT** DALHART, TX

START TO FINISH: 10 MIN.
MAKES: 8 SERVINGS

- 4 cups shredded carrots
- ¾ to 1½ cups raisins
- ¼ cup mayonnaise
- 2 tablespoons sugar
- 2 to 3 tablespoons 2% milk

Place carrots and raisins in a large bowl. In a small bowl, combine the mayonnaise, sugar and enough milk to achieve dressing consistency. Pour over carrot mixture; toss to coat.

top tip
Over Noodles

When I made Grandma's Chicken 'n' Dumpling Soup, I used boneless chicken and added a little flour and milk to thicken the soup. Then I served it over buttered noodles, and it was delicious!

—**TERIPERRY** TASTEOFHOME.COM

Creamy Dilled Cucumber Salad

This fresh-tasting savory side dish, a Norwegian favorite, was a staple at all of our family holidays. It adds a refreshing crunch to any meal.

—**PATTY LANOUE STEARNS** TRAVERSE CITY, MI

PREP: 20 MIN. + CHILLING
MAKES: 6 SERVINGS

- 2 **English cucumbers, thinly sliced**
- 1 **teaspoon salt**
- 1½ **cups (12 ounces) sour cream**
- ¼ **cup thinly sliced red onion**
- ¼ **cup snipped fresh dill**
- 2 **tablespoons white wine vinegar**
- 2 **garlic cloves, minced**
- 1 **teaspoon sugar**
- 1 **teaspoon coarsely ground pepper**

1. Place cucumbers in a colander over a bowl; sprinkle with salt and toss. Let stand 15 minutes. Squeeze and blot dry with paper towels.

2. In a large bowl, combine the remaining ingredients; stir in cucumbers. Refrigerate, covered, at least 1 hour.

Broccoli Rice Casserole

When I was little, serving this dish was the only way my mother could get me to eat broccoli. It's an excellent recipe and especially good with poultry.

—**JENNIFER FULLER** BALLSTON SPA, NY

PREP: 15 MIN. • **BAKE:** 30 MIN.
MAKES: 8 SERVINGS

- 1½ **cups water**
- ½ **cup butter, cubed**
- 1 **tablespoon dried minced onion**
- 2 **cups uncooked instant rice**
- 1 **package (16 ounces) frozen chopped broccoli, thawed**
- 1 **can (10¾ ounces) condensed cream of mushroom soup, undiluted**
- 1 **jar (8 ounces) process cheese sauce**

1. In a large saucepan, bring the water, butter and onion to a boil. Stir in rice. Remove from the heat; cover and let stand for 5 minutes or until water is absorbed.

2. Stir in the broccoli, soup and cheese sauce. Transfer to a greased 2-qt. baking dish. Bake, uncovered, at 350° for 30-35 minutes or until bubbly.

Roasted Harvest Vegetables

Here is my favorite side dish to serve any time we're having company. I like to pair it with any kind of roasted meat.

—AMY LOGAN MILL CREEK, PA

PREP: 20 MIN. • **BAKE:** 30 MIN.
MAKES: 9 SERVINGS

- 8 small red potatoes, quartered
- 2 small onions, quartered
- 1 medium zucchini, halved and sliced
- 1 medium yellow summer squash, halved and sliced
- ½ pound fresh baby carrots
- 1 cup fresh cauliflowerets
- 1 cup fresh broccoli florets
- ¼ cup olive oil
- 1 tablespoon garlic powder
- 1½ teaspoons dried rosemary, crushed
- ½ teaspoon dried thyme
- ¼ teaspoon salt
- ¼ teaspoon pepper

1. Place vegetables in a large bowl. In a small bowl, whisk the remaining ingredients; drizzle over vegetables and toss to coat.
2. Transfer to two greased 15-in. x 10-in. x 1-in. baking pans. Bake, uncovered, at 400° for 30-35 minutes or until tender, stirring occasionally.

Layered Tortellini Salad

My tortellini salad combines layers of flavors and textures, and its colors are amazing. It's perfect for a salad luncheon. Other cheese options are Havarti, fontina or Monterey Jack.

—NITA RAUSCH DALLAS, TX

PREP: 30 MIN. + CHILLING
MAKES: 12 SERVINGS (1½ CUPS DRESSING)

- ½ cup buttermilk
- ½ cup plain yogurt
- ¼ cup mayonnaise
- 1 teaspoon sugar
- ¼ teaspoon salt
- ¼ teaspoon dill weed
- ¼ teaspoon dried basil
- ⅛ teaspoon white pepper

SALAD

- 1 package (9 ounces) refrigerated cheese tortellini
- 2 cups shredded red cabbage
- 6 cups fresh baby spinach
- 1 block (8 ounces) part-skim mozzarella cheese, cubed
- 1 cup cherry tomatoes, halved
- 1 small red onion, thinly sliced
- 8 bacon strips, cooked and crumbled
- ½ cup crumbled feta cheese

1. For dressing, place the first eight ingredients in a blender. Cover and process until blended; process 1-2 minutes longer or until smooth.
2. Cook tortellini according to package directions. Drain and rinse in cold water.
3. In a large glass bowl, layer the cabbage, spinach and tortellini. Top with mozzarella cheese, tomatoes, onion, bacon and feta cheese. Cover and refrigerate for at least 3 hours. Drizzle with dressing; toss to coat.

1. In a large skillet, saute the summer squash, zucchini, mushrooms and onion in oil until tender; drain.

2. In a large bowl, combine the vegetable mixture, cheese, soup, sour cream and salt. Transfer to a greased 11-in. x 7-in. baking dish. Combine cracker crumbs and butter. Sprinkle over vegetable mixture.

3. Bake, uncovered, at 350° for 25-30 minutes or until bubbly.

Glazed Sweet Potatoes

Fresh sweet potatoes Mom grew disappeared fast at our family table when she served them with this easy, flavorful glaze. She still makes them this way, and now they've become favorites with her grandchildren as well!

—ROSEMARY PRYOR PASADENA, MD

PREP: 30 MIN. • **BAKE:** 30 MIN.
MAKES: 8 SERVINGS

> 2 **pounds sweet potatoes or 2 cans (15¾ ounces each) sweet potatoes, drained**
> ¼ **cup butter, cubed**
> ¼ **cup maple syrup**
> ¼ **cup packed brown sugar**
> ¼ **teaspoon ground cinnamon**

1. If using fresh sweet potatoes, place in a large saucepan or Dutch oven; cover with water. Bring to a boil. Reduce heat; cover and cook 25-40 minutes or until tender. Drain; cool slightly and peel. Cut into chunks.

2. Preheat oven to 350°. Place sweet potatoes in a 2-qt. baking dish. In a small saucepan, combine butter, syrup, brown sugar and cinnamon; bring to a boil, stirring constantly. Pour over potatoes.

3. Bake, uncovered, 30-40 minutes or until heated through.

Summer Squash Mushroom Casserole

With its crunchy topping, this rich and creamy side is a wonderful dish to take to potlucks and picnics. It goes well with a wide variety of entrees.

—JENNIFER WALLACE CANAL WINCHESTER, OH

PREP: 20 MIN. • **BAKE:** 25 MIN.
MAKES: 10 SERVINGS

> 2 **medium yellow summer squash, diced**
> 1 **large zucchini, diced**
> ½ **pound sliced fresh mushrooms**
> 1 **cup chopped onion**
> 2 **tablespoons olive oil**
> 2 **cups (8 ounces) shredded cheddar cheese**
> 1 **can (10¾ ounces) condensed cream of mushroom soup, undiluted**
> ½ **cup sour cream**
> ½ **teaspoon salt**
> 1 **cup crushed butter-flavored crackers (about 25 crackers)**
> 1 **tablespoon butter, melted**

Creamy Chicken Rice Soup

I came up with this thick flavorful soup while making some adjustments to a favorite stovetop chicken casserole. It makes a tasty lunch with half a sandwich or a salad and a roll.

—JANICE MITCHELL AURORA, CO

START TO FINISH: 30 MIN.
MAKES: 5 SERVINGS

- ½ cup chopped onion
- 1 medium carrot, chopped
- 1 celery rib, chopped
- 1 tablespoon canola oil
- ½ teaspoon minced garlic
- 2 cans (14½ ounces each) chicken broth
- ⅓ cup uncooked long grain rice
- ¾ teaspoon dried basil
- ¼ teaspoon pepper
- 3 tablespoons all-purpose flour
- 1 can (5 ounces) evaporated milk
- 1 package (9 ounces) frozen diced cooked chicken, thawed

1. In a large saucepan, saute the onion, carrot, celery in oil until tender. Add garlic; cook 1 minute longer. Stir in the broth, rice, basil and pepper. Bring to a boil. Reduce heat; cover and simmer for 15 minutes or until rice is tender.

2. In a small bowl, combine flour and milk until smooth; stir into soup. Bring to a boil; cook and stir for 2 minutes or until thickened. Stir in chicken; heat through.

? Did you know?

Soup was originally called "sop," a medieval stew that was poured over slices of bread to soak up the liquid.

Creamy Slaw

This colorful coleslaw is a longtime favorite. Cabbage, carrots and green pepper are blended with a tasty dressing that gets its zest from a hint of mustard. When Mom set this slaw on the table, it disappeared fast.

—DIANNE ESPOSITE NEW MIDDLETOWN, OH

PREP: 10 MIN. + CHILLING
MAKES: 6-8 SERVINGS

- 3 to 4 cups shredded cabbage
- 1 cup shredded carrots
- 1 cup thinly sliced green pepper
- ½ cup mayonnaise
- ¼ cup lemon juice
- 1 to 2 tablespoons sugar
- 1 tablespoon prepared mustard
- 1 teaspoon celery seed
- 1 teaspoon salt

In a large salad bowl, toss the cabbage, carrots and green pepper. In a small bowl, whisk the remaining ingredients. Pour over cabbage mixture and toss to coat. Chill for at least 2-3 hours.

Shrimp Salad

I remember my mother making this when I was a child. It's became a traditional Fourth of July side dish for our family.

—DELORES HILL HELENA, MT

PREP: 15 MIN. + CHILLING
MAKES: 9 SERVINGS

- 2⅓ cups uncooked small pasta shells
- ⅓ pound cooked salad shrimp
- 3 celery ribs, chopped
- 1 small onion, chopped
- 4 radishes, halved and sliced
- 4 hard-cooked eggs, chopped
- 1 cup mayonnaise
- 1 tablespoon prepared mustard
- 1½ teaspoons salt
- ⅛ teaspoon pepper

1. Cook pasta according to package directions. Meanwhile, in a large bowl, combine the shrimp, celery, onion, radishes and eggs. In a small bowl, combine mayonnaise, mustard, salt and pepper.

2. Drain pasta and rinse in cold water; add to shrimp mixture. Add dressing mixture; toss to coat. Cover and refrigerate for at least 2 hours.

Orange Spinach Salad

The combination of mustard-onion dressing with juicy oranges, cheese and crunchy sweet almonds is a joy for every taste bud! We eat this salad several times a week.

—JENNIFER RYTTING WEST JORDAN, UT

START TO FINISH: 30 MIN.
MAKES: 16 SERVINGS (1 CUP EACH)

- ¼ **cup sugar**
- ½ **cup slivered almonds**
- 1 **bunch romaine, torn**
- 1 **package (6 ounces) fresh baby spinach**
- ½ **pound sliced fresh mushrooms**
- 3 **cups (12 ounces) shredded Swiss cheese**
- 1 **medium red onion, sliced**
- ½ **pound sliced bacon, cooked and crumbled**
- 1 **can (15 ounces) mandarin oranges, drained**

POPPY SEED DRESSING

- ⅓ **cup white vinegar**
- ⅓ **cup sugar**
- ¼ **cup finely chopped onion**
- 2 **tablespoons Dijon mustard**
- ¾ **teaspoon salt**
- ¾ **cup canola oil**
- 2 **teaspoons poppy seeds**

1. In a small heavy skillet, melt sugar over low heat. Add almonds and stir to coat. Cook and stir 3-5 minutes or until golden brown. Spread onto a greased sheet of foil; break apart if necessary.
2. In a large bowl, combine the romaine, spinach, mushrooms, cheese, red onion, bacon and oranges.
3. For dressing, in a blender, combine the vinegar, sugar, onion, mustard and salt; cover and process until blended. While processing, gradually add oil in a steady stream. Stir in poppy seeds.
4. Pour dressing over salad and toss to coat. Sprinkle with sugared almonds. Serve immediately.

Makeover Corn Pudding

My mother-in-law, Hazel, made this recipe for my husband when he was growing up. I learned how to make it, but with all that butter and cheese I know it's high in fat and calories. This makeover version is just as comforting and one we'll serve for generations to come.

—ARLENE SPENCER OCONOMOWOC, WI

PREP: 15 MIN. • **BAKE:** 50 MIN.
MAKES: 12 SERVINGS

- ⅓ **cup all-purpose flour**
- 2 **tablespoons sugar**
- 1 **cup fat-free milk**
- ¾ **cup egg substitute**
- 1 **tablespoon butter, melted**
- 1 **teaspoon salt**
- 8 **cups frozen corn, thawed**
- 1 **can (14¾ ounces) cream-style corn**
- 1 **cup (4 ounces) shredded sharp cheddar cheese**

1. In a large bowl, combine flour and sugar. Whisk in the milk, egg substitute, butter and salt. Stir in the corn, cream-style corn and cheese.
2. Pour into a 13-in. x 9-in. baking dish coated with cooking spray. Bake, uncovered, at 375° for 50-55 minutes or until a knife inserted near the center comes out clean.

Creamed Garden Potatoes and Peas

Spring has comfort foods, too. New potatoes and peas are treated to a creamy sauce in this delicious side dish.

—JANE UPHOFF CUNNINGHAM, KS

START TO FINISH: 25 MIN.
MAKES: 12 SERVINGS

- 2 **pounds small red potatoes, quartered**
- 3 **cups fresh or frozen peas**
- 1 **cup water**
- 2 **tablespoons chopped onion**
- 2 **tablespoons butter**
- 3 **tablespoons plus 1 teaspoon all-purpose flour**
- 1½ **teaspoons salt**
- ¼ **teaspoon pepper**
- 2 **cups 2% milk**
- 1 **cup half-and-half cream**

1. Place potatoes in a large saucepan and cover with water. Bring to a boil. Reduce heat; cover and simmer for 8-12 minutes or until tender. Drain.

2. Meanwhile, place peas and water in a small saucepan. Bring to a boil. Reduce heat; cover and simmer for 3-5 minutes or until tender. Drain.

3. In a large saucepan, saute onion in butter until tender. Stir in the flour, salt and pepper until blended; gradually add milk and cream. Bring to a boil; cook and stir for 2 minutes or until thickened. Stir in potatoes and peas; heat through.

Salami Pasta Salad

The first time I tasted this delicious salad was at my wedding, and I recall, even in the blur of that day, the recipe was in high demand. That was years ago, and I'm still asked to bring it to cookouts and parties!

—SARAH RYAN GENEVA, OH

START TO FINISH: 20 MIN.
MAKES: 9 SERVINGS

- 2 **cups uncooked small pasta shells**
- ¾ **cup chopped green pepper**
- ¾ **cup chopped fresh tomatoes**
- ½ **cup chopped pepperoni**
- ½ **cup cubed hard salami**
- ½ **cup whole ripe olives, quartered**
- 2 **ounces provolone cheese, cubed**
- ⅓ **cup chopped onion**

DRESSING

- ⅓ **cup canola oil**
- ¼ **cup red wine vinegar**
- 2 **tablespoons sugar**
- 1½ **teaspoons salt**
- 1½ **teaspoons dried oregano**
- ½ **teaspoon pepper**

1. Cook pasta according to package directions; drain and rinse in cold water. Place in a large bowl; add the green pepper, tomatoes, pepperoni, salami, olives, cheese and onion.

2. In a small bowl, whisk the dressing ingredients. Pour over pasta mixture; toss to coat. Cover and refrigerate until serving.

Beef Macaroni Soup
kid FRIENDLY

You'll love my quick version of classic beef macaroni soup. Loaded with veggies and pasta, it's just as good as the original but without all the fuss.

—DEBRA BAKER GREENVILLE, NC

START TO FINISH: 25 MIN.
MAKES: 5 SERVINGS

- 1 **pound ground beef**
- 2 **cups frozen mixed vegetables**
- 1 **can (14½ ounces) diced tomatoes, undrained**
- 1 **can (14½ ounces) beef broth**
- ¼ **teaspoon pepper**
- ½ **cup uncooked elbow macaroni**

In a large saucepan, cook beef over medium heat until no longer pink; drain. Stir in the mixed vegetables, tomatoes, broth and pepper. Bring to a boil; add macaroni. Reduce heat; cover and simmer for 8-10 minutes or until macaroni and vegetables are tender.

Sweet Holiday Carrots

Pineapple, honey and dried cranberries give these carrots an extra touch of sweetness. This is probably the best side dish to serve with a turkey or a honey baked ham.

—DONNA MARIE RYAN TOPSFIELD, MA

START TO FINISH: 30 MIN.
MAKES: 5 SERVINGS

- 8 **medium carrots, sliced**
- ½ **cup water**
- 1 **can (8 ounces) crushed pineapple, undrained**
- ½ **cup chopped peeled tart apple**
- ½ **cup dried cranberries**
- ⅓ **cup honey**
- 1 **tablespoon lemon juice**
- ½ **teaspoon salt**
- 1 **tablespoon butter, melted**
- 1 **tablespoon all-purpose flour**
- ½ **teaspoon ground cinnamon**
- ½ **cup chopped walnuts, toasted**

1. Place carrots and water in a large saucepan. Bring to a boil; reduce heat. Cover and simmer 5 minutes.

2. Add pineapple, apple, cranberries, honey, lemon juice and salt; cook 3-4 minutes or until carrots are crisp-tender, stirring occasionally.

3. Combine butter, flour and cinnamon; stir into pan. Bring to a boil; cook and stir 2 minutes or until sauce is thickened. Sprinkle with walnuts before serving.

top tip — Just Add Broth

My husband and I loved the Beef Macaroni Soup. But we thought it needed more broth. Next time I will make it with 2 cans of broth and an extra ¼ cup of noodles.

—JDANZ2010 TASTEOFHOME.COM

Everything Stuffing

My husband and father both go crazy for this stuffing! It also freezes well so we can enjoy it long after Thanksgiving has passed.
—**BETTE VOTRAL** BETHLEHEM, PA

PREP: 30 MIN. • **COOK:** 3 HOURS
MAKES: 9 SERVINGS

- ½ **pound bulk Italian sausage**
- 4 **cups seasoned stuffing cubes**
- 1½ **cups crushed corn bread stuffing**
- ½ **cup chopped toasted chestnuts or pecans**
- ½ **cup minced fresh parsley**
- 1 **tablespoon minced fresh sage or 1 teaspoon rubbed sage**
- ⅛ **teaspoon salt**
- ⅛ **teaspoon pepper**
- 1¾ **cups sliced baby portobello mushrooms**
- 1 **package (5 ounces) sliced fresh shiitake mushrooms**
- 1 **large onion, chopped**
- 1 **medium apple, peeled and chopped**
- 1 **celery rib, chopped**
- 3 **tablespoons butter**
- 1 **can (14½ ounces) chicken broth**

1. In a large skillet, cook sausage over medium heat until no longer pink; drain. Transfer to a large bowl. Stir in the stuffing cubes, corn bread stuffing, chestnuts, parsley, sage, salt and pepper.

2. In the same skillet, saute the mushrooms, onion, apple and celery in butter until tender. Stir into stuffing mixture. Add enough broth to reach desired moistness. Transfer to a 4-qt. slow cooker. Cover and cook on low for 3 hours, stirring once.

ULTIMATE *Comfort* ## Caramel Sweet Potatoes

The sauce is the star of this recipe. It really does taste like butterscotch. It is a nice side dish for poultry or ham.
—**MARY JO PATRICK** NAPOLEON, OH

PREP: 25 MIN. • **BAKE:** 25 MIN.
MAKES: 10 SERVINGS

- 6 **medium sweet potatoes, peeled and cut into 1-inch chunks**
- ½ **cup packed brown sugar**
- ½ **cup corn syrup**
- ¼ **cup milk**
- 2 **tablespoons butter**
- ½ **to 1 teaspoon salt**
- ½ **teaspoon ground cinnamon**

1. Place sweet potatoes in a Dutch oven; cover with water. Bring to a boil. Reduce heat; cover and simmer for 20 minutes or until crisp-tender.

2. Drain and transfer to a greased 13-in. x 9-in. baking dish. Bake, uncovered, at 325° for 15 minutes.

3. Meanwhile, in a small saucepan, combine the remaining ingredients. Bring to a boil; pour over sweet potatoes. Bake 10-15 minutes longer or until glazed, basting frequently.

Layered Lettuce Salad

This is a great-tasting salad that can be made for most any occasion. It looks so pretty for a buffet or on the dinner table. My family loves it.

—JULIA BURKHOLDER ROBESONIA, PA

PREP: 15 MIN. + CHILLING
MAKES: 12 SERVINGS

- 1 medium head lettuce, torn
- 1 cup minced fresh parsley
- 4 hard-cooked eggs, sliced
- 2 large tomatoes, chopped
- 1 package (10 ounces) frozen peas, thawed and patted dry
- 6 bacon strips, cooked and crumbled
- 1 cup (4 ounces) shredded cheddar cheese
- 1 small red onion, chopped

DRESSING

- 1½ cups mayonnaise
- ½ cup sour cream
- 1 teaspoon dill weed
- ¾ teaspoon dried basil
- ½ teaspoon salt
- ⅛ teaspoon pepper
  Fresh dill sprigs, optional

In a large salad bowl, layer in order the lettuce, parsley, eggs, tomatoes, peas, bacon, cheese and onion. In a small bowl, combine mayonnaise, sour cream, dill, basil, salt and pepper. Carefully spread on top of salad. Cover and refrigerate for several hours or overnight. Garnish with dill sprigs if desired.

Did you know?

Butternut squash is one of the longest keeping vegetables. When properly stored in a cool, dark place (a pantry, basement or closet), it can last more than 3 months.

Butternut Squash Casserole

When we lived in Zimbabwe, Mom couldn't get sweet potatoes, which the family loved. So, instead she made this creamy casserole with butternut squash, spices and a touch of sugar. It soon became a family favorite.

—SUSAN HANSEN AUBURN, AL

PREP: 30 MIN. • **BAKE:** 30 MIN.
MAKES: 6 SERVINGS

- 2 medium butternut squash, peeled and cut into chunks
- ½ cup sugar
- 2 eggs
- ¼ cup milk
- 2 tablespoons butter
- 1 teaspoon vanilla extract
- ¼ teaspoon ground cinnamon
- ¼ teaspoon ground nutmeg

1. Place squash in a large saucepan and cover with water; bring to a boil. Reduce heat; cover and simmer for 12-16 minutes or until tender. Drain.
2. In a small bowl, beat squash until smooth. Add the remaining ingredients; beat well. Spoon into a 1½-qt. baking dish coated with cooking spray. Cover and bake at 350° for 30-35 minutes or until a thermometer inserted near the center reads 160°.

This is my mother-in-law's recipe, but I've made it so often I feel as though it's my own! Squash and apples remind me of fall in New England, and they taste fabulous when baked together.

—**JUDITH HAWES** CHELMSFORD, MA

Squash-Apple Bake

PREP: 15 MIN. • **BAKE:** 50 MIN.
MAKES: 4-6 SERVINGS

- 1 medium buttercup or butternut squash (about 1¼ pounds), peeled and cut into ¾-inch slices
- 2 medium apples, peeled and cut into wedges
- ½ cup packed brown sugar
- 1 tablespoon all-purpose flour
- ¼ cup butter, melted
- ½ teaspoon salt
- ½ teaspoon ground mace

1. Arrange squash in a 2-qt. baking dish. Top with apple wedges. Combine the remaining ingredients; spoon over apples.

2. Bake, uncovered, at 350° for 50-60 minutes or until tender.

Creamy Twice-Baked Potatoes

With a rich cream cheese filling, these twice-baked spuds are the perfect thing to serve meat-and-potato lovers.

—LINDA WHEELER HARRISBURG, PA

PREP: 1¼ HOURS • **BAKE:** 20 MIN.
MAKES: 2 SERVINGS

- 2 medium baking potatoes
- 2 tablespoons butter, softened
- 1 tablespoon 2% milk
- ¼ teaspoon salt
- 1 package (3 ounces) cream cheese, cubed
- 2 tablespoons sour cream
  Paprika

1. Pierce potatoes and bake at 375° for 1 hour or until tender. When cool enough to handle, cut a thin slice off the top of each potato and discard. Scoop out pulp, leaving a thin shell.

2. In a small bowl, mash the pulp with butter, milk and salt. Stir in cream cheese and sour cream. Spoon into potato shells. Sprinkle with paprika.

3. Place on a baking sheet. Bake, uncovered, at 350° for 20-25 minutes or until heated through and tops are golden brown.

Spiral Pasta Salad

I am always on the go, so I appreciate recipes that I can prepare ahead of time. This salad topped with a homemade dressing is easy to fix when I have a few spare moments. It's perfect for taking along on picnics or just about any outing.

—DARLENE KILEEL RIVERVIEW, NB

START TO FINISH: 30 MIN.
MAKES: 6 SERVINGS

- 3 cups cooked drained spiral pasta
- ½ cup chopped green pepper
- ½ cup sliced celery
- ½ cup chopped tomato
- ½ cup shredded carrot

DRESSING
- ¼ cup canola oil
- ¼ cup cider vinegar
- ¼ cup chopped onion
- 2 tablespoons ketchup
- 4 teaspoons sugar
- ½ teaspoon salt, optional
- ¼ teaspoon garlic powder
- ¼ teaspoon dried oregano
- ¼ teaspoon ground mustard
- ¼ teaspoon paprika

In a large bowl, combine the pasta, green pepper, celery, tomato and carrot. In a small bowl, whisk the dressing ingredients. Pour over salad and toss to coat. Refrigerate until serving.

Creamed Peas and Carrots

A delicate cream sauce gently seasoned with salt and pepper is all it takes to turn peas and carrots into an elegant side.

—**GAYLEEN GROTE** BATTLEVIEW, ND

START TO FINISH: 25 MIN.
MAKES: 4 SERVINGS

- 4 **medium carrots, sliced**
- 2 **cups frozen peas**
- 1 **tablespoon cornstarch**
- ¼ **teaspoon salt**
- ⅛ **teaspoon pepper**
- ½ **cup heavy whipping cream**

1. Place carrots in a large saucepan; add 1 in. of water. Bring to a boil. Reduce heat; cover and simmer for 5-8 minutes or until crisp-tender.
2. Add peas; return to a boil. Reduce heat; cover and simmer 5-10 minutes longer or until vegetables are tender. Drain, reserving ½ cup cooking liquid. Return vegetables and reserved liquid to the pan.
3. In a small bowl, combine the cornstarch, salt, pepper and cream until smooth. Stir into vegetables. Bring to a boil; cook and stir for 1-2 minutes or until thickened.

Jazzed-Up Green Bean Casserole

After trying many variations of this old standby, I decided to give it a little extra kick. The crunchy texture, cheesy goodness and bacon make it a hit at any holiday get-together.

—**SCOTT RUGH** PORTLAND, OR

PREP: 20 MIN. • **COOK:** 5½ HOURS
MAKES: 10 SERVINGS

- 2 **packages (16 ounces each) frozen cut green beans, thawed**
- 2 **cans (10¾ ounces each) condensed cream of mushroom soup, undiluted**
- 1 **can (8 ounces) sliced water chestnuts, drained**
- 1 **cup 2% milk**
- 6 **bacon strips, cooked and crumbled**
- 1 **teaspoon pepper**
- ⅛ **teaspoon paprika**
- 4 **ounces process cheese (Velveeta), cubed**
- 1 **can (2.8 ounces) French-fried onions**

In a 4-qt. slow cooker, combine the green beans, soup, water chestnuts, milk, bacon, pepper and paprika. Cover and cook on low for 5-6 hours or until beans are tender; stir in cheese. Cover and cook for 30 minutes or until cheese is melted. Sprinkle with onions.

Breads

BREAKING BREAD IS ONE OF LIFE'S SIMPLE JOYS—THESE RECIPES TASTE
EVEN BETTER WHEN SHARED WITH SOMEONE YOU LOVE.

**RUSTIC
PUMPKIN BREAD**
PAGE 220

**PEPPERY
HUSH PUPPIES**
PAGE 229

**HERBED ONION
FOCACCIA**
PAGE 240

kid FRIENDLY Chocolate Chocolate Chip Muffins

The title says it all! These extra chocolaty muffins feature nutritious ingredients like whole wheat flour and applesauce to make a lighter muffin. Because these treats are so delicious and surprisingly healthy, we even serve them for breakfast at the school where I work.

—**THERESA HARRINGTON** SHERIDAN, WY

PREP: 20 MIN. • **BAKE:** 20 MIN./BATCH
MAKES: 32 MUFFINS.

- 2½ cups all-purpose flour
- 1¾ cups whole wheat flour
- 1¾ cups packed brown sugar
- ½ cup baking cocoa
- 1¼ teaspoons salt
- 1 teaspoon baking powder
- 1 teaspoon baking soda
- 2 egg whites
- 1 egg
- 2 cups unsweetened applesauce
- 1¾ cups fat-free milk
- 2 tablespoons canola oil
- 2½ teaspoons vanilla extract
- 1¼ cups semisweet chocolate chips

1. In a large bowl, combine the flours, brown sugar, cocoa, salt, baking powder and baking soda. In another bowl, whisk the egg whites, egg, applesauce, milk, oil and vanilla. Stir into dry ingredients just until moistened. Fold in chocolate chips.
2. Coat muffin cups with cooking spray; fill three-fourths full with batter. Bake at 350° for 18-20 minutes or until a toothpick inserted near the center comes out clean. Cool for 5 minutes before removing from pans to wire racks. Serve warm.

Pumpkin Spice Bread

One bite and you'll agree—this bread tastes just like pumpkin pie without the crust. During autumn your family will request this one often.

—**DELORA LUCAS** BELLE, WV

PREP: 10 MIN. • **BAKE:** 1 HOUR + COOLING
MAKES: 2 LOAVES

- 3 cups sugar
- 1 cup vegetable oil
- 4 eggs, lightly beaten
- 1 can (15 ounces) solid-pack pumpkin
- 3½ cups all-purpose flour
- 1 teaspoon baking soda
- 1 teaspoon salt
- 1 teaspoon ground cinnamon
- 1 teaspoon ground nutmeg
- ½ teaspoon baking powder
- ½ teaspoon ground cloves
- ½ teaspoon ground allspice
- ½ cup water

1. In a large bowl, combine sugar, oil and eggs. Add pumpkin and mix well. Combine the flour, baking soda, salt, cinnamon, nutmeg, baking powder, cloves and allspice; add to the pumpkin mixture alternately with water, beating well after each addition.
2. Pour into two greased 9x5-in. loaf pans. Bake at 350° for 60-65 minutes or until a toothpick inserted near the center comes out clean. Cool in pans 10 minutes before removing to a wire rack to cool completely.

? Did you know?

Libby's processes 85 percent of the canned pumpkin on the planet in Morton, Illinois, which calls itself the pumpkin capital of the world.

Blueberry Quick Bread

This sweet bread recipe has won a blue ribbon at our state fair, perhaps because the crushed pineapple and coconut give it a mild but delicious twist. It makes two loaves, so you can freeze one for a future treat.

—LOIS EVEREST GOSHEN, IN

PREP: 25 MIN. • **BAKE:** 50 MIN. + COOLING
MAKES: 2 LOAVES (12 SLICES EACH)

- ⅔ cup butter, softened
- 1¼ cups sugar blend
- 2 eggs
- 4 egg whites
- 1½ teaspoons lemon juice
- 3 cups all-purpose flour
- 3¾ teaspoons baking powder
- ½ teaspoon salt
- ½ cup fat-free milk
- 2 cups fresh or frozen blueberries
- 1 cup canned unsweetened crushed pineapple, drained
- ½ cup chopped pecans or walnuts
- ½ cup flaked coconut

1. In a large bowl, cream butter and sugar blend until light and fluffy. Beat in the eggs, egg whites and lemon juice. Combine the flour, baking powder and salt; gradually add to creamed mixture alternately with milk, beating well after each addition. Fold in blueberries, pineapple, pecans and coconut.

2. Transfer to two 8x4-in. loaf pans coated with cooking spray. Bake at 350° for 50-60 minutes or until a toothpick inserted near the center comes out clean. Cool for 10 minutes before removing loaves from pans to wire racks.

EDITOR'S NOTE *This recipe was tested with Splenda sugar blend. If using frozen blueberries, do not thaw before adding to batter.*

Here's a recipe that couldn't be much quicker or easier. It doesn't really matter what you serve these rolls with; the garlic and Parmesan flavors go great with just about any meal.
—**LORI ABAD** EAST HAVEN, CT

Garlic-Cheese Crescent Rolls

START TO FINISH: 20 MIN.
MAKES: 8 SERVINGS

- 1 tube (8 ounces) refrigerated crescent rolls
- 3 tablespoons butter, melted
- 1½ teaspoons garlic powder
- 1 teaspoon dried oregano
- 2 tablespoons grated Parmesan cheese

1. Separate crescent dough into eight triangles. Roll up from the wide end and place point side down 2 in. apart on an ungreased baking sheet. Curve ends to form a crescent.

2. Combine the butter, garlic powder and oregano; brush over rolls. Sprinkle with cheese.

3. Bake at 375° for 10-12 minutes or until golden brown. Serve warm.

Surprise Sausage Bundles

Kielbasa and sauerkraut star in a tasty filling for these scrumptious stuffed rolls, which make a great dinner with soup or salad. My family also loves leftover bundles right out of the refrigerator for a quick lunch.

—**BARB RUIS** GRANDVILLE, MI

PREP: 45 MIN. + RISING • **BAKE:** 20 MIN.
MAKES: 16 SERVINGS

- 6 bacon strips, diced
- 1 cup chopped onion
- 1 can (16 ounces) sauerkraut, rinsed and well drained
- ½ pound smoked kielbasa or Polish sausage, coarsely chopped
- 2 tablespoons brown sugar
- ½ teaspoon garlic salt
- ¼ teaspoon caraway seeds
- ⅛ teaspoon pepper
- 1 package (16 ounces) hot roll mix
- 2 eggs

- 1 cup warm water (120° to 130°)
- 2 tablespoons butter, softened
  Poppy seeds

1. In a large skillet, cook bacon until crisp; remove to paper towels. Reserve 2 tablespoons drippings. Saute onion in drippings until tender. Stir in the sauerkraut, sausage, brown sugar, garlic salt, caraway and pepper. Cook and stir for 5 minutes. Remove from the heat; add bacon. Set aside to cool.

2. In a large bowl, combine contents of the roll mix and its yeast packet. Stir in one egg, water and butter to form a soft dough. Turn onto a floured surface; knead until smooth and elastic, about 5 minutes. Cover dough with a large bowl; let stand for 5 minutes.

3. Divide dough into 16 pieces. On a floured surface, roll out each piece into a 4-in. circle. Top each with ¼ cup filling. Fold dough around filling, forming a ball; pinch edges to seal. Place seam side down on greased baking sheets. Cover loosely with plastic wrap that has been coated with cooking spray. Let rise in a warm place for 15 minutes.

4. Beat remaining egg; brush over bundles. Sprinkle with poppy seeds. Bake at 350° for 16-17 minutes or until golden brown. Serve warm.

FREEZE OPTION *Freeze cooled bundles in a freezer container, separating layers with waxed paper. To use, reheat bundles on a greased baking sheet in a preheated 325° oven until heated through.*

Honey-Wheat Oatmeal Bread

My husband and I are grain farmers and we also have beehives on our property. The beekeepers keep us well stocked with honey so I'm always looking for ways to use it along with our products.

—WANNETTA EHNES EAGLE BEND, MN

PREP: 10 MIN. • **BAKE:** 3 HOURS
MAKES: 1 LOAF (2 POUNDS, 20 SLICES)

- 1¼ cups water (70° to 80°)
- ½ cup honey
- 2 tablespoons canola oil
- 1½ teaspoons salt
- 1½ cups bread flour
- 1½ cups whole wheat flour
- 1 cup quick-cooking oats
- 1 package (¼ ounce) active dry yeast

1. In bread machine pan, place all the ingredients in the order suggested by the manufacturer. Select the basic bread setting. Choose the crust color and the loaf size if available.

2. Bake according to bread machine directions (check dough after 5 minutes of mixing; add 1 to 2 tablespoons of water or flour if needed).

Sour Cream Yeast Rolls

These rolls are the perfect finishing touch for any meal. They represent genuine comfort food like Mom used to make.

—CHRISTINE FRAZIER AUBURNDALE, FL

PREP: 35 MIN. + RISING • **BAKE:** 25 MIN.
MAKES: 1 DOZEN

- 2½ to 3 cups all-purpose flour
- 2 tablespoons sugar
- 1 package (¼ ounce) active dry yeast
- 1 teaspoon salt
- 1 cup (8 ounces) sour cream
- ¼ cup water
- 3 tablespoons butter, divided
- 1 egg

1. In a large bowl, combine 1½ cups flour, sugar, yeast and salt. In a small saucepan, heat the sour cream, water and 2 tablespoons butter to 120°-130°; add to the dry ingredients. Beat on medium speed for 2 minutes. Add egg and ½ cup flour; beat 2 minutes longer. Stir in enough remaining flour to form a soft dough.

2. Turn onto a floured surface; knead until smooth and elastic, about 6-8 minutes. Place in a greased bowl, turning once to grease the top. Cover and let rise in a warm place until doubled, about 1 hour.

3. Punch dough down. Turn onto a lightly floured surface; divide into 12 pieces. Shape each into a ball. Place in a greased 13x9-in. baking pan. Cover and let rise until doubled, about 30 minutes.

4. Bake at 375° for 25-30 minutes or until golden brown. Melt remaining butter; brush over rolls. Remove from pan to a wire rack.

Blueberry Yogurt Muffins

With the addition of vanilla yogurt, these quick and easy muffins turn out soft and tender. My husband loves having them for breakfast on mornings when he is rushing out the door.

—CINDI BUDREAU NEENAH, WI

PREP: 15 MIN. • **BAKE:** 20 MIN.
MAKES: 6 MUFFINS.

- 1 **cup all-purpose flour**
- 6 **tablespoons sugar**
- ¼ **teaspoon salt**
- ¼ **teaspoon baking powder**
- ¼ **teaspoon baking soda**
- 1 **egg**
- ½ **cup vanilla yogurt**
- 3 **tablespoons canola oil**
- 2 **tablespoons 2% milk**
- ½ **cup fresh or frozen blueberries**

1. In a small bowl, combine the flour, sugar, salt, baking powder and baking soda. In another bowl, combine the egg, yogurt, oil and milk. Stir into dry ingredients just until moistened. Fold in blueberries.

2. Fill greased or paper-lined muffin cups three-fourths full. Bake at 350° for 20-22 minutes or until a toothpick inserted near the center comes out clean. Cool for 5 minutes before removing from pan to a wire rack. Serve warm.

NOTE *If using frozen blueberries, use without thawing to avoid discoloring the batter.*

Fluffy Biscuits

If you're looking for a basic flaky biscuit, this recipe is the best. These golden brown rolls bake up tall, light and tender and make an exceptional treat served warm.

—NANCY HORSBURGH EVERETT, ON

START TO FINISH: 30 MIN.
MAKES: 1 DOZEN

- 2 **cups all-purpose flour**
- 4 **teaspoons baking powder**
- 3 **teaspoons sugar**
- ½ **teaspoon salt**
- ½ **cup shortening**
- 1 **egg**
- ⅔ **cup 2% milk**

1. In a small bowl, combine the flour, baking powder, sugar and salt. Cut in the shortening until the mixture resembles coarse crumbs. Whisk egg and milk; stir into dry ingredients just until moistened.

2. Turn onto a well-floured surface; knead 20 times. Roll out to ¾-in. thickness; cut with a floured 2½-in. biscuit cutter. Place on a lightly greased baking sheet.

3. Bake at 450° for 8-10 minutes or until golden brown. Serve warm.

ITALIAN BISCUITS *Add 1 teaspoon Italian seasoning to the flour mixture.*

ULTIMATE *Comfort* Rustic Pumpkin Bread

I received this recipe from a co-worker who made it for an office party. It is so yummy and tender that I now make it every year at the holidays to give as a special treat.

—**SANDY SANDAVAL** SANDY VALLEY, NV

PREP: 25 MIN. • **BAKE:** 1 HOUR + COOLING
MAKES: 2 LOAVES (16 SLICES EACH)

- 3 cups sugar
- 1 can (15 ounces) solid-pack pumpkin
- 1 cup canola oil
- 4 eggs
- ⅔ cup water
- 3½ cups all-purpose flour
- 2 teaspoons baking soda
- 1 teaspoon salt
- 1 teaspoon ground cinnamon
- 1 teaspoon ground nutmeg
- ½ teaspoon ground cloves
- ½ cup chopped pecans

TOPPING
- ⅓ cup all-purpose flour
- ¼ cup packed brown sugar
- ½ teaspoon ground cinnamon
- 2 tablespoons cold butter
- ¼ cup chopped pecans

1. In a large bowl, beat the sugar, pumpkin, oil, eggs and water until blended. In a large bowl, combine the flour, baking soda, salt, cinnamon, nutmeg and cloves; gradually beat into the pumpkin mixture until blended. Stir in pecans.

2. Pour into two greased 9x5-in. loaf pans. For topping, in a small bowl, combine the flour, brown sugar and cinnamon; cut in butter until mixture resembles coarse crumbs. Stir in the pecans. Sprinkle over batter.

3. Bake at 350° for 60-65 minutes or until a toothpick inserted near the center comes out clean. Cool for 10 minutes before removing from pans to wire racks.

Irish Soda Bread

This traditional bread can be made with an assortment of mix-ins such as dried fruit and nuts, but I like it with a handful of raisins.

—**GLORIA WARCZAK** CEDARBURG, WI

PREP: 15 MIN. • **BAKE:** 30 MIN.
MAKES: 6-8 SERVINGS

- 2 cups all-purpose flour
- 2 tablespoons brown sugar
- 1 teaspoon baking powder
- 1 teaspoon baking soda
- ½ teaspoon salt
- 3 tablespoons butter
- 2 eggs
- ¾ cup buttermilk
- ⅓ cup raisins

1. In a large bowl, combine the flour, brown sugar, baking powder, baking soda and salt. Cut in the butter until crumbly. In a small bowl, whisk 1 egg and buttermilk. Stir into flour mixture just until moistened. Fold in raisins.

2. Knead on a floured surface for 1 minute. Shape into a round loaf; place on a greased baking sheet. Cut a ¼-in.-deep cross in top of loaf. Beat remaining egg; brush over loaf.

3. Bake at 375° for 30-35 minutes or until golden brown.

CARAWAY IRISH SODA BREAD *Add 1 to 2 tablespoons caraway seeds to the dry ingredients.*

Lemon Pound Cake Muffins

I make these lemony muffins for all kinds of occasions. My family is always asking for them. They have a rich texture and a sweet and tangy flavor. All I can say is they're just sooo good!

—**LOLA BAXTER** WINNEBAGO, MN

PREP: 15 MIN. • **BAKE:** 20 MIN.
MAKES: 1 DOZEN

- ½ cup butter, softened
- 1 cup sugar
- 2 eggs
- ½ cup sour cream
- 1 teaspoon vanilla extract
- ½ teaspoon lemon extract
- 1¾ cups all-purpose flour
- ½ teaspoon salt
- ¼ teaspoon baking soda

GLAZE

- 2 cups confectioners' sugar
- 3 tablespoons lemon juice

1. In a large bowl, cream the butter and sugar until light and fluffy. Add eggs, one at a time, beating well after each addition. Beat in the sour cream and extracts. Combine the flour, salt and baking soda; add to the creamed mixture just until moistened.

2. Fill greased or paper-lined muffin cups three-fourths full. Bake at 400° for 18-20 minutes or until a toothpick inserted near the center comes out clean. Cool for 5 minutes before removing from pan to a wire rack.

3. Combine the glaze ingredients; drizzle over muffins. Serve warm.

Sweet Milk Dinner Rolls

A hint of sweetness in these tender buns brings in many compliments. Served warm with butter or jam, they're a big hit at any meal.

—**MERLE DYCK** ELKFORD, BC

PREP: 20 MIN. + RISING • **BAKE:** 35 MIN.
MAKES: 16 ROLLS

- 1 package (¼ ounce) active dry yeast
- 2 cups warm milk (110° to 115°)
- ½ cup sugar
- 2 tablespoons butter, melted
- 1 teaspoon salt
- 4 to 5 cups all-purpose flour

1. In a large bowl, dissolve yeast in warm milk. Add the sugar, butter, salt and 3 cups flour. Beat until smooth. Add enough remaining flour to form a soft dough.

2. Turn onto a floured surface; knead until smooth and elastic, about 6-8 minutes. Place in a greased bowl, turning once to grease top. Cover and let rise in a warm place until doubled, about 1 hour.

3. Punch dough down. Turn onto a floured surface; divide into 16 pieces. Shape each into a ball. Place 2 in. apart on greased baking sheets. Cover and let rise until doubled, about 30 minutes.

4. Bake at 350° for 35-40 minutes or until golden brown. Remove from pans to wire racks. Serve warm.

Jumbo Caramel Banana Muffins

Love banana bread? Then you'll be thrilled with my flavorful muffins. They're drizzled with sweet caramel icing, and the flavor is exceptional!

—KATHERINE MCCLELLAND

DEEP BROOK, NS

PREP: 20 MIN. • **BAKE:** 25 MIN. + COOLING
MAKES: 6 MUFFINS.

- ¼ **cup shortening**
- 1 **cup sugar**
- 1 **egg**
- 1½ **cups mashed ripe bananas (about 3 large)**
- 1 **teaspoon vanilla extract**
- 1½ **cups all-purpose flour**
- 1 **teaspoon baking soda**
- ¼ **teaspoon salt**

CARAMEL ICING

- 2 **tablespoons butter**
- ¼ **cup packed brown sugar**
- 1 **tablespoon 2% milk**
- ½ **cup confectioners' sugar**

1. In a large bowl, cream shortening and sugar until light and fluffy. Beat in egg. Beat in the bananas and vanilla. Combine the flour, baking soda and salt; add to creamed mixture just until moistened.

2. Fill paper-lined jumbo muffin cups three-fourths full. Bake at 350° for 23-28 minutes or until a toothpick inserted near the center comes out clean. Cool for 5 minutes before removing from pan to a wire rack to cool completely.

3. For icing, in a small saucepan, melt butter over medium heat. Stir in brown sugar and milk; bring to a boil. Cool slightly. Beat in confectioners' sugar until smooth. Transfer mixture to a small resealable plastic bag; cut a small hole in a corner of bag and drizzle over the muffins.

Easy Batter Rolls

The first thing my guests ask when they come for dinner is if I'm serving these dinner rolls. They are all smiles when I assure them the answer is yes.

—THOMASINA BRUNNER GLOVERSVILLE, NY

PREP: 30 MIN. + RISING • **BAKE:** 15 MIN.
MAKES: 1 DOZEN

- 3 **cups all-purpose flour**
- 2 **tablespoons sugar**
- 1 **package (¼ ounce) active dry yeast**
- 1 **teaspoon salt**
- 1 **cup water**
- 2 **tablespoons butter**
- 1 **egg**
  Melted butter

1. In a large bowl, combine 2 cups of flour, sugar, yeast and salt. In a saucepan, heat water and butter to 120°-130°. Add to dry ingredients; beat until blended. Add egg; beat on low speed for 30 seconds, then on high for 3 minutes. Stir in remaining flour (batter will be stiff). Do not knead. Cover and let rise in a warm place until doubled, about 30 minutes.

2. Stir dough down. Fill greased muffin cups half full. Cover and let rise until doubled, about 4 minutes.

3. Bake at 350° for 15-20 minutes or until golden brown. Cool for 1 minute before removing from pan to a wire rack. Brush tops with melted butter.

Sunflower Seed Bread

For the Buttery Herb Loaves, I used a dough hook and it turned out fine. I like to add ½ cup unsalted sunflower seeds to the bread—it makes great toast!

—GWM TASTEOFHOME.COM

Buttery Herb Loaves

This is one of my family's favorite bread recipes. They love it with a warm bowl of soup when there's a chill in the air.

—LILLIAN HATCHER PLAINFIELD, IL

PREP: 45 MIN. + RISING
BAKE: 20 MIN. + COOLING
MAKES: 2 LOAVES (16 SLICES EACH)

- 4 **to 5 cups all-purpose flour**
- 1 **package (¼ ounce) active dry yeast**
- ¼ **cup sugar**
- 1 **teaspoon salt**
- 1¼ **cups 2% milk**
- ⅓ **cup butter, cubed**
- 2 **eggs**
  FILLING
- ½ **cup butter, softened**
- 1 **garlic clove, minced**
- ½ **teaspoon dried minced onion**
- ½ **teaspoon dried basil**
- ½ **teaspoon caraway seeds**
- ¼ **teaspoon dried oregano**
- ⅛ **teaspoon cayenne pepper**

1. In a large bowl, combine 2 cups flour, yeast, sugar and salt. In a small saucepan, heat milk and butter to 120°-130°. Add to dry ingredients; beat just until moistened. Add eggs; beat until smooth. Stir in enough remaining flour to form a soft dough.

2. Turn dough onto a floured surface; knead until smooth and elastic, about 6-8 minutes. Place in a greased bowl, turning once to grease top. Cover and let rise in a warm place until doubled, about 1 hour.

3. In a small bowl, combine filling ingredients; set aside. Punch down dough; divide in half. Turn onto a lightly floured surface. Roll each portion into a 15x9-in. rectangle. Spread filling over each to within ½ in. of edges. Roll up jelly-roll style, starting with a short side; pinch seams to seal and tuck ends under.

4. Place seam side down in two greased 9x5-in. loaf pans. Cover and let rise in a warm place until doubled, about 30 minutes.

5. Bake at 350° for 20-25 minutes or until loaves are golden brown. Cool for 10 minutes before removing from pans to wire racks to cool completely.

Dill-Onion Batter Bread

This dough doesn't require any kneading so it's very easy to make. The loaf comes out tender and has a pleasant dill flavor. I serve it with soups, salads and a variety of different entrees.

—**GLORIA HUEY** PORT ALLEGANY, PA

PREP: 15 MIN. + RISING
BAKE: 30 MIN. + COOLING
MAKES: 1 LOAF (16 SLICES)

- 1 package (¼ ounce) active dry yeast
- ¼ cup warm water (110° to 115°)
- 1 cup warm 2% milk (110° to 115°)
- 2 tablespoons butter, softened
- 2 tablespoons sugar
- 1 egg
- 2 teaspoons dill seed
- 2 teaspoons dried minced onion
- ½ teaspoon salt
- 3 cups all-purpose flour

1. In a large bowl, dissolve yeast in warm water. Add the milk, butter, sugar, egg, dill seed, onion, salt and 1½ cups flour. Beat on medium speed for 3 minutes. Stir in remaining flour (batter will be sticky). Do not knead. Cover and let rise in a warm place until doubled, about 1 hour.

2. Stir the batter down. Spoon into a greased 9x5-in. loaf pan. Cover and let dough rise until nearly doubled, about 45 minutes.

3. Bake at 350° for 30-35 minutes or until golden brown (cover loosely with foil if top browns too quickly). Cool for 10 minutes before removing from pan to a wire rack.

kid FRIENDLY Pumpkin Cheesecake Muffins

PREP: 25 MIN. • **BAKE:** 15 MIN.
MAKES: 2 DOZEN

- 3 cups all-purpose flour
- 2 cups sugar
- 2 teaspoons baking soda
- 2 teaspoons baking powder
- 1 teaspoon salt
- 1 teaspoon ground cinnamon
- 4 eggs
- 1 can (15 ounces) solid-pack pumpkin
- 1½ cups canola oil

CREAM CHEESE FILLING
- 1 package (8 ounces) cream cheese, softened
- ½ cup sugar
- 1 egg
- 1 tablespoon all-purpose flour

PRALINE TOPPING
- ⅔ cup chopped pecans
- ⅓ cup packed brown sugar
- 2 tablespoons sour cream

1. In a large bowl, combine the first six ingredients. In another bowl, whisk the eggs, pumpkin and oil. Stir into dry ingredients just until moistened. Fill greased or paper-lined muffin cups one-third full.

2. For filling, beat the cream cheese, sugar, egg and flour until smooth. Drop by tablespoonfuls into center of each muffin. Top with remaining batter.

3. For the topping, in a small bowl, combine the pecans, brown sugar and sour cream; spoon over batter. Bake at 400° for 15-18 minutes or until a toothpick inserted in the muffin comes out clean. Cool for 5 minutes before removing from pans to wire racks. Serve warm. Refrigerate leftovers.

My mother-in-law came up with these tender treats by combining a few of her favorite muffin recipes. Chock-full of pumpkin, they feature both a sweet cream cheese filling and crunchy praline topping. —LISA POWELSON SCOTT CITY, KS

Lemon Crumb Muffins

I love to have the dough for these muffins ready and waiting in the refrigerator when company comes. They bake up in just 20 minutes and taste delicious warm. The cakelike texture makes them perfect for breakfast, dessert or snacking.

—CLAUDETTE BROWNLEE KINGFISHER, OK

PREP: 25 MIN. • **BAKE:** 20 MIN./BATCH
MAKES: 40 MUFFINS.

- 6 cups all-purpose flour
- 4 cups sugar
- ¾ teaspoon baking soda
- ¾ teaspoon salt
- 8 eggs
- 2 cups (16 ounces) sour cream
- 2 cups butter, melted
- 3 tablespoons grated lemon peel
- 2 tablespoons lemon juice

TOPPING
- ¾ cup all-purpose flour
- ¾ cup sugar
- ¼ cup cold butter, cubed

GLAZE
- ½ cup sugar
- ⅓ cup lemon juice

1. In a large bowl, combine the flour, sugar, baking soda and salt. In another bowl, combine the eggs, sour cream, butter, lemon peel and juice. Stir into dry ingredients just until moistened. Fill greased or paper-lined muffin cups three-fourths full.

2. In a small bowl, combine flour and sugar; cut in butter until the mixture resembles coarse crumbs. Sprinkle over batter.

3. Bake at 350° for 20-25 minutes or until a toothpick inserted near the center comes out clean. Cool for 5 minutes before removing from pans to wire racks. In a small bowl, whisk glaze ingredients; drizzle over warm muffins. Serve warm.

Orange Nut Bread & Cream Cheese Spread

This delectable sweet bread was my mother's favorite. Every bite gives you a burst of orange and a little crunch from the chopped walnuts.

—KAREN SUE GARBACK-PRISTERA
ALBANY, NY

PREP: 40 MIN. • **BAKE:** 35 MIN. + COOLING
MAKES: 3 MINI LOAVES (6 SLICES EACH) AND 1 CUP SPREAD

- ⅓ cup butter, softened
- ⅔ cup sugar
- 2 eggs
- ½ teaspoon orange extract
- ½ teaspoon vanilla extract
- 2 cups all-purpose flour
- 1 teaspoon baking powder
- ½ teaspoon salt
- ¼ teaspoon baking soda
- 1 cup orange juice
- 1 cup chopped walnuts

SPREAD
- 1 package (8 ounces) cream cheese, softened
- 2 tablespoons orange juice
- 1 tablespoon confectioners' sugar
- 1 teaspoon grated orange peel

1. In a large bowl, cream butter and sugar until light and fluffy. Add eggs, one at a time, beating well after each addition. Beat in extracts.

2. Combine the flour, baking powder, salt and baking soda; add to creamed mixture alternately with orange juice. Fold in walnuts.

3. Transfer to three greased 5¾x3x2-in. loaf pans. Bake at 350° for 35-40 minutes or until a toothpick inserted near the center comes out clean. Cool for 10 minutes before removing from pans to wire racks.

4. In a small bowl, beat the cream cheese, orange juice, confectioners' sugar and orange peel until well blended. Chill until serving. Serve with bread.

Did you know?
The first pop-up toaster for home use came out in 1926, two years before consumers could buy prepared sliced bread.

Cornmeal Dinner Rolls

A flavorful sidekick to chilis, soups and stews, these biscuits can also stand alone as a snack with a simple pat of butter and drizzle of honey.

—**BRYNN RADER** OLYMPIA, WA

PREP: 35 MIN.+ RISING • **BAKE:** 15 MIN.
MAKES: 2½ DOZEN

- 2 **cups whole milk**
- ½ **cup sugar**
- ½ **cup butter, cubed**
- ⅓ **cup cornmeal**
- 1¼ **teaspoons salt**
- 1 **package (¼ ounce) active dry yeast**
- ¼ **cup warm water (110° to 115°)**
- 2 **eggs**
- 4¾ **to 5¾ cups all-purpose flour**

TOPPING

- 2 **tablespoons butter, melted**
- 1 **tablespoon cornmeal**

1. In a large saucepan, combine the milk, sugar, butter, cornmeal and salt. Bring to a boil over medium heat, stirring constantly. Reduce heat; cook and stir 5-8 minutes or until thickened. Cool to 110°-115°.

2. In a small bowl, dissolve yeast in warm water. In a large bowl, combine the eggs, cornmeal mixture, yeast mixture and 2 cups flour; beat until smooth. Stir in enough of remaining flour to form a soft dough (dough will be sticky).

3. Turn dough onto a floured surface; knead until smooth and elastic, about 6-8 minutes. Place in a greased bowl, turning once to grease the top. Cover with plastic wrap; let rise in a warm place until doubled, about 1 hour.

4. Punch dough down. Turn onto a lightly floured surface; divide into 30 balls. Place 2 in. apart on greased baking sheets. Cover with a clean kitchen towel; let rise in a warm place until doubled, about 45 minutes.

5. Uncover rolls; brush with melted butter and sprinkle with cornmeal. Bake at 375° for 13-17 minutes or until golden brown. Remove from pans to wire racks; serve warm.

Parmesan Herb Loaf

This savory loaf is one of my very best quick bread recipes. I like to serve slices accompanied by individual ramekins filled with extra virgin olive oil infused with herbs for dipping.

—**DIANNE CULLEY** NESBIT, MS

PREP: 15 MIN. • **BAKE:** 30 MIN.
MAKES: 1 LOAF (8 SERVINGS)

- 1¼ **cups all-purpose flour**
- 3 **tablespoons plus 1 teaspoon grated Parmesan cheese, divided**
- 1½ **teaspoons sugar**
- 1½ **teaspoons dried minced onion**
- 1¼ **teaspoons Italian seasoning, divided**
- ½ **teaspoon baking powder**
- ¼ **teaspoon baking soda**
- ¼ **teaspoon salt**
- ½ **cup sour cream**
- 2 **tablespoons plus 2 teaspoons 2% milk**
- 4½ **teaspoons butter, melted**
- 1 **egg white, lightly beaten**

1. In a small bowl, combine the flour, 3 tablespoons Parmesan cheese, sugar, onion, 1 teaspoon Italian seasoning, baking powder, baking soda and salt. In another bowl, whisk the sour cream, milk and butter. Stir into the dry ingredients just until moistened.

2. Turn onto a floured surface; knead for 1 minute. Shape into a round loaf; place on a baking sheet coated with cooking spray. With kitchen scissors, cut a ¼-in.-deep cross in top of loaf. Brush with egg white. Sprinkle with the remaining cheese and Italian seasoning.

3. Bake at 350° for 30-35 minutes or until golden brown. Serve warm.

Lemon Bread

You'll often find me baking this sunshiny-sweet bread in the kitchen when we are expecting company. It has a texture similar to a pound cake and it tastes just as rich, with a slight hint of lemon.

—KATHY SCOTT LINGLE, WY

PREP: 10 MIN. • **BAKE:** 45 MIN. + COOLING
MAKES: 1 LOAF (12 SLICES)

- ½ **cup butter, softened**
- 1 **cup sugar**
- 2 **eggs**
- 2 **tablespoons lemon juice**
- 1 **tablespoon grated lemon peel**
- 1½ **cups all-purpose flour**
- 1 **teaspoon baking powder**
- ⅛ **teaspoon salt**
- ½ **cup 2% milk**

GLAZE

- ½ **cup confectioners' sugar**
- 2 **tablespoons lemon juice**

1. In a large bowl, cream butter and sugar until light and fluffy. Beat in the eggs, lemon juice and peel. Combine the flour, baking powder and salt; gradually stir into creamed mixture alternately with milk, beating well after each addition.

2. Pour into a greased 8x4-in. loaf pan. Bake at 350° for 45 minutes or until a toothpick inserted near the center comes out clean.

3. Combine glaze ingredients. Remove bread from pan; immediately drizzle with glaze. Cool bread on a wire rack. Serve warm.

Italian Sweet Bread

My golden brown bread offers satisfying sweetness in every slice. The hearty round loaves rise well and cut beautifully. With an egg wash and a light sprinkling of Italian seasoning, the bread looks pretty, too.

—KIM OOMS COTTAGE GROVE, MN

PREP: 10 MIN. + RISING
BAKE: 20 MIN. + COOLING
MAKES: 2 LOAVES (16 SLICES EACH)

- 1 **cup warm 2% milk (70° to 80°)**
- 1 **egg, lightly beaten**
- 2 **tablespoons butter, softened**
- ¼ **cup sugar**
- 1 **teaspoon salt**
- 3 **cups all-purpose flour**
- 2 **teaspoons active dry yeast**

EGG WASH

- 1 **egg**
- 1 **tablespoon water**
  Italian seasoning, optional

1. In bread machine pan, place the first seven ingredients in the order suggested by manufacturer. Select dough setting (check dough after 5 minutes of mixing; add 1 to 2 tablespoons of water or flour if needed).

2. When the cycle is completed, turn dough onto a floured surface. Divide in half. Shape each portion into a ball; flatten slightly. Place in two greased 9-in. round baking pans. Cover and let rise until doubled, about 45 minutes.

3. Beat egg and water; brush over the dough. Sprinkle with Italian seasoning if desired. Bake loaves at 350° for 20-25 minutes or until golden brown. Remove loaves from pans to wire racks to cool.

NOTE *We recommend you do not use a bread machine's time-delay feature for this recipe.*

Hawaiian Dinner Rolls

Pineapple and coconut give a subtle sweetness to these golden rolls, and leftovers are perfect for sandwiches.

—**KATHY KURTZ** GLENDORA, CA

PREP: 35 MIN. + RISING • **BAKE:** 15 MIN.
MAKES: 15 ROLLS

- 1 can (8 ounces) crushed pineapple, undrained
- ¼ cup warm pineapple juice (70° to 80°)
- ¼ cup water (70° to 80°)
- 1 egg
- ¼ cup butter, cubed
- ¼ cup nonfat dry milk powder
- 1 tablespoon sugar
- 1½ teaspoons salt
- 3¼ cups bread flour
- 2¼ teaspoons active dry yeast
- ¾ cup flaked coconut

1. In bread machine pan, place the first 10 ingredients in order suggested by manufacturer. Select dough setting (check the dough after 5 minutes of mixing; add 1 to 2 tablespoons of water or flour if needed). Just before final kneading (your machine may audibly signal this), add coconut.

2. When the cycle is complete, turn the dough onto a lightly floured surface. Cover with plastic wrap; let the dough rest for 10 minutes. Divide into 15 portions; roll each into a ball. Place in a greased 13x9-in. baking pan.

3. Cover and let rise in a warm place for 45 minutes or until doubled. Bake at 375° for 15-20 minutes or until golden brown.

NOTE *We recommend you do not use a bread machine's time-delay feature for this recipe.*

Peppery Hush Puppies

For our family, a good fish dinner just isn't complete without a side of these zesty hush puppies. You can also serve them alone as a spicy snack.

—**CAROLYN GRIFFIN** MACON, GA

PREP: 10 MIN. • **COOK:** 30 MIN.
MAKES: 6 DOZEN

- 2 cups cornmeal
- 1 cup plus 3 tablespoons all-purpose flour
- 2 teaspoons baking powder
- 1½ teaspoons sugar
- 1 teaspoon salt
- ½ teaspoon baking soda
- 1 egg
- ⅔ cup water
- ½ cup buttermilk
- ½ cup butter, melted
- 1 cup grated onion
- 2 jalapeno peppers, seeded and chopped
- 1 small green pepper, chopped
  Oil for deep-fat frying

1. In a large bowl, combine cornmeal, flour, baking powder, sugar, salt and baking soda. In another bowl, whisk the egg, water, buttermilk and butter. Stir in the onion, jalapenos and green pepper. Stir into dry ingredients just until moistened.

2. In an electric skillet or deep-fat fryer, heat oil to 375°. Drop batter by teaspoonfuls, a few at a time, into hot oil. Fry until golden brown on both sides. Drain hush puppies on paper towels. Serve warm.

NOTE *Wear disposable gloves when cutting hot peppers; the oils can burn skin. Avoid touching your face.*

ULTIMATE *Comfort* Cheddar Garlic Biscuits

A friend gave me the recipe for these savory biscuits. They're easy to make! Biscuit mix is combined with a little minced onion, garlic powder and cheese to create golden drop biscuits that bake in a flash.
—**FRANCES POSTE** WALL, SD

START TO FINISH: 25 MIN.
MAKES: 15 BISCUITS

- 2 **cups biscuit/baking mix**
- ½ **cup shredded cheddar cheese**
- ½ **teaspoon dried minced onion**
- ⅔ **cup 2% milk**
- ¼ **cup butter, melted**
- ½ **teaspoon garlic powder**

1. Preheat oven to 450°. Combine biscuit mix, cheese and onion in a large bowl. Stir in milk until a soft dough forms; stir 30 seconds.

2. Drop by rounded tablespoonfuls 2 in. apart onto ungreased baking sheets. Bake 8-10 minutes or until golden brown. Combine butter and garlic powder; brush over biscuits. Serve warm.

Baker's Dozen Yeast Rolls

A yummy honey-garlic topping turns easy dinner rolls into something extra-special. A batch of these goes great with a pot of chili or soup. They're also delicious served alongside a main-dish salad.
—**TASTE OF HOME TEST KITCHEN**

PREP: 25 MIN. + RISING
BAKE: 15 MIN. + COOLING
MAKES: 13 ROLLS

- 2 **to 2½ cups all-purpose flour**
- 2 **tablespoons sugar**
- 1 **package (¼ ounce) quick-rise yeast**
- ½ **teaspoon salt**
- ¾ **cup warm water (120° to 130°)**
- 2 **tablespoons plus 4 teaspoons butter, melted, divided**
- ¾ **cup shredded sharp cheddar cheese**
- 2 **teaspoons honey**
- ⅛ **teaspoon garlic salt**

1. In a large bowl, combine 1½ cups flour, sugar, yeast and salt. Add water and 2 tablespoons butter; beat on medium speed for 3 minutes or until smooth. Stir in cheese and enough remaining flour to form a soft dough.

2. Turn dough onto a lightly floured surface; knead until smooth and elastic, about 4-6 minutes. Cover and let rest for 10 minutes. Divide into 13 pieces. Shape each into a ball. Place in a greased 9-in. round baking pan. Cover and let rise in a warm place until doubled, about 30 minutes.

3. Preheat oven to 375°. Bake 11-14 minutes or until lightly browned. Combine honey, garlic salt and remaining butter; brush over rolls. Remove from pan to wire rack.

Swiss Beer Bread

The recipe is a favorite because it isn't greasy like other cheese breads I have tried. It will not last long, though!

—**DEBI WALLACE** CHESTERTOWN, NY

PREP: 15 MIN. • **BAKE:** 50 MIN. + COOLING
MAKES: 1 LOAF (12 SLICES)

- **4 ounces Jarlsberg or Swiss cheese**
- **3 cups all-purpose flour**
- **3 tablespoons sugar**
- **3 teaspoons baking powder**
- **1½ teaspoons salt**
- **½ teaspoon pepper**
- **1 bottle (12 ounces) beer or nonalcoholic beer**
- **2 tablespoons butter, melted**

1. Divide cheese in half. Cut half of cheese into ¼-inch cubes; shred remaining cheese. In a large bowl, combine the flour, sugar, baking powder, salt and pepper. Stir beer into dry ingredients just until moistened. Fold in cheese.

2. Transfer to a greased 8x4-in. loaf pan. Drizzle with butter. Bake at 375° for 50-60 minutes or until a toothpick inserted near the center comes out clean. Cool for 10 minutes before removing from pan to a wire rack.

Blue-Ribbon Rye Bread

Our family had a little bread business, selling homemade loaves to neighbors and other people in the community, including this rye that won best of show at our county fair.

—**SUSANNE SPICKER** NORTH OGDEN, UT

PREP: 40 MIN. + RISING
BAKE: 20 MIN. + COOLING
MAKES: 3 LOAVES (12 SLICES EACH)

- **1 package (¼ ounce) active dry yeast**
- **1 tablespoon sugar**
- **2¼ cups warm water (110° to 115°)**
- **¼ cup packed brown sugar**
- **¼ cup shortening**
- **¼ cup molasses**
- **1 tablespoon caraway seeds**
- **1 teaspoon salt**
- **1 cup rye flour**
- **3½ to 4 cups all-purpose flour**

1. In a large bowl, dissolve yeast and sugar in warm water. Stir in the brown sugar, shortening, molasses, caraway seeds and salt. Add the rye flour and 1¾ cups all-purpose flour; beat until smooth. Stir in enough remaining all-purpose flour to form a soft dough.

2. Turn dough onto a floured surface; knead until smooth and elastic, about 6-8 minutes. Place in a greased bowl, turning once to grease the top. Cover and let rise in a warm place until doubled, about 1 hour.

3. Punch dough down; shape into three loaves. Place on greased baking sheets. Cover and let rise until doubled, about 1 hour.

4. Bake at 350° for 20-25 minutes or until golden brown. Remove from pans to wire racks to cool.

My mother made this bread for years, but she used date filling. I loved her bread so much that I made my own with cranberries. It has a slightly tart filling and a sweet streusel topping, and each slice shows off the enticing ruby swirl.

—**DARLENE BRENDEN** SALEM, OR

Cranberry Swirl Loaf

PREP: 30 MIN. + RISING
BAKE: 40 MIN. + COOLING
MAKES: 1 LOAF (16 SLICES)

- ⅓ cup sugar
- 1 package (¼ ounce) quick-rise yeast
- ½ teaspoon salt
- 3 to 3½ cups all-purpose flour
- ½ cup water
- ½ cup milk
- ⅓ cup butter, cubed

FILLING

- 1 cup chopped fresh or frozen cranberries
- ¼ cup packed brown sugar
- ¼ cup water
- 1 tablespoon butter
- 1 tablespoon lemon juice
- ½ cup chopped walnuts, optional

TOPPING

- 2 tablespoons all-purpose flour
- 2 tablespoons sugar
- 2 tablespoons cold butter, divided

1. In a large bowl, mix the sugar, yeast, salt and 1 cup flour. In a small saucepan, heat water, milk and butter to 120°-130°. Add to dry ingredients; beat on medium speed 2 minutes. Stir in enough remaining flour to form a soft dough.

2. Turn dough onto a floured surface; knead until smooth and elastic, about 6-8 minutes. Place in a greased bowl, turning once to grease the top. Cover with plastic wrap and let rise in a warm place until doubled, about 1 hour.

3. Meanwhile, in a small saucepan, combine cranberries, brown sugar and water. Cook over medium heat until the cranberries are soft, about 15 minutes. Remove from heat; stir in butter, lemon juice and, if desired, walnuts. Cool.

4. Punch down dough. Turn onto a lightly floured surface; roll into a 20x10-in. rectangle. Spread filling to within ½ in. of edges. Roll up jelly-roll style, starting with a long side; pinch seam to seal. Transfer to a greased 9x5-in. loaf pan, arranging in a slight zigzag fashion to fit.

5. For the topping, in a small bowl, combine the flour and sugar; cut in 1 tablespoon butter until crumbly. Melt remaining butter; brush over dough. Sprinkle with crumb mixture. Cover with a towel; let rise in a warm place until doubled, about 40 minutes. Preheat oven to 350°.

6. Bake 40-45 minutes or until golden brown. Carefully remove from pan to a wire rack to cool.

Go-Go Garlic Bread

My family simply devours this savory garlic bread. And I'm always asked for the recipe when I make it for guests. I call it go-go bread because it's gone before I know it!
—**DOLORES BRIGHAM** INGLEWOOD, CA

START TO FINISH: 25 MIN.
MAKES: 12 SERVINGS

- ½ cup butter, softened
- ½ cup mayonnaise
- 1 tablespoon grated Parmesan cheese
- 2 teaspoons minced garlic
- ½ teaspoon Italian seasoning
- ⅛ teaspoon seasoned salt
- ½ cup shredded Monterey Jack cheese
- 1 loaf French bread (about 20 inches), halved lengthwise

1. In a small bowl, beat butter and mayonnaise until smooth. Beat in the Parmesan cheese, garlic, Italian seasoning and seasoned salt. Stir in Monterey Jack cheese. Spread over cut sides of bread.

2. Place on an ungreased baking sheet. Bake at 350° for 10-15 minutes or until cheese is melted. Slice and serve warm.

Use the Proper Pan

Whenever you bake bread, use aluminum pans with a dull rather than a shiny or dark finish. Glass baking dishes and dark finishes will produce darker crusts.

ULTIMATE *Comfort*

Judy's Chocolate Chip Banana Bread

I received this recipe from my co-worker and dear friend Judy 32 years ago. When she gave it to me she said, "You will never need another banana bread recipe." She was almost right. I added lots of chocolate chips for the chocolate lovers in my family.

—DEBRA KEISER ST. CLOUD, MN

PREP: 20 MIN. • **BAKE:** 1 HOUR + COOLING
MAKES: 1 LOAF (16 SLICES)

- ½ cup butter, softened
- 1¼ cups sugar
- 2 eggs
- 1 cup mashed ripe bananas (about 2 medium)
- ¼ cup buttermilk
- 1 teaspoon vanilla extract
- 2 cups all-purpose flour
- 1 teaspoon baking powder
- ¾ teaspoon baking soda
- ½ teaspoon salt
- ¾ cup semisweet chocolate chips
- ¼ cup chopped walnuts, optional

1. Preheat oven to 350°. Line bottom of a greased 9x5-in. loaf pan with parchment paper; grease paper.

2. In a large bowl, beat butter and sugar until crumbly. Add eggs, one at a time, beating well after each addition. Beat in the bananas, buttermilk and vanilla. In another bowl, mix flour, baking powder, baking soda and salt; stir into creamed mixture. Fold in the chocolate chips and, if desired, the walnuts.

3. Transfer to prepared pan. Bake 60-65 minutes or until a toothpick inserted in center comes out clean. Cool 10 minutes before removing from pan to a wire rack; remove paper.

Icebox Butterhorns

If you like a roll that melts in your mouth, try my mom's recipe. She had a way with the dough, giving it just the right touch to turn out beautiful buttery rolls every time.

—JUDY CLARK ELKHART, IN

PREP: 15 MIN. + CHILLING • **BAKE:** 15 MIN.
MAKES: 2 DOZEN

- 2 packages (¼ ounce each) active dry yeast
- ¼ cup warm water (110° to 115°)
- 2 cups warm milk (110° to 115°)
- ¾ cup butter, melted
- ½ cup sugar
- 1 egg
- 1 teaspoon salt
- 6½ cups all-purpose flour
  Additional melted butter

1. In a small bowl, dissolve yeast in warm water. In a large bowl, combine the milk, butter, sugar, egg, salt, yeast mixture and 3 cups flour; beat on medium speed until smooth. Stir in enough remaining flour to form a soft dough (dough will be sticky).

2. Do not knead. Place in a greased bowl, turning once to grease the top. Cover with plastic wrap and refrigerate overnight.

3. Punch down dough. Turn onto a lightly floured surface; divide in half. Roll each into a 12-in. circle; cut each into 12 wedges. Roll up wedges from the wide ends. Place 2 in. apart on greased baking sheets, point side down. Cover with kitchen towels; let rise in a warm place until doubled, about 1 hour.

4. Bake at 350° for 15-20 minutes or until golden brown. Immediately brush with additional melted butter. Remove from pans to wire racks to cool.

Lemony Zucchini Bread

Flecks of zucchini give a third dimension to the popular lemon and poppy seed combination in this wonderful quick bread.

—CAROL FUNK RICHARD, SK

PREP: 25 MIN. • **BAKE:** 50 MIN. + COOLING
MAKES: 2 LOAVES (16 SLICES EACH)

- 4 cups all-purpose flour
- 1½ cups sugar
- 1 package (3.4 ounces) instant lemon pudding mix
- 1½ teaspoons baking soda
- 1 teaspoon baking powder
- 1 teaspoon salt
- 4 eggs
- 1¼ cups milk
- 1 cup canola oil
- 3 tablespoons lemon juice
- 1 teaspoon lemon extract
- 2 cups shredded zucchini
- ¼ cup poppy seeds
- 2 teaspoons grated lemon peel

1. In a large bowl, combine the flour, sugar, pudding mix, baking soda, baking powder and salt. In another bowl, whisk the eggs, milk, oil, lemon juice and extract. Stir into the dry ingredients just until moistened. Fold in the zucchini, poppy seeds and lemon peel.
2. Pour into two greased 9x5-in. loaf pans. Bake at 350° for 50-55 minutes or until a toothpick inserted near the center comes out clean. Cool for 10 minutes before removing from pans to wire racks to cool completely.

? Did you know?

Banana nut bread became a mainstream item in the 1930s when mass marketing of baking power and baking soda was on the rise.

Nut-Topped Strawberry Rhubarb Muffins

If the muffin top is your favorite part, you will be delighted with these tasty treats. Pecans, cinnamon and brown sugar give sweet crunch to every bite.

—AUDREY STALLSMITH HADLEY, PA

PREP: 25 MIN. • **BAKE:** 20 MIN. + COOLING
MAKES: 1½ DOZEN

- 2¾ cups all-purpose flour
- 1⅓ cups packed brown sugar
- 2½ teaspoons baking powder
- ½ teaspoon baking soda
- ½ teaspoon ground cinnamon
- ¼ teaspoon salt
- 1 egg
- 1 cup buttermilk
- ½ cup canola oil
- 2 teaspoons vanilla extract
- 1 cup chopped fresh strawberries
- ¾ cup diced fresh or frozen rhubarb

TOPPING
- ½ cup chopped pecans
- ⅓ cup packed brown sugar
- ½ teaspoon ground cinnamon
- 1 tablespoon cold butter

1. In a large bowl, combine the first six ingredients. In another bowl, whisk the egg, buttermilk, oil and vanilla. Stir into the dry ingredients just until moistened. Fold in strawberries and rhubarb. Fill greased or paper-lined muffin cups two-thirds full.
2. In a small bowl, combine the pecans, brown sugar and cinnamon. Cut in butter until mixture resembles coarse crumbs. Sprinkle over batter.
3. Bake at 400° for 20-25 minutes or until a toothpick inserted near the center comes out clean. Cool for 5 minutes before removing from pans to wire racks. Serve warm.

NOTE *If using frozen rhubarb, measure rhubarb while still frozen, then thaw completely. Drain in a colander, but do not press liquid out.*

Apple Streusel Muffins

My family enjoys these muffins with a coffee cake texture as a quick breakfast or a snack on the run. The drizzle of glaze makes them pretty enough for company.
—**DULCY GRACE** ROARING SPRING, PA

PREP: 20 MIN. • **BAKE:** 15 MIN. + COOLING
MAKES: 1 DOZEN

- 2 cups all-purpose flour
- 1 cup sugar
- 1 teaspoon baking powder
- ½ teaspoon baking soda
- ½ teaspoon salt
- 2 eggs
- ½ cup butter, melted
- 1¼ teaspoons vanilla extract
- 1½ cups chopped peeled tart apples

STREUSEL TOPPING
- ⅓ cup packed brown sugar
- 1 tablespoon all-purpose flour
- ⅛ teaspoon ground cinnamon
- 1 tablespoon cold butter

GLAZE
- 1½ cups confectioners' sugar
- 1 to 2 tablespoons milk
- 1 teaspoon butter, melted
- ¼ teaspoon vanilla extract
- ⅛ teaspoon salt

1. In a large bowl, combine the flour, sugar, baking powder, baking soda and salt. In another bowl, combine the eggs, butter and vanilla; stir into dry ingredients just until moistened (batter will be stiff). Fold in apples.
2. Fill greased or paper-lined muffin cups three-fourths full. In a small bowl, combine the brown sugar, flour and cinnamon; cut in butter until crumbly. Sprinkle over batter.
3. Bake at 375° for 15-20 minutes or until a toothpick inserted near center comes out clean. Cool for 5 minutes before removing from pan to a wire rack to cool completely. Combine glaze ingredients; drizzle over muffins.

Challah

This traditional Jewish loaf is often called egg bread because it uses more eggs than most bread recipes. The golden color and delicious flavor make it hard to resist.
—**TASTE OF HOME TEST KITCHEN**

PREP: 30 MIN. + RISING
BAKE: 30 MIN. + COOLING
MAKES: 2 LOAVES (16 SLICES EACH)

- 2 packages (¼ ounce each) active dry yeast
- 1 cup warm water (110° to 115°)
- ½ cup canola oil
- ⅓ cup sugar
- 1 tablespoon salt
- 4 eggs
- 6 to 6½ cups all-purpose flour

TOPPING
- 1 egg
- 1 teaspoon cold water
- 1 tablespoon sesame or poppy seeds, optional

1. In a large bowl, dissolve yeast in warm water. Add the oil, sugar, salt, eggs and 4 cups flour. Beat until smooth. Stir in enough remaining flour to form a firm dough. Turn onto a floured surface; knead until smooth and elastic, about 6-8 minutes. Place in a greased bowl, turning once to grease top. Cover and let rise in a warm place until doubled, about 1 hour.
2. Punch dough down. Turn onto a lightly floured surface; divide in half. Divide each portion into thirds. Shape each piece into a 15-in. rope.
3. Place three ropes on a greased baking sheet and braid; pinch ends to seal and tuck under. Repeat with remaining dough. Cover and let rise until doubled, about 1 hour.
4. Beat the egg and cold water; brush over braids. Sprinkle with sesame or poppy seeds if desired. Bake at 350° for 30-35 minutes or until golden brown. Remove to wire racks to cool.

Old-Fashioned Brown Bread

At Kings Head Inn, which is part of the Kings Landing Historical Settlement, our favorite meal to serve is Thanksgiving dinner. We prepare a traditional meal including roast turkey, mashed potatoes, homemade pickles, cranberry jelly and this delicious brown bread.

—**PATRICIA DONNELLY** KINGS LANDING, NB

PREP: 20 MIN. + RISING
BAKE: 35 MIN. + COOLING
MAKES: 2 LOAVES (16 SLICES EACH)

- 2⅓ **cups boiling water**
- 1 **cup old-fashioned oats**
- ½ **cup butter, cubed**
- ⅓ **cup molasses**
- 5½ **to 6½ cups all-purpose flour**
- 5 **teaspoons active dry yeast**
- 2 **teaspoons salt**

1. In a large bowl, pour boiling water over oats. Stir in butter and molasses. Let stand until mixture cools to 120°-130°, stirring occasionally.
2. In another bowl, combine 3½ cups of the flour, yeast and salt. Beat in oat mixture until blended. Stir in enough remaining flour to form a soft dough.
3. Turn dough onto a floured surface; knead until smooth and elastic, about 6-8 minutes. Place in a greased bowl, turning once to grease the top. Cover and let rise in a warm place until doubled, about 1 hour.
4. Punch dough down. Turn onto a lightly floured surface; divide in half. Shape into loaves. Place in two greased 9x5-in. loaf pans. Cover and let rise until doubled, about 30 minutes.
5. Bake at 375° for 35-40 minutes or until golden brown. Remove from pans to wire racks to cool.

Sweet Potato Crescents

I often serve these light-as-air crescent rolls as part of our Thanksgiving dinner. They make a delightful accompaniment to any menu.

—**REBECCA BAILEY** FAIRBURY, NE

PREP: 30 MIN. + RISING • **BAKE:** 15 MIN.
MAKES: 3 DOZEN

- 2 packages (¼ ounce each) active dry yeast
- 1 cup warm water (110° to 115°)
- 1 can (15¾ ounces) cut sweet potatoes, drained and mashed
- ½ cup sugar
- ½ cup shortening
- 1 egg
- 1½ teaspoons salt
- 5 to 5½ cups all-purpose flour
- ¼ cup butter, melted

1. In a large bowl, dissolve yeast in water; let stand for 5 minutes. Beat in the sweet potatoes, sugar, shortening, egg, salt and 3 cups flour. Add enough remaining flour to form a stiff dough.

2. Turn dough onto a floured surface; knead until smooth and elastic, about 6-8 minutes. Place in a greased bowl, turning once to grease top. Cover and let rise in a warm place until doubled, about 1 hour.

3. Punch dough down; divide into thirds. Roll each portion into a 12-in. circle; cut each into 12 wedges. Brush with butter. Roll up from the wide end and place, pointed end down, 2 in. apart on greased baking sheets. Cover dough and let rise until doubled, about 40 minutes.

4. Bake at 375° for 13-15 minutes or until golden brown. Remove from pans to wire racks.

Grandma Russell's Bread

PREP: 30 MIN. + RISING • **BAKE:** 20 MIN.
MAKES: 2 LOAVES OR 2 DOZEN ROLLS

- 1 package (¼ ounce) active dry yeast
- ⅓ cup warm water (110° to 115°)
- ½ cup sugar, divided
- 1 cup milk
- ½ cup butter, cubed
- 1 tablespoon salt
- 1 cup mashed potatoes
- 2 eggs, beaten

- 5 to 6 cups all-purpose flour
  CINNAMON FILLING
- ¼ cup butter, melted
- ¾ cup sugar
- 1 tablespoon ground cinnamon

1. In a large bowl, combine the yeast, warm water and 1 teaspoon sugar; set aside. In a saucepan, heat milk, butter, salt and remaining sugar until butter is melted. Remove from the heat; stir in potatoes until smooth. Cool to lukewarm; add eggs and mix well.

2. To yeast mixture, add the potato mixture and 5 cups flour. Stir in enough remaining flour to make a soft dough. Turn onto a floured surface and knead until smooth and elastic, about 6-8 minutes. Place in a greased bowl, turning once to grease top. Cover and let rise in a warm place until doubled, about 1½ hours.

3. Punch down and divide in half.
For white bread: Shape two loaves and place in greased 8x4-in. loaf pans.
For cinnamon bread: Roll each half into a 16x8-in. rectangle. Brush with melted butter; combine sugar and cinnamon and sprinkle over butter. Starting at the narrow end, roll up into a loaf, sealing the edges and ends. Place in greased 8x4-in. loaf pans.
For cinnamon rolls: Roll each half into an 18x12-in. rectangle. Brush with melted butter and sprinkle with cinnamon-sugar. Starting at the narrow end, roll up and seal edges and ends. Cut each into 12 pieces of 1½ in. Place in greased 9-in. round baking pans.

4. To bake: Cover and let rise until doubled. Bake loaves at 375° for 20 minutes; bake rolls at 375° for 25-30 minutes. Cover with foil if they brown too quickly.

I remember as a child always smelling fresh homemade bread and rolls whenever I walked into Grandma's house. The warm slices were delicious and melted in my mouth!

—JANET POLITO NAMPA, ID

Herbed Onion Focaccia

My recipe makes three savory flat breads, but don't be surprised to see them all disappear from your dinner table!

—**MELANIE EDDY** SYRACUSE, KS

PREP: 40 MIN. + RISING • **BAKE:** 20 MIN.
MAKES: 3 LOAVES

- 1 package (¼ ounce) active dry yeast
- 1½ cups warm water (110° to 115°), divided
- 1 teaspoon sugar
- 6 tablespoons olive oil, divided
- 2 teaspoons salt
- 4 to 4½ cups all-purpose flour
- 3 tablespoons finely chopped green onions
- 1½ teaspoons minced fresh rosemary or ½ teaspoon dried rosemary, crushed
- 1½ teaspoons small fresh sage leaves or ½ teaspoon rubbed sage
- 1½ teaspoons minced fresh oregano or ½ teaspoon dried oregano
  Seasoned olive oil or additional olive oil, optional

1. In a large bowl, dissolve yeast in ½ cup warm water. Add sugar; let stand 5 minutes. Add 4 tablespoons oil, salt, 2 cups flour and remaining water. Beat until smooth. Stir in enough remaining flour to form a soft dough.

2. Turn dough onto a floured surface; knead until smooth and elastic, about 6-8 minutes. Place in a greased bowl, turning once to grease top. Cover and let rise in a warm place until doubled, about 1 hour.

3. Punch dough down. Divide into three portions. Cover and let rest for 10 minutes. Shape each portion into an 8-in. circle; place on greased baking sheets. Cover and let rise until doubled, about 30 minutes. Using the end of a wooden spoon handle, make several ¼-in. indentations in each loaf.

4. Brush with remaining oil. Sprinkle with green onions, rosemary, sage and oregano. Bake loaves at 400° for 20-25 minutes or until golden brown. Remove to wire racks. Serve with olive oil for dipping if desired.

Overnight Honey-Wheat Rolls

These yeast rolls don't require kneading, and the make-ahead dough saves you time on the day of your meal. But the best part is the hint of sweet honey—it really adds to the flavor.

—**LISA VARNER** EL PASO, TX

PREP: 30 MIN. + CHILLING • **BAKE:** 10 MIN.
MAKES: 1½ DOZEN

- 1 package (¼ ounce) active dry yeast
- 1¼ cups warm water (110° to 115°), divided
- 2 egg whites
- ⅓ cup honey
- ¼ cup canola oil
- 1 teaspoon salt
- 1½ cups whole wheat flour
- 2½ cups all-purpose flour
  Melted butter, optional

1. In a small bowl, dissolve yeast in ¼ cup warm water. In a large bowl, beat egg whites until foamy. Add the yeast mixture, honey, oil, salt, whole wheat flour and remaining water. Beat on medium speed for 3 minutes. Beat until smooth. Stir in enough of the all-purpose flour to form a soft dough (dough will be sticky). Cover and refrigerate overnight.

2. Punch dough down. Turn onto a floured surface; divide in half. Shape each portion into nine balls. To form knots, roll each ball into a 10-in. rope; tie into a knot. Tuck ends under.

3. Place rolls 2 in. apart on greased baking sheets. Cover and let rise until doubled, about 50 minutes.

4. Bake at 375° for 10-12 minutes or until golden brown. Brush with melted butter if desired.

Desserts

GET OUT THE MIXING BOWL. THE SWEETS YOU'VE BEEN DREAMING OF ARE ABOUT TO COME TRUE.

**DELUXE
PUMPKIN CHEESECAKE**
PAGE 247

**SPECIAL
MOCHA CUPCAKES**
PAGE 250

**CARROT
LAYER CAKE**
PAGE 276

Cheesecake with Raspberry Sauce

Cheesecake is our family tradition for holidays and special occasions. When my daughter was away from home for her birthday, I made this and shipped it to her (with candles) on dry ice. I'm planning to make it for her wedding in June.

—JEANETTE VOLKER WALTON, NE

PREP: 1 HOUR • **BAKE:** 50 MIN. + CHILLING
MAKES: 16 SERVINGS

- 1¾ cups graham cracker crumbs
- ¼ cup sugar
- ⅓ cup butter, melted

FILLING

- 5 packages (8 ounces each) cream cheese, softened
- 1 cup sugar
- 1 cup (8 ounces) sour cream
- ½ cup heavy whipping cream
- 2 teaspoons vanilla extract
- 7 eggs, lightly beaten

SAUCE/TOPPING

- 1 package (12 ounces) frozen unsweetened raspberries, thawed
- ½ cup sugar
- 2 cups heavy whipping cream
- ½ cup confectioners' sugar
- 1 teaspoon vanilla extract

1. Place a greased 10-in. springform pan on a double thickness of heavy-duty foil (about 18 in. square). Securely wrap foil around pan.

2. In a small bowl, combine cracker crumbs and sugar; stir in butter. Press onto the bottom and 1 in. up the sides of prepared pan. Place on a baking sheet. Bake at 350° for 5-8 minutes. Cool on a wire rack.

3. In a large bowl, beat cream cheese and sugar until smooth. Beat in the sour cream, heavy cream and vanilla. Add eggs; beat on low speed just until combined. Pour into crust. Place springform pan in a large baking pan; add 1 in. of hot water to larger pan.

4. Bake at 350° for 50-60 minutes or until center is just set and top appears dull. Remove springform pan from water bath. Cool on a wire rack for 10 minutes. Carefully run a knife around edge of pan to loosen. Cool 1 hour

longer. Refrigerate overnight. Remove sides of pan.

5. For sauce, place raspberries and sugar in a food processor; cover and process until blended. For topping, in a small bowl, beat heavy cream until it begins to thicken. Add confectioners' sugar and vanilla; beat until soft peaks form. Serve cheesecake with raspberry sauce and topping.

Icebox Cake

You don't have to be a baker to turn out an impressive dessert. This cake is made from chocolate wafers and whipping cream and only takes 15 minutes to make.

—CINDY HAWKINS NEW YORK, NY

PREP: 15 MIN. + CHILLING
MAKES: 10-12 SERVINGS

- 2 cups heavy whipping cream
- 2 tablespoons confectioners' sugar
- 1 teaspoon vanilla extract
- 1 package (9 ounces) chocolate wafers
    Chocolate curls, optional

1. In a large bowl, beat cream until soft peaks form. Add sugar and vanilla; beat until stiff. Spread heaping teaspoonfuls on the cookies. Make six stacks of cookies; turn stacks on edge and place on a serving platter, forming a 14-in.-long cake.

2. Frost top and sides with remaining whipped cream. Garnish with chocolate curls if desired. Refrigerate for 4-6 hours before serving.

Did you know?

Depending on where you live, icebox cake is also known as zebra or ripple cake. And now with the icebox extinct, some folks refer to it as refrigerator cake.

Strawberry Cheesecake Ice Cream

Light and refreshing, this dreamy, creamy dessert is perfect for warm afternoons. Great for scooping into cones, the frozen fluff won't melt as fast as regular ice cream.

—DEBRA GOFORTH NEWPORT, TN

PREP: 10 MIN. + FREEZING
MAKES: 2 QUARTS

- 1 package (8 ounces) cream cheese, softened
- ⅓ cup refrigerated French vanilla nondairy creamer
- ¼ cup sugar
- 1 teaspoon grated lemon peel
- 1 carton (16 ounces) frozen whipped topping, thawed
- 2 packages (10 ounces each) frozen sweetened sliced strawberries, thawed

In a large bowl, beat the cream cheese, creamer, sugar and lemon peel until blended. Fold in whipped topping and strawberries. Transfer to a freezer container; freeze for 4 hours or until firm. Remove from the freezer 10 minutes before serving.

ULTIMATE *Comfort* Banana Cream Pie

Cream pies are my mom's specialty, and this dreamy dessert has a wonderful banana flavor. It looks so pretty topped with almonds, and it cuts easily, too.

—JODI GRABLE SPRINGFIELD, MO

PREP: 10 MIN. • **COOK:** 15 MIN. + CHILLING
MAKES: 8 SERVINGS

- 1 cup sugar
- ¼ cup cornstarch
- ½ teaspoon salt
- 3 cups 2% milk
- 2 eggs, lightly beaten
- 3 tablespoons butter
- 1½ teaspoons vanilla extract
- 1 pastry shell (9 inches), baked
- 2 large firm bananas
- 1 cup heavy whipping cream, whipped

1. In a large saucepan, combine sugar, cornstarch, salt and milk until smooth. Cook and stir over medium-high heat until thickened and bubbly. Reduce heat; cook and stir 2 minutes longer. Remove from heat. Stir a small amount of hot filling into eggs; return all to pan. Bring to a gentle boil; cook and stir 2 minutes longer.

2. Remove from heat. Gently stir in butter and vanilla. Press plastic wrap onto surface of custard; refrigerate, covered, 30 minutes.

3. Spread half of the custard into pastry shell. Slice bananas; arrange over filling. Pour remaining custard over bananas. Spread with whipped cream. Refrigerate 6 hours or overnight.

Strawberry-Rhubarb Crumb Pie

Everyone seems to have a rhubarb patch here in Maine. This pie won first prize at our church fair; I hope it's a winner at your house, too!

—**PAULA PHILLIPS** EAST WINTHROP, ME

PREP: 15 MIN. • **BAKE:** 45 MIN.
MAKES: 8 SERVINGS

- 1 **egg**
- 1 **cup sugar**
- 2 **tablespoons all-purpose flour**
- 1 **teaspoon vanilla extract**
- ¾ **pound rhubarb rib, cut into ½-inch pieces or sliced frozen rhubarb, (about 3 cups)**
- 1 **pint fresh strawberries, halved**
- 1 **unbaked pie shell (9 inches)**

TOPPING

- ¾ **cup all-purpose flour**
- ½ **cup packed brown sugar**
- ½ **cup quick-cooking or old-fashioned oats**
- ½ **cup cold butter, cubed**

1. In a large bowl, beat egg. Beat in the sugar, flour and vanilla until well blended. Gently stir in rhubarb and strawberries. Pour into pastry shell.
2. For topping, in a small bowl, combine the flour, brown sugar and oats; cut in butter until crumbly. Sprinkle over fruit.
3. Bake at 400° for 10 minutes. Reduce heat to 350° bake for 35 minutes longer or until crust is golden brown and filling is bubbly. Cool on a wire rack.
NOTE *If using frozen rhubarb, measure rhubarb while still frozen, then thaw completely. Drain in a colander, but do not press liquid out.*

Lemon-Blueberry Pound Cake

This is a refreshing dessert, perfect with ice cream, and a staple at our family barbecues. The trick is to add the glaze in three stages so each layer soaks into the cake.

—**REBECCA LITTLE** PARK RIDGE, IL

PREP: 25 MIN. • **BAKE:** 55 MIN. + COOLING
MAKES: 12 SERVINGS

- ⅓ **cup butter, softened**
- 4 **ounces cream cheese, softened**
- 2 **cups sugar**
- 3 **eggs**
- 1 **egg white**
- 1 **tablespoon grated lemon peel**
- 2 **teaspoons vanilla extract**
- 2 **cups fresh or frozen unsweetened blueberries**
- 3 **cups all-purpose flour, divided**
- 1 **teaspoon baking powder**
- ½ **teaspoon baking soda**
- ½ **teaspoon salt**
- 1 **cup (8 ounces) lemon yogurt**

GLAZE

- 1½ **cups confectioners' sugar**
- ¼ **cup lemon juice**

1. Grease and flour a 10-in. fluted tube pan. In a large bowl, cream the butter, cream cheese and sugar until blended. Add eggs and egg white, one at a time, beating well after each addition. Beat in lemon peel and vanilla.
2. Toss blueberries with 2 tablespoons flour. In another bowl, mix the remaining flour with baking powder, baking soda and salt; add to creamed mixture alternately with yogurt, beating after each addition just until combined. Fold in blueberry mixture.
3. Transfer batter to prepared pan. Bake at 350° for 55-60 minutes or until a toothpick inserted in center comes out clean. Cool in pan 10 minutes before removing to wire rack; cool for 15 minutes.
4. In a small bowl, mix confectioners' sugar and lemon juice until smooth. Gradually brush onto warm cake, about one-third at a time, allowing glaze to soak into cake before adding more. Cool completely.
EDITOR'S NOTE *For easier removal of cake, use solid shortening when greasing a fluted or plain tube pan.*

ULTIMATE *Comfort* Layered Turtle Cheesecake

After receiving a request for a special turtle cheesecake and not finding a good recipe, I created my own. Everyone is thrilled with the results, and this remains a favorite at the coffee shop where I work.

—SUE GRONHOLZ BEAVER DAM, WI

PREP: 40 MIN. • **BAKE:** 1¼ HOURS + CHILLING
MAKES: 12 SERVINGS

- 1 cup all-purpose flour
- ⅓ cup packed brown sugar
- ¼ cup finely chopped pecans
- 6 tablespoons cold butter, cubed

FILLING

- 4 packages (8 ounces each) cream cheese, softened
- 1 cup sugar
- ⅓ cup packed brown sugar
- ¼ cup plus 1 teaspoon all-purpose flour, divided
- 2 tablespoons heavy whipping cream
- 1½ teaspoons vanilla extract
- 4 eggs, lightly beaten
- ½ cup milk chocolate chips, melted and cooled
- ¼ cup caramel ice cream topping
- ⅓ cup chopped pecans

GANACHE

- ½ cup milk chocolate chips
- ¼ cup heavy whipping cream
- 2 tablespoons chopped pecans
  Additional caramel ice cream topping, optional

1. Place a greased 9-in. springform pan on a double thickness of heavy-duty foil (about 18 in. square). Securely wrap foil around pan.

2. In a small bowl, combine the flour, brown sugar and pecans; cut in butter until crumbly. Press onto the bottom of prepared pan. Place pan on a baking sheet. Bake at 325° for 12-15 minutes or until set. Cool on a wire rack.

3. In a large bowl, beat cream cheese and sugars until smooth. Beat in ¼ cup flour, cream and vanilla. Add eggs; beat on low speed just until blended. Remove 1 cup batter to a small bowl; stir in melted chocolate. Spread over crust.

4. In another bowl, mix caramel topping and remaining flour; stir in pecans. Drop by tablespoonfuls over chocolate batter. Top with remaining batter. Place springform pan in a large baking pan; add 1 in. of hot water to larger pan.

5. Bake at 325° for 1¼ to 1½ hours or until center is just set and top appears dull. Remove springform pan from water bath; remove foil. Cool cheesecake on a wire rack for 10 minutes. Loosen sides from pan with a knife; cool 1 hour longer. Refrigerate overnight.

6. For ganache, place chips in a small bowl. In a small saucepan, bring cream just to a boil. Pour over chips; whisk until smooth. Cool slightly, stirring occasionally.

7. Remove sides of springform pan. Spread ganache over cheesecake; sprinkle with pecans. Refrigerate until set. If desired, drizzle with additional caramel topping before serving.

Ready for the ultimate pumpkin recipe? This cheesecake has a unique gingersnap crust and rich, luscious swirls of cream cheese and pumpkin. If you want something extra special for dessert, this is it. —**SHARON SKILDUM** MAPLE GROVE, MN

Deluxe Pumpkin Cheesecake

PREP: 35 MIN. • **BAKE:** 50 MIN. + CHILLING
MAKES: 12 SERVINGS

- 1 cup crushed gingersnap cookies (about 20 cookies)
- ⅓ cup finely chopped pecans
- ¼ cup butter, melted
- 4 packages (8 ounces each) cream cheese, softened, divided
- 1½ cups sugar, divided
- 2 tablespoons cornstarch
- 2 teaspoons vanilla extract
- 4 eggs
- 1 cup canned pumpkin
- 2 teaspoons ground cinnamon
- 1½ teaspoons ground nutmeg

GARNISH

- Chocolate syrup, caramel ice cream topping, whipped topping and additional crushed gingersnap cookies, optional

1. Place a greased 9-in. springform pan on a double thickness of heavy-duty foil (about 18 in. square). Securely wrap foil around pan.

2. In a small bowl, combine the cookie crumbs, pecans and butter. Press onto the bottom of prepared pan. Place on a baking sheet. Bake at 350° for 8-10 minutes or until set. Cool on a wire rack.

3. For filling, in a large bowl, beat 1 package of cream cheese, ½ cup sugar and cornstarch until smooth, about 2 minutes. Beat in remaining cream cheese, one package at a time until smooth. Add remaining sugar and vanilla. Add eggs; beat on low speed just until combined.

4. Place 2 cups filling in a small bowl; stir in the pumpkin, cinnamon, and nutmeg. Remove ¾ cup pumpkin filling; set aside. Pour remaining pumpkin filling over crust; top with remaining plain filling. Cut through with a knife to swirl. Drop reserved pumpkin filling by spoonfuls over cheesecake; cut through with a knife to swirl.

5. Place springform pan in a large baking pan; add 1 in. of hot water to larger pan. Bake at 350° for 55-65 minutes or until center is just set and top appears dull. Remove springform pan from water bath. Cool on a wire rack for 10 minutes. Carefully run a knife around edge of pan to loosen; cool 1 hour longer. Refrigerate overnight.

6. Garnish with chocolate syrup, caramel sauce, whipped topping and additional crushed gingersnaps if desired.

Vanilla Custard Cups

When I was living with my mother, she loved custard, so I'd make this comforting dessert for us each week. There's no chance of getting tired of this treat!
—**BILLIE BOHANNAN** IMPERIAL, CA

PREP: 10 MIN. • **BAKE:** 30 MIN.
MAKES: 2 SERVINGS

- 1 egg
- 1 cup milk
- 3 tablespoons brown sugar
- ¾ teaspoon vanilla extract
- ⅛ teaspoon salt, optional
- ⅛ teaspoon ground nutmeg

1. In a small bowl, beat the egg, milk, brown sugar, vanilla and salt if desired until blended. Pour into two ungreased 6-oz. custard cups. Sprinkle with nutmeg.

2. Place cups in a 9-in. square baking pan. Fill pan with hot water to a depth of 1 in. Bake, uncovered, at 350° for 30-35 minutes or until a knife inserted near the center comes out clean.

top tip — Kettle Trick

For the Vanilla Custard Cups, put the pan with the cups inside the oven before adding water to the pan. Then use a kettle or pot to pour hot water into the pan. This way you don't have to worry about spilling water from the baking dish while putting it in the oven.

Oat Apple Crisp

When making this crisp, I use a yellow cake mix instead of flour. It's different than a traditional crisp, but in the most delicious way possible.

—RUBY HODGE RICHLAND CENTER, WI

PREP: 25 MIN. • **BAKE:** 45 MIN.
MAKES: 8 SERVINGS

- 7 cups thinly sliced peeled tart apples (about 7 medium)
- 1 cup sugar
- 1 tablespoon all-purpose flour
- 1 teaspoon ground cinnamon
  Dash salt
- ¼ cup water
- 1 package (9 ounces) yellow cake mix
- ¾ cup quick-cooking oats
- ⅓ cup butter, softened
- ¼ cup packed brown sugar
- ¼ teaspoon baking powder
- ¼ teaspoon baking soda
  Vanilla ice cream

1. Place apples in a greased 2½ qt. shallow baking dish. In a small bowl, combine the sugar, flour, cinnamon and salt; sprinkle over apples. Drizzle with water. In a large bowl, combine the cake mix, oats, butter, brown sugar, baking powder and baking soda. Sprinkle over apples.

2. Bake, uncovered, at 350° for 45-50 minutes or until apples are tender and topping is golden brown. Serve warm with ice cream.

Honey Pecan Pie

There's nothing like a good old-fashioned piece of pecan pie to make someone feel welcome. This honey-infused version is southern hospitality at it finest.

—CATHY HUDAK WADSWORTH, OH

PREP: 25 MIN. • **BAKE:** 45 MIN. + COOLING
MAKES: 8 SERVINGS

- 4 eggs
- 1 cup chopped pecans
- 1 cup light corn syrup
- ¼ cup sugar
- ¼ cup packed brown sugar
- 2 tablespoons butter, melted
- 1 teaspoon vanilla extract
- ½ teaspoon salt
- 1 unbaked pastry shell (9 inches)

TOPPING

- 3 tablespoons butter
- ⅓ cup packed brown sugar
- 3 tablespoons honey
- 1½ cups pecan halves

1. In a large bowl, combine the eggs, pecans, corn syrup, sugars, butter, vanilla and salt. Pour into pastry shell. Bake at 350° for 30 minutes.

2. In a small saucepan, melt butter over medium heat. Stir in brown sugar and honey until combined. Stir in pecan halves until coated. Spoon over pie.

3. Bake 15-20 minutes longer or until a knife inserted near the center comes out clean. Cool completely on a wire rack. Refrigerate leftovers.

Cherry Cream Cheese Dessert

Pretty layers of graham cracker crumbs, creamy filling and fruit topping make this dessert stand out. For a nice change, you can substitute blueberry pie filling or another fruit flavor for the cherry filling called for in the recipe.

—**MELODY MELLINGER** MYERSTOWN, PA

START TO FINISH: 15 MIN.
MAKES: 8 SERVINGS

- ¾ **cup graham cracker crumbs (about 12 squares)**
- 2 **tablespoons sugar**
- 2 **tablespoons butter, melted**

FILLING

- 1 **package (8 ounces) cream cheese, softened**
- 1 **can (14 ounces) sweetened condensed milk**
- ⅓ **cup lemon juice**
- 1 **teaspoon vanilla extract**
- 1 **can (21 ounces) cherry pie filling**

1. In a bowl, combine the cracker crumbs, sugar and butter. Divide among eight dessert dishes, about 4 rounded teaspoonfuls in each.

2. In a small bowl, beat cream cheese until smooth. Gradually add milk until blended. Beat in lemon juice and vanilla. Spoon ¼ cup into each dish. Top with pie filling, about ¼ cup in each.

Dark Chocolate Cream Pie

Even though I don't personally care for chocolate, this is one of my favorite desserts to make for my chocolate-loving friends. The filling is simple to cook and begins to set up in the shell right away.

—**KEZIA SULLIVAN** SACKETS HARBOR, NY

PREP: 30 MIN. + CHILLING
MAKES: 8 SERVINGS

- 1¼ **cups sugar**
- ¼ **cup cornstarch**
- ¼ **teaspoon salt**
- 3 **cups milk**
- 3 **ounces unsweetened chocolate, chopped**
- 4 **egg yolks, lightly beaten**
- 3 **tablespoons butter**
- 1½ **teaspoons vanilla extract**
- 1 **pastry shell (9 inches), baked**

1. In a large saucepan, combine the sugar, cornstarch and salt. Stir in milk and chocolate. Cook and stir over medium-high heat until thickened and bubbly. Reduce heat; cook and stir 2 minutes longer. Remove from the heat.

2. Stir a small amount of hot filling into egg yolks; return all to the pan, stirring constantly. Bring to a gentle boil; cook and stir 2 minutes longer. Remove from the heat.

3. Gently stir in butter and vanilla. Spoon into pastry shell. Cool on a wire rack. Cover and chill for at least 3 hours.

Special Mocha Cupcakes

These extra-rich, extra-luscious cupcakes smell wonderful while baking. Topped with a fluffy frosting and chocolate sprinkles, they taste even better!

—MARY BILYEU ANN ARBOR, MI

PREP: 25 MIN. • **BAKE:** 20 MIN. + COOLING
MAKES: 1 DOZEN

- 1 **cup sugar**
- ½ **cup cold brewed coffee**
- ½ **cup canola oil**
- 2 **eggs**
- 3 **teaspoons cider vinegar**
- 3 **teaspoons vanilla extract**
- 1½ **cups all-purpose flour**
- ⅓ **cup baking cocoa**
- 1 **teaspoon baking soda**
- ½ **teaspoon salt**

MOCHA FROSTING

- 3 **tablespoons milk chocolate chips**
- 3 **tablespoons semisweet chocolate chips**
- ⅓ **cup butter, softened**
- 2 **cups confectioners' sugar**
- 1 **to 2 tablespoons brewed coffee**
- ½ **cup chocolate sprinkles**

1. Preheat oven to 350°. In a large bowl, beat sugar, coffee, oil, eggs, vinegar and vanilla until well blended. In a small bowl, combine flour, cocoa, baking soda and salt; gradually beat into coffee mixture until blended.

2. Fill paper-lined muffin cups three-fourths full. Bake 20-25 minutes or until a toothpick inserted in center comes out clean. Cool 10 minutes before removing from pan to a wire rack to cool.

3. For frosting, in a microwave, melt chips and butter; stir until smooth. Transfer to a large bowl. Gradually beat in confectioners' sugar and enough coffee to achieve desired consistency. Pipe frosting onto cupcakes. Top with sprinkles; gently press down.

Old-Fashioned Rice Pudding

This comforting dessert is a wonderful way to end any meal. As a girl, I always waited eagerly for the first heavenly bite of rice pudding. Today, my husband likes to top his with a scoop of ice cream.

—SANDRA MELNYCHENKO GRANDVIEW, MB

PREP: 10 MIN. • **BAKE:** 1 HOUR
MAKES: 6 SERVINGS

- 3½ cups 2% milk
- ½ cup uncooked long grain rice
- ⅓ cup sugar
- ½ teaspoon salt
- ½ cup raisins
- 1 teaspoon vanilla extract
  Ground cinnamon, optional

1. In a large saucepan, combine the milk, rice, sugar and salt if desired. Bring to a boil over medium heat, stirring constantly. Pour into a greased 1½-qt. baking dish.
2. Cover and bake at 325° for 45 minutes, stirring every 15 minutes. Add raisins and vanilla; cover and bake for 15 minutes longer or until rice is tender. Sprinkle with cinnamon if desired. Serve warm or chilled. Store in the refrigerator.

Raspberry & White Chocolate Cheesecake

My mom makes this cheesecake a lot because it's so good and really pretty. She calls it a go-to recipe. Someday I'll try to make it myself.

—PEGGY ROOS MINNEAPOLIS, MN

PREP: 40 MIN. • **BAKE:** 1¾ HOURS + CHILLING
MAKES: 16 SERVINGS

- 1 package (10 ounces) frozen sweetened raspberries, thawed
- 1 tablespoon cornstarch

CRUST
- 1 cup all-purpose flour
- 2 tablespoons sugar
- ½ cup cold butter

FILLING
- 4 packages (8 ounces each) cream cheese, softened
- 1½ cups sugar
- 1¼ cups heavy whipping cream
- 2 teaspoons vanilla extract
- 2 eggs, lightly beaten
- 12 ounces white baking chocolate, melted and cooled

1. In a small saucepan, mix raspberries and cornstarch until blended. Bring to a boil; cook and stir 1-2 minutes or until thickened. Press through a fine-mesh strainer into a bowl; discard seeds. Cool completely.
2. Preheat oven to 350°. Place a greased 9x3-in. deep springform pan on a double thickness of heavy-duty foil (about 18 in. square). Wrap foil securely around pan.
3. For crust, in a small bowl, mix flour and sugar. Cut in butter until crumbly. Press onto bottom of prepared pan. Place pan on a baking sheet. Bake 20-25 minutes or until golden brown. Cool on a wire rack. Reduce oven setting to 325°.
4. For filling, in a large bowl, beat cream cheese and sugar until smooth. Beat in cream and vanilla. Add eggs; beat on low speed just until blended. Stir in cooled chocolate. Pour half of the mixture over crust. Spread with half of the raspberry puree. Top with remaining batter. Drop remaining puree by tablespoonfuls over top. Cut through batter with a knife to swirl.
5. Place springform pan in a larger baking pan; add 1 in. of hot water to larger pan. Bake 1¾ to 2 hours or until edge of cheesecake is set and golden. (Center of cheesecake will jiggle when moved.) Remove springform pan from water bath. Cool cheesecake on a wire rack for 10 minutes. Loosen cheesecake from pan with a knife; remove foil. Cool 1 hour longer. Refrigerate overnight. Remove rim from pan.

Lemon Ladyfinger Dessert

We whipped up this rich and creamy treat for when you need a taste of spring. Five ingredients and 20 minutes are all you need to make this impressive dessert.

—TASTE OF HOME TEST KITCHEN

PREP: 20 MIN. + CHILLING
MAKES: 12 SERVINGS

- 2 packages (3 ounces each) ladyfingers, split
- 3 cups heavy whipping cream
- 1 package (8 ounces) cream cheese, softened
- ½ cup lemon curd
- ⅔ cup confectioners' sugar

1. Set aside 5 ladyfingers; line the sides and bottom of a lightly greased 9-in. springform pan with remaining ladyfingers. In a large bowl, beat cream until stiff peaks form; set aside.
2. In another large bowl, beat cream cheese and curd until smooth; add sugar. Beat on medium for 1 minute. Fold in whipped cream. Spread half of cream cheese mixture into prepared pan. Arrange reserved ladyfingers in a spoke pattern over top. Spread with remaining cream cheese mixture. Cover and chill overnight.

Biltmore's Bread Pudding

This classic recipe from the historic Biltmore Estate in North Carolina has fans from all over the country, and it's no surprise why. It bakes evenly, is easy to make, and turns out buttery and rich.

— BILTMORE ESTATE ASHEVILLE, NC

PREP: 15 MIN. • **BAKE:** 40 MIN.
MAKES: 12 SERVINGS

- 8 cups cubed day-old bread
- 9 eggs
- 2¼ cups whole milk
- 1¾ cups heavy whipping cream
- 1 cup sugar
- ¾ cup butter, melted
- 3 teaspoons vanilla extract
- 1½ teaspoons ground cinnamon

CARAMEL SAUCE
- 1 cup sugar
- ¼ cup water
- 1 tablespoon lemon juice
- 2 tablespoons butter
- 1 cup heavy whipping cream

1. Place bread cubes in a greased 13-in. x 9-in. baking dish. In a large bowl, whisk the eggs, milk, cream, sugar, butter, vanilla and cinnamon. Pour evenly over bread.
2. Bake, uncovered, at 350° for 40-45 minutes or until a knife inserted near the center comes out clean. Let stand for 5 minutes before cutting.
3. Meanwhile, in a small saucepan, bring the sugar, water and lemon juice to a boil. Reduce heat to medium; cook until sugar is dissolved and mixture turns a golden amber color. Stir in butter until melted. Add cream. Remove from the heat. Serve with bread pudding.

 **Did you know?**
Not all that different from French toast, bread pudding was first devised as an easy way to use up stale bread. Just remember, the better the bread you use, the better your pudding will be, so don't shy away from fun flavors.

Frosty Coffee Pie

This pie was inspired by my husband, who loves coffee ice cream, and his mom, who makes a cool, creamy dessert using pudding mix. This dish brings both great tastes together.

—APRIL TIMBOE SILOAM SPRINGS, AR

PREP: 15 MIN. + FREEZING
MAKES: 8 SERVINGS

- ¼ cup hot fudge ice cream topping, warmed
- 1 chocolate crumb crust (9 inches)
- 3 cups coffee ice cream, softened
- 1 package (5.9 ounces) instant chocolate pudding mix
- ½ cup cold strong brewed coffee
- ¼ cup cold 2% milk
- 1¾ cups whipped topping
- 1 cup marshmallow creme
- ¼ cup miniature semisweet chocolate chips

1. Spread ice cream topping into crust. In a large bowl, beat the ice cream, dry pudding mix, coffee and milk until blended; spoon into crust.

2. In another bowl, combine the whipped topping and marshmallow creme; spread over top. Sprinkle with chocolate chips. Cover and freeze until firm.

ULTIMATE *Comfort* German Chocolate Cake

This cake is my husband's favorite! Every bite has a light crunch from the pecans, a sweet taste of coconut and a drizzle of chocolate.

—JOYCE PLATFOOT WAPAKONETA, OH

PREP: 30 MIN. • **BAKE:** 30 MIN. + COOLING
MAKES: 12 SERVINGS

- 4 ounces German sweet chocolate, chopped
- ½ cup water
- 1 cup butter, softened
- 2 cups sugar
- 4 eggs, separated
- 1 teaspoon vanilla extract
- 2½ cups cake flour
- 1 teaspoon baking soda
- ½ teaspoon salt
- 1 cup buttermilk

FROSTING

- 1½ cups sugar
- 1½ cups evaporated milk
- ¾ cup butter
- 5 egg yolks, beaten
- 2 cups flaked coconut
- 1½ cups chopped pecans
- 1½ teaspoons vanilla extract

ICING

- 1 teaspoon shortening
- 2 ounces semisweet chocolate

1. Line three greased 9-in. round baking pans with waxed paper. Grease waxed paper and set aside. In small saucepan, melt chocolate with water over low heat; cool.

2. Preheat oven to 350°. In a large bowl, cream butter and sugar until light and fluffy. Beat in 4 egg yolks, one at a time, beating well after each addition. Blend in melted chocolate and vanilla. Combine flour, baking soda and salt; add to the creamed mixture alternately with buttermilk, beating well after each addition.

3. In a small bowl and with clean beaters, beat the 4 egg whites until stiff peaks form. Fold a fourth of the egg whites into creamed mixture; fold in remaining whites.

4. Pour batter into prepared pans. Bake 24-28 minutes or until a toothpick inserted in center comes out clean. Cool 10 minutes before removing from pans to wire racks to cool completely.

5. For frosting, in a small saucepan, heat sugar, milk, butter and egg yolks over medium-low heat until mixture is thickened and golden brown, stirring constantly. Remove from heat. Stir in coconut, pecans and vanilla extract. Cool until thick enough to spread. Spread a third of the frosting over each cake layer and stack the layers.

6. In a microwave, melt chocolate and shortening; stir until smooth; drizzle over cake.

Buttermilk Pound Cake

This cake is the one I make most often. It is a truly Southern classic, and one I think can't be beat. Once people taste it, they won't go back to their other recipes.
—**GRACIE HANCHEY** DE RIDDER, LA

PREP: 10 MIN. • **BAKE:** 70 MIN. + COOLING
MAKES: 16-20 SERVINGS

- 1 cup butter, softened
- 2½ cups sugar
- 4 eggs
- 3 cups all-purpose flour
- ¼ teaspoon baking soda
- 1 cup buttermilk
- 1 teaspoon vanilla extract
  Confectioners' sugar, optional

1. In a large bowl, cream butter and sugar until light and fluffy. Add eggs, one at a time, beating well after each addition. Combine flour and baking soda; add alternately with buttermilk and beat well. Stir in vanilla.

2. Pour into a greased and floured 10-in. fluted tube pan. Bake at 325° for 70 minutes or until a toothpick inserted near the center comes out clean. Cool in pan for 15 minutes before removing to a wire rack to cool completely. Dust with confectioners' sugar if desired.

kid FRIENDLY Monster Caramel Apples

Bring back a childhood favorite by making this timeless treat. These caramel-covered apples take a dip in crushed Oreos before getting drizzled with white candy coating. How will you dunk and decorate yours?
—**KAREN ANN BLAND** GOVE, KS

PREP: 40 MIN. • **COOK:** 30 MIN. + COOLING
MAKES: 8-10 SERVINGS

- 8 to 10 medium apples
- 8 to 10 wooden sticks
- 32 Oreo cookies, coarsely chopped
- 1 cup butter, cubed
- 2 cups packed brown sugar
- 1 can (14 ounces) sweetened condensed milk
- 1 cup light corn syrup
- 1 teaspoon vanilla extract
- 8 squares (1 ounce each) white candy coating, coarsely chopped
- ½ cup orange and brown sprinkles

1. Wash and thoroughly dry apples; insert a wooden stick into each. Place on a waxed paper-lined baking sheet; chill. Place cookie crumbs in a shallow dish; set aside.

2. In a heavy 3-qt. saucepan, combine butter, brown sugar, milk and corn syrup; bring to a boil over medium-high heat. Cook and stir until mixture reaches 248° (firm-ball stage) on a candy thermometer, about 30-40 minutes. Remove from the heat; stir in vanilla.

3. Dip each apple into hot caramel mixture to completely coat, then dip the bottom in cookie crumbs, pressing lightly to adhere. Return to baking sheet to cool.

4. In a microwave, melt candy coating; stir until smooth. Transfer to a small plastic bag; cut a small hole in a corner of bag. Drizzle coating over apples. Decorate with sprinkles.

MONSTER CARAMEL PEARS
Substitute pears for the apples.
NOTE *We recommend that you test your candy thermometer before each use by bringing water to a boil; the thermometer should read 212°. Adjust your recipe temperature up or down based on your test.*

top tip Wash Away Apple Wax

Be sure to wash apples in warm water to rinse away the waxy coating. This will help the caramel stick to the apple better.

Lemon-Berry Shortcake

Here's a quick-and-easy way to satisfy a craving for something summery. The homemade shortcake layer is not overly sweet but makes the perfect base for a crown of whipped cream and berries.

—MERYL HERR GRAND RAPIDS, MI

PREP: 30 MIN. • **BAKE:** 20 MIN. + COOLING
MAKES: 8 SERVINGS

- 1⅓ **cups all-purpose flour**
- ½ **cup sugar**
- 2 **teaspoons baking powder**
- ¼ **teaspoon salt**
- 1 **egg**
- ⅔ **cup buttermilk**
- ¼ **cup butter, melted**
- 1 **tablespoon lemon juice**
- 1 **teaspoon grated lemon peel**
- 1 **teaspoon vanilla extract**
- 1 **cup sliced fresh strawberries**

TOPPING
- 1½ **cups sliced fresh strawberries**
- 1 **tablespoon lemon juice**
- 1 **teaspoon sugar**
- 2 **cups reduced-fat whipped topping**

1. In a large bowl, combine the flour, sugar, baking powder and salt. In another bowl, combine the egg, buttermilk, butter, lemon juice, lemon peel and vanilla. Stir into dry ingredients just until moistened. Fold in strawberries. Pour into a greased and floured 9-in. round baking pan.
2. Bake at 350° for 20-25 minutes or until a toothpick inserted near the center comes out clean. Cool for 10 minutes before removing from pan to a wire rack to cool completely.
3. For topping, in a large bowl, combine the strawberries, lemon juice and sugar. Cover and refrigerate until serving. Spread whipped topping over cake. Drain strawberries; arrange over top.

ULTIMATE *Comfort* Caramel-Pecan Apple Pie

Caramel-Pecan Apple Pie reminds me of being back home in Virginia at my granny's table. The smell of this sweet pie in the oven perfumes the whole house.

—JEAN CASTRO SANTA ROSA, CA

PREP: 45 MIN. • **BAKE:** 55 MIN. + COOLING
MAKES: 8 SERVINGS

- 7 **cups sliced peeled tart apples**
- 1 **teaspoon lemon juice**
- 1 **teaspoon vanilla extract**
- ¾ **cup chopped pecans**
- ⅓ **cup packed brown sugar**
- 3 **tablespoons sugar**
- 4½ **teaspoons ground cinnamon**
- 1 **tablespoon cornstarch**
- ¼ **cup caramel ice cream topping, room temperature**
- 1 **unbaked pastry shell (9 inches)**
- 3 **tablespoons butter, melted**

STREUSEL TOPPING
- ¾ **cup all-purpose flour**
- ⅔ **cup chopped pecans**
- ¼ **cup sugar**
- 6 **tablespoons cold butter**
- ¼ **cup caramel ice cream topping, room temperature**

1. In a large bowl, toss apples with lemon juice and vanilla. Combine the pecans, sugars, cinnamon and cornstarch; add to apple mixture and toss to coat. Pour caramel topping over bottom of pastry shell; top with apple mixture (shell will be full). Drizzle with butter.
2. In a small bowl, combine the flour, pecans and sugar. Cut in butter until mixture resembles coarse crumbs. Sprinkle over filling.
3. Bake at 350° for 55-65 minutes or until filling is bubbly and topping is browned. Immediately drizzle with caramel topping. Cool on a wire rack.

Peanut Butter Pudding Dessert

Here's a fun, layered dessert that will appeal to all ages. If you want it even nuttier, you can use chunky peanut butter, and if you're not a fan of cashews, substitute your favorite nut.

—BARBARA SCHINDLER NAPOLEON, OH

PREP: 25 MIN. • **BAKE:** 25 MIN. + CHILLING
MAKES: 12-16 SERVINGS

- 1 cup all-purpose flour
- ½ cup cold butter, cubed
- 1½ cups chopped cashews, divided
- 1 package (8 ounces) cream cheese, softened
- ⅓ cup creamy peanut butter
- 1 cup confectioners' sugar
- 1 carton (12 ounces) frozen whipped topping, thawed, divided
- 2⅔ cups cold milk
- 1 package (3.9 ounces) instant chocolate pudding mix
- 1 package (3.4 ounces) instant vanilla pudding mix
- 1 milk chocolate candy bar (1.55 ounces), coarsely chopped

1. Place flour and butter in a food processor; cover and process until mixture resembles coarse crumbs. Add 1 cup cashews; pulse a few times until combined.
2. Press into a greased 13x9-in. baking dish. Bake at 350° for 25-28 minutes or until golden brown. Cool completely on a wire rack.
3. In a small bowl, beat the cream cheese, peanut butter and confectioners' sugar until smooth. Fold in 1 cup whipped topping. Spoon over crust.
4. In another bowl, whisk milk and both pudding mixes for 2 minutes. Let stand for 2 minutes or until soft-set. Spread over cream cheese layer. Top with remaining whipped topping.

Sprinkle with chopped candy bar and remaining cashews. Cover and refrigerate for at least 1 hour before serving.

Chocolate-Covered Cheesecake Squares

Satisfy your cheesecake craving in one amazing bite. These squares are party favorites and perfect for the holidays when there are so many sweets to choose from.

—ESTHER NEUSTAETER LA CRETE, AB

PREP: 1½ HOURS + FREEZING
MAKES: 49 SQUARES

- 1 cup graham cracker crumbs
- ¼ cup finely chopped pecans
- ¼ cup butter, melted

FILLING
- 2 packages (8 ounces each) cream cheese, softened
- ½ cup sugar
- ¼ cup sour cream
- 2 eggs, lightly beaten
- ½ teaspoon vanilla extract

COATING
- 24 ounces semisweet chocolate, chopped
- 3 tablespoons shortening

1. Line a 9-in. square baking pan with foil and grease the foil. In a small bowl, combine the graham cracker crumbs, pecans and butter. Press into prepared pan; set aside.
2. In a large bowl, beat the cream cheese, sugar and sour cream until smooth. Add eggs and vanilla; beat on low speed just until combined. Pour over crust. Bake at 325° for 35-40 minutes or until center is almost set. Cool on a wire rack. Freeze overnight.
3. In a microwave, melt chocolate and shortening; stir until smooth. Cool slightly.
4. Using foil, lift cheesecake out of pan. Gently peel off foil; cut cheesecake into 1¼-in. squares. Work with a few pieces at a time for dipping; keep remaining squares refrigerated until ready to dip.
5. Using a toothpick, completely dip squares, one at a time, in melted chocolate; allow excess to drip off. Place on waxed paper-lined baking sheets. Spoon additional chocolate over the tops if necessary to coat. (Reheat chocolate if needed to finish dipping.) Let stand for 20 minutes or until set. Store in an airtight container in the refrigerator or freezer.

Chocolate Mousse

A friend shared this rich velvety mousse recipe with me. I love to cook and have tons of recipes, but this one is a favorite.
—**JUDY SPENCER** SAN DIEGO, CA

PREP: 20 MIN. + CHILLING
MAKES: 2 SERVINGS

- ¼ cup semisweet chocolate chips
- 1 tablespoon water
- 1 egg yolk, lightly beaten
- 1½ teaspoons vanilla extract
- ½ cup heavy whipping cream
- 1 tablespoon sugar
  Whipped cream, optional

1. In a small saucepan, melt chocolate chips with water; stir until smooth. Stir a small amount of hot chocolate mixture into egg yolk; return all to the pan, stirring constantly. Cook and stir for 2 minutes or until slightly thickened. Remove from the heat; stir in vanilla. Cool, stirring several times.
2. In a small bowl, beat whipping cream until it begins to thicken. Add sugar; beat until soft peaks form. Fold in cooled chocolate mixture. Cover and refrigerate for at least 2 hours. Garnish with whipped cream if desired.

Spice Cupcakes

These spicy cupcakes have been in my family for years. When I was growing up, it seemed these cupcakes were always in the freezer, just waiting to be snitched, one at a time!
—**CARLA HODENFIELD** RAY, ND

PREP: 40 MIN. • **BAKE:** 20 MIN. + COOLING
MAKES: 14 CUPCAKES

- 2 cups water
- 1 cup raisins
- ½ cup shortening
- 1 cup sugar
- 1 egg
- 1¾ cups all-purpose flour
- ¾ teaspoon baking powder
- ½ teaspoon salt
- ½ teaspoon each ground allspice, cinnamon and nutmeg
- ¼ teaspoon baking soda
- ¼ teaspoon ground cloves
- ¼ cup chopped walnuts

FROSTING

- 1 cup packed brown sugar
- ⅓ cup half-and-half cream
- ¼ teaspoon salt
- 3 tablespoons butter
- 1 teaspoon vanilla extract
- 1¼ cups confectioners' sugar
  Coarsely chopped walnuts, optional

1. In a large saucepan, bring water and raisins to a boil. Reduce heat; simmer for 10 minutes. Remove from heat and cool to room temperature (do not drain).
2. Meanwhile, in a large bowl, cream shortening and sugar until light and fluffy. Beat in egg. Stir in raisins. Combine dry ingredients; add to creamed mixture until well blended. Stir in walnuts.
3. Fill paper-lined muffin cups three-fourths full. Bake at 350° for 20-25 minutes or until a toothpick comes out clean. Cool for 10 minutes; remove from pan to a wire rack.
4. For frosting, in a large saucepan, combine the brown sugar, cream and salt. Bring to a boil over medium-low heat; cook and stir until smooth. Stir in butter and vanilla. Remove from the heat; cool slightly. Stir in confectioners' sugar until smooth. Frost cupcakes; top with nuts if desired.

Sunny Peaches & Cream Pie

I've always thought this pie was as delicious as it is beautiful. It's not just a summer dessert, either. I also make it for the holidays, using strawberries and strawberry gelatin.

—LORRAINE WRIGHT GRAND FORKS, BC

PREP: 25 MIN. • **COOK:** 5 MIN. + CHILLING
MAKES: 8 SERVINGS

- 1¼ cups graham cracker crumbs
- ¼ cup sugar
- 6 tablespoons margarine, melted

FILLING
- 4 ounces cream cheese, softened
- ½ cup confectioners' sugar
- ½ cup frozen whipped topping, thawed

TOPPING
- 1 package (3 ounces) peach gelatin
- 1 package (3 ounces) cook-and-serve vanilla pudding mix
- 1¼ cups water
- 2 cups sliced peeled fresh peaches or canned sliced peaches

1. In a small bowl, mix cracker crumbs and sugar; stir in margarine. Press onto the bottom and up the sides of an ungreased 9-in. pie plate. Bake at 375° for 6-8 minutes or until lightly browned. Cool completely on a wire rack.

2. For filling, in a small bowl, mix cream cheese and confectioners' sugar until blended. Fold in whipped topping. Carefully spread over crust; refrigerate until set.

3. For topping, in a small saucepan, combine gelatin and pudding mix; stir in water. Bring just to a boil over medium-low heat, stirring constantly; remove from the heat. Cool 5 minutes.

4. Arrange peach slices over filling. Spoon gelatin mixture over peaches. Refrigerate for 4 hours or until chilled.

Italian Cream Cheese Cake

Buttermilk makes every bite of this awesome dessert melt in your mouth. I rely on this recipe year-round for special dinners and reunions because I never have to worry about bringing home leftovers.

—JOYCE LUTZ CENTERVIEW, MO

PREP: 40 MIN. • **BAKE:** 20 MIN. + COOLING
MAKES: 12 SERVINGS

- ½ cup butter, softened
- ½ cup shortening
- 2 cups sugar
- 5 eggs, separated
- 1 teaspoon vanilla extract
- 2 cups all-purpose flour
- 1 teaspoon baking soda
- 1 cup buttermilk
- 1½ cups flaked coconut
- 1 cup chopped pecans

CREAM CHEESE FROSTING
- 2 packages (one 8 ounces, one 3 ounces) cream cheese, softened
- ¾ cup butter, softened
- 6 cups confectioners' sugar
- 1½ teaspoons vanilla extract
- ¾ cup chopped pecans

1. In a large bowl, cream the butter, shortening and sugar until light and fluffy. Beat in egg yolks and vanilla. Combine flour and baking soda; add to creamed mixture alternately with buttermilk. Beat just until combined. Stir in coconut and pecans.

2. In a small bowl, beat egg whites until stiff peaks form. Fold a fourth of the egg whites into batter, then fold in remaining whites. Pour into three greased and floured 9-in. round baking pans.

3. Bake at 350° for 20-25 minutes or until a toothpick inserted near the center comes out clean. Cool for 10 minutes before removing from pans to wire racks to cool completely.

4. In a large bowl, beat cream cheese and butter until smooth. Beat in confectioners' sugar and vanilla until fluffy. Stir in pecans. Spread frosting between layers and over top and sides of cake. Store in the refrigerator.

Ginger-Streusel Pumpkin Pie

I love to bake and have spent a lot of time making goodies for my family and friends. The streusel topping gives this pie a special touch your family will love.

—SONIA PARVU SHERRILL, NY

PREP: 25 MIN. • **BAKE:** 55 MIN. + COOLING
MAKES: 8 SERVINGS

- 1 sheet refrigerated pie pastry
- 3 eggs
- 1 can (15 ounces) solid-pack pumpkin
- 1½ cups heavy whipping cream
- ½ cup sugar
- ¼ cup packed brown sugar
- 1½ teaspoons ground cinnamon
- ½ teaspoon salt
- ¼ teaspoon ground allspice
- ¼ teaspoon ground nutmeg
- ¼ teaspoon ground cloves

STREUSEL
- 1 cup all-purpose flour
- ½ cup packed brown sugar
- ½ cup cold butter, cubed
- ½ cup chopped walnuts
- ⅓ cup finely chopped crystallized ginger

1. On a lightly floured surface, unroll pastry. Transfer pastry to a 9-in. pie plate. Trim pastry to ½ in. beyond edge of plate; flute edges.

2. In a large bowl, whisk the eggs, pumpkin, cream, sugars, cinnamon, salt, allspice, nutmeg and cloves. Pour into pastry shell. Bake at 350° for 40 minutes.

3. In a small bowl, combine flour and brown sugar; cut in butter until crumbly. Stir in walnuts and ginger. Gently sprinkle over filling.

4. Bake 15-25 minutes longer or until a knife inserted near the center comes out clean. Cool on a wire rack. Refrigerate leftovers.

Lemon Dream Cheesecake

This cheesecake bakes like a dream with no cracks. Plus it cuts well and everyone loves the light lemon flavor—a refreshing treat any time of year.

—BONNIE JOST MANITOWOC, WI

PREP: 30 MIN. • **BAKE:** 55 MIN. + CHILLING
MAKES: 16 SERVINGS

- 2 cups graham cracker crumbs
- 6 tablespoons butter, melted
- ¼ cup sugar

FILLING
- 4 packages (8 ounces each) cream cheese, softened
- 1 cup sugar
- ½ cup heavy whipping cream
- ¼ cup lemon juice
- 2 tablespoons all-purpose flour
- 1 tablespoon grated lemon peel
- 2½ teaspoons vanilla extract
- 1 teaspoon lemon extract
- 10 drops yellow food coloring, optional
- 5 eggs, lightly beaten

1. Preheat oven to 325°. In a small bowl, combine cracker crumbs, butter and sugar. Press onto bottom and 2 in. up sides of a greased 10-in. springform pan. Place pan on a baking sheet. Bake 10 minutes. Cool on a wire rack.

2. In a large bowl, beat cream cheese and sugar until smooth. Beat in cream, lemon juice, flour, lemon peel, extracts and food coloring if desired. Add eggs; beat on low speed just until combined. Pour into crust. Return pan to baking sheet.

3. Bake 55-65 minutes or until center is almost set. Cool on a wire rack 10 minutes. Carefully run a knife around edge of pan to loosen; cool 1 hour. Refrigerate overnight. Remove sides of pan.

Banana Cupcakes

Go bananas when baking, especially when you have a bunch to use up. Very ripe bananas are the secret to these down-home cupcakes.

—**JANE DEARING** NORTH LIBERTY, IN

PREP: 25 MIN. • **BAKE:** 20 MIN. + COOLING
MAKES: 1½ DOZEN

- ½ cup shortening
- 1½ cups sugar
- 2 eggs
- 1 cup mashed ripe bananas (about 2 medium)
- 1 teaspoon vanilla extract
- 2 cups all-purpose flour
- ¾ teaspoon baking soda
- ½ teaspoon baking powder
- ½ teaspoon salt
- ½ cup buttermilk

LEMON BUTTER FROSTING

- 2 cups confectioners' sugar
- ⅓ cup butter, softened
- 3 tablespoons mashed ripe banana
- 1 tablespoon lemon juice

1. In a large bowl, cream shortening and sugar until light and fluffy. Add eggs, one at a time, beating well after each addition. Beat in bananas and vanilla. Combine the flour, baking soda, baking powder and salt; add to creamed mixture alternately with buttermilk, beating well after each addition.

2. Fill paper-lined muffin cups two-thirds full. Bake at 375° for 18-22 minutes or until a toothpick inserted near the center comes out clean. Cool for 10 minutes before removing from pan to a wire rack to cool completely.

3. In a small bowl, combine the frosting ingredients; beat until light and fluffy. Frost cupcakes.

This is my ode to all things chocolate. Each layer of this coffee-spiked cake is smothered in silky ganache for a phenomenally rich and satisfying dessert. —**TARRA KNIGHT** BENBROOK, TX

Deep &
Dark Ganache Cake

PREP: 40 MIN. + COOLING
BAKE: 30 MIN. + COOLING
MAKES: 24 SERVINGS

- **6 ounces bittersweet chocolate, chopped**
- **1½ cups hot brewed coffee**
- **4 eggs**
- **3 cups sugar**
- **¾ cup canola oil**
- **2 teaspoons vanilla extract**
- **2½ cups all-purpose flour**
- **1 cup baking cocoa**
- **2 teaspoons baking soda**
- **¾ teaspoon baking powder**
- **1¼ teaspoons salt**
- **1½ cups buttermilk**

GANACHE FROSTING

- **16 ounces bittersweet chocolate, chopped**
- **2 cups heavy whipping cream**
- **5 teaspoons light corn syrup**

1. Preheat oven to 325°. Line bottoms of three greased 8-in.-square baking pans with parchment paper; grease paper.

2. Place chocolate in a small bowl. Pour hot coffee over chocolate; stir with a whisk until smooth. Cool slightly.

3. In a large bowl, beat eggs on high speed until lemon-colored. Gradually add sugar, oil, vanilla and chocolate mixture, beating until well blended. In another bowl, mix flour, cocoa, baking soda, baking powder and salt; add to chocolate mixture alternately with buttermilk, beating well after each addition.

4. Transfer to prepared pans. Bake 30-35 minutes or until a toothpick inserted in center comes out clean. Cool 10 minutes before removing from pans to wire racks; remove paper. Cool

completely.

5. For ganache, place chocolate in a large bowl. In a small saucepan, bring cream and corn syrup just to a boil. Pour over chocolate; stir with a whisk until smooth.

6. Let stand at room temperature to cool and thicken slightly, about 45 minutes, stirring occasionally. (Mixture will be very soft, but will thicken when spread onto cake.)

7. Place one cake layer on a serving plate; spread with ⅓ cup ganache. Repeat layers. Top with remaining cake layer. Spread remaining ganache over top and sides of cake.

TWO-LAYERED DEEP & DARK GANACHE CAKE & CUPCAKES

Prepare cake as directed, using twelve paper-lined muffin cups and two greased and parchment-lined 8-in.-square baking pans. Fill muffin cups three-fourths full; bake at 375° for 15-17 minutes or until a toothpick comes out clean. Divide remaining batter between prepared cake pans. Reduce oven setting to 325°; bake cake layers as directed. Yield: One 2-layered cake and 1 dozen cupcakes (24 servings).

Banana Split
Brownie Cake

Everything we love about a banana split is beautifully layered into the most awesome cake ever. The only thing this cake is missing is a cherry on top.
—**TASTE OF HOME TEST KITCHEN!**

PREP: 20 MIN. + FREEZING
MAKES: 14 SERVINGS

- **2 packages (13 ounces each) fudge brownies**
- **1 quart strawberry ice cream, softened**
- **3 large firm bananas, halved lengthwise**

- **1 cup hot fudge ice cream topping, warmed**
- **1 quart vanilla ice cream, softened**
- **¾ cup chopped pecans**

1. Arrange brownies in a greased 9-in. springform pan, cutting to fit and filling in small holes. Spread with strawberry ice cream. Cover and freeze for 3 hours or until firm.

2. Arrange bananas over ice cream, cutting to fit as needed. Spread with fudge topping and vanilla ice cream. Sprinkle with pecans. Cover tightly and freeze overnight. May be frozen for up to 2 months.

3. Remove from the freezer 10 minutes before serving. Carefully run a knife around the edge of pan to loosen; remove sides of pan.

EDITOR'S NOTE *This recipe was prepared with Little Debbie fudge brownies.*

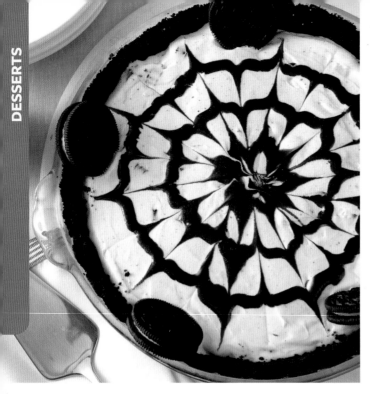

Frozen Mud Pie

Using a knife to swirl the chocolate gives this dessert a fun design. It's a simple treat that will be a new family favorite.

—DEBBIE TERENZINI-WILKERSON

LUSBY, MD

PREP: 40 MIN. + FREEZING
MAKES: 8 SERVINGS

- 1½ **cups Oreo cookie crumbs**
- 1½ **teaspoons sugar, optional**
- ¼ **cup butter, melted**
- 4 **cups chocolate chip or coffee ice cream, softened**
- ¼ **cup chocolate syrup, divided**
  Additional Oreo cookies, optional

1. In a small bowl, combine cookie crumbs and sugar if desired. Stir in butter. Press onto the bottom and up the sides of an ungreased 9-in. pie plate. Refrigerate for 30 minutes.

2. Spoon 2 cups ice cream into crust. Drizzle with half the chocolate syrup; swirl with knife. Carefully top with remaining ice cream. Drizzle with remaining syrup; swirl with a knife. Cover and freeze until firm.

3. Remove from the freezer 10-15 minutes before serving. Garnish with whole cookies if desired.

Blueberry-Rhubarb Crumble

A dollop of whipped topping adds a nice finishing touch to this satisfying crumble. Sometimes I drizzle a little flavored coffee creamer on top instead of the whipped topping.

—NANCY SOUSLEY LAFAYETTE, IN

PREP: 15 MIN. • **BAKE:** 45 MIN. + COOLING
MAKES: 12 SERVINGS

- 6 **cups fresh or frozen unsweetened blueberries**
- 4 **cups diced fresh or frozen rhubarb**
- 1 **cup sugar**
- ¼ **cup all-purpose flour**

TOPPING
- 1 **cup quick-cooking oats**
- 1 **cup packed brown sugar**
- ½ **cup all-purpose flour**
- ½ **teaspoon ground nutmeg**
- ½ **teaspoon ground cinnamon**
- ½ **cup cold butter**
  Whipped cream, optional

1. In a large bowl, combine the blueberries, rhubarb, sugar and flour. Transfer to a greased 13-in. x 9-in. baking dish.

2. For topping, in a large bowl, combine the oats, brown sugar, flour, nutmeg and cinnamon; cut in butter until crumbly. Sprinkle over fruit mixture.

3. Bake at 350° for 45-55 minutes or until the fruit is bubbly and topping is golden brown. Let cool for 10 minutes. Serve warm; dollop with whipped cream if desired.

kid FRIENDLY Ice Cream Cookie Dessert

Our family loves dessert, and this chocolaty, layered treat is one of Mom's most-requested recipes, and you only need five ingredients to make it happen.

—**KIMBERLY LAABS** HARTFORD, WI

PREP: 15 MIN. + FREEZING
MAKES: 12 SERVINGS

- 1 package (15½ ounces) Oreo cookies
- ¼ cup butter, melted
- ½ gallon vanilla ice cream, softened
- 1 jar (16 ounces) hot fudge ice cream topping, warmed
- 1 carton (8 ounces) frozen whipped topping, thawed

1. In a large bowl, combine 3¾ cups cookie crumbs and butter. Press into a greased 13-in. x 9-in. dish. Spread with ice cream; cover and freeze until set.
2. Drizzle fudge topping over ice cream; cover and freeze until set.

Spread with whipped topping; sprinkle with remaining cookie crumbs. Cover and freeze for 2 hours or until firm. Remove from the freezer 10 minutes before serving.

Chocolate Almond Cake

When our son and daughter were teenagers, our house was the hang-out for them and their friends. This rich cake was always popular with the kids.

—**CHAR SAFLEY** RALEIGH, NC

PREP: 15 MIN. • **BAKE:** 65 MIN. + COOLING
MAKES: 12-16 SERVINGS

- 1 package German chocolate cake mix (regular size)
- 1 package (3.9 ounces) instant chocolate fudge pudding mix
- 1¼ cups water
- ½ cup canola oil
- 4 eggs
- 3 teaspoons almond extract
- 2¾ cups semisweet chocolate chips, divided
- 6 tablespoons refrigerated regular or amaretto-flavored nondairy creamer
- 1 tablespoon sliced almonds

1. In a large bowl, combine the cake, pudding mix, water, oil, eggs and extract; beat until combined. Stir in 2 cups chocolate chips.
2. Pour into a greased and floured 10-in. fluted tube pan. Bake at 350° for 65-70 minutes or until a toothpick inserted near the center comes out clean. Cool for 10 minutes before removing from pan to a wire rack to cool completely.
3. In a small saucepan, combine the creamer and remaining chocolate chips. Cook over low heat until chips are melted; stir until smooth. Cool for 45 minutes. Drizzle over cake. Garnish with almonds.

Black Forest Torte

If you want to pull out all the stops for a dessert that says "wow," here is the recipe. This beauty is stacked with layers of chocolate cake and cream filling and then crowned with cherries.

—**DORIS GROTZ** YORK, NE

PREP: 1¼ HOURS • **BAKE:** 15 MIN. + COOLING
MAKES: 16 SERVINGS

- ⅔ cup butter, softened
- 1¾ cups sugar
- 4 eggs
- 1¼ cups water
- 4 ounces unsweetened chocolate, chopped
- 1 teaspoon vanilla extract
- 1¾ cups all-purpose flour
- 1 teaspoon baking powder
- ¼ teaspoon baking soda

CHOCOLATE FILLING

- 6 ounces German sweet chocolate
- ¾ cup butter, cubed
- ½ cup sliced almonds, toasted

CREAM FILLING

- 3 cups heavy whipping cream
- 2 tablespoons sugar
- 2 teaspoons vanilla extract

TOPPING

- 1 cup cherry pie filling
- 3 cups sliced almonds, toasted

1. In a large bowl, cream butter and sugar until light and fluffy. Add eggs, one at a time, beating well after each addition. Beat in water just until blended.

2. In a microwave, melt chocolate; stir until smooth. Stir in vanilla until blended. Combine the flour, baking powder and baking soda; add to creamed mixture alternately with chocolate mixture beating well after each addition.

3. Pour into four greased and floured 9-in. round baking pans. Bake at 350° for 15-20 minutes or until a toothpick inserted near the center comes out clean. Cool for 10 minutes before removing from pans to wire racks to cool completely.

4. For chocolate filling, in a microwave, melt chocolate; stir until smooth. Stir in butter until smooth. Add almonds.

5. For cream filling, in a small bowl, beat cream until it begins to thicken. Add sugar and vanilla; beat until soft peaks form.

6. To assemble, place one cake on a serving platter; spread with a fourth of the chocolate filling and a fourth of the cream filling. Repeat layers twice. Top with remaining cake and chocolate filling.

7. Place 1½ cups of the remaining cream filling in a pastry bag with a large star pastry tip. Pipe around edge of cake. Fill center with cherry pie filling. Spread remaining cream filling over sides of cake; press almonds into sides. Store in the refrigerator.

Grandma's Red Velvet Cake

No one thinks it's Christmas in our family without this cake. I baked the first one for Christmas in 1963 when I found the recipe in the newspaper and my mother kept the tradition going into the '80s. It's different than other red velvet cakes I've tasted over the years; the icing is as light as snow.

—**KATHRYN DAVISON** CHARLOTTE, NC

PREP: 30 MIN. • **BAKE:** 20 MIN. + COOLING
MAKES: 14 SERVINGS

- ½ **cup butter, softened**
- 1½ **cups sugar**
- 2 **eggs**
- 2 **bottles (1 ounce each) red food coloring**
- 1 **tablespoon white vinegar**
- 1 **teaspoon vanilla extract**
- 2¼ **cups cake flour**
- 2 **tablespoons baking cocoa**
- 1 **teaspoon baking soda**
- 1 **teaspoon salt**
- 1 **cup buttermilk**

FROSTING

- 1 **tablespoon cornstarch**
- ½ **cup cold water**
- 2 **cups butter, softened**
- 2 **teaspoons vanilla extract**
- 3½ **cups confectioners' sugar**

1. Preheat oven to 350°. In a large bowl, cream butter and sugar until light and fluffy. Add eggs, one at a time, beating well after each addition. Beat in food coloring, vinegar and vanilla. Combine flour, cocoa, baking soda and salt; add to creamed mixture alternately with buttermilk, beating well after each addition.
2. Pour into two greased and floured 9-in. round baking pans. Bake for 20-25 minutes or until a toothpick inserted in center comes out clean. Cool 10 minutes before removing from pans to wire racks to cool completely.

3. For frosting, in a small saucepan, combine cornstarch and water until smooth. Cook and stir over medium heat for 2-3 minutes or until thickened and opaque. Cool to room temperature.
4. In a large bowl, beat butter and vanilla until light and fluffy. Beat in cornstarch mixture. Gradually add confectioners' sugar; beat until frosting is light and fluffy. Spread frosting between layers and over top and sides of cake.

Chocolate Almond Cheesecake

This cheesecake is easy to make but it's definitely not easy to wait till the next day to eat it. However, it's a spectacular make-ahead dessert for a party.

—**DARLENE BRENDEN** SALEM, OR

PREP: 25 MIN. + CHILLING
BAKE: 50 MIN. + CHILLING
MAKES: 12-16 SERVINGS

CRUST

- 1 **package (9 ounces) chocolate wafer cookies, crushed (about 2 cups)**
- ¼ **cup sugar**
- ¼ **teaspoon ground cinnamon**
- ¼ **cup butter, melted**

FILLING

- 2 **packages (8 ounces each) cream cheese, softened**
- 1 **cup sugar**
- 1 **cup (8 ounces) sour cream**
- 8 **ounces semisweet chocolate, melted and cooled**
- ½ **teaspoon almond extract**
- 2 **eggs, lightly beaten**

TOPPING

- 1 **cup (8 ounces) sour cream**
- ¼ **teaspoon baking cocoa**
- 2 **tablespoons sugar**
- ½ **teaspoon almond extract**

1. In a small bowl, combine crust ingredients; reserve 2 tablespoons for garnish. Press remaining crumbs evenly onto the bottom and 2 in. up the sides of a 9-in. springform pan. Chill.
2. For filling, in a large bowl, beat cream cheese and sugar until smooth. Beat in the sour cream, chocolate and extract. Add eggs; beat on low speed just until combined. Pour into crust.
3. Place pan on a baking sheet. Bake at 350° for 40 minutes (filling will not be set). Remove from oven and let stand for 5 minutes.
4. Meanwhile, combine topping ingredients. Gently spread over filling. Sprinkle with reserved crumbs. Bake 10 minutes longer.
5. Cool on a wire rack for 10 minutes. Carefully run a knife around edge of pan to loosen; cool 1 hour longer. Refrigerate overnight.

Fresh Cherry Pie

This ruby-red treat is just sweet enough, with a hint of almond and a good level of cinnamon. The cherries peeking out of the lattice crust look enticing.

—**JOSIE BOCHEK** STURGEON BAY, WI

PREP: 25 MIN. • **BAKE:** 55 MIN. + COOLING
MAKES: 8 SERVINGS

- 1¼ cups sugar
- ⅓ cup cornstarch
- 1 cup cherry juice blend
- 4 cups fresh tart cherries, pitted or frozen pitted tart cherries, thawed
- ½ teaspoon ground cinnamon
- ¼ teaspoon ground nutmeg
- ¼ teaspoon almond extract

PASTRY

- 2 cups all-purpose flour
- ½ teaspoon salt
- ⅔ cup shortening
- 5 to 7 tablespoons cold water

1. In a large saucepan, combine sugar and cornstarch; gradually stir in cherry juice until smooth. Bring to a boil; cook and stir for 2 minutes or until thickened. Remove from the heat. Add the cherries, cinnamon, nutmeg and extract; set aside.

2. In a large bowl, combine flour and salt; cut in shortening until crumbly. Gradually add cold water, tossing with a fork until a ball forms. Divide pastry in half so that one ball is slightly larger than the other.

3. On a lightly floured surface, roll out larger ball to fit a 9-in. pie plate. Transfer pastry to pie plate; trim even with edge of plate. Add filling. Roll out remaining pastry; make a lattice crust. Trim, seal and flute edges.

4. Bake at 425° for 10 minutes. Reduce heat to 375°; bake 45-50 minutes longer or until crust is golden brown. Cool on a wire rack.

Toffee Ice Cream Dessert

A woman at my church gave me the recipe for this delicious frozen treat. It's a great dessert for a gathering at any time of year because you can prepare it ahead and store it in the freezer.

—SHARON PAVLIKOWSKI
VIRGINIA BEACH, VA

PREP: 15 MIN. + CHILLING
MAKES: 12-15 SERVINGS

- 1 package (10 ounces) butter cookies, crushed (3 cups crumbs)
- ½ cup butter, melted
- 1 cup cold milk
- 2 packages (3.4 ounces each) instant vanilla pudding mix
- 1 quart vanilla ice cream, softened
- 1 carton (8 ounces) frozen whipped topping, thawed
- 2 Heath candy bars (1.4 ounces each), crushed

1. In a small bowl, combine cookie crumbs and butter. Press into a 13-in. x 9-in. dish; refrigerate.

2. In a bowl, whisk milk and pudding mixes for 2 minutes. Fold in ice cream. Spread over crust. Top with whipped topping. Cover and refrigerate for at least 2 hours. Sprinkle with crushed candy bars before serving.

Invent Your Own Dessert

Use the recipe for Toffee Ice Cream Dessert to make your own treat. Try different types of cookie crumbs, fun flavors of ice cream and pudding and your favorite candy bar to top it off.

kid FRIENDLY ## Chocolate Cream Cheese Cupcakes

I got this recipe for filled cupcakes from a dear friend many years ago. I make them a lot for my family and for church functions because they're different from other cupcakes, and they're so irresistible.

—VIVIAN MORRIS CLEBURNE, TX

PREP: 30 MIN. • **BAKE:** 25 MIN. + COOLING
MAKES: 20 CUPCAKES

- 1 package (8 ounces) cream cheese, softened
- 1½ cups sugar, divided
- 1 egg
- 1 teaspoon salt, divided
- 1 cup (6 ounces) semisweet chocolate chips
- 1½ cups all-purpose flour
- ¼ cup baking cocoa
- 1 teaspoon baking soda
- 1 cup water
- ⅓ cup canola oil
- 1 tablespoon white vinegar

FROSTING
- 3¾ cups confectioners' sugar
- 3 tablespoons baking cocoa
- ½ cup butter, melted
- 6 tablespoons milk
- 1 teaspoon vanilla extract
- ⅓ cup chopped pecans

1. For filling, in a small mixing bowl, beat cream cheese and ½ cup sugar until smooth. Beat in egg and ½ teaspoon salt until combined. Fold in chocolate chips; set aside.

2. In a bowl, combine the flour, cocoa, baking soda, and remaining sugar and salt. In another bowl, whisk the water, oil and vinegar; stir into dry ingredients just until moistened.

3. Fill paper-lined muffin cups half full with batter. Drop filling by heaping tablespoonfuls into the center of each. Bake at 350° for 24-26 minutes or until a toothpick inserted in cake comes out clean. Cool for 10 minutes before removing from pans to wire racks to cool completely.

4. For frosting, in a large mixing bowl, combine confectioners' sugar, cocoa, butter, milk and vanilla; beat until blended. Frost cupcakes; sprinkle with pecans. Store in the refrigerator.

Butterscotch Peach Cobbler

I use canned peaches instead of fresh so I can reserve some of the syrup to make a warm butterscotch sauce. Any leftover sauce can be refrigerated and reheated for a second helping. It's also delicious drizzled over vanilla ice cream.

—**ELLEN MERICK** NORTH POLE, AK

PREP: 20 MIN. + STANDING
BAKE: 50 MIN. + COOLING
MAKES: 10-12 SERVINGS

- 2 cans (29 ounces each) sliced peaches
- ½ cup packed brown sugar
- 6 tablespoons quick-cooking tapioca
- 1 teaspoon ground cinnamon, optional
- 1 teaspoon lemon juice
- 1 teaspoon vanilla extract

TOPPING

- 1 cup all-purpose flour
- 1 cup sugar
- 1 teaspoon baking powder
- ½ teaspoon salt
- ¼ cup cold butter, cubed
- 2 eggs, lightly beaten

BUTTERSCOTCH SAUCE

- ½ cup packed brown sugar
- 2 tablespoons all-purpose flour
- ⅛ teaspoon salt
- ¼ cup butter, melted
- 2 tablespoons lemon juice
  Vanilla ice cream, optional

1. Drain peaches, reserving ½ cup syrup for the sauce. In a large bowl, combine peaches, brown sugar, tapioca, cinnamon if desired, lemon juice and vanilla. Transfer to an ungreased 11-in. x 7-in. baking dish. Let stand for 15 minutes.

2. In a large bowl, combine the flour, sugar, baking powder and salt; cut in butter until mixture resembles coarse crumbs. Stir in eggs. Drop by spoonfuls onto peach mixture; spread evenly. Bake at 350° for 50-55 minutes or until filling is bubbly and a toothpick inserted in topping comes out clean. Cool for 10 minutes.

3. In a small saucepan, combine the brown sugar, flour, salt, butter and reserved peach syrup. Bring to a boil over medium heat; cook and stir for 1 minute or until thickened. Remove from the heat; add lemon juice. Serve with cobbler and ice cream if desired.

Carrot-Spice Cake with Caramel Frosting

This cake starts with a mix, but it's loaded with extras like pineapple and coconut to give it that from-scratch flavor.

—**NORA FITZGERALD** SEVIERVILLE, TN

PREP: 45 MIN. • **BAKE:** 25 MIN. + COOLING
MAKES: 12 SERVINGS

- 1 package spice cake mix (regular size)
- 1 package (3.4 ounces) instant vanilla pudding mix
- 4 eggs
- ¾ cup water
- ½ cup sour cream
- ¼ cup canola oil
- 1 cup shredded carrots
- 1 can (8 ounces) unsweetened crushed pineapple, drained
- ½ cup flaked coconut
- ½ cup chopped pecans
- ¼ cup raisins

FROSTING

- 1 cup butter, softened
- 1 package (8 ounces) cream cheese, softened
- 6 cups confectioners' sugar
- ½ cup caramel ice cream topping
- 1 to 2 tablespoons 2% milk

1. In a large bowl, combine the cake mix, pudding mix, eggs, water, sour cream and oil; beat on low speed for 30 seconds. Beat on medium for 2 minutes. Fold in the carrots, pineapple, coconut, pecans and raisins just until blended. Pour into two greased and floured 9-in. round baking pans.

2. Bake at 350° for 25-30 minutes or until a toothpick inserted near the center comes out clean. Cool for 10 minutes before removing from pans to wire racks to cool completely.

3. For frosting, in a large bowl, beat butter and cream cheese until fluffy. Add the confectioners' sugar, ice cream topping and enough milk to achieve desired consistency. Spread frosting between layers and over the top and sides of cake. Store in the refrigerator.

Lime Cheesecake

Being from the Sunshine State, I love any recipe containing citrus. This one, featuring lime, is quick to mix up and disappears almost as fast.

—ROBIN SPIRES TAMPA, FL

PREP: 30 MIN. + CHILLING
MAKES: 12 SERVINGS

   3 **cups graham cracker crumbs**
   ⅔ **cup sugar**
   ⅔ **cup butter, melted**
FILLING
   2 **envelopes unflavored gelatin**
   1 **cup lime juice**
   ¼ **cup cold water**
   1½ **cups sugar**
   5 **eggs, lightly beaten**
   2 **teaspoons grated lime peel**
   2 **packages (8 ounces each) cream cheese, softened**
   ½ **cup butter, softened**
   ½ **cup heavy whipping cream**

1. In a large bowl, combine the graham cracker crumbs, sugar and butter. Press onto the bottom and 2 in. up the sides of a greased 9-in. springform pan. Cover and refrigerate for at least 30 minutes.

2. In a small saucepan, sprinkle gelatin over lime juice and cold water; let stand for 1 minute. Stir in the sugar, eggs and lime peel. Cook and stir over medium heat until mixture reaches 160°. Remove from the heat.

3. In a large bowl, beat cream cheese and butter until fluffy. Gradually beat in gelatin mixture. Cover and refrigerate for 45 minutes or until partially set, stirring occasionally.

4. In a small bowl, beat cream until stiff peaks form; fold into lime mixture. Spoon into crust. Cover and refrigerate for 3-4 hours or until set. Just before serving, remove sides of pan. Refrigerate leftovers.

Caramel-Pecan Cheesecake Pie

Cheesecake meets pecan pie in this simple-to-make dessert. Every slice reveals its beautiful layers of rich cream cheese and caramel-nut topping.

—BECKY RUFF MC GREGOR, IA

PREP: 15 MIN. • **BAKE:** 35 MIN. + CHILLING
MAKES: 6-8 SERVINGS

   1 **sheet refrigerated pie pastry**
   1 **package (8 ounces) cream cheese, softened**
   ½ **cup sugar**
   4 **eggs**
   1 **teaspoon vanilla extract**
   1¼ **cups chopped pecans**
   1 **jar (12¼ ounces) fat-free caramel ice cream topping**
      Additional fat-free caramel ice cream topping, optional

1. Preheat oven to 375°. Line a 9-in. deep-dish pie plate with pastry. Trim and flute edges. In a small bowl, beat cream cheese, sugar, 1 egg and vanilla until smooth. Spread into pastry shell; sprinkle with pecans.

2. In a small bowl, whisk remaining eggs; gradually whisk in caramel topping until blended. Pour slowly over pecans.

3. Bake 35-40 minutes or until lightly browned (loosely cover edges with foil after 20 minutes if pie browns too quickly). Cool on a wire rack 1 hour. Refrigerate 4 hours or overnight before slicing. If desired, garnish with additional caramel ice cream topping.

EDITOR'S NOTE *This recipe was tested with Smucker's ice cream topping.*

4. Beat marshmallow mixture until light and fluffy. Spread over pie; sprinkle with remaining almonds.

Zucchini Cupcakes

PREP: 20 MIN. • **BAKE:** 20 MIN. + COOLING
MAKES: 1½ TO 2 DOZEN

- 3 **eggs**
- 1⅓ **cups sugar**
- ½ **cup canola oil**
- ½ **cup orange juice**
- 1 **teaspoon almond extract**
- 2½ **cups all-purpose flour**
- 2 **teaspoons ground cinnamon**
- 2 **teaspoons baking powder**
- 1 **teaspoon baking soda**
- 1 **teaspoon salt**
- ½ **teaspoon ground cloves**
- 1½ **cups shredded zucchini**

CARAMEL FROSTING

- 1 **cup packed brown sugar**
- ½ **cup butter, cubed**
- ¼ **cup 2% milk**
- 1 **teaspoon vanilla extract**
- 1½ **to 2 cups confectioners' sugar**

1. In a large bowl, beat the eggs, sugar, oil, orange juice and extract. Combine dry ingredients; gradually add to egg mixture and mix well. Stir in zucchini.
2. Fill paper-lined muffin cups two-thirds full. Bake at 350° for 20-25 minutes or until toothpick inserted near the center comes out clean. Cool for 10 minutes before removing to a wire rack.
3. For frosting, combine the brown sugar, butter and milk in a saucepan. Bring to a boil over medium heat; cook and stir for 2 minutes or until thickened. Remove from the heat; stir in vanilla. Cool to lukewarm.
4. Gradually beat in confectioners' sugar until frosting reaches spreading consistency.

Marshmallow-Almond Key Lime Pie

It's great to see that many grocers now carry Key limes, which give this pie its distinctive sweet-tart flavor. But unlike other Key lime pies, this one has a smooth marshmallow top layer that makes it a crowd favorite.

—JUDY CASTRANOVA NEW BERN, NC

PREP: 40 MIN. • **BAKE:** 15 MIN. + CHILLING
MAKES: 8 SERVINGS

- 1 **cup all-purpose flour**
- 3 **tablespoons brown sugar**
- 1 **cup slivered almonds, toasted, divided**
- ¼ **cup butter, melted**
- 1 **tablespoon honey**
- 1 **can (14 ounces) sweetened condensed milk**
- 1 **package (8 ounces) cream cheese, softened, divided**
- ½ **cup Key lime juice**
- 1 **tablespoon grated Key lime peel**
  Dash salt
- 1 **egg yolk**
- 1¾ **cups miniature marshmallows**
- 4½ **teaspoons butter**
- ½ **cup heavy whipping cream**

1. Place the flour, brown sugar and ½ cup almonds in a food processor. Cover and process until blended. Add melted butter and honey; cover and process until crumbly. Press onto the bottom and up the sides of a greased 9-in. pie plate. Bake at 350° for 8-10 minutes or until crust is lightly browned. Cool on a wire rack.
2. In a large bowl, beat the milk, 5 ounces cream cheese, lime juice, peel and salt until blended. Add egg yolk; beat on low speed just until combined. Pour into crust. Bake for 15-20 minutes or until center is almost set. Cool on a wire rack.
3. In a large saucepan, combine marshmallows and butter. Cook and stir over medium-low heat until melted. Transfer to a large bowl. Add cream and remaining cream cheese; beat until smooth. Cover and refrigerate until chilled.

I asked my grandmother for this recipe after trying these irresistible spice cupcakes at her home. I love their creamy caramel frosting. They're such a scrumptious dessert you actually forget you're eating your vegetables.

—VIRGINIA LAPIERRE GREENSBORO BEND, VT

Strawberry Patch Frost

The taste of strawberry comes through in three different ways in this milkshake-meets-sundae treat. It's perfect for sharing with someone special.

—TASTE OF HOME TEST KITCHEN

START TO FINISH: 5 MIN.
MAKES: 1 SERVING.

- 2 **tablespoons strawberry jam**
- 1 **teaspoon water**
- 3 **scoops strawberry ice cream**
- ½ **cup sliced fresh strawberries**
- ¼ **cup heavy whipping cream or half-and-half cream**
- 1 **cup chilled strawberry or raspberry sparkling water**
  Whipped cream
  Colored sprinkles

In a tall glass, combine strawberry jam and water. Add ice cream, strawberries and cream. Top with sparkling water. Garnish with whipped cream and sprinkles. Serve immediately.

Pretzel Dessert

This is one of my mom's favorite desserts. The salty pretzel crust goes great with the sweet cream cheese filling, and you can top it with different flavors.

—ERIN FRAKES MOLINE, IL

PREP: 30 MIN. + CHILLING
MAKES: 12-16 SERVINGS

- 2 **cups crushed pretzels**
- ¾ **cup butter, melted**
- 2 **tablespoons sugar**

FILLING

- 1 **package (8 ounces) cream cheese, softened**
- 1 **cup sugar**
- 1 **carton (8 ounces) frozen whipped topping, thawed**

TOPPING

- 2 **packages (3 ounces each) strawberry gelatin**
- 2 **cups boiling water**
- ½ **cup cold water**

1. In a large bowl, combine the pretzels, butter and sugar. Press into an ungreased 13-in. x 9-in. baking dish. Bake at 350° for 10 minutes. Cool completely.

2. In a large bowl, beat cream cheese and sugar until smooth. Stir in whipped topping. Spread over pretzel crust. Cover and refrigerate until chilled.

3. For topping, in a small bowl, dissolve gelatin in boiling water. Add cold water; chill until partially set. Carefully pour over filling. Cover and refrigerate for 4-6 hours or until firm. Cut into squares.

Raspberry Chocolate Cake

The filling in this layered chocolate cake gets its flavor from a little raspberry liqueur and melted raspberry jam. I've been tweaking this recipe, adding a bit of this and a bit of that, to get it just right.

—MARLENE SANDERS PARADISE, TX

PREP: 45 MIN. + STANDING
BAKE: 35 MIN. + COOLING
MAKES: 16 SERVINGS

- 3 **cups sugar**
- 2¾ **cups all-purpose flour**
- 1 **cup baking cocoa**
- 2 **teaspoons baking soda**
- 1½ **teaspoons salt**
- ¾ **teaspoon baking powder**
- 1¼ **cups buttermilk**
- ¾ **cup canola oil**
- 3 **teaspoons vanilla extract**
- 3 **eggs**
- 1½ **cups strong brewed coffee, room temperature**

FILLING

- 3 **tablespoons all-purpose flour**
- 6 **tablespoons 2% milk**
- 6 **tablespoons shortening**
- 3 **tablespoons butter, softened**
- 3 **cups confectioners' sugar**
- 2 **tablespoons raspberry liqueur**
- ¼ **teaspoon salt**
- 2 **drops red food coloring, optional**
- 4 **tablespoons seedless raspberry jam, melted, divided**

FROSTING

- 1 **package (8 ounces) cold cream cheese**
- ⅓ **cup butter, softened**
- ½ **cup baking cocoa**
- 1 **tablespoon raspberry liqueur**
- 4 **cups confectioners' sugar**

1. Line three greased 9-in. round baking pans with waxed paper and grease paper; set aside. In a large bowl, combine the first six ingredients. Combine the buttermilk, oil and vanilla; add to the dry ingredients. Add eggs, one at a time, beating well after each addition; beat for 2 minutes. Gradually add coffee (batter will be thin).

2. Pour batter into prepared pans. Bake at 350° for 35-40 minutes or until a toothpick inserted near the center comes out clean. Cool for 10 minutes before removing from pans to wire racks to cool completely.

3. For filling, in a small saucepan, whisk together flour and milk until smooth. Cook over medium heat for 1 minute or until thickened, stirring constantly. Remove from the heat and let stand until cool.

4. In a large bowl, cream shortening and butter until light and fluffy. Gradually add confectioners' sugar and mix well. Gradually add cooled milk mixture; beat for 4 minutes or until light and fluffy. Beat in liqueur, salt and food coloring if desired.

5. Level tops of cakes, if necessary. Place one layer on a serving plate; spread with about 2 tablespoons jam. Place remaining layers on waxed paper; spread one of the remaining layers with remaining jam. Let stand for 30 minutes.

6. Spread ½ cup filling over cake on the plate to within ¼ in. of edges. Top with jam-covered cake, then spread with remaining filling. Top with remaining cake layer.

7. In a large bowl, beat cream cheese and butter until smooth. Beat in cocoa and liqueur. Gradually beat in confectioners' sugar until light and fluffy. Frost top and sides of cake. Store in the refrigerator.

Did you know?

Black raspberries, not to be confused with blackberries, have a rich, distinct flavor that makes them ideal for jams and preserves. You can distinguish black raspberries from blackberries by their hollow core.

ULTIMATE *Comfort*

Carrot Layer Cake

My sister gave me this recipe for what she calls the ultimate carrot cake, and it really lives up to the name. When people taste it, they're bowled over by the tender, not-too-sweet cake and unexpected pecan filling.

—LINDA VAN HOLLAND INNISFAIL, AB

PREP: 55 MIN. • **BAKE:** 35 MIN. + COOLING
MAKES: 16-20 SERVINGS

FILLING
- 1 cup sugar
- 2 tablespoons all-purpose flour
- ¼ teaspoon salt
- 1 cup heavy whipping cream
- ½ cup butter
- 1 cup chopped pecans
- 1 teaspoon vanilla extract

CAKE
- 1¼ cups canola oil
- 2 cups sugar
- 2 cups all-purpose flour
- 2 teaspoons ground cinnamon
- 2 teaspoons baking powder
- 1 teaspoon baking soda
- 1 teaspoon salt
- 4 eggs
- 4 cups finely shredded carrots
- 1 cup raisins
- 1 cup chopped pecans

FROSTING
- ¾ cup butter, softened
- 2 packages (3 ounces each) cream cheese, softened
- 1 teaspoon vanilla extract
- 3 cups confectioners' sugar

1. In a large heavy saucepan, combine sugar, flour and salt. Stir in cream; add butter. Cook and stir over medium heat until the butter is melted; bring to a boil. Reduce heat. Simmer, uncovered, for 30 minutes, stirring occasionally. Stir in nuts and vanilla. Cool and set aside.

2. In a large bowl, beat oil and sugar until well blended. Combine the flour, cinnamon, baking powder, baking soda and salt; add to the creamed mixture alternately with eggs, beating well after each addition. Stir in the carrots, raisins and nuts.

3. Pour into three greased and floured 9-in. round baking pans. Bake at 350° for 35-40 minutes or until a toothpick inserted near the center comes out clean. Cool in pans 10 minutes before removing to wire racks to cool completely.

4. For frosting, in a small bowl, beat the butter, cream cheese and vanilla until fluffy. Gradually beat in sugar until smooth. Spread filling between cake layers. Frost the sides and top of cake. Store in the refrigerator.

top tip

Make-Ahead Assembly

After I put the filling between the layers, I put the cake in the fridge for the next day. Then I make the frosting and finish the cake. This way the layers are set and don't slide when you frost the cake.

—THEFAMILYBAKER
TASTEOFHOME.COM

Cookies & Bars

THERE'S NOTHING LIKE A WARM, FRESH-BAKED COOKIE
TO REMIND YOU OF HOME SWEET HOME.

**FROSTED
PUMPKIN COOKIES**
PAGE 281

**CHUNKY
PECAN BARS**
PAGE 288

**JUMBO CHOCOLATE
CHIP COOKIES**
PAGE 282

Chocolate Billionaires

I received this recipe from a friend while living in Texas. When we moved, I made sure to take it with me. Everyone raves about these chocolate and caramel bites.

—JUNE HUMPHREY STRONGSVILLE, OH

PREP: 45 MIN. + CHILLING
MAKES: ABOUT 2 POUNDS

- 1 package (14 ounces) caramels
- 3 tablespoons water
- 1½ cups chopped pecans
- 1 cup crisp rice cereal
- 3 cups milk chocolate chips
- 1½ teaspoons shortening

1. Line two baking sheets with waxed paper; grease the paper and set aside. In a large heavy saucepan, combine the caramels and water; cook and stir over low heat until smooth. Stir in pecans and cereal until coated. Drop by teaspoonfuls onto prepared pans. Refrigerate for 10 minutes or until firm.

2. Meanwhile, in a microwave, melt chocolate chips and shortening; stir until smooth. Dip candy into chocolate, coating all sides; allow excess to drip off. Place on prepared pans. Refrigerate until set. Store in an airtight container.

kid FRIENDLY S'more Bars

Once school starts, it can be hard for kids to let go of summer. But these great-tasting bars will bring back sweet campfire memories, whether they're served for dessert or as an after-school snack.

—LISA MORIARTY WILTON, NH

PREP: 20 MIN. • **BAKE:** 25 MIN. + COOLING
MAKES: 1½ DOZEN

- ½ cup butter, softened
- ¾ cup sugar
- 1 egg
- 1 teaspoon vanilla extract
- 1⅓ cups all-purpose flour
- ¾ cup graham cracker crumbs
- 1 teaspoon baking powder
- ⅛ teaspoon salt
- 5 milk chocolate candy bars (1.55 ounces each)
- 1 cup marshmallow creme

1. In a large bowl, cream butter and sugar until light and fluffy. Beat in egg and vanilla. Combine the flour, cracker crumbs, baking powder and salt; gradually add to creamed mixture. Set aside ½ cup for topping.

2. Press remaining mixture into a greased 9-in. square baking pan. Place candy bars over crust; spread with marshmallow creme. Crumble remaining graham cracker mixture over top.

3. Bake at 350° for 25-30 minutes or until golden brown. Cool on a wire rack. Cut into bars. Store in an airtight container.

Toasty Tip

For the S'more Bars, I used 10 large marshmallows cut in half instead of the creme and placed the cut side down. They browned just like on a campfire. Fabulous!!

—JKJJJ2009 TASTEOFHOME.COM

White Chocolate Peppermint Crunch

This is my favorite candy to make at Christmas. Not only is it easy, it's delicious as well. I like to place small bags or boxes of it inside gift baskets.

—NANCY SHELTON BOAZ, KY

PREP: 15 MIN. + CHILLING
MAKES: ABOUT 1½ POUNDS

- 2 tablespoons butter, divided
- 1 pound white candy coating, coarsely chopped
- 1 tablespoon canola oil
- 1 cup crushed peppermint candies or candy canes

1. Line a baking sheet with foil and grease the foil with 1 tablespoon butter; set aside.
2. In a microwave-safe bowl, melt candy coating; stir until smooth. Stir in oil and remaining butter until smooth. Stir in peppermint candies.
3. Pour onto prepared baking sheet, spreading to desired thickness. Refrigerate for 30 minutes or until firm. Break into pieces. Store in an airtight container in the refrigerator.

Cappuccino Brownies

There's something magical in coffee that intensifies the flavor of chocolate. These three-layer wonders freeze well, but somehow most of them disappear before they reach the freezer.

—SUSIE JONES BUHL, ID

PREP: 30 MIN. + CHILLING
BAKE: 25 MIN. + COOLING
MAKES: 2 DOZEN

- 8 ounces bittersweet chocolate, chopped
- ¾ cup butter, cut up
- 2 tablespoons instant coffee granules
- 1 tablespoon hot water

- 4 eggs
- 1½ cups sugar
- 2 teaspoons vanilla extract
- 1 cup all-purpose flour
- ½ teaspoon salt
- 1 cup chopped walnuts

TOPPING

- 1 package (8 ounces) cream cheese, softened
- 6 tablespoons butter, softened
- 1½ cups confectioners' sugar
- 1 teaspoon ground cinnamon
- 1 teaspoon vanilla extract

GLAZE

- 4 teaspoons instant coffee granules
- 1 tablespoon hot water
- 5 ounces bittersweet chocolate, chopped
- 2 tablespoons butter
- ½ cup heavy whipping cream

1. In a microwave, melt chocolate and butter; stir until smooth. Cool slightly. Dissolve coffee granules in hot water. In a large bowl, beat eggs and sugar. Stir in vanilla, chocolate mixture and coffee mixture. Combine flour and salt; gradually add to chocolate mixture until blended. Fold in walnuts.
2. Transfer to a greased and floured 13x9-in. baking pan. Bake at 350° for 25-30 minutes or until a toothpick inserted near the center comes out clean. Cool completely on a wire rack.
3. For topping, in a large bowl, beat cream cheese and butter until blended. Add confectioners' sugar, cinnamon and vanilla; beat on low speed until combined. Spread over bars. Refrigerate until firm, about 1 hour.
4. For glaze, dissolve coffee granules in hot water. In a microwave, melt chocolate and butter; cool slightly. Stir in cream and coffee mixture. Spread over cream cheese layer. Let stand until set. Serve or cover and freeze for up to 1 month.

TO USE FROZEN BROWNIES *Thaw at room temperature. Cut into bars. Refrigerate leftovers.*

Peanut Butter Cookies

This cookie recipe is a treasured family heirloom since it is the only one my grandmother ever recorded! When my mother was married, she insisted her mother write down one recipe for her. That was a real effort, because Grandma was a pioneer-type cook who used a little of this or that till it felt right.

—**JANET HALL** CLINTON, WI

PREP: 15 MIN. • **BAKE:** 10 MIN./BATCH
MAKES: 3 DOZEN

- 1 cup shortening
- 1 cup peanut butter
- 1 cup sugar
- 1 cup packed brown sugar
- 3 eggs
- 3 cups all-purpose flour
- 2 teaspoons baking soda
- ¼ teaspoon salt

1. In a large bowl, cream shortening, peanut butter and sugars until light and fluffy. Add eggs, one at a time, beating well after each addition. Combine the flour, baking soda and salt; add to creamed mixture and mix well.

2. Roll into 1½-in. balls. Place 3 in. apart on ungreased baking sheets. Flatten with a fork or meat mallet if desired. Bake at 375° for 10-15 minutes. Remove to wire racks.

Spiced Almond Cookies

I usually make a big batch of these and freeze the dough. That way when I need a tray of sweets, I take a log out of the freezer, thaw it and make fresh cookies in minutes. These are my all-time favorite!

—**WANDA DAILY** MILWAUKIE, OR

PREP: 15 MIN. + CHILLING • **BAKE:** 15 MIN.
MAKES: 7 DOZEN

- 1 cup butter, softened
- ½ cup shortening
- 1 cup packed brown sugar
- 1 cup sugar
- 2 eggs
- 4 cups all-purpose flour
- 2 teaspoons ground cinnamon
- 1 teaspoon baking soda
- 1 teaspoon salt
- 1 teaspoon ground cloves
- 1 teaspoon allspice
- 1 cup slivered almonds

1. In a bowl, cream the butter, shortening and sugars until light and fluffy. Add eggs and beat well. Combine dry ingredients; stir into creamed mixture along with nuts. Shape into three 9x1½-in. rolls; wrap in plastic wrap. Refrigerate 2-3 days for spices to blend.

2. Preheat oven to 350°. Unwrap and cut into ¼-in. slices. Place 2 in. apart on ungreased baking sheets. Bake 12-14 minutes or until set. Remove to wire racks.

Dark Chocolate Orange Truffles

I love chocolate truffles, so you can imagine my delight when I came across these dark and decadent confections. The hint of orange makes them deliciously different from other candies.

—**THERESA YOUNG** MCHENRY, IL

PREP: 10 MIN. + CHILLING
MAKES: 2½ DOZEN

- **1** **package (12 ounces) dark chocolate chips**
- **¾** **cup heavy whipping cream**
- **1** **teaspoon orange extract**
- **⅓** **cup sugar**

In a microwave, melt chocolate; stir until smooth. Gradually stir in cream until blended. Stir in extract. Cool to room temperature, stirring occasionally. Refrigerate until firm. Shape into ¾-in. balls. Roll in sugar.

Frosted Pumpkin Cookies

These caramel frosted cookies are our favorites! They freeze and travel well, especially if you let the icing dry completely, then layer the cookies between sheets of waxed paper.

—**LEONA LUTTRELL** SARASOTA, FL

PREP: 25 MIN. • **BAKE:** 15 MIN./BATCH
MAKES: 6½ DOZEN

- **1** **cup shortening**
- **2** **cups packed brown sugar**
- **1** **can (15 ounces) solid-pack pumpkin**
- **4** **cups all-purpose flour**
- **2** **teaspoons baking powder**
- **2** **teaspoons baking soda**
- **2** **teaspoons ground cinnamon**
- **⅛** **teaspoon salt**
- **1** **cup chopped pecans**
- **1** **cup chopped dates**

CARAMEL FROSTING
- **½** **cup butter, cubed**
- **1½** **cups packed brown sugar**
- **¼** **cup 2% milk**
- **1** **teaspoon maple flavoring**
- **½** **teaspoon vanilla extract**
- **2** **to 2½ cups confectioners' sugar**

1. In a large bowl, cream shortening and brown sugar until light and fluffy. Beat in pumpkin. Combine the flour, baking powder, baking soda, cinnamon and salt; gradually add to pumpkin mixture and mix well. Stir in pecans and dates.

2. Drop by rounded teaspoonfuls 2 in. apart onto ungreased baking sheets. Bake at 375° for 13-15 minutes or until firm.

3. Meanwhile, for frosting, combine the butter, brown sugar and milk in a small saucepan. Bring to a boil over medium heat, stirring constantly; boil for 3 minutes. Remove from the heat; stir in maple flavoring and vanilla.

4. Cool slightly; beat in enough confectioners' sugar to achieve spreading consistency. Remove cookies to wire racks; frost while warm.

ULTIMATE *Comfort* Jumbo Chocolate Chip Cookies

These huge cookies are very popular with my family. No one can resist the sweet chocolaty taste.

—**LORI SPORER** OAKLEY, KS

PREP: 15 MIN. + CHILLING
BAKE: 15 MIN./BATCH • **MAKES:** 2 DOZEN

- ⅔ cup shortening
- ⅔ cup butter, softened
- 1 cup sugar
- 1 cup packed brown sugar
- 2 eggs
- 2 teaspoons vanilla extract
- 3½ cups all-purpose flour
- 1 teaspoon baking soda
- 1 teaspoon salt
- 2 cups (12 ounces) semisweet chocolate chips
- 1 cup chopped pecans

1. In a large bowl, cream shortening, butter and sugars until light and fluffy. Beat in eggs and vanilla. Combine the flour, baking soda and salt; add to creamed mixture and mix well. Fold in the chocolate chips and pecans. Chill for at least 1 hour.

2. Drop by ¼ cupfuls 2 in. apart onto greased baking sheets. Bake at 375° for 13-15 minutes or until golden brown. Cool for 5 minutes before removing to wire racks.

Terrific Toffee

PREP: 10 MIN. • **COOK:** 25 MIN. + STANDING
MAKES: ABOUT 2 POUNDS

- 1½ teaspoons plus 1 cup butter, divided
- 1 cup (6 ounces) semisweet chocolate chips
- 1 cup milk chocolate chips
- 1 cup sugar
- 3 tablespoons water
- 2 cups coarsely chopped almonds, toasted, divided

1. Butter a large baking sheet with 1½ teaspoons butter; set aside. In a small bowl, combine semisweet and milk chocolate chips; set aside.

2. In a heavy saucepan, combine the sugar, water and remaining butter. Cook and stir over medium heat until a candy thermometer reaches 290° (soft-crack stage). Remove from the heat; stir in 1 cup almonds. Immediately pour onto prepared baking sheet.

3. Sprinkle with chocolate chips; spread with a knife when melted. Sprinkle with remaining almonds. Let stand until set, about 1 hour.

4. Break into 2-in. pieces. Store in an airtight container.

ENGLISH TOFFEE *Omit semisweet chocolate chips and almonds. Prepare toffee as directed; omit stirring in the almonds. Spread in pan and cool. Melt 1 cup milk chocolate chips in a microwave at 30% power or in a saucepan over low heat; stir until smooth. Spread over toffee and sprinkle with 1 cup chopped pecans. Let stand until set, about 1 hour.*

HAZELNUT TOFFEE *Omit milk chocolate chips and almonds. Prepare toffee as directed; stirring ⅓ cup chopped hazelnut. Spread in pan and cool. Melt 2 cups semisweet chocolate chips in a microwave at 50% power or in a saucepan over low heat; stir until smooth. Spread over toffee and sprinkle with ½ cup finely chopped hazelnuts. Let stand until set, about 1 hour.*

NOTE *We recommend that you test your candy thermometer before each use by bringing water to a boil; the thermometer should read 212°. Adjust your recipe temperature up or down based on your test.*

Nutty, buttery toffee is one of those must-make treats my family requests for the holidays. You can also try variations to make English or Hazelnut Toffee. —**CAROL GILLESPIE** CHAMBERSBURG, PA

Whole Wheat Toffee Sandies

Crisp and loaded with goodies, these cookies are my husband's favorite. I used to bake them in large batches when our four sons still lived at home. Now I whip them up for our grandchildren.
—**ALICE KAHNK** KENNARD, NE

PREP: 35 MIN. • **BAKE:** 15 MIN./BATCH
MAKES: ABOUT 12 DOZEN

- 1 **cup butter, softened**
- 1 **cup sugar**
- 1 **cup confectioners' sugar**
- 1 **cup canola oil**
- 2 **eggs**
- 1 **teaspoon almond extract**
- 3½ **cups all-purpose flour**
- 1 **cup whole wheat flour**
- 1 **teaspoon baking soda**
- 1 **teaspoon cream of tartar**
- 1 **teaspoon salt**
- 2 **cups chopped almonds**
- 1 **package (8 ounces) milk chocolate English toffee bits**
  Additional sugar

1. In a large bowl, cream butter and sugars until light and fluffy. Beat in the oil, eggs and extract. Combine the flours, baking soda, cream of tartar and salt; gradually add to creamed mixture and mix well. Stir in almonds and toffee bits.
2. Shape into 1-in. balls; roll in sugar. Place on ungreased baking sheets and flatten with a fork. Bake at 350° for 12-14 minutes or until lightly browned.

? Did you know?

The world's best-selling cookie, the Oreo, debuted in 1912 with two flavors: original and lemon meringue.

Chocolate Lover's Dream Cookies

My daughter won first prize in the cookie division of a local chocolate festival with these—beating out a number of adult bakers. These rich chocolate cookies with white chocolate chips are scrumptious.
—**PAULA ZSIRAY** LOGAN, UT

PREP: 15 MIN. • **BAKE:** 15 MIN./BATCH
MAKES: 3½ DOZEN

- 6 **tablespoons canola oil**
- ¼ **cup butter, softened**
- ¾ **cup packed brown sugar**
- ½ **cup sugar**
- 2 **eggs**
- 1 **teaspoon vanilla extract**
- 1¼ **cups all-purpose flour**
- ½ **cup baking cocoa**
- ¼ **teaspoon baking powder**
- 1 **cup white baking chips**
- 1 **cup (6 ounces) semisweet chocolate chips**

1. In a large bowl, beat the oil, butter and sugars until well blended. Add eggs, one at a time, beating well after each addition. Beat in vanilla. Combine the flour, cocoa and baking powder; gradually add to oil mixture and mix well. Stir in chips.
2. Drop by rounded tablespoonfuls 2 in. apart onto ungreased baking sheets. Bake at 350° for 12-15 minutes or until edges begin to brown. Cool for 1 minute before removing from pans to wire racks.

Angel Sugar Crisps

Whenever I've taken these to church coffees, I've had women come into the kitchen and want me to share the recipe. The brown sugar gives the cookie its unique flavor and texture.

—ANNABEL COX OLIVET, SD

PREP: 25 MIN. • **BAKE:** 10 MIN.
MAKES: 4 DOZEN

- ½ cup butter, softened
- ½ cup shortening
- ½ cup sugar
- ½ cup packed brown sugar
- 1 egg
- 1 teaspoon vanilla extract
- 2 cups all-purpose flour
- 1 teaspoon baking soda
- 1 teaspoon cream of tartar
- ½ teaspoon salt
  Water
  Additional white or colored sugar

In a bowl, cream butter, shortening, sugars, egg and vanilla until light and fluffy. Sift together flour, soda, cream of tartar and salt. Add to creamed mixture; mix until blended. Shape into large marble-size balls. Dip half of ball into water, then in sugar. Place, sugared side up, on ungreased baking sheets. Bake at 400° for 6 minutes or until done. Cool.

ULTIMATE *Comfort* Fudge Nut Brownies

There's no brownie recipe or mix I've ever tried that's better than this! You can mix it in one bowl in just a few minutes. My husband's grandmother passed the recipe on; now our son makes these brownies for after-school snacks.

—BECKY ALBRIGHT NORWALK, OH

PREP: 15 MIN. • **BAKE:** 25 MIN.
MAKES: ABOUT 24 BROWNIES

- 1⅓ cups all-purpose flour
- 2 cups sugar
- ¾ cup baking cocoa
- 1 teaspoon baking powder
- ½ teaspoon salt
- ½ cup chopped nuts
- ⅔ cup vegetable oil
- 4 eggs, lightly beaten
- 2 teaspoons vanilla extract
- 1 cup chopped nuts, optional

In a bowl, combine first six ingredients. In another bowl, combine oil, eggs and vanilla; add to dry ingredients. Do not overmix. Spread in a 13x9-in. baking pan. Sprinkle with nuts if desired. Bake at 350° for 20-25 minutes or until toothpick inserted in center comes out clean.

Chocolate Almond Brittle

Here in Kern County, there are thousands of acres of almond orchards. I like to experiment with recipes to try to come up with something new. This candy is the result of a lot of taste-testing.

—**PAT PARSONS** BAKERSFILED, CA

PREP: 15 MIN. + COOLING
MAKES: ABOUT 1 POUND.

- 1 **cup sugar**
- ½ **cup light corn syrup**
- ⅛ **teaspoon salt**
- 1 **cup coarsely chopped almonds**
- 1 **tablespoon butter**
- 1 **teaspoon vanilla extract**
- 1½ **teaspoons baking soda**
- ¾ **pound dark or milk chocolate candy coating**

1. In a 1½-qt. microwave-safe bowl, combine the sugar, corn syrup and salt. Microwave, uncovered, on high for 2½ minutes. Stir in almonds; cook on high for 2½ minutes. Add the butter and vanilla; cook on high for 1 minute.
2. Stir in baking soda. As soon as the mixture foams, quickly pour onto a greased metal baking sheet. Cool completely. Break into 2-in. pieces.
3. Melt chocolate coating in a microwave. Dip one side of brittle in chocolate and place on waxed paper to harden. Store in an airtight container.
NOTE *This recipe was tested in a 1,100-watt microwave.*

Did you know?

Legend has it that around 1890, a woman was making taffy in her kitchen and accidentally added baking soda instead of cream of tartar. When she realized her mistake, she added peanuts and brittle was born.

Sugar Cookie Cutouts

Each Christmas, my brother, sister and I would eagerly wait for Grandpa and Grandma to arrive with these cookies in tow. Now I must have over 100 different cookie cutters and have had fun putting them to use with this recipe over the years.

—ELIZABETH WALTERS WATERLOO, IA

PREP: 30 MIN. + CHILLING
BAKE: 10 MIN./BATCH + COOLING
MAKES: 8 DOZEN

- 1 **cup butter, softened**
- 1 **cup sugar**
- 2 **eggs**
- ¼ **cup half-and-half cream**
- 3 **cups all-purpose flour**
- 2 **teaspoons baking powder**
- 1 **teaspoon baking soda**
- ½ **teaspoon salt**

FROSTING
- ½ **cup butter, softened**
- 4 **cups confectioners' sugar**
- 1 **teaspoon vanilla extract**
- 2 **to 4 tablespoons half-and-half cream**
  Food coloring and colored sugar, optional

1. In a large bowl, cream butter and sugar until light and fluffy. Add eggs, one at a time, beating well after each addition. Beat in cream. Combine the flour, baking powder, baking soda and salt; gradually add to creamed mixture and mix well. Cover and refrigerate for 3 hours or until easy to handle.

2. On a lightly floured surface, roll out dough to ⅛-in. thickness. Cut with floured 2½-in. cookie cutters. Place 1 in. apart on ungreased baking sheets. Bake at 325° for 6-8 minutes or until edges are lightly browned. Remove to wire racks to cool.

3. In another large bowl, cream butter, sugar, vanilla and enough cream to achieve spreading consistency. Add food coloring if desired. Frost cookies. Sprinkle with colored sugar if desired.

kid FRIENDLY Peanut Butter Kiss Cookies

It's amazing to everyone who tries these that they only use 5 ingredients. Baking cookies doesn't get much easier than this.

—DEE DAVIS SUN CITY, AZ

PREP: 20 MIN. • **BAKE:** 10 MIN. + COOLING
MAKES: 2 DOZEN

- 1 **cup peanut butter**
- 1 **cup sugar**
- 1 **egg**
- 1 **teaspoon vanilla extract**
- 24 **milk chocolate kisses**

1. In a large bowl, cream peanut butter and sugar until light and fluffy. Add egg and vanilla; beat until blended.

2. Roll into 1¼-in. balls. Place 2 in. apart on ungreased baking sheets. Bake at 350° for 10-12 minutes or until tops are slightly cracked.

3. Immediately press one chocolate kiss into the center of each cookie. Cool for 5 minutes before removing from pans to wire racks.

EDITOR'S NOTE *This recipe does not contain flour. Reduced-fat or generic brands of peanut butter are not recommended for this recipe.*

Chunky Pecan Bars

Most folks can't stop at just one of these fudgy, nutty bars. They remind people of pecan pie with a chocolate twist.

—**HAZEL BALDNER** AUSTIN, MN

PREP: 15 MIN. • **BAKE:** 20 MIN. + COOLING
MAKES: 4 DOZEN

- 1½ **cups all-purpose flour**
- ½ **cup packed brown sugar**
- ½ **cup cold butter, cubed**

FILLING
- 3 **eggs**
- ¾ **cup sugar**
- ¾ **cup dark corn syrup**
- 2 **tablespoons butter, melted**
- 1 **teaspoon vanilla extract**
- 1¾ **cups semisweet chocolate chunks**
- 1½ **cups coarsely chopped pecans**

1. In a small bowl, combine the flour and brown sugar; cut in butter until crumbly. Press into a greased 13x9-in. baking pan. Bake at 350° for 10-15 minutes or until golden brown.

2. Meanwhile, in a large bowl, whisk the eggs, sugar, corn syrup, butter and vanilla until blended. Stir in chocolate chunks and pecans. Pour over crust.

3. Bake for 20-25 minutes or until set. Cool completely on a wire rack. Cut into bars. Store in an airtight container in the refrigerator.

Slice 'n' Bake Lemon Gems

Rolled in colorful sprinkles, these melt-in-your-mouth cookies can be decorated for any holiday or special occasion.

—**DELORES EDGECOMB** ATLANTA, NY

PREP: 25 MIN. + CHILLING
BAKE: 10 MIN./BATCH + COOLING
MAKES: 28 COOKIES

- ¾ **cup butter, softened**
- ½ **cup confectioners' sugar**
- 1 **tablespoon grated lemon peel**
- 1 **cup all-purpose flour**
- ½ **cup cornstarch**
- ¼ **cup colored nonpareils**

LEMON ICING
- 1 **cup confectioners' sugar**
- 2 **tablespoons lemon juice**
- ½ **teaspoon grated lemon peel**

1. In a small bowl, cream butter and confectioners' sugar until light and fluffy. Beat in lemon peel. Combine flour and cornstarch; gradually add to creamed mixture and mix well. Cover and refrigerate for 1 hour or until easy to handle.

2. Shape into a 1¾-in.-diameter roll; roll in nonpareils. Wrap in plastic wrap. Refrigerate for 2-3 hours or until firm.

3. Preheat oven to 375°. Unwrap and cut into ¼-in. slices. Place 1 in. apart on ungreased baking sheets. Bake 9-11 minutes or until set and edges are lightly browned. Cool 1 minute before removing to wire racks to cool completely.

4. In a small bowl, combine icing ingredients. Spread over cookies.

Berry Shortbread Dreams

Raspberry, blackberry, strawberry ... use whatever kind of seedless jam you like to fill these buttery cookies. They practically melt in your mouth.

—MILDRED SHERRER FORT WORTH, TX

PREP: 20 MIN. + CHILLING • **BAKE:** 15 MIN.
MAKES: ABOUT 3½ DOZEN

- 1 **cup butter, softened**
- ⅔ **cup sugar**
- ½ **teaspoon almond extract**
- 2 **cups all-purpose flour**
- ⅓ **to ½ cup seedless raspberry jam**

GLAZE
- 1 **cup confectioners' sugar**
- ½ **teaspoon almond extract**
- 2 **to 3 teaspoons water**

1. In a large bowl, cream butter and sugar until light and fluffy. Beat in extract; gradually add flour until dough forms a ball. Cover and refrigerate for 1 hour or until dough is easy to handle.

2. Roll into 1-in. balls. Place 1 in. apart on ungreased baking sheets. Using the end of a wooden spoon handle, make an indentation in the center. Fill with jam.

3. Bake at 350° for 14-18 minutes or until edges are lightly browned. Remove to wire racks to cool.

4. Spoon additional jam into cookies if desired. Combine confectioners' sugar, extract and enough water to achieve drizzling consistency; drizzle over cookies.

Snickerdoodles

The history of this whimsically named treat is widely disputed, but the popularity of this classic cinnamon-sugar-coated cookie is undeniable! Add this version to your holiday cookie collection.

—TASTE OF HOME TEST KITCHEN

START TO FINISH: 25 MIN.
MAKES: 2½ DOZEN

- ½ **cup butter, softened**
- 1 **cup plus 2 tablespoons sugar, divided**
- 1 **egg**
- ½ **teaspoon vanilla extract**
- 1½ **cups all-purpose flour**
- ¼ **teaspoon baking soda**
- ¼ **teaspoon cream of tartar**
- 1 **teaspoon ground cinnamon**

1. In a large bowl, cream butter and 1 cup sugar until light and fluffy. Beat in egg and vanilla. Combine the flour, baking soda and cream of tartar; gradually add to the creamed mixture and mix well. In a small bowl, combine cinnamon and remaining sugar.

2. Shape dough into 1-in. balls; roll in cinnamon-sugar. Place 2 in. apart on ungreased baking sheets. Bake at 375° for 10-12 minutes or until lightly browned. Remove to wire racks to cool.

These soft, chewy cookies go over big with my grandchildren. They love helping me decorate them, too —**JOAN TRUAX** PITTSBORO, IN

Gingerbread People

PREP: 45 MIN. + CHILLING
BAKE: 10 MIN./BATCH + COOLING
MAKES: 2½ DOZEN

- 6 tablespoons butter, softened
- ¾ cup packed dark brown sugar
- ½ cup molasses
- 1 egg
- 2 teaspoons vanilla extract
- 1 teaspoon grated lemon peel
- 3 cups all-purpose flour
- 3 teaspoons ground ginger
- 1½ teaspoons baking powder
- 1¼ teaspoons ground cinnamon
- ¾ teaspoon baking soda
- ¼ teaspoon salt
- ¼ teaspoon ground cloves
  Decorating icing and assorted candies

1. In a large bowl, cream butter and brown sugar until light and fluffy. Beat in molasses, egg, vanilla and lemon peel. In another bowl, whisk flour, ginger, baking powder, cinnamon, baking soda, salt and cloves; gradually beat into creamed mixture. Divide dough in half. Shape each into a disk; wrap in plastic wrap. Refrigerate 30 minutes or until easy to handle.

2. Preheat oven to 350°. On a lightly floured surface, roll each portion to ¼-in. thickness. Cut with a floured 4-in. gingerbread man cookie cutter.

3. Place 2 in. apart on greased baking sheets. Bake 7-9 minutes or until edges are firm. Remove from pans to wire racks to cool completely. Decorate as desired.

TO DECORATE WITH ROYAL ICING *In a bowl, combine 2 cups confectioners' sugar, 2 tablespoons plus 2 teaspoons water, 4½ teaspoons meringue powder and ¼ teaspoon cream of tartar; beat on low speed just until combined. Beat on high 4-5 minutes or until stiff peaks form. If desired, tint with food coloring and pipe with a pastry bag and small pastry tips. Keep unused icing covered at all times; beat again on high to restore texture as necessary. Yield: 1 cup icing.*

Chocolate Peanut Butter Candy

With just three ingredients, these peanut butter and chocolate-swirl treats take only a few moments to whip up. And there's no cooking or baking involved.

—**HOLLY DEMERS** ABBOTSFORD, BC

PREP: 10 MIN. + CHILLING
MAKES: ABOUT 2½ POUNDS

- 1 pound white candy coating, coarsely chopped
- 1½ cups creamy peanut butter
- 2 cups (12 ounces) semisweet chocolate chips

1. In a large microwave-safe bowl, melt candy coating; stir until smooth. Stir in peanut butter; thinly spread onto a waxed paper-lined baking sheet.

2. In another microwave-safe bowl, melt chocolate chips; stir until smooth. Drizzle over candy coating mixture; cut through mixture with a knife to swirl the chocolate. Chill until firm.

3. Break into pieces. Store in an airtight container in the refrigerator.

Soft Chewy Caramels

One of my first experiences with cooking was helping my mother make these caramels for Christmas. We'd make up to 12 batches each year. Today I do at least 95 percent of the cooking at home, but my wife does most of the baking.

—**ROBERT SPRENKLE** HURST, TX

PREP: 5 MIN. • **COOK:** 20 MIN. + COOLING
MAKES: ABOUT 2½ POUNDS

- 1 tablespoon plus 1 cup butter, divided
- 2¼ cups packed brown sugar
- 1 can (14 ounces) sweetened condensed milk
- 1 cup dark corn syrup

1. Line a 15x10x1-in. pan with foil; grease the foil with 1 tablespoon butter. In a heavy saucepan over medium heat, melt remaining butter. Add the brown sugar, milk and corn syrup. Cook and stir until candy thermometer reads 250° (hard-ball stage).

2. Pour into prepared pan (do not scrape saucepan). Cool completely before cutting.

NOTE *We recommend that you test your candy thermometer before each use by bringing water to a boil; the thermometer should read 212°. Adjust your recipe temperature up or down based on your test.*

Lemon Bars

Basic lemon bars have been popular for years. The wonderful tangy flavor is a nice change from chocolate-laden desserts.

—**ETTA SOUCY** MESA, AZ

PREP: 10 MIN. • **BAKE:** 45 MIN. + COOLING
MAKES: 9 SERVINGS

- 1 cup all-purpose flour
- ½ cup butter, softened
- ¼ cup confectioners' sugar

FILLING

- 2 eggs
- 1 cup sugar
- 2 tablespoons all-purpose flour
- ½ teaspoon baking powder
- 2 tablespoons lemon juice
- 1 teaspoon grated lemon peel
  Additional confectioners' sugar

1. In a bowl, combine the flour, butter and confectioners' sugar. Pat into an ungreased 8-in. square baking pan. Bake at 350° for 20 minutes.

2. For filling, in a small bowl, beat eggs. Add the sugar, flour, baking powder, lemon juice and peel; beat until frothy. Pour over the crust. Bake 25 minutes longer or until light golden brown. Cool on a wire rack. Dust with confectioners' sugar. Cut into bars.

top tip · Flavored Caramels

I've been making these caramels for years, and I've had great success adding different flavors of extracts such as rum and orange. I wrap the individual candies in wax paper and give them as gifts during holidays. Everyone loves them!

—**ROMANCE1982** TASTEOFHOME.COM

Caramel Marshmallow Delights

Caramel-dipped marshmallows with a Rice Krispie coating are a fun take on cereal bars. Our children like to bring these sweet and chewy treats to school to share on their birthday.

—SUSAN KERR CROWN POINT, IN

PREP: 25 MIN. + CHILLING
MAKES: 5-6 DOZEN

- 1 **package (10 ounces) crisp rice cereal**
- 1 **can (14 ounces) sweetened condensed milk**
- ½ **cup butter, cubed**
- 1 **package (14 ounces) caramels**
- 1 **package (16 ounces) large marshmallows**

1. Place cereal in a large bowl; set aside. In a double boiler or metal bowl over simmering water, combine the milk, butter and caramels, stirring until smooth. Remove from the heat.
2. With a fork, quickly dip marshmallows into hot mixture; allow excess to drip off. Roll in cereal. Place on a foil-lined pan; chill for 30 minutes. Remove from the pan and refrigerate in an airtight container.

Butterscotch Shortbread

After sampling these tender cookies in a specialty store, I knew I had to duplicate them. My version has lots of butterscotch chips and toffee bits. I give away dozens as home-baked gifts.

—SANDY MCKENZIE BRAHAM, MN

PREP: 30 MIN. + CHILLING
BAKE: 10 MIN./BATCH + COOLING
MAKES: 4½ DOZEN

- 1 **cup butter, softened**
- ½ **cup confectioners' sugar**
- 1 **teaspoon vanilla extract**
- 1¾ **cups all-purpose flour**
- ½ **cup cornstarch**
- ¼ **teaspoon salt**
- ½ **cup butterscotch chips, finely chopped**
- ½ **cup milk chocolate English toffee bits**

1. In a large bowl, cream butter and confectioners' sugar until light and fluffy. Beat in vanilla. Combine flour, cornstarch and salt; gradually add to creamed mixture and mix well. Fold in butterscotch chips and toffee bits. Cover and refrigerate 1 hour or until easy to handle.
2. Preheat oven to 350°. On a lightly floured surface, roll out dough to ¼-in. thickness. Cut with a floured 2-in. fluted round cookie cutter. Place 1 in. apart on ungreased baking sheets.
3. Bake 10-12 minutes or until lightly browned. Remove to wire racks.

1. In a bowl, beat the eggs, sugar, oil and pumpkin until well blended. Combine the flour, cinnamon, baking powder, baking soda and salt; gradually add to pumpkin mixture and mix well. Pour into an ungreased 15-in. x 10-in. x 1-in. baking pan. Bake at 350° for 25-30 minutes or until set. Cool completely.

2. For icing, beat the cream cheese, confectioners' sugar, butter and vanilla in a small bowl. Add enough milk to achieve spreading consistency. Spread over bars. Store in the refrigerator.

Oatmeal Chip Cookies

Sometimes a traditional oatmeal chocolate chip cookie is all it takes to warm someone's day—and this simple recipe makes enough to cheer up a crowd.

—**RUTH ANN STELFOX** RAYMOND, AB

PREP: 25 MIN. + CHILLING • **BAKE:** 15 MIN.
MAKES: ABOUT 7 DOZEN

- 2 **cups butter, softened**
- 2 **cups sugar**
- 2 **cups packed brown sugar**
- 4 **eggs**
- 2 **teaspoons vanilla extract**
- 6 **cups quick-cooking oats**
- 3 **cups all-purpose flour**
- 2 **teaspoons baking soda**
- 1 **teaspoon salt**
- 2 **cups (12 ounces) semisweet chocolate chips**

1. In a large bowl, cream butter and sugars until light and fluffy. Beat in eggs and vanilla. Combine the oats, flour, baking soda and salt; gradually add to creamed mixture and mix well. Stir in chocolate chips. Chill dough for 1 hour or until firm.

2. Roll dough into 1½ in. balls; place on greased baking sheets. Bake at 350° for 11-13 minutes or until lightly browned. Remove from pans to wire racks.

Pumpkin Bars

What could be more appropriate for a Halloween treat than a pan of pumpkin-flavored bars? Actually, my family loves them any time of year.

—**BRENDA KELLER** ANDALUSIA, AL

PREP: 15 MIN. • **BAKE:** 25 MIN. + COOLING
MAKES: 2 DOZEN

- 4 **eggs**
- 1⅔ **cups sugar**
- 1 **cup canola oil**
- 1 **can (15 ounces) solid-pack pumpkin**
- 2 **cups all-purpose flour**
- 2 **teaspoons ground cinnamon**
- 2 **teaspoons baking powder**
- 1 **teaspoon baking soda**
- 1 **teaspoon salt**

ICING

- 1 **package (3 ounces) cream cheese, softened**
- 2 **cups confectioners' sugar**
- ¼ **cup butter, softened**
- 1 **teaspoon vanilla extract**
- 1 **to 2 tablespoons milk**

Ice Cream Kolachkes

These sweet pastries have Polish and Czech roots and can also be spelled *kolaches*. They are usually filled with poppy seeds, nuts, jam or a mashed fruit mixture, so the ice cream is a unique twist.

—DIANE TURNER BRUNSWICK, OH

PREP: 1 HOUR + CHILLING
BAKE: 10 MIN./BATCH • **MAKES:** 10 DOZEN

- 2 **cups butter, softened**
- 1 **pint vanilla ice cream, softened**
- 4 **cups all-purpose flour**
- 2 **tablespoons sugar**
- 2 **cans (12 ounces each) apricot and/ or raspberry cake and pastry filling**
- 1 **to 2 tablespoons confectioners' sugar, optional**

1. In the bowl of a heavy-duty stand mixer, beat butter and ice cream until blended (mixture will appear curdled). Add flour and sugar; mix well. Divide dough into four portions; cover and refrigerate for 2 hours or until easy to handle.

2. On a lightly floured surface, roll one portion of dough into a 12– x 10–in. rectangle; cut into 2-in. squares. Place a teaspoonful of filling in the center of each square. Overlap two opposite corners of dough over filling; pinch tightly to seal. Place 2 in. apart on ungreased baking sheets. Repeat with remaining dough and filling.

3. Bake at 350° for 11-14 minutes or until bottoms are lightly browned. Cool for 1 minute before removing from pans to wire racks. Sprinkle with confectioners' sugar if desired.

NOTE *This recipe was tested with Solo brand cake and pastry filling. Look for it in the baking aisle.*

kid FRIENDLY Pretzel Cereal Crunch

A festive container of this salty-sweet treat was left in my mailbox several years ago, and it was eaten in a heartbeat! When my neighbor shared the recipe, I started making it with a touch of peanut butter.

—**CINDY LUND** VALLEY CENTER, CA

PREP: 20 MIN. + COOLING
MAKES: ABOUT 9 CUPS

- 1¼ cups Golden Grahams
- 1¼ cups Apple Cinnamon Cheerios
- 1¼ cups miniature pretzels
- 1 cup chopped pecans, toasted
- 1 package (10 to 12 ounces) white baking chips
- 2 tablespoons creamy peanut butter

In a large bowl, combine the cereals, pretzels and pecans. In a microwave-safe bowl, melt chips; stir until smooth. Stir in peanut butter. Drizzle over cereal mixture; toss to coat. Spread evenly on a waxed paper-lined baking sheet. Cool completely; break into pieces. Store in an airtight container.

Mackinac Fudge

PREP: 5 MIN. • **COOK:** 25 MIN. + CHILLING
MAKES: 3 POUNDS (10 DOZEN PIECES)

- 2 teaspoons plus 1 cup butter, divided
- 4 cups sugar
- 1 cup 2% milk
- 25 large marshmallows
- 1 package (11½ ounces) milk chocolate chips
- 2 cups (12 ounces) semisweet chocolate chips
- 2 ounces unsweetened chocolate, chopped
- 1 teaspoon vanilla extract
  Decorating icing and sprinkles, optional

1. Line a 13x9-in. pan with foil; grease the foil with 2 teaspoons butter.
2. In a large heavy saucepan, combine the sugar, milk and remaining butter. Bring to a rapid boil over medium heat, stirring constantly. Cook, without stirring, for 2 minutes. Remove from the heat.
3. Stir in marshmallows until melted. Add all chocolate; stir until melted. Stir in vanilla. Immediately spread into prepared pan; cool for 1 hour.
4. Score into 1-in. squares. Refrigerate, covered, for 3 hours or until firm. Using foil, lift out fudge. Remove foil; cut fudge. Store between layers of waxed paper in airtight containers. Decorate as desired.

? Did you know?

Covering only 3.8 square miles, Mackinac Island, Michigan, is home to more than 15 fudge shops.

When I was married, a lady at my parents' church gave me this version of a popular Michigan treat. I sometimes pipe a bit of frosting on each piece for decoration during the holidays. —**KRISTEN EKHOFF** AKRON, IN

Mackinac Fudge

Ultimate Double Chocolate Brownies

We live in the city, but within just a block of our house we can see cattle grazing in a grassy green pasture. It's a sight that I never tire of. As someone who grew up in the country, I love home-style recipes like these from-scratch brownies.

—**CAROL PREWETT** CHEYENNE, WY

PREP: 15 MIN. • **BAKE:** 35 MIN.
MAKES: 3 DOZEN

- ¾ cup baking cocoa
- ½ teaspoon baking soda
- ⅔ cup butter, melted, divided
- ½ cup boiling water
- 2 cups sugar
- 2 eggs
- 1⅓ cups all-purpose flour
- 1 teaspoon vanilla extract
- ¼ teaspoon salt
- ½ cup coarsely chopped pecans
- 2 cups (12 ounces) semisweet chocolate chunks

1. In a large bowl, combine cocoa and baking soda; blend ⅓ cup melted butter. Add boiling water; stir until well blended. Stir in sugar, eggs and remaining butter. Add flour, vanilla salt. Stir in the pecans and chocolate chunks.

2. Pour into a greased 13-in. x 9-in. baking pan. Bake at 350° for 35-40 minutes or until brownies begin to pull away from sides of pan. Cool.

kid FRIENDLY Whoopie Pies

These soft cupcakelike treats have been a favorite of mine for many years. They're especially fun to assemble with kids.

—**RUTH ANN STELFOX** RAYMOND, AB

PREP: 15 MIN.
BAKE: 5 MIN./BATCH + COOLING
MAKES: 1½ DOZEN

- 1 cup butter, softened
- 1½ cups sugar
- 2 eggs
- 2 teaspoons vanilla extract
- 4 cups all-purpose flour
- ¾ cup baking cocoa
- 2 teaspoons baking soda
- ½ teaspoon salt
- 1 cup water
- 1 cup buttermilk

FILLING

- 2 cups confectioners' sugar
- 2 cups marshmallow creme
- ½ cup butter, softened
- 2 teaspoons vanilla extract

1. In a large bowl, cream butter and sugar until light and fluffy. Beat in eggs and vanilla. Combine flour, cocoa, baking soda and salt; add to creamed mixture alternately with water and buttermilk, beating after each addition.

2. Drop by tablespoonfuls 2 in. apart onto greased baking sheets. Bake at 375° for 5-7 minutes or until set. Remove to wire racks to cool completely.

3. In a small bowl, beat filling ingredients until fluffy. Spread on the bottoms of half of the cookies; top with remaining cookies.

Did you know?

Amish women would bake these sandwich desserts with leftover cake batter and put them in the farmers' lunchboxes, causing the farmers to shout, "Whoopie!"

Frosted Molasses Cookies

My frosted spice cookies are always the first item to disappear at the holiday bake sales. That's why I call them "The Best Christmas Cookies."

—**MURIEL LERDAL** HUMBOLDT, IA

PREP: 30 MIN.
BAKE: 10 MIN./BATCH + COOLING
MAKES: 7½ DOZEN

- 1 cup butter, softened
- 1 cup packed brown sugar
- 2 eggs
- 1 cup dark molasses
- 1 teaspoon vanilla extract
- 4½ cups all-purpose flour
- 1 tablespoon ground ginger
- 1 tablespoon ground cinnamon
- 2 teaspoons baking soda
- 1 teaspoon salt
- ¼ teaspoon ground allspice
- 1 cup buttermilk

FROSTING
- ¼ cup shortening
- ¼ cup butter, softened
- ½ teaspoon vanilla extract
- 2 cups confectioners' sugar
- ¼ teaspoon ground ginger
- 4 teaspoons 2% milk
- Colored sprinkles, optional

1. In a large bowl, cream the butter and brown sugar until light and fluffy. Beat in the eggs, molasses and vanilla. Combine the flour, ginger, cinnamon, baking soda, salt and allspice; add to creamed mixture alternately with buttermilk, beating well after each addition.

2. Drop by tablespoonfuls 2 in. apart onto greased baking sheets. Bake at 375° for 7-9 minutes or until set. Remove to wire racks to cool.

3. For frosting, in a small bowl, cream shortening and butter until light and fluffy. Beat in vanilla. Gradually beat in confectioners' sugar and ginger. Add milk; beat until light and fluffy. Spread over cookies. Decorate with sprinkles if desired. Store in an airtight container.

ULTIMATE *Comfort* Cookie Dough Truffles

The filling at the center of these candies tastes like genuine chocolate chip cookie dough...without the worry of raw eggs.

—**LANITA DEDON** SLAUGHTER, LA

PREP: 1 HOUR + CHILLING
MAKES: 5½ DOZEN

- ½ cup butter, softened
- ¾ cup packed brown sugar
- 1 teaspoon vanilla extract
- 2 cups all-purpose flour
- 1 can (14 ounces) sweetened condensed milk
- ½ cup miniature semisweet chocolate chips
- ½ cup chopped walnuts
- 1½ pounds dark chocolate candy coating, coarsely chopped

1. In a large bowl, cream the butter and brown sugar until light and fluffy. Beat in vanilla. Gradually add flour, alternately with milk, beating well after each addition. Stir in chocolate chips and walnuts.

2. Shape into 1-in. balls; place on waxed paper-lined baking sheets. Loosely cover and refrigerate for 1-2 hours or until firm.

3. In a microwave, melt candy coating; stir until smooth. Dip balls in coating; allow excess to drip off. Place on waxed paper-lined baking sheets. Refrigerate until firm, about 15 minutes. If desired, remelt remaining candy coating and drizzle over candies. Store in the refrigerator.

Oatmeal Surprise Cookies

How do you make an oatmeal raisin cookie even better? Use chocolate-covered raisins, of course. I also like to add pumpkin pie spice to give them a warm, fall flavor.

—**REBECCA CLARK** WARRIOR, AL

PREP: 20 MIN. • **BAKE:** 15 MIN./BATCH
MAKES: 3 DOZEN

- 1 **cup butter, softened**
- ¾ **cup packed brown sugar**
- ½ **cup sugar**
- 2 **eggs**
- 1½ **cups all-purpose flour**
- 1 **teaspoon baking soda**
- 1 **teaspoon pumpkin pie spice**
- 2¾ **cups quick-cooking oats**
- 1½ **cups chocolate-covered raisins**

1. In a large bowl, cream butter and sugars until light and fluffy. Beat in eggs. Combine the flour, baking soda and pumpkin pie spice; gradually add to creamed mixture and mix well. Stir in oats and raisins.

2. Drop by tablespoonfuls 2 in. apart onto greased baking sheets. Flatten slightly. Bake at 350° for 13-15 minutes or until golden brown. Cool for 5 minutes before removing to wire racks. Store in an airtight container.

top tip

Eggs to Room Temperature

Baking with room-temperature eggs will help the whites and yolks mix more evenly through the batter. This makes a better, lighter cookie texture. Simply place the eggs in a bowl of warm tap water for 10 to 15 minutes.

White Chocolate Pumpkin Dreams

Penuche is a type of fudge made with brown sugar, butter, cream and nuts. Here, these soft pecan pumpkin cookies get topped with a frosting that mimics the flavors of this sweet candy.

—**JEAN KLECKNER** SEATTLE, WA

PREP: 25 MIN. + COOLING • **BAKE:** 15 MIN.
MAKES: ABOUT 4½ DOZEN

- 1 **cup butter, softened**
- ½ **cup sugar**
- ½ **cup packed brown sugar**
- 1 **egg**
- 2 **teaspoons vanilla extract**
- 1 **cup canned pumpkin**
- 2 **cups all-purpose flour**
- 3½ **teaspoons pumpkin pie spice**
- 1 **teaspoon baking powder**
- 1 **teaspoon baking soda**
- ¼ **teaspoon salt**
- 1 **package (11 ounces) vanilla or white chips**
- 1 **cup chopped pecans**

PENUCHE FROSTING

- ½ **cup packed brown sugar**
- 3 **tablespoons butter**
- ¼ **cup milk**
- 1½ **to 2 cups confectioners' sugar**

1. In a large bowl, cream butter and sugars until light and fluffy. Beat in the egg, vanilla and pumpkin. Combine dry ingredients; gradually add to the creamed mixture and mix well. Stir in chips and pecans.

2. Drop by rounded teaspoonfuls 2 in. apart onto ungreased baking sheets. Bake at 350° for 12-14 minutes or until firm. Remove to wire racks to cool.

3. For frosting, combine brown sugar and butter in a small saucepan. Bring to a boil; cook over medium heat for 1 minute or until slightly thickened. Cool for 10 minutes. Add milk; beat until smooth. Beat in enough confectioners' sugar to reach desired consistency. Spread over cooled cookies.

Chocolate Caramel Cracker Bars

Made on Saturday and gone by Monday, these Chocolate Caramel Bars go even quicker at bake sales. They taste like homemade Twix bars.

—**ALLY BILLHORN** WILTON, IA

PREP: 15 MIN. • **COOK:** 10 MIN. + CHILLING
MAKES: 27 BARS

- 1 **teaspoon plus ¾ cup butter, cubed**
- 45 **Club crackers (2½x1 inch)**
- 1 **can (14 ounces) sweetened condensed milk**
- ½ **cup packed brown sugar**
- 3 **tablespoons light corn syrup**
- 1 **cup (6 ounces) semisweet chocolate chips**

1. Line a 9-in. square baking pan with foil and grease the foil with 1 teaspoon butter. Arrange a single layer of crackers in the pan.

2. In a large saucepan, combine the milk, brown sugar, corn syrup and remaining butter. Bring to a boil over medium heat, stirring occasionally. Reduce heat to maintain a low boil; cook and stir for 7 minutes. Remove from the heat. Evenly spread a third of the mixture over the crackers. Repeat cracker and caramel layers twice.

3. Immediately sprinkle chocolate chips over caramel; let stand 3-5 minutes or until glossy. Spread over top. Cover and refrigerate for 2 hours or until chocolate is set. Using foil, lift layers out of pan; cut into 3x1-in. bars.

Chocolate Caramel Cracker Bars $1.⁻

Toffee Cranberry Crisps

I've had more friends request this recipe than any other cookie recipe I bake. The combination of cranberries, chocolate chips and toffee bits is wonderful.

—**ANN QUAERNA** LAKE GENEVA, WI

PREP: 15 MIN. + CHILLING
BAKE: 10 MIN./BATCH • **MAKES:** 5½ DOZEN

- 1 **cup butter, softened**
- ¾ **cup sugar**
- ¾ **cup packed brown sugar**
- 1 **egg**
- 1 **teaspoon vanilla extract**
- 1½ **cups all-purpose flour**
- 1½ **cups quick-cooking oats**
- 1 **teaspoon baking soda**
- ¼ **teaspoon salt**
- 1 **cup dried cranberries**
- 1 **cup miniature semisweet chocolate chips**
- 1 **cup milk chocolate English toffee bits**

1. In a large bowl, cream butter and sugars until light and fluffy. Beat in egg and vanilla. Combine the flour, oats, baking soda and salt; gradually add to creamed mixture and mix well. Stir in the cranberries, chocolate chips and toffee bits.

2. Shape into three 12-in. logs; wrap each in plastic wrap. Refrigerate for 2 hours or until firm. Unwrap and cut into ½-in. slices. Place 2 in. apart on lightly greased baking sheets.

3. Bake at 350° for 8-10 minutes or until golden brown. Remove to wire racks to cool.

Back-to-School Cookies

These cookies have become a favorite for almost anyone who tries them. They also make a delicious after-school treat, especially with a cold glass of milk.

—**FRANCES PIERCE** WADDINGTON, NY

PREP: 30 MIN. • **BAKE:** 10 MIN./BATCH
MAKES: 6½ DOZEN

- 1 **cup butter-flavored shortening**
- 1 **cup creamy peanut butter**
- 2 **cups packed brown sugar**
- 4 **egg whites**
- 1 **teaspoon vanilla extract**
- 2 **cups all-purpose flour**
- 1 **teaspoon baking soda**
- ½ **teaspoon baking powder**
- 2 **cups crisp rice cereal**
- 1½ **cups chopped nuts**
- 1 **cup flaked coconut**
- 1 **cup quick-cooking oats**

1. In a large bowl, cream the shortening, peanut butter and brown sugar until light and fluffy. Beat in egg whites and vanilla. Combine the flour, baking soda and baking powder; gradually add to creamed mixture and mix well. Stir in the cereal, nuts, coconut and oats.

2. Drop by rounded tablespoonfuls 2 in. apart onto ungreased baking sheets. Flatten with a fork, forming a crisscross pattern. Bake at 375° for 7-8 minutes. Remove to wire racks.

NOTE *Reduced-fat peanut butter is not recommended for this recipe.*

1. Line baking sheets with waxed paper; lightly coat with cooking spray and set aside. Butter the sides of a heavy saucepan with 1 teaspoon butter. Cube remaining butter; place in pan. Add the corn syrup, brown sugar and salt. Cook and stir until sugar is melted.
2. Gradually stir in milk. Cook and stir over medium heat until mixture comes to a boil. Cook and stir until a candy thermometer reads 248° (firm-ball stage), about 16 minutes. Remove from the heat; stir in vanilla. Gently stir in pecans. Drop by rounded teaspoonfuls onto prepared baking sheets. Refrigerate until firm, about 12 minutes.
3. In a microwave, melt chips and shortening; stir until smooth. Drizzle over clusters. Chill until firm. Store in the refrigerator.

NOTE *We recommend that you test your candy thermometer before each use by bringing water to a boil; the thermometer should read 212°. Adjust your recipe temperature up or down based on your test.*

Pecan Clusters

I made these turtle-like concoctions for a sweets exchange, and when my dad saw them on the counter waiting to be boxed up, he said they looked like they came from a candy shop. That's the best compliment I've ever received.

—**CARRIE BURKE** CONWAY, MA

PREP: 1¼ HOURS + CHILLING
MAKES: ABOUT 6 DOZEN

- 1 teaspoon plus 1 cup butter, divided
- 1 cup light corn syrup
- 2¼ cups packed brown sugar
- ⅛ teaspoon salt
- 1 can (14 ounces) sweetened condensed milk
- 1 teaspoon vanilla extract
- 1½ pounds pecan halves, toasted
- ¾ cup milk chocolate chips
- ¾ cup semisweet chocolate chips
- 4 teaspoons shortening

Raspberry Delights

These buttery bars have a rich crust holding the sweet jam topping. During the summer or holidays, they're always a hit.

—**GEORGIANA HAGMAN** LOUISVILLE, KY

PREP: 10 MIN. • **BAKE:** 25 MIN. + COOLING
MAKES: 3 DOZEN

- 1 cup butter, softened
- 1 cup sugar
- 2 egg yolks
- 2 cups all-purpose flour
- 1 cup coarsely ground pecans
- 1 cup raspberry jam

1. In a large bowl, cream butter and sugar until light and fluffy. Beat in egg yolks. Gradually add flour and mix well. Stir in the pecans.
2. Spread half into a lightly greased 13-in. x 9-in. baking pan. Top with jam. Drop remaining dough by teaspoonfuls over jam.
3. Bake at 350° for 25-30 minutes or until top is golden brown. Cool on a wire rack. Cut into bars.

Almond Cheesecake Bars

My sister-in-law shared the recipe for these delicious bars. I bring them to many functions, and everyone always asks for the recipe.

—MARY COUSER MAPLE PLAIN, MN

PREP: 20 MIN. • **BAKE:** 35 MIN. + COOLING
MAKES: 3 DOZEN

- 2 cups all-purpose flour
- 1 cup butter, softened
- ½ cup confectioners' sugar

FILLING

- 1 package (8 ounces) cream cheese, softened
- ½ cup sugar
- 1 teaspoon almond extract
- 2 eggs, lightly beaten

FROSTING

- 1½ cups confectioners' sugar
- ¼ cup butter, softened
- 1 teaspoon almond extract
- 4 to 5 teaspoons milk

1. Combine the flour, butter and confectioners' sugar; press onto the bottom of a greased 13-in. x 9-in. baking pan. Bake at 350° for 20-25 minutes or until golden brown.

2. For filling, in a small bowl, beat the cream cheese, sugar and extract until smooth. Add eggs; beat on low speed just until combined. Pour over crust. Bake for 15-20 minutes or until center is almost set. Cool on a wire rack.

3. Combine the frosting ingredients until smooth; spread over bars. Store in the refrigerator.

Buttery Spritz Cookies

These tender little cookies always remind people of the holidays. The dough is easy to work with, so it's fun to make these into a variety of festive shapes for all different occasions.

—BEVERLY LAUNIUS SANDWICH, IL

PREP: 20 MIN. • **BAKE:** 10 MIN./BATCH
MAKES: 7½ DOZEN

- 1 cup butter, softened
- 1¼ cups confectioners' sugar
- 1 egg
- 1 teaspoon vanilla extract
- ½ teaspoon almond extract
- 2½ cups all-purpose flour
- ½ teaspoon salt
  Food coloring, optional
  Colored sugar and decorating candies, optional

1. In a large bowl, cream butter and confectioners' sugar until light and fluffy. Beat in egg and extracts. Combine flour and salt. Gradually add to creamed mixture; mix well. Tint with food coloring if desired.

2. Using a cookie press fitted with the disk of your choice, press dough 2 in. apart onto ungreased baking sheets. Decorate as desired.

3. Bake at 375° for 6-8 minutes or until set (do not brown). Remove to wire racks to cool.

General Index

Use this index to search for recipes by food category or major ingredient.
Recipes marked **K** are kid-friendly favorites, and recipes marked **U** are must-try ultimate comfort foods.

Alphabetical Index

Recipes marked 🅚 are kid-friendly favorites, and recipes marked 🆄 are must-try ultimate comfort foods.

INDEXES

Specific Icon Index

Throughout this index, we used Ⓚ to identify kid-friendly recipes and Ⓤ for must-try ultimate comfort foods.